LAND OF
REFUGE

PERSPECTIVES ON ISRAEL STUDIES

S. Ilan Troen, Natan Aridan, Donna Divine, David Ellenson,
Arieh Saposnik, and Jonathan Sarna, *editors*

Sponsored by the Ben-Gurion Research Institute for the Study of Israel
and Zionism of the Ben-Gurion University of the Negev and
the Schusterman Center for Israel Studies of Brandeis University

LAND OF REFUGE

Immigration to Palestine, 1919-1927

Gur Alroey

translated by Deborah Stern

INDIANA UNIVERSITY PRESS

This book is a publication of

Indiana University Press
Office of Scholarly Publishing
Herman B Wells Library 350
1320 East 10th Street
Bloomington, Indiana 47405 USA

iupress.org

Manufactured in the United States of America

First Printing 2024

Cataloging information is available from the LIbrary of Congress.

ISBN 978-0-253-07006-7 (hardcover)
ISBN 978-0-253-07007-4 (paperback)
ISBN 978-0-253-07008-1 (e-book)

Originally published as *Eretz Miklat: Ha'hagirah Le'Eretz Israel, 1919–1927*
by Gur Alroey © 2021, The Ben-Gurion University of the Negev

On Saturday morning, October 7, 2023, the festival of Simhat Torah, Hamas and the Islamic Jihad launched a barbaric pogrom against the residents of communities near Gaza and in southern Israel. The terrorists—members of those organizations and Palestinian civilians—crossed the border, invaded Israel, murdered, slaughtered, burned, raped, abused, looted, and kidnapped innocent people, Jews and others, whoever was in their path.

The writing of *Land of Refuge* was completed before the bloodbath in southern Israel. A direct line connects the "Simhat Torah Pogrom" to the pogroms perpetrated in Ukraine at the time of the civil war (and described in the book). What was true for the Jewish people then remains true today: Israel is and will remain a land of refuge, a land of life and fulfillment, for the Jews in Israel and abroad.

Land of Refuge is dedicated to the memory of **Shahar (Deborah) Troen-Mathias**, the great-granddaughter of Zissel Malcah Pearlmutter, who was murdered in Derazhne, Ukraine, by Petliura's troops, and her husband, **Shlomi David Mathias.**

This loyal, brave couple, whose lives were devoted to art, work, and peace, were brutally murdered while desperately protecting their son and their home on Kibbutz Holit, near the border of the Gaza Strip.

May their memory, and the memory of all those murdered, be a blessing.

CONTENTS

PREFACE

My first book, *Imigrantim: Ha-Hagira ha-Yehudit le-Eretz-Yisrael be-Reshit ha-Me'a ha-Esrim* [Immigrants: Jewish Migration to Palestine in the Early Twentieth Century], was published in Hebrew in 2004 (an expanded version was later published in English as *An Unpromising Land: Jewish Migration to Palestine in the Early Twentieth Century*). I examined the Second Aliya in the historical context of mass Jewish migration from eastern Europe in the late nineteenth and early twentieth centuries. For me, *Imigrantim* was the starting point for the study of Jewish migration. I continued to follow those ordinary Jews in additional articles and books I wrote about Jewish migration, including but not limited to immigration to Palestine. The more I delved into the history of migration, the more I realized that I could only understand its dynamics, characteristics, and causes if I looked at them from the perspective of the individual migrants and their families. Migrants are the main heroes of the drama of migration, which starts in the country of origin and ends many years after they have arrived at their destination.

Land of Refuge opens with an excerpt from Irving Howe's monumental, inspirational work *World of Our Fathers* that expresses the spirit of this book: "A story is the essential unit of our life, offering the magical imperatives of 'so it began' and 'so it came to an end.' A story encompasses us, justifies our stay, prepares our leaving. Here, in these pages, is the story of the Jews, bedraggled and inspired, who came from eastern Europe. Let us now praise obscure men." Let us also praise the obscure, bedraggled, inspired Jews who went to Palestine from Islamic countries.

The French-Jewish author and playwright Georges Perec believed that if we want to understand migration from Europe to the United States, we must follow the personal story of each of those millions of immigrants. He attempted to break down the human mosaic of the immigrant population and examine every stone in it individually. As he wrote,

> five million emigrants from Italy
> four million emigrants arriving from Ireland
> one million emigrants arriving from Sweden
> six million arriving from Germany
> three million emigrants arriving from Austria and Hungary
> three million five hundred thousand emigrants arriving from Russia and the
>   Ukraine
> five million emigrants arriving from Great Britain
> eight hundred thousand emigrants arriving from Norway
> six hundred thousand emigrants arriving from Greece
> four hundred thousand emigrants arriving from Turkey
> four hundred thousand emigrants arriving from the Netherlands
> six hundred thousand emigrants arriving from France
> three hundred thousand emigrants arriving from Denmark
> . . . rather than simply saying: in thirty years
> sixteen million emigrants passed through Ellis Island
> attempting to give palpable form
> to what those sixteen million individual stories were,
> the sixteen million stories, identical and distinct,
> of the men, women, and children driven
> from their native land by famine or poverty,
> or by political, racial, or religious oppression,
> leaving everything behind—village, family, friends—
> taking months and years to set aside
> the money needed for the trip,
> finding themselves here, in a hall so vast that they never
> would have dared imagine that there could anywhere
> exist so big a place,
> lined up by fours,
> waiting their turn.[1]

The distinction that Perec makes here is important and real. It should be adopted with respect to immigration to Palestine as well, specifically in the context of the British Mandate. To understand the complexity of this distinction, we must extricate the Jewish migrants from the Zionist arch-narrative and from quantitative statistics and make them the official heroes of the drama of migration. The main heroes of *Land of Refuge* are Howe's bedraggled, obscure Jews, some of whom really wanted to go to America but could not get in and had to make do with Palestine instead. Here center stage is taken not by the pioneers of the Third Aliya, members of the Labor Battalion, and founders of the first kibbutzim but by ordinary Jewish refugees and emigrants fleeing for their lives from eastern Europe and Islamic countries. Through their personal stories as told here we can come to understand those Jews who crossed border after border and the Mediterranean Basin to embark on new lives in Palestine.

Chronologically, *Land of Refuge* is a sequel to *An Unpromising Land*, although it differs in the range of topics and issues covered. *An Unpromising Land* ends with the outbreak of World War I. *Land of Refuge* starts with the military regime in Palestine following the British conquest; it focuses on the causes of emigration and the journey to Palestine. It explores the migrants' fears and misgivings before they arrived on the shores of Palestine. The focus is on the personal experiences, stories, and testimonies of the refugees, immigrants, and olim; these add an important layer to our understanding of Yishuv society during the Mandate period. *Land of Refuge* is not just a chapter in the history of the Yishuv. It is an integral part of the historiography of Jewish migration in the first half of the twentieth century.

I would like to thank those who assisted me throughout the writing of this book: Dr. Yigal Sitry, director of the Central Zionist Archives; Anat Banin, head of the Photograph Collection; and the entire devoted staff of the archives who spared neither time nor effort and demonstrated extraordinary patience in helping me with all my questions and requests. Thank you also to the dedicated staff of the Center for Jewish History in New York. Special thanks go to Professor Gary Zola, executive director of the Jacob Rader Marcus Center of the American Jewish Archives in Cincinnati, for his generous hospitality and warmth during the time I spent in the archives. I would also like to thank Professor Ilan Troen who accepted my manuscript and found it suitable for publication in his series for Indiana University Press. Ilan also gave me a photo of his grandmother's grave. His grandmother was murdered in a pogrom during the civil war in Ukraine and the photo was placed in the book. The Troen family history tragically repeated itself when Ilan's daughter and son-in-law were murdered by Hamas terrorists in the Simchat Torah pogrom in Israel on October 7, 2023. This book is dedicated to them. And, special thanks to the Indiana Press team: Anna Francis, Nancy Lightfoot, Laura Abrams, and Stephen Williams.

I am also grateful to Dr. Galia Hasharoni, a student of mine who, while searching for sources for her own research, drew my attention to important historical documents that contributed greatly to my study. I am indebted to Chaim Sonnenfeld, a great-grandson of Rabbi Yosef Chaim Sonnenfeld, the first rabbi of the Eda Haredit in Jerusalem, for his graciousness and endless patience whenever I needed help with Yiddish. I thank Reuven Salomons, perpetual auditor and student, whom I consulted when I had difficulty understanding texts in German.

My thanks also go to Deborah Stern for translating the book from Hebrew to English. I have worked with Deborah for many years and am surprised each time anew by the accuracy and brilliance of her translation and especially by how well she manages to preserve my writing style. Finally, I am grateful to Hilla Klor, my partner in writing the book and editor of the Hebrew edition.

LAND OF
REFUGE

Figure 0.1. Child survivors of the pogrom in Khodorkov, May 1919. Photo courtesy of the National Library of Israel.

Introduction

The photograph and poem with which this book begins epitomize its central theme: The bloodbath in Ukraine, Yemen, and the Orumiyeh region of Iran between 1917 and 1921 and the story of the persecuted refugees and migrants who experienced the events of those years firsthand are an essential part of the study of immigration to Palestine in the 1920s. Viewing the Third Aliya and Fourth Aliya solely from the perspective of the halutzim or that of the Polish-Jewish petty bourgeoisie misses the mark in terms of historical truth because it detaches immigration to Palestine from its broad historical context and ignores the dramatic, tragic events the Jews of Ukraine and Orumiyeh experienced in the years before the Holocaust.

Four children in rags, survivors of the carnage, face a photographer who memorialized the aftermath of the May 1919 pogrom in the Khodorkov shtetl (Kiev Governorate). The children's faces are blackened with soot; their hands are bandaged; and they look panic-stricken, confused, and stunned by the terror they have just experienced. The boy in the center of the picture looks to be about six or seven. The other three are clearly teenagers. The girl on the left, with the exposed breast, is supporting her injured, bandaged arm. It is presumably no coincidence that the girl is facing the camera lens in such an undignified, immodest way. Perhaps the photographer was hinting that she had been raped during the pogrom, as many Jewish women in Ukraine were during the civil war.[1] We have no way of knowing if the four were related, but they certainly knew one another. We have no idea who helped them or what happened to them afterward. Did they go to the United States or Palestine? Did they stay in Ukraine and eventually perish in the Holocaust, or did they survive? We have no further details about the picture or the people in it, but we do have eyewitnesses to what happened in Khodorkov during the pogrom.

> Although the defenders mustered and fought the gang, they quickly discovered that they could not withstand them. Some were killed in the fighting. The others fled up the road toward the Popelnia station, which is twenty parasangs from Khodorkov. But the ruffians pursued them twenty parasangs from the town and cut down the fugitives mercilessly. The entire road was covered in dead bodies. After finishing off the defenders, the murderers returned to the city and started to wipe out the Jews in the city. They killed them viciously: killed, butchered, threw their victims into the Irpin River, condemned them to burn. They murdered men and women, old and young, even small children and suckling infants. They knew no mercy. Almost all their victims were killed with cold steel. Only those who were thrown into the river were shot to finish them off. They set fire to the homes and the other buildings. They took about thirty people to Meir Ribak's stable, shut the doors, and set fire to the stable. Everyone in the stable was burned. No one survived. After the massacre, farmers with carts were sent to collect the bodies lying in the fields and on the roads, so that they wouldn't stink up the air. For four days the farmers brought heaps and heaps of dead bodies to the Khodorkov cemetery and buried them in other people's graves. One hundred twenty victims in one grave. But they were unable to collect all the victims. Many were left lying in the fields and on the roads and were eaten by dogs and wild animals. Even afterwards, farmers kept finding large numbers of bodies in gardens and fields and they brought them to town for burial. Up to two thousand people were murdered.[2]

Kiev: A Poem; and Two Drafts of a Poem in Memory of Tetiev
Ya'akov Orland

All my life I have written of Tetiev.
After three score and ten, nearly eighty years—
I am still writing of Tetiev.
In all my scrawls—Tetiev is there, if only at the tip of my pen.
Whether I said Kiev, Kishinev, Galați, or Constanța,
Whether I said Constantinople,
Jaffa, Tel Hai, Kefar Giladi, Migdal, Tiberias,
Or spoke of Jerusalem, Tel Aviv, and Haifa—be it long ago or here and now . . .
Tetiev has stalked me constantly.
Like an enemy.
Like a huntsman, trapping and despoiling quarry.

Throughout my youth and young adulthood,
My wanderings around the world,
My kin,
Even my parents' blessings
And my airs' metaphorical wings—
All their footsteps are dogged by the day of Tetiev.
It pursues me relentlessly
Since the early morn when I—hitherto a lad haunted by ghostly dreams—
Called out to a God who didn't answer.[3]

In the summer of 1921, after a long journey, Eliezer and Batya Orland arrived in Palestine with their seven-year-old son, Ya'akov. They had survived a brutal pogrom in Tetiev, Ukraine, by the skin of their teeth. Four thousand Jews in the town had been murdered, including eight members of their family.[4] Ya'akov, five years old at the time, had hidden in the garbage barrel in their yard. Through a crack in the barrel, he watched his relatives being murdered and saw his grandfather's severed head rolling at his feet. In a lull between attacks, he fled with his mother to a nearby church, where they found refuge. After the pogrom, his family went to Kiev, the capital of Ukraine. From there, they crossed the Dnieper and Dniester Rivers to Bessarabia and lived in Kishinev for about a year.

In January 1921, the Orlands reached the port city of Constanța; from there, they sailed to Palestine via Constantinople.[5] They lived first in Kefar Giladi and then moved from place to place: Tel Yosef, Migdal, Tiberias, Jerusalem, and Tel Aviv. In Jerusalem, Ya'akov attended the Tachkemoni school, and after his family moved to Tel Aviv, he attended the Herzliya Gymnasium. He graduated from the Hebrew Gymnasium in the Rehavia neighborhood of Jerusalem. Throughout his life in Palestine and Israel, Ya'akov retained the "anguish of silence and the landscape of speechlessness" that had seared him with fear at the bottom of that garbage barrel in the Ukrainian shtetl. In 1985, while in his seventies, he wrote, "From the age of five, Tetiev has filled me with horror and fear as a chaotic, bloody town, merciless and corpse-strewn, that would be best obliterated from under God's heaven. But such is the scorn of fate that Tetiev was not obliterated; only its Jews were. Its forests are thicker than ever, the acacias are growing madly, and the lilacs yearn. There is always something there. Bits of memories of Tetiev have burned and scorched me on and off since the pogroms in April 1919, which I witnessed and was physically involved in."[6] The pogrom was a significant event in Ya'akov Orland's life. It shaped his personality and remained with him throughout his years in Palestine and Israel until his dying day: "All my life I have been writing Tetiev. After seventy years, or the threshold of eighty—I am still writing Tetiev."[7]

The Orlands were not the only family to go to Palestine after surviving a pogrom. Many refugees arrived in Palestine in the 1920s who, like Orland, carried with them the trauma of the Ukrainian civil war and the murder of their family members,. The refugees were part of a larger wave of migrants, most of whom hoped to go to the United States. Scattering throughout eastern and central Europe, they tried desperately, against all odds, to obtain the precious visa for the United States, which had closed its gates to immigration at one of the Jewish people's hardest times.

Along with the refugees from the Ukrainian pogroms, Jews who had lost their livelihoods in Poland, Bolshevik Russia, Iraq, Iran, and Yemen arrived in Palestine in the 1920s. The severe famine in Russia claimed many casualties, while the economic crisis in Poland drove the Jews into desperate, unrelenting poverty. Iraq heavily taxed its middle class, thereby eroding the status of Jewish merchants. In Yemen and Iran, Jews were persecuted and marginalized both socially and economically. Halutzim and members of youth movements also arrived in those years, drawn by Zionist ideology and the desire to build a just, equal society in Palestine.

The historiography of the *Yishuv* (Jews living in Palestine before the 1948 establishment of the state of Israel) has divided immigration to Palestine in the 1920s into two waves with different social compositions and motivations. The Third Aliya (1919–1923) has always been identified by Zionist historians as halutzic aliya, whereas the Fourth Aliya (1924–1928) is characterized as bourgeois and petty bourgeois. The young people of the Third Aliya came from the pioneering youth movements. They settled in the periphery of Palestine, founded the Labor Battalion, established moshavim and kibbutzim, and farmed the land. The members of the Fourth Aliya settled in the big cities and worked in skilled trades and commerce.

This division into two waves, however, does not faithfully reflect Jewish immigration to Palestine in the 1920s. The vast majority of Jews who entered the country in those years did not belong unequivocally to either of those waves from an ideological or social standpoint. Had they been asked, they no doubt would not have known whether they were part of the third wave or the fourth. Most were refugees and immigrants, survivors of the bloodbath in Ukraine or the pogroms in Orumiyeh; for them, Palestine was a last resort or land of refuge after the countries across the Atlantic had refused to let them in.

Although the familiar division into waves of aliya took shape in the minds of their contemporaries, that does not mean historians must accept it unquestioningly. The economic historian Nachum Gross, for instance, has proposed examining the Mandate period based on long-term processes such as economic growth or immigrant absorption rather than short periods such as waves of immigration. Gross maintains that the distinction between the Third Aliya and the Fourth Aliya is dubious because the immigrants were socioeconomically diverse at the time of the Third Aliya; a large proportion of them came from a distinctly Polish, middle-class background.[8]

I accept Gross's fundamental assertion that the boundaries of the Third Aliya and Fourth Aliya were fuzzy. Unlike Gross, however, my research indicates that the boundaries of the study were dictated not by the economy of Palestine but by European geopolitics after World War I and by the Zionist and British immigration policies that took shape in the 1920s. The heroes of *Land of Refuge* are ordinary immigrants, those who carried Jewish people's suffering on their backs and decided to migrate with their families from Europe, North Africa, and Asia to Palestine. Some were welcomed by the Zionist establishment; others came despite it and against its recommendation. At the heart of this story is not their actions in Palestine after they settled there but the bumpy road they traveled on their way, from their vacillations about emigrating until their arrival on the shores of Palestine. The hardships of integration and acclimatization in the new land are therefore not addressed in this work.

The 1920s were fateful years for Jewish immigrants. The geopolitical situation had changed unrecognizably after World War I, making their lives more difficult: the Russian and Austro-Hungarian empires had broken up, and the new countries that had arisen ex nihilo atop their ruins violated the Jews' rights and worsened their living conditions. In the brutal civil war that broke out in Ukraine, one hundred thousand Jews were murdered or wounded, and tens of thousands became refugees throughout Europe. In Palestine, the new British Mandate instituted immigration regulations that limited the entry of Jews. The United States passed immigration quota laws in 1921 and 1924 and finally closed its gates to the immigrants. The American quota laws changed the direction of Jewish migration, as tens of thousands of Jews had no choice but to go to Palestine instead of America. Once in Palestine, they surprisingly energized the Zionist enterprise and helped it strengthen its demographic, economic, and social hold on the country.

The pogroms against Russian Jewry in the late nineteenth and early twentieth centuries formed an inseparable part of the Zionist narrative and ethos. They were perceived as proof that Zionism was right and served as an impetus for further immigration to Palestine. The pogroms in the southern Pale of Settlement in 1881 spurred Leon Pinsker to write *Autoemancipation* and led to the founding of the Hibbat Zion movement. The first members of Bilu arrived in Palestine, followed by the farmers of the First Aliya. The Kishinev pogrom, on the eve of Passover 1903, came as a severe shock to the Jewish world and the Zionist movement. Forty-nine Jews were murdered, and a delegation headed by Chaim Nachman Bialik was dispatched to investigate the pogroms. The delegation's mission was to take testimony from the victims and to gather the investigative material necessary to bring the accused to justice. In 1904 and 1905, more than three thousand Jews were murdered in hundreds of outbreaks of violence in the southern Pale of Settlement. The first halutzim of the Second Aliya arrived in Palestine at that time, and they brought with them the idea of Jewish self-defense.

The Third Aliya and Fourth Aliya are not usually identified with the pogroms in Ukraine. Despite the destruction wreaked in the Ukrainian civil war, Zionist historiography has not attributed great importance to it. After the Balfour Declaration and the British promise to establish the national home of the Jewish people in Palestine, there was no longer an ideological need for pogroms and the murder of Jews to justify the Zionist idea. In 1964, Am Oved published the thousand-page *Sefer ha-Aliya ha-Shelishit* (The book of the Third Aliyah).[9] Its editor, Yehuda Erez, set forth the history of the Third Aliya from the training camps in eastern Europe to the establishment of the Labor Battalion and the first kibbutzim and workers' moshavim in the Jezreel Valley. Wrinkled halutzim nearing the end of their days recalled starting out in Palestine, describing it with great nostalgia. Thus, the slaughter of Ukrainian Jewry faded from the national collective memory and was not etched in it as a decisive historical event like the pogroms in 1881 and the Kishinev pogrom.

Historical scholarship has also done little to link immigration to Palestine in the 1920s with the carnage during the Ukrainian civil war. Baruch Ben-Avram and Henry Near dealt critically with the Third Aliya period in their book *Iyunim ba-Aliya ha-Shelishit: Dimui u-Metsiut* (Studies in the Third Aliyah: image and reality). They noted a disparity between the image and reality but ignored the murder of Ukrainian Jewry, which they did not consider a major factor in immigration to Palestine.[10] David Shapira and Moshe Lissak's studies about the start of immigration to Palestine also completely disregard the impact of the pogroms.[11] In her book *Be-Meruts Kaful Neged ha-Zeman* (Dual race against time), about immigration policy in the 1930s, Aviva Halamish notes that there was a large number of aliya applicants in the early 1920s because "eastern European Jewry suffered from persecution and pogroms. The plight of Ukrainian Jewry was particularly grave, as they found themselves on the battlefield between the Whites and the Reds in the winter of 1918/1919. From late 1917 until 1920, some 75,000 Jews were killed there, tens of thousands were wounded, women were raped, and a great deal of Jewish-owned property was plundered and destroyed."[12] In *Mi-Bayit Leumi li-Medina ba-Derekh* (From national home to a state in the making), Halamish addresses factors that pushed eastern European Jews to emigrate. Among them were the pogroms in Ukraine.[13] Halamish is the exception that proves the rule. However, although she does emphasize anti-Jewish discrimination and persecution in her study of immigration to Palestine in the 1930s, even she does not portray the pogroms as a constitutive event that should be used as the basis for exploring immigration to Palestine in the 1920s.[14]

In this volume, I consider immigration to Palestine in a broader historical context. I maintain that it is impossible to understand the essence of that immigration without addressing the slaughter of Ukrainian Jewry and its consequences for eastern European Jews. It was a national catastrophe on a scale previously unknown to modern Jewry, although it was overshadowed by the extermination of European Jewry during World War II. The pogroms in Ukraine are a thread running through this book from the first chapter to the last, as they are relevant to various aspects of immigration to Palestine.

The story of immigration to Palestine between 1919 and 1927 is not only an eastern European one. About 10 percent of the immigrants in those years came from Iran, Iraq, Yemen, and the Maghreb. In Orumiyeh, Armenians massacred Jews; in Yemen, the Jews were degraded, persecuted, and discriminated against. Bereft of hope and financial prospects, they viewed Palestine as a lifeline and refuge. Arriving overland, they became an integral part of the immigrant population in the 1920s. Any perspective that does not consider all the immigrants to Palestine during the Mandate period, and in the 1920s in particular, is deficient and may skew our understanding of history.

One of the outstanding characteristics of immigration between the two world wars was regulation by means of laws and orders. Before World War I, migration policies were open and free. People could leave their homes and go to any country without a passport or visa. They needed only to pass their medical exams and prove to immigration officials that they had enough money to live on while starting out in the new land. After the war, conservative migration policies limited immigrants' choice of destinations. The United States passed laws imposing quotas for each country of origin, and in Palestine, the Mandatory government issued immigration permits ("certificates") sparingly, and only for various categories of immigrants.

The development of the Mandatory and Zionist immigration policies, political influences on the distribution of the certificates, and the bureaucratic procedures involved in entering Palestine directly impacted immigration to Palestine in the 1920s. Immigrants had to cross a field of administrative thorns to obtain visas and aliya certificates. Some had a hard time understanding the ever-changing immigration laws, and many were forced to rely on assistance from the Palestine Offices and Jewish migration societies that had been established in Europe.

One outcome of the new global and Mandatory immigration policies was the establishment of a hierarchical bureaucracy that dealt with all aspects of immigration to Palestine. By focusing on immigration policy, we can trace the Zionist movement's deliberations regarding the character of Jewish immigration to Palestine and its dilemma as to the desirability of different categories of immigrants amid pogroms, government persecution, and economic hardship between 1919 and 1927. An aliya bureau headed by Professor Hermann Pick was established to resolve this dilemma. In addition, the Zionist movement established Palestine Offices in the main countries of origin of Jewish migration as well as aliya bureaus in Jaffa, Haifa, and Jerusalem. In meetings held after World War I, the Zionist General Council and the Zionist Congress decided to establish a Palestine Office in every country where there were Jews who wanted to go to Palestine. These offices would be subordinate to the Zionist Organization and would receive instructions from the Aliya Department.

Palestine Offices were indeed established in most countries of origin of Jewish migration, and they helped immigrants from the decision-making stage through their arrival in Palestine. The Aliya Department, based first in London and later in Jerusalem, issued instructions to the Palestine Offices in accordance with Zionist and British immigration policy. Coastal aliya bureaus were established in Haifa and Jaffa. In addition, a bureau in Jerusalem handled arrangements for the immigrants' entry into Palestine and offered them assistance in their first days in the country.

Alongside the refugees from the pogroms and ordinary immigrants were the other heroes of the book—the professional and executive echelons of the aliya bureaus. They were the ones who greeted the immigrants and removed bureaucratic obstacles. The most prominent of them were the directors of the aliya bureaus in Jaffa (Joshua Gordon), Haifa (Levi Shvueli), and Jerusalem (Ze'ev Leibowitz) and the directors of the Palestine Offices in Europe and around the world, especially Warsaw (Chaim Barlas) and Trieste (Giuseppe Fano). These were highly experienced experts who were intimately familiar with the complexity of the immigration procedures, who dealt with big and small problems concerning entry into the country, and who were ready to suggest sound solutions and methods of action. On more than one occasion, they found themselves between a rock (British and Zionist immigration policy) and a hard place (refugees and immigrants desperate to reach Palestine). In the mid-1920s, Joshua Gordon published an impressive and comprehensive study of various aspects of immigration to Palestine in the first decade of the British Mandate. Gordon addressed the various difficulties and problems the Aliya Department had to contend with after immigration resumed in the first years of the Mandatory regime.[15]

One methodological challenge for scholars of immigration, and especially of immigration to Palestine, concerns the difficulty of understanding the complexities of the various reasons and motivations for immigration. The decision to uproot oneself from one's native land and move to a new country is a complicated and difficult one. There is no one consideration or single motivation to emigrate but rather a whole slew of interrelated considerations and motivations. It is not always possible to isolate one component that led to someone moving to a different country. Consequently, terminology is crucial if we want to understand the entire range of factors that brought the immigrants/*olim*/refugees to Palestine. These terms embody a long list of reasons and motives, and they help us understand the real weight of the push and pull factors in the countries of origin and destination.

Few words in the Hebrew language other than *aliya* have had such a powerful impact on shaping the collective memory and on how Israeli society interprets history, expresses its national narrative, and delineates its borders. The word *aliya* embodies a wide world of values that encompasses the totality of thoughts and feelings evoked upon arrival in the Land of Israel. Literally, *aliya* means movement from a low place to a high place, but in Hebrew it has taken on another sense: Jews coming from the Diaspora to settle in the Land of Israel. The biblical commentators gave the word *aliya* its values connotation, and the Zionist movement made it a central component of national activity. Aliya is not immigration; in the Zionist discourse, there is a clear, sharp distinction between *olim* (ideological immigrants) to the Land of Israel and immigrants to other destinations.

The distinctions between aliya, immigration, and refugeeism and between olim, immigrants, and refugees are among the cornerstones in Zionist thought. Zionist historiography accepted unquestioningly the basic assumption that the first three waves of aliya were pioneering ones and that the Jews who arrived in those years were olim and not immigrants. Jews who went to Palestine starting in the late nineteenth century have been regarded as full-fledged olim. The ideological baggage embodied in the term *aliya* is so deeply rooted in the Hebrew language that it became hard to distinguish between Jewish immigrants to Palestine and olim. Thus, the Zionist narrative was differentiated from the history of general Jewish migration. It turned aliya into a unique, exceptional phenomenon unparalleled in the history of the Jewish people and other nations.

The first historians of the so-called aliyot recognized that the newcomers included some large groups that were not involved in rural settlement and did not advocate communal living and farming. Yehuda Slutsky, for example, asserted in his book *Mavo le-Toldot Tenu'at ha-'Avoda ha-Yisre'elit* (Introduction to the history of the labour movement in Israel) that the terms *Second Aliya* and *Third Aliya* have two senses: a chronological sense—that is, all Jews who arrived in Palestine in 1904–1914 and 1919–1923; and a sociological-ideological sense, which encompassed a certain subset of olim who brought with them specific national and social views.[16] Thus, Israeli historiography absolved itself of having to discuss all immigrants and focused instead on the founders of the moshavot from the First Aliya and the pioneering builders from the Second Aliya and the Third Aliya.

Nevertheless, even in later studies, preference is given to the word *aliya* over other words describing the movement of people from place to place. Halamish, for instance, claims that "the use of the word *aliya* in an essay written in Hebrew does not indicate the adoption of a values-based stance; rather, replacing it with other terms is evidence of ideological bias."[17] Avi Picard, in his book about aliya in the 1950s, takes a similar position, arguing that the use of the term *aliya* for the immigration of Jews to the Land of Israel "has values-based significance. However, the use of the term *immigration* also attests to a values-based stance that negates the unique significance of Jews coming to the Land of Israel; therefore it is not neutral. Treating aliya as immigration makes it hard to understand the motivations of the olim and of the establishment that brought them over."[18]

Historical scholarship on the waves of immigration to Palestine has focused mostly on the integration of the so-called olim and their contribution to the Yishuv. The questions asked deal with the localities they established and the cities in which they settled; the political groupings to which they belonged; the institutions that assisted them and those they themselves founded; and the economic, social, and emotional hardships they experienced in their first years in the country. Immigration to Palestine as a historical event, separate from political or settlement activity in Palestine, has rarely been studied. Five studies have addressed immigration itself rather than aspects of absorption and settlement: Moshe Mossek's *Palestine Immigration Policy under Sir Herbert*

Samuel: British, Zionist, and Arab Attitudes; Aviva Halamish's *Be-Meruts Kaful Neged ha-Zeman*; Magdalena Wrobel Bloom's *Social Networks and the Jewish Migration between Poland and Palestine, 1924–1928*; Meir Margalit's *Ha-Shavim be-Dim'a: Ha-Yerida bi-Tekufat ha-Mandat ha-Beriti*; and Hagit Lavsky's *The Creation of the German-Jewish Diaspora: Interwar German-Jewish Immigration to Palestine, the USA, and England*. These are certainly not representative of scholarship in general.

In their books, Mossek and Halamish discuss immigration policy; Lavsky examines German-Jewish migration in the 1920s and 1930s to three destination countries—Palestine, the United States, and England—from a comparative perspective; Wrobel examines the practical aspects of migration; and Margalit looks at Jews who went to Palestine but for various reasons chose not to stay. Moshe Yakir wrote *Toldot ha-Mahlaka la-Aliya shel ha-Histadrut ha-Tsiyonit: Ha-Shanim ha-Rishonot 1919–1927* (The history of the Zionist Organization Aliya Department: the early years, 1919–1927), as an internal Jewish Agency publication from 2006.[19] His in-depth study, which describes the activity of the aliya bureau and the Palestine Offices in Europe in the first decade of the Mandate, contributed greatly to this volume.

Land of Refuge is devoted to the early stages of the migration process, from the vacillations and internal wrestling about whether to emigrate and where to go through the migrants' administrative registration, the start of their journey, the voyage itself, and their arrival on the shores of Palestine. The discussion ends with the immigrants' arrival on the shores of Jaffa or Haifa or at some overland border crossing. The book begins in 1919 with the resumption of immigration to Palestine after the British conquest and ends in 1927, when departures exceeded arrivals and immigration stopped almost completely. Furthermore, by 1927, the entire bureaucratic array of aliya bureaus had been established, the British and Zionist immigration policies had taken shape, and there were no additional dramatic decisions that affected the scope or social composition of immigration.

The primary sources in this volume consist of correspondence between the Palestine Offices and coastal aliya bureaus and the central aliya bureau in Jerusalem. The documents, which are stored in the Central Zionist Archives in Jerusalem, are diverse and rich in content and information: minutes of meetings, lists of applicants for immigration and of people entering the country, letters from Jews expressing interest in immigrating to Palestine and references from their relatives, contracts and agreements with shipping companies, literature offering guidance to immigrants, and many other documents pertaining to immigration to Palestine. Also important are the National Archives of the United Kingdom in the London suburb of Kew; Mandatory government documents stored there provide the British perspective on immigration to Palestine.

The book consists of six chapters. The first chapter examines immigration to Palestine in the broad context of general Jewish migration: the number of Jewish migrants and their destinations, the reasons for the quota laws passed in 1921 and 1924, and the migration societies established in the 1920s to help Jewish migrants through the societies' cooperation with the Zionist Organization. The second chapter focuses on the push factors in the countries of origin: the pogroms in Ukraine, economic hardship in Bolshevik Russia and Poland, and the Zionist youth movements that pressed their members to settle in Palestine and fulfill the Zionist ideal. The third chapter deals with the British and Zionist policies governing immigration to Palestine in the wake of the violence in 1920–1921 and the refugees from the Ukrainian civil war who started to reach Palestine in increasing numbers. The fourth chapter follows the bureaucracy of immigration: the travel papers needed to go to Palestine, the cost of immigration, and the hardships with which the immigrants had to contend from the moment they contacted the local Palestine Office until they reached the shores of Palestine. The fifth chapter deals with the final stage of the journey, from the Jewish immigrants' encounter with the Arab boatmen, to the medical exams on board the ship and at the quarantine camp, to the immigrant homes in Haifa, Jaffa, and Jerusalem. The sixth and final chapter focuses on immigration from Asia and the Maghreb and compares the Palestine Offices' attitude toward immigrants from Islamic countries with their attitude toward immigrants from eastern Europe.

1

New Times, New Tunes

Between 1875 and 1914, approximately 2.5 million Jews emigrated overseas from eastern Europe, changing the face of the Jewish world unrecognizably. New Jewish centers sprouted up ex nihilo, while others shrank. The United States was the main destination; smaller numbers of Jews went to Argentina, Canada, Australia, South Africa, and Palestine. The outbreak of World War I in the summer of 1914 put an end to emigration from eastern Europe westward and to Palestine. Maritime routes were blocked, trains carried soldiers to the battlefield instead of taking emigrants to the ports of departure, ships were nationalized, and land borders were closed.

Despite the bloodbath on the European continent and the difficulty of crossing seas and countries in wartime, Jews continued to attempt to immigrate to the United States in roundabout ways. Many Jews who had emigrated shortly before World War I were now cut off from the families they had left behind. Fearing for their fate, they pressured Jewish aid organizations to find ways of bringing their relatives over or at least contacting them. A new migration route opened during the war via Siberia, China, and Japan to ports on the West Coast of the United States, and from there to cities on the East Coast. In contrast, Palestine was closed completely to immigration, and many people there died of starvation and illness, were deported, or left the country for fear of being drafted into the Ottoman army. The Jewish community in Palestine (known as the *Yishuv*), which had numbered eighty-five thousand people on the eve of World War I, was down to fifty thousand by the end of the war.

Immigration began to increase again shortly after the war ended and soon regained its previous dimensions. In certain senses, the Jewish migration of the

1920s can be seen as a continuation of prewar migration. But despite the similarities, including the fact that the Jews followed similar routes for migration,
this period was really a distinct chapter, unique and exceptional in the history
of Jewish migration in general and Jewish immigration to Palestine in particular. The geopolitical situation had changed beyond recognition, affecting the
scope of migration and its demographic makeup: although migration societies were founded to aid Jewish migrants, the Russian and Austro-Hungarian
empires had broken apart; US quota laws enacted in 1921 and 1924 put an end
to the liberal American immigration policy; and one hundred thousand Jews
were murdered or wounded in hundreds of pogroms in the Ukrainian civil
war from 1917 to 1920. Palestine gradually became the preferred destination
for Jewish migration.

Immigration to Palestine in the 1920s was an inseparable part of overall Jewish migration; it cannot be understood out of its broad historical context. Most
Jewish migrants—whether they went to the United States, South America, or
Palestine—came from the same geographical region and faced the same difficulties: overcoming conservative immigration policies in the various destination countries, obtaining travel papers and visas, planning migration routes,
purchasing tickets for the voyage, and obtaining current information before
setting out. Into the postwar chaos came Jewish migration societies and the
Zionist movement, attempting to put order into the migration process and help
Jewish migrants reach their destinations.

In the following pages we will examine Jewish immigration to the various
destinations—with special emphasis on the United States—from the war years
until the gates of the United States were closed. We will look at the American
quota laws and their impacts on immigration to Palestine, discuss the reasons
for the establishment of Jewish migration societies in the 1920s and their cooperation with the Zionist Organization, and, finally, examine the impact of the
geopolitical changes of the 1920s on immigration to Palestine.

Jewish Migration during World War I

World War I put a sudden end to eastern European Jews' immigration to the
United States and cut off immigrant families from their relatives who had remained behind. The Jews who had settled in the United States, worried about
the news from war-torn Europe, pressured Jewish aid organizations for ways
of restoring contact and suggestions as to how their relatives could be brought
over to America. Parents, children, and other concerned relatives requested

assistance in locating family members who had fled from the battle zones and who had vanished without a trace.

The Hebrew Immigrant Aid Society (HIAS) was established in New York in 1892 by eastern European Jewish immigrants who wanted to assist other Jews just starting out in the United States. It was based on a similarly named organization founded in 1881, which disbanded in 1883. The second HIAS was founded the same year that the US government opened the immigration station on Ellis Island. This was no coincidence. The HIAS hoped to ease immigrants' shock on arrival in the United States as much as possible and help them get through the entry procedure smoothly and without undue hardship. One of its first activities was to station representatives on Ellis Island to mediate between the immigration officials and the Jewish immigrants. The representatives, wearing blue hats with the letters *HIAS* embroidered on them, greeted the newcomers with a warm, calming welcome that expressed solidarity and brotherly concern. The representatives explained the laws governing entry into the United States, translated the immigration inspectors' questions from English to Yiddish, helped immigrants convert their rubles or kronen into dollars, and even gave legal advice to those who were turned back. The HIAS representatives also had a restraining influence on the Ellis Island authorities, who were inclined to reject immigrants and prevent them from entering New York. Representatives of HIAS would continue to assist immigrants as they adjusted to their everyday lives in the United States: they helped them find work, enroll in English classes at night, and wire money to their relatives in Europe. The organization expanded its activity during World War I and especially afterward in the 1920s and 1930s; it also started operations beyond US borders, providing aid to emigrants before they left their countries of origin.[1]

During World War I, HIAS was the natural organization to turn to for those searching for relatives with whom they had lost contact during the chaos of the war.[2] The following two examples are typical of hundreds of letters sent to the HIAS leadership during this time: On September 13, 1915, Celis Levitt contacted HIAS asking for help finding her father so that she could resume contact with him. "Perhaps you can help me make contact with my father, whom I have not heard from in almost a year." Her father, Leib Rubinstein, lived in the Suwałki Governorate in Poland. Levitt noted, "I sent him money at the beginning of the year, but the money never reached him, according to a trace by the bank here that wired the money to Russia. I last heard from him in November 1914. He was suffering from terrible hardship and lacked the absolute necessities of life."[3] Levitt added that she had also lost contact with her sister-in-law Rosa Seriesko and her eight children, who lived in the war zone on the Polish-German border; the last news of her had come from Białystok. In another letter, Rabbi Abraham Halevi Lipschitz of Fall River, Massachusetts, asked HIAS to help him locate his "unfortunate [sons] who remained in Russia and from whom I have had no word for several months." Rabbi Lipschitz wrote,

> They lived in the small town of Slabada, known as Miraslov, in the Suwałki Governorate. They then traveled from the Vilna Governorate to the home of my brother-in-law, Rabbi Avraham Yitzhak Finkelstein. I sent them money and received a reply, but I have not heard anything in months. They may have been exiled from there or remained under German protection. In any case, according to numerous sources you are in touch with many organizations and benevolent institutions in Europe. I therefore hope you will be so good as to support me with your good, sound advice regarding how I should go about achieving my goal of finding out where they are.[4]

World War I caused chaos, confusion, uncertainty, and economic hardship among the Jewish (and non-Jewish) population in eastern Europe. Following the Russian invasion of Galicia, hundreds of thousands of Jews fled or were expelled to western Austria, especially Vienna. Those who remained under czarist occupation were exiled to the Russian interior. This was a personal and community trauma and an economic catastrophe for hundreds of thousands of Jews who became destitute refugees overnight, at the mercy of Jewish aid organizations in Europe and the United States. There are no accurate figures regarding the number of Jewish refugees during World War I. Mordechai Alt-shuler estimates the number at around half a million, whereas Jonathan Frankel believes there were a million Jewish refugees by the end of 1915.[5] The relatives of Celis Levitt and of Rabbi Lipschitz were no doubt part of that wave of refugees that inundated Europe, losing all contact with their families overseas.

Leon Sanders, the president of HIAS from 1909 to 1917, described in his annual address how the war had affected European Jewry. In his overview of his organization's activity in 1915, he expressed profound concern for the fate of the Jews of eastern Europe, depicting their terrible plight in bleak tones.

> Fate, ever cruel to the Jews, has picked out with unerring hand the Jews of Russia, of Poland, and Galicia for a special unmerited place in this world-tragedy. Their homes have become the battleground of Eastern Europe.... Six hundred thousand Jews were suddenly, without warning, expelled from their homes in the war zone, and compelled to leave, often at dead of night, without conveyance, or inhumanly boxed in freight cars—the young, the

Table 1.1. Jewish immigration to the United States, 1915–1918.

Year	Total immigration	Jews	Jews as pct. of total immigrants
1915	327,000	26,000	8.0
1916	299,000	15,000	5.1
1917	295,000	17,000	5.8
1918	111,000	4,000	3.6
Total	1,032,000	62,000	6.0

Source: Hersch, "International Migration," 474.

aged, the crippled, the sick, the mother in labor, even the soldiers in their country's cause—and to wander into the interior of Russia.[6]

Jews continued to immigrate to the United States even during the war, despite the hardships of refugee life and the closure of maritime routes. However, they did so in smaller numbers than before, and the decrease in Jewish immigration was sharper than that in non-Jewish immigration.

Approximately sixty-two thousand Jews entered the United States during World War I, constituting 6 percent of total immigration. Some arrived on the West Coast from Chinese and Japanese ports. These Jews were part of a larger group of twenty thousand refugees who fled the Bolsheviks and the war zone in Europe and reached the Ural Mountains. A small number of them took the Trans-Siberian Railway across the Siberian prairies to Vladivostok and Harbin; some then continued to the port city of Yokohama, Japan. The presence of Jewish refugees in these three Far Eastern cities led to increased activity by HIAS: for the first time in the organization's history, it opened an extension outside the United States. In the years that followed, additional branches were opened in Europe.[7]

Jewish migration from the Far East stopped when the war ended and the maritime routes from western European ports reopened. Jewish refugees no longer traveled to Harbin, Vladivostok, and Yokohama, and HIAS gradually scaled down its activity. In 1920, the organization's representatives returned to the United States, and the HIAS branch in Yokohama was closed.[8] HIAS activity in the Far East was important not only in the context of Jewish migration during World War I but also in terms of the organization's strategic decision to aid Jewish migrants outside the borders of the United States. Through its work in China, Japan, and Russia, HIAS consolidated its status as a leading organization involved in Jewish migration, which in the 1920s and 1930s became the most pressing issue for the Jewish people.

The Social Composition of Jewish Migration in the 1920s

Between 1920 and 1929, more than 620,00 Jews emigrated from eastern Europe to all destination countries. Until 1924, the United States was the preferred destination for Jewish migrants, but after it closed its gates, immigration to other countries increased: more than one hundred thousand Jews immigrated to Palestine, more than sixty-seven thousand to Argentina, forty thousand to Canada, twenty-one thousand to Brazil, and eight thousand to South Africa.

We see from table 1.2 that the United States' closure of its gates in 1924 triggered a change in Jewish migration trends: total Jewish migration dropped by more than 40 percent. New migration routes opened up and alternative destinations were found, especially in South America, and Palestine's share of immigrants increased. The quota law directly impacted all destinations, especially Palestine.

As we can see in figure 1.1, more than 342,000 Jews arrived in the United States in the 1920s, constituting 55 percent of all Jewish migration in that period. Table 1.3 shows that Jewish immigration to the United States declined in the 1920s as a proportion of total immigration. In 1921 and 1922, Jews accounted for 15 and 17 percent of total immigrants, respectively, whereas after 1925, the figure was less than 4 percent. In Canada, Jews constituted 3.7 percent of immigrants on average, and in Argentina, they accounted for an average of 4.8 percent of total immigration.

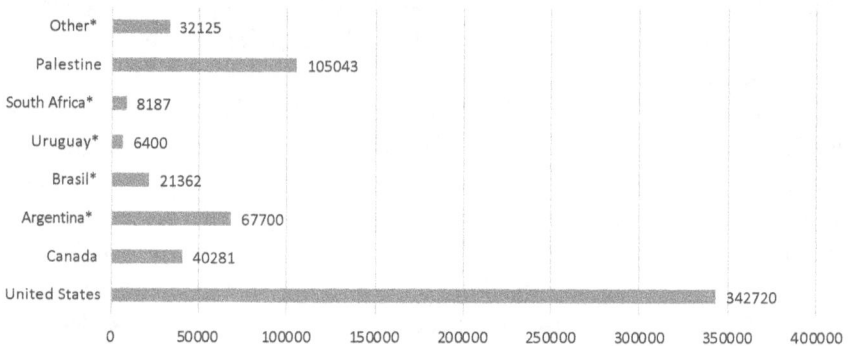

Figure 1.1. Jewish migration by destination, 1920–1929.

Table 1.2. Jewish immigration by destination and year, before and after the quota law.

Years	Total countries	USA	Canada	Argentina	Brazil	Uruguay	South Africa	Palestine	Other
1920–1924	398,776	286,560	18,331	34,864	–	–	–	48,021	11,000
1925–1929	225,042	56,160	21,950	32,836	21,362	6,400	8,187	57,022	21,125

Source: Linfield, *Jewish Migration*, 40.

Table 1.3. Jewish immigration to the United States, 1919–1929.

Year	No. of Jewish immigrants	Jews as pct. of total immigrants
1919	3,055	2.16
1920	14,292	3.32
1921	119,036	14.78
1922	53,524	17.29
1923	49,719	9.51
1924	49,989	7.07
1925	10,292	3.50
1926	10,267	3.37
1927	11,483	3.43
1928	11,639	3.79
1929	12,479	4.46
Total	345,775	7.79

Source: Linfield, *Jewish Migration,* 40; Kaznelson, *L'Immigrazione degli ebrei,* 78–81.

The outstanding feature of Jewish immigration to all countries was its family nature. Between 1899 and 1914, 56 percent of Jewish immigrants to the United States were male and 44 percent were female. In contrast, among non-Jewish immigrants, males were estimated at 68 percent and females at 32 percent. The trend changed in the 1920s, when more Jewish females (54.5 percent) immigrated to the United States than Jewish males (45.6 percent). The main reason for the change was family reunification after the closure of the US gates: as part of the quotas stipulated in the law, visas were issued to women whose husbands had immigrated before the war.

A high proportion of female immigrants generally indicates a high proportion of children as well. Indeed, as figure 1.3 shows, the age distribution of Jewish immigrants to the United States differed from that of non-Jewish immigrants. Between 1899 and 1914, the proportion of children among Jewish immigrants to the United States was twice that among non-Jewish immigrants. About 24 percent of the Jews were aged fourteen and under, compared with only 12 percent of the non-Jews. In those same years, 70 percent of Jewish immigrants were between fourteen and forty-four, and 6 percent were over forty-four. After World War I, the age composition of the Jewish immigrants changed. The proportion of Jewish children shot up to 30 percent in 1921–1924, dropping to 23 percent after the quota law took effect in 1924. The proportion of immigrants aged fourteen to forty-four before and after the enactment of the

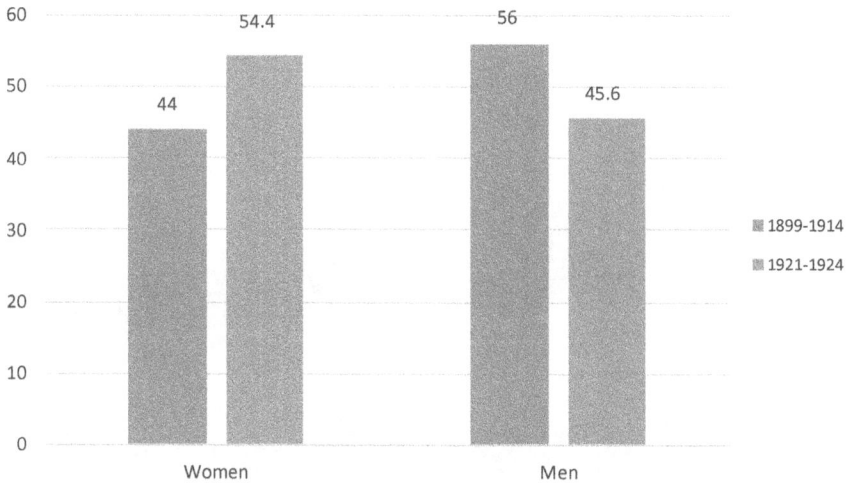

Figure 1.2. Jewish immigration to the United States by sex, 1899–1914 and 1921–1924. Source: Hersch, "Jewish Migrations," 421–22.

quota law is estimated at 58 and 54 percent, respectively. And the proportion of immigrants over age forty-four increased steeply compared with the period of free immigration: 23 percent in 1925–1927 versus 13 percent in 1921–1924.

US immigration statistics divided occupations into three categories: professional, skilled, and miscellaneous. Skilled workers included tradespeople,

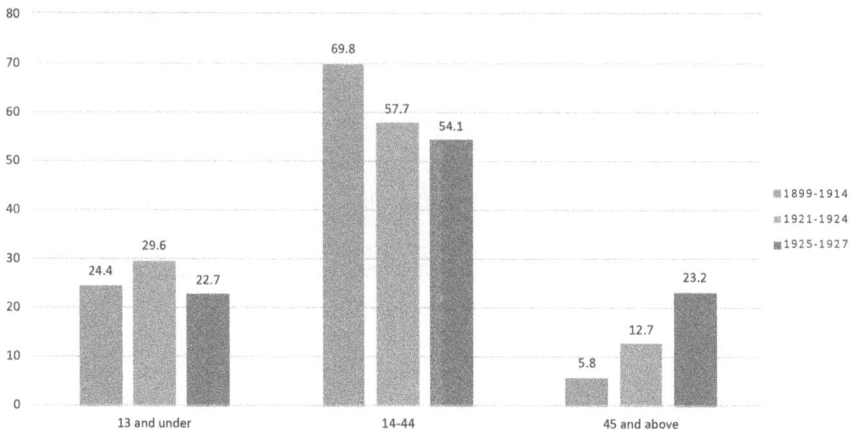

Figure 1.3. Jewish immigration to the United States by age, 1899–1914, 1921–1924, and 1925–1927. Source: Hersch, "Jewish Migrations," 422.

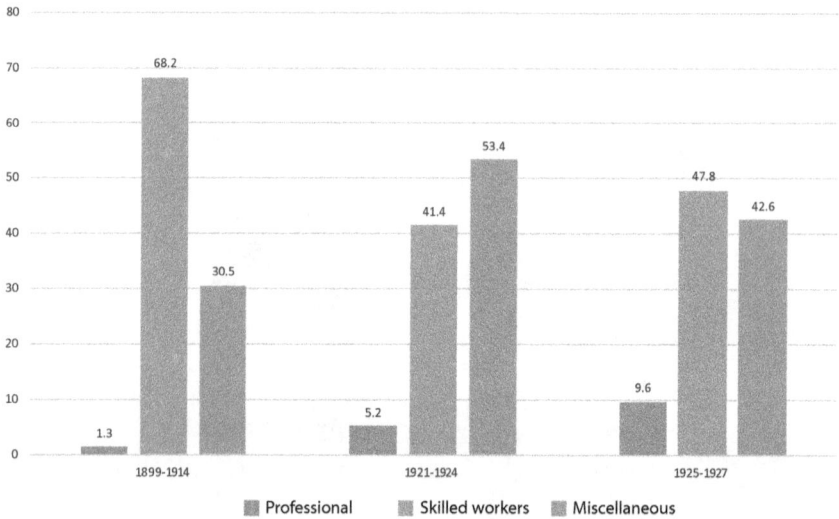

Figure 1.4. Jewish immigration to the United States by occupation, 1899–1914, 1921–1924, and 1925–1927. Source: Hersch, "Jewish Migrations," 424.

industrial workers, and white-collar workers. The "miscellaneous" category was broad and diverse, encompassing farm workers, unskilled workers, and domestic workers as well as industrialists, merchants, and middlemen.

Two-thirds of Jewish immigrants in the United States in the 1920s (more than half a million individuals) were skilled workers, most of them (329,000) employed in the garment industry. The rest worked in the wood, food, metal, paper, and textile industries.

The occupations of Jewish immigrants to the United States, too, differed before and after the war. Table 1.4 shows the changes in the occupational

Table 1.4. Occupations of Jewish immigrants in the United States (pct.).

Occupation	1899–1914	1921–1924
Agriculture	2.6	3.0
Industry	65.6	36.3
Commerce	9.2	17.1
Professionals	1.3	5.4
Unskilled workers	21.3	38.2
Total	**100.0**	**100.0**

Source: Hersch, "Jewish Migrations," 424.

composition of Jewish immigration to the United States in the 1920s. The proportion of unskilled workers rose, especially due to the large number of newly arrived women and children, while the proportion of industrial workers dropped. In addition, the proportions of Jewish immigrants working in commerce and the liberal professions increased in the 1920s.

The Butterfly Effect: The Quota Laws of 1921 and 1924

When I got the departure papers, I borrowed 25 million marks, and I went to Warsaw to get information about my trip to America. Unfortunately, however, I didn't get any good news in Warsaw. I went to HIAS and showed them my papers, but they said that the quotas for 1924 and 1925 had already been filled by people in the first and second categories. If I wanted to, they said, I could register for 1926, but it could turn out that the 1926 quota will also be filled by those in the first and second categories. It could well be that we will never get to go at all.[9]

This is how Wolf Lewkowicz of Łódź described to his nephew Sol Zissman in America being turned down for a visa to the United States. In the first half of the 1920s, the US government toughened its immigration policy, enacting two quota laws that drastically reduced the number of immigrants, and especially the number of Jews, admitted into the country. Like many Polish Jews, Lewkowicz was trying to leave Poland due to his dire financial situation but encountered bureaucratic and legal obstacles posed by American consuls applying the policy rigidly, preventing him and many others from entering the United States.

The roots of the stringent American immigration policy, which led to the closure of the country's gates in 1924, lay in American attitudes toward immigrants during the second half of the nineteenth century. Between 1820 and 1880, some ten million immigrants arrived in the United States. A quarter million of them were from Asia, most of them Chinese, and these gradually became an unwanted ethnic minority. They were different from the surrounding society, with a unique culture, a different way of life, and even their own justice system. The native-born white population persecuted them, seeing them as an inferior ethnic group that threatened the character of American society. In the 1870s and 1880s, fear of Chinese domination led to the enactment of several laws intended to limit immigration from Asia. The Chinese Exclusion Act, passed on May 6, 1882, stopped migration from China to the United States almost entirely. In many senses, this law was a watershed in US immigration policy, the harbinger of a long series of restrictive immigration laws.[10]

The Immigration Act of 1882, passed on August 3, further limited immigration to the United States. This law banned not only Asians but also criminals, the mentally ill, the intellectually disabled, and all those who could not take care of themselves and their families and were liable to become a burden on society.[11] The laws of May and August 1882 illustrate the change in US legislative policy, which became increasingly tougher until the final closure of the gates in 1924. Each law expanded on the previous one and was usually more stringent. The various immigration laws passed until the quota laws of the 1920s set forth eight categories whose members were barred from entering the United States: contract workers, Asians, criminals, "moral degenerates" and people with bad reputations, the ill or disabled, the poor, revolutionaries, and the illiterate.

In his book *World of Our Fathers*, Irving Howe maintains, "Irksome as such laws were from the point of view of the immigrants and their defenders, none constituted nearly so great a threat as the recurrent proposal that persons unable to read or write their own language be barred."[12] According to Howe, this would dramatically reduce free immigration, and whenever such a bill came up for debate in Congress, the ethnic communities that would be affected mobilized to fight it. Three times literacy bills reached Congress, and three times presidents vetoed them: Grover Cleveland in 1897, William Howard Taft in 1913, and Woodrow Wilson in 1915. One American Jewish leader who opposed such legislation was Louis Marshall, an attorney with German-born parents who for many years headed the American Jewish Committee. Marshall argued that not knowing how to read and write was in itself an insufficient reason to consider an immigrant "undesirable," as educated immigrants were not necessarily more beneficial. In fact, the anarchists and socialists whom many Americans were afraid of tended to come from the educated classes and were often fluent in more than one language.[13]

The quota laws of 1921 and 1924 were the last laws enacted to limit immigration to the United States. In the 1880s, Americans had been worried about Chinese immigrants, and the exclusion laws had been directed against them, but forty years later, it was the Jews and Italians who concerned them. Between 1907 and 1910, a congressional committee headed by Senator William Dillingham studied the impact of immigration on American society. In 1911, the Dillingham Commission issued a thorough, comprehensive report that filled forty-two volumes. It addressed a long list of topics: the relationship between immigration and crime, the integration of immigrants in major industrial cities, literacy skills in English, housing conditions, and occupations.[14] The authors of the report warned against continued free immigration from Europe and recommended limiting it by means of quotas. The conclusions of

אירגעבורטסטאג 35 איר

„עפעס אזוי זיינינ טעניטען קומען מיך היינט באגריסען צו מיינע אימינינעם..."

(די וואך איז געווארטען) 35 יאר זינט מ'האט אין נ.י. 'ארקער האפען אוועקגעשטעלם ,די סטאטשו או ליבערטי.")

Figure 1.5. "So few people are coming today to congratulate me on my birthday." This week is the thirty-fifth anniversary of the placement of the Statue of Liberty in New York Harbor. *Der Groyser Kundes,* November 4, 1921.

the report, published before World War I, were the main motivation for the enactment of the quota laws a decade later.

Senator Dillingham was the first to introduce the idea of quotas. The first quota law, introduced by chair of the House Immigration Committee Albert Johnson, would suspend immigration to the United States for two years until a permanent immigration policy could be drawn up and enshrined in law. At first there was to be an annual quota for each country of 5 percent of the number of nationals of that country living in the United States in 1910. The House passed the bill but with the annual quota reduced to just 3 percent. The quota did not apply to foreigners under eighteen who were descendants or first-degree relatives of US citizens. Nor did it apply to intellectuals, artists, and professionals; these groups were given special status. President Wilson opposed the bill, but he was nearing the end of his term. When Warren Harding became president in 1921, he promoted the bill and signed it into law.[15]

Some of the arguments of the senators opposed to immigration were anti-semitic, xenophobic, and anti-European. They were afraid that the immigrants coming to the United States en masse posed a threat to the majority society and would undermine its stability. They argued that the immigrants—particularly Jews and Italians—had been unable to integrate in the host society and had created threatening ethnic enclaves. Representative Albert Johnson of Washington quoted US Consular Service director Wilbur Carr as describing the Jews as filthy, dangerous, and unpatriotic.[16] Johnson added that the United States was inundated with "abnormally twisted," "unassimilable" Jews who were "filthy, un-American and often dangerous in their habits."[17] The term *un-American* had undergone a transformation over the years. At first it had been used to describe opponents to immigration on the grounds that they were undermining the American ethos of a nation of immigrants open to all; by the 1920s, however, it was used derogatorily to refer to immigrants who would apparently never be Americans.

The Emergency Quota Act of 1921 (the "Johnson Act") allotted to each country an immigration quota equal to 3 percent of the number of its nationals living in the United States in 1910. The bill, passed in the Senate by a vote of 78–1, did not include in the quota asylum-seekers persecuted on religious grounds in their countries. The Immigration Act of 1924 (the "Johnson-Reed Act") then reduced the quota to just 2 percent and changed the reference year. It had become clear to the authors of the bill that the results of the 1910 census permitted the entry of too many immigrants from southern and eastern Europe, so they set 1890—when the number of Jews and Italians in the United States was much lower—as the base year. The new law also stipulated that visas would be issued in the countries of origin instead of at Ellis Island; the US consuls in those countries were authorized to reject or approve immigration applications.

These changes in US immigration laws had a tremendous impact on eastern European Jews who wanted to emigrate, as they now were unable to enter the United States. The story of Rachel Tauber is typical: After fleeing to Romania in 1920 from Myastkovka, Ukraine, she waited in vain for a visa to the United States. Eventually, she moved to Palestine instead. "Until aid came from America, until the letters went there and back and they arranged for the money, it took five months. When the money arrived, we went with Avraham and Otti to Bucharest, where we received the money and the visa." But in Bucharest they were told by the American consul, "Just yesterday the order came from America not to let immigrants from Russia enter America. . . . So we wrote to America . . . and we remained in Bucharest and waited for the visa to come from Palestine."[18] Tauber was not the only one who waited in vain. In the following

Table 1.5. Immigration quotas to the United States by nationality, 1925–1927.

Northwestern Europe and Scandinavia		Eastern and southern Europe		Other countries	
Country	Quota	Country	Quota	Country	Quota
Germany	51,227	Poland	5,982	Africa	1,100
Great Britain and Northern Ireland	34,007	Italy	3,845	Armenia	124
Ireland	28,567	Czechoslovakia	3,073	Australia	121
Sweden	9,561	Russia	2,248	Palestine	100
Norway	6,453	Yugoslavia	671	Syria	100
France	3,954	Romania	603	Turkey	100
Denmark	2,789	Portugal	503	Egypt	100
Switzerland	2,081	Hungary	473	New Zealand and the Pacific Islands	100
Netherlands	1,648	Lithuania	344	Other	1,900
Austria	785	Latvia	142		
Belgium	512	Spain	131		
Finland	471	Estonia	124		
Danzig	228	Albania	100		
Iceland	100	Bulgaria	100		
Luxembourg	100	Greece	100		
Total	142,483	Total	18,439	Total	3,745

Source: Statistical Abstract of the United States (Washington, DC: US Dept. of Commerce, US GPO, 1929), 100.

chapters, we will see that tens of thousands of refugees and migrants like her who hoped to go to America were rejected by the American consuls and finally went to Palestine for lack of any other choice.

Table 1.5 shows that 86.5 percent of the quotas were reserved for immigrants from northern Europe and Scandinavia; 11.2 percent were for eastern and southern Europeans; and 2.3 percent were for people from the Middle East, Africa, and the Pacific. Only 8,230 people were permitted to immigrate to the United States from Poland and Russia. Thus, it comes as no surprise that the quotas were filled quickly and obtaining a visa became a complicated, nearly

Figure 1.6. Waiting in line at the HIAS offices in Warsaw (HIAS Archives).

impossible bureaucratic task. Long lines of prospective immigrants stretched outside American consulates in the hope of obtaining longed-for visas. Lillian Gorenstein recounts how her mother set out early in the morning to stand in line at the US consulate, leaving her small children in a tiny rented apartment on Nalewki Street. She waited weeks to get a visa.

One's place in line was valuable, and hustlers and thieves took advantage of the situation to cheat the people waiting. Sometimes they stole their numbers in line and sold them on the black market. Gorenstein said, "One day while Ma was standing in line, a man came over to her and told her that he could help her reach the consulate much faster, if she would just give him her number. He showed her a few other numbers and so she believed him and handed him hers also. She never saw the man again. She had to start all over, and it took her over six weeks to reach the same place in the line."[19]

The masses of Jews hoping to emigrate did not find tolerant, accepting officials at the American consulates. In most cases, their requests, entreaties, and pleas did no good, as the consular workers abided by every clause of the immigration law. Visa applicants encountered arrogant officials and sometimes even antisemitic ones who were repulsed by Jews. The historian Tara Zahra gives an example of the discriminatory attitude of the US consul in Warsaw: A Jewish woman named Esther Reisfeld was applying for visas for herself and her two daughters, ages fourteen and fifteen. Her husband was already a US citizen, so according to the Johnson-Reed Act, she was eligible for a visa. At the consulate, she was given an intelligence test, which she failed because she did not correctly answer such questions as the following: What is more neces-sary, the fly or the butterfly? How many feathers does a goose have? How many stars are there in heaven? Which is heavier, one pound of corn or one pound of feathers? How many legs does an American cat have? Reisfeld was labeled mentally defective and was denied the visa.[20]

The quota laws dramatically changed the procedure for entering the United States. Until World War I, the entry procedure had taken place within the United States. Even after immigrants disembarked, they did not know whether the American immigration officials would let them in. After quotas were set and immigrants had to get an official visa from the US consulate before embarking, the center of gravity moved to the country of origin, and the immigrants set out knowing that they would be admitted into the United States.

The new immigration laws also posed a challenge for American Jews, who had to contend with their ramifications. The restrictions on immigration prompted Jews to try to enter the country by various illegal means: they slipped across the Mexico-Texas border, entered on false passports via Cuba, and paid smugglers to take them in. The American Jewish leadership faced a dilemma: on the one hand, they felt solidarity with the plight of the Jewish refugees from eastern Europe; on the other hand, as law-abiding US citizens, they could not give their imprimatur to lawbreaking. The historian Libby Garland maintains that the efforts of the American Jewish leadership at that time focused mainly on mitigating the law and finding loopholes that would enable individuals and special groups to enter the country.[21]

For want of an alternative for the thousands of Jews hoping to immigrate to the United States, Palestine became a destination in demand. In the space of one decade, the Yishuv tripled in size—from a population of 60,000 in 1919 to 180,000 in 1929. The year 1925 was a turning point in the history of Jewish mi-gration: for the first time, more immigrants entered Palestine than the United States. What Zionism had failed to do in four decades was accomplished by two antisemitic US senators who closed the gates of the United States, making Palestine the main destination for Jewish migration.

Jewish Immigration Societies

Barriers to emigration also existed in the countries of origin. Freedom of movement in Europe was limited, and the right to travel from country to country became a political tool for the new countries that had arisen after the war.[22] The restrictions on movement were anchored in an official set of travel and border-control documents that made it possible to identify citizens. These papers became ideal means of closing borders and keeping out ethnic groups that did not belong to the country's nationality. Passports became a visible sign of a country's sovereignty and translated the abstract presence of the sovereign into everyday reality.[23] This "belonging on paper," as the historian Yaron Jean terms it, was particularly problematic for eastern European Jews, many of whom had become refugees during the war and were wandering through Europe without any papers. These people had difficulty finding a place for themselves in the new order. Furthermore, the new immigration laws confused them, leaving them to rely on rumors and dubious advice from travel agents with their own agenda.

An article titled "The Migration Crisis," printed in the journal *Ha-Tsefira*, succinctly expressed the migration difficulties of the early 1920s in the countries of origin and destination. "The chief immigration official in America announces that he sees no way out of the crisis other than stopping the issuance of travel papers." Similarly, the Zionist Executive issued an "order to the Palestine Offices to stop migration." Canada imposed obstacles for immigrants, "threatening to send them back to their places." "Everywhere the migrants go . . . we hear the locking of gates." But there were difficulties in the countries of origin as well: "In addition, doors are being shut somewhat even in the countries the migrants are leaving. New orders are being promulgated in Poland regarding the issuance of travel papers," while Soviet Russia "is not allowing anyone to leave the country at all."[24] These circumstances made things difficult for migrants in general, and Jewish migrants in particular:

> Everywhere, most of all, and to the greatest extent, the Jews are suffering.
> [This is] already [the case] simply because they are forced to emigrate
> because their homes have been burned on top of them, because death pursues
> them, because people's cruelty gives them no rest. . . . The emigration crisis is
> obvious. Soon the sound of the cry of the wretched condemned to annihilation will break out. Yet in the final hour there is hope, namely, the organization and resolution of emigration. We must establish committees for the
> Jewish emigrants. Be aware that future generations will hold you to account,
> because when arrangements and order could have helped, you did nothing.[25]

Even experienced immigration activists who had been experts in the intricacies of the immigration bureaucracy before World War I had a hard time understanding the new laws and the impact they would have on Jewish migration. A HIAS representative in Germany, for example, asked the American consul a series of questions even before the first quota law was passed, to understand what migrants had to do in order to enter the United States: "First, regarding the Polish travel documents . . . what type of travel documents do you accept? . . . And do you issue visas immediately based on travel papers issued by the Polish consul? Second, regarding travel papers from Ukraine, White Russia . . . and other countries that previously belonged to the Russian Empire . . . do you accept all these travel papers for the purpose of issuing visas?"[26]

The Jewish emigrants' suffering and helplessness in the face of geopolitical changes led to the establishment of dozens of Jewish migration societies throughout Europe in the 1920s. Their primary mission was to provide prospective emigrants with reliable, authoritative information and help them carry out their decision. In early June 1921, the Jewish Colonization Association (ICA) organized a conference in Brussels to find solutions to the prevailing migration problems. Thirty-two delegates representing twenty organizations took part in the conference—the first in the 1920s and one of many that would take place in the coming years. The conference delegates exchanged valuable information and reiterated the need for coordination among all organizations dealing with migration. They called for the establishment of a single emigration council that would coordinate and streamline the work of the migration societies. The conference ended without any real results. In late September of that year, however, another emigration conference was held in Prague at the initiative of HIAS. At the end of this conference the participants decided to establish the Faraynigten Komitet far Yidishe Oysvanderung (United Jewish Emigration Committee, or Emigdirect).[27]

Prominent Jewish public figures were elected to the board of directors, secretariat, and plenum of Emigdirect, including Leo Motzkin, Ze'ev Latzky-Bertholdi, Myron Kreinin, Vladimir Tiomkin, Ilja Dijour, Elias Tcherikower, Jacob Lestschinsky, and Dr. Julius Brutzkus.[28] Motzkin opened the conference, describing its objective as being "to send abroad the Jews who have been harmed by the pogroms and to open the immigration countries to them." Kreinin described the bleak situation of Russian Jewry: "Four million Jews are in the most dire state of emergency. Antisemitism is increasing. The pogroms in Ukraine and White Russia are going on regularly. The government is helpless to fight the various groups."[29] Latzky-Bertholdi spoke of "the need to establish an emigration bank that will try to coordinate all emigration-related activities."[30]

Table 1.6. Money transfers via HIAS from Americans to their relatives in Poland, 1920–1925.

Year	Sum transferred ($)	No. of migrants
1920	1,042,728	14,292
1921	5,386,791	119,036
1922	5,052,002	53,524
1923	2,186,307	49,989
1924	1,725,331	10,292
1925	1,421,966	10,267
Total	16,815,125	257,400
	[equivalent to $250,280,163 in 2021]	

Source: Szajkowski, "American Jewish Overseas Relief," 246.

The founding conference of Emigdirect passed a series of resolutions that immediately and directly made life easier for Jewish emigrants, helping them make the decision to emigrate and to carry it out. The participants voted to ensure collaboration among the various migration societies; publish reliable, up-to-date information for Jewish emigrants; negotiate with consuls from immigration countries for entry visas; aid Jewish emigrants in the ports of departure; and help immigrants find work in their new land. The greatest challenge for Emigdirect was to establish a bank that would handle the financial management of Jewish emigration, particularly exchanging and transferring money in various currencies, selling tickets for the voyage, and providing loans and financial aid to emigrants.[31]

Emigdirect took on responsibility for negotiating with the shipping companies for lower fares and better conditions on the voyage. Until the founding of Emigdirect, each migration society had operated individually, and their successes had been limited. The united organization was able to exert more pressure on the shipping companies, with good results. When the United States closed its gates to immigrants, Emigdirect worked on lowering fares to South America. It purchased hundreds of tickets from the various shipping companies and sold them directly to the immigrants at reduced prices, thus sparing them from having to deal with travel agents or shipping companies themselves.[32]

One of Emigdirect's first activities was to publish a Yiddish-language migration newspaper titled *Di Idishe Emigratsie*, which provided the emigrants with the information they needed. Migration-related newspapers were nothing new in the Jewish world. At the start of the twentieth century, the ICA information bureau had put out a twice a month entitled *Der Yudisher Emigrant*, with articles on a range of topics related to emigration to various countries. Printing and distribution of the *Der Yudisher Emigrant* stopped when World War I broke out and did not resume after the war. The new Emigdirect publication became a vital source of information for Jewish emigrants. The articles and commentary dealt with all aspects of Jewish emigration: Jewish communities in South America, Jewish emigration via France, emigration from Russia, the emigration bank established in Kishinev, immigration to Palestine and the cost of living in Tel Aviv, the US immigration laws and efforts to repeal them, the struggle against the shipping companies, and much more.

In late 1926, HIAS, the ICA, and Emigdirect merged to form a single society by the name of HICEM. The name of the new organization reflected all three of its components: Hias-ICa-EMigdirect. Twenty-three local migration societies in eighteen countries collaborated with HICEM and made use of its services.[33] In its first nine months, 70,000 people passed through the society's offices, 12,000 received legal advice, and more than 31,000 emigrants were sent by HICEM to various destination countries.[34]

At a press conference held by HICEM a year after its founding, Elias Tcherikower, a member of the board, explained its importance and its method of operation: "After the war, which completely halted Jewish emigration, committees and societies were established in many countries to come to the aid of the Jewish emigrant." These migration societies "varied in their outlooks and methods, but in the end all arrived at the clear recognition that emigration is a field of action in which one cannot work in isolation." Only through joint, coordinated work can anything be achieved, Tcherikower maintained. "Protecting Jewish migrants from the shipping company scoundrels, settling them in a foreign land, seeking new lines of work and immigration locations—these are all matters that can be resolved only by uniting all the societies in one center."[35]

HICEM spent time and money on training the migrants before their departure for their destination. "Agricultural courses have been established, and we are sure that those who attend these courses will become pioneers of Jewish productivization in the immigration countries and will not do some other sort of work there," Tcherikower explained to the Jewish journalists. "We have established courses in crafts, taking into account the crafts needed in the immigration countries. Courses have been offered in English and Spanish, and 750 migrants have learned these languages in them."[36] HICEM helped the migrants after they arrived at their destinations, too. It remained in touch with

Figure 1.7. Prospective emigrants at the HIAS office in Warsaw (YIVO).

Jewish organizations in the destination countries and sent them money to offer vocational courses so as to help the immigrants find work and integrate in the surrounding society.

One of HICEM's main activities was to find new destinations for Jewish emigrants. A delegation that traveled to South America concluded that Argentina, Brazil, and Uruguay would be good countries for Jewish immigration. Conditions in these countries were better than they had been in the United States in the 1880s, when the first immigrants from eastern Europe had arrived. In these South American countries, *landsmanshaftn* (associations of people from the same town or region in the old country) and other aid organizations sprouted up to support the immigrants and help them make a new start in the new land. The HICEM delegation estimated that South America could take in 20,000 Jewish immigrants a year. In Argentina, an association by the name of Soprotimis, founded in 1922, helped immigrants purchase and settle land, as well as find work in the colonies of Baron Hirsch. Soprotimis also operated in Montevideo, Uruguay, and two other associations were established in Brazil: Benficiente in Rio de Janeiro and Ezra in São Paulo.[37]

Emigdirect, HICEM, and Immigration to Palestine

The Jewish migration societies did not assist those who wanted to go to Palestine; instead, they referred them to the Palestine Offices, run by the Zionist Executive in all the countries of origin of Jewish emigration. The Palestine Offices (which will be discussed at length in chapter 4) were not established ex nihilo; they operated in the same geographical regions as the international migration societies, contended with the same difficulties, and sometimes even collaborated with them. A comparison of the patterns of activity of the Zionist Organization's Aliya Department with those of the international Jewish migration societies shows numerous similarities: the Zionist movement encouraged emigrants to enroll in Hebrew-language courses and agricultural training programs in Europe before going to Palestine, provided financial support for Jews considering immigration to Palestine, offered reliable, up-to-date information about settlement in Palestine, negotiated with the shipping companies for better conditions on the voyage, and was in ongoing contact with the Mandatory government in Palestine regarding immigration policy.

The establishment of Emigdirect and HICEM inspired hope in the Aliya Department that cooperation between the Zionist movement and the non-Zionist migration societies could further and assist in immigration to Palestine. Although HIAS, the ICA, and Emigdirect were not Zionist organizations, they advocated aid to Jewish emigrants irrespective of their destination and political or ideological worldview. An opinion piece printed in *Doar Hayom* argued that collaboration between HICEM and the Yishuv in Palestine was essential, and that HICEM had no choice but to support and aid the Zionist settlement enterprise. "Whereas the attitude of HIAS, Emigdirect, and the ICA toward building the national home in Palestine was until now passive if not negative, the merger of these three associations is not physical but chemical and the joint association created from them has new properties" that none of the individual organizations had before the merger. According to this opinion piece, HICEM's success was contingent "not only on its financial means" but also "on the extent of the psychological understanding of the character and true needs of the Jewish people" and on the new geopolitical situation. "These days, [HICEM] will not come across big industrial lands in the United States of America with cities that are developing from one day to the next, that can swallow millions of Jews one by one and give them a quick, ready-made livelihood. In such times, our immigrants need to conquer nature and the primordial wilds, settle bit by bit in empty wilderness countries, and bear on their backs the entire heavy, dangerous burden of the New Yishuv."[38]

The migration societies had learned from experience that it was almost impossible to settle Jews in remote, unfamiliar countries and turn them into farmers against their will. "The cities of Australia, South Africa, and the like can take in only a few immigrants. A spacious receptacle for our emigrants can only exist today in new localities that are based on Jewish agriculture." "[HICEM] will seek out empty corners for settlement in all ends of the earth, and Palestine will, by hook or by crook, be within its field of vision." HICEM, the article in *Doar Hayom* argued, would conclude that Palestine was the only suitable destination for Jewish emigrants. "The new settlements can only be built on autonomous foundations, which will require great expenditure of finances and energy—and the Yishuv in Palestine, which already has an administrative apparatus and a ready-made political platform, will no longer look extremely dear and harsh in comparison."[39] The migration society must immediately and without delay enter into "negotiations with the Zionist Executive in London and with the aliya offices in the Diaspora and in Palestine regarding coordinating and sharing the work."[40] In such a way, "our international migration workers [will] come to participate in building up the Land of Israel, not based on a national consciousness but on external, objective necessity." The collaboration, however, should focus on settlement, and not on arrangements for migration: "We have enough aliya offices, whereas we do not have sufficient means to conquer the land we are standing on. . . . Broad horizons for large-scale national work are available to [HICEM] for the migration that is taking shape—and if it does not stray, its path will lead to Zion."[41]

Although the Jewish migration societies focused most of their efforts in the 1920s on South America, they did cooperate with the Zionist Organization. In 1926 Professor Hermann Pick, director of the Aliya Department, was asked at a press conference for details of the negotiations conducted by Emigdirect and HIAS with the Zionist Organization. He replied, "The negotiations cannot yet be publicized, but it can almost be determined that they have had positive results and that activity in this regard will begin soon."[42]

Emigdirect, HIAS, and HICEM indeed helped the Zionist movement and immigrants who chose to go to Palestine. They supported *halutzim* whose aliya had been delayed and who were stuck in Europe with no source of livelihood; they raised funds in the United States for immigration to South America and Palestine; and they provided financial support for immigrant homes in Europe that the Zionist movement sometimes had difficulty funding.[43] Sometimes the Jewish migration societies asked the Palestine Offices to help a particular individual. In August 1926, for instance, the Palestine Office in Warsaw asked the

Aliya Department in Jerusalem to expedite the aliya of "the orphan Svintzky, a refugee from Ukraine." According to the letter, the request had come from the ICA and HIAS. "To this day this letter of ours has not been answered. Nor does the English consulate have any instructions regarding an entry permit for this orphan. Both the HIAS migration society and ICA are demanding that we enable this orphan to immigrate."[44]

In 1924, the Zionist Organization offered HIAS an original outline for collaboration in sending immigrants to Palestine. The Mandatory immigration laws limited the number of Jews permitted to enter the country, but they allowed unlimited entry of "persons of means." According to the Mandatory definition, a "person of means" was someone in possession of 500 pounds sterling ($2,250) or the equivalent in property (jewelry, goods, tools, etc.). The Zionist Organization proposed using American Jewish money to bring in as many immigrants as possible under the category of persons of means. "American Jewry can help a lot with this. . . . The immigrants have relatives in America who can lend them the money they lack, and thus enable them to be classified in one of the aforementioned categories and obtain a visa for Palestine. HIAS, which is in touch with all the American Jews who are interested in Jewish migration, whether for general humanitarian reasons or national reasons and by virtue of its sense of connection to their people there, is the organization best suited to embark on such an action and raise the funds for immigration to Palestine."[45]

The Zionist Organization pledged to provide HIAS with lists of candidates who had relatives in the United States and had been found suitable for immigration to Palestine, and HIAS would be asked to locate their relatives in America. With American Jewish money, loans from their relatives in America, and the help of HIAS (which was based in the United States), the Zionist movement hoped to move the Jewish immigrants into the category of "persons of means." From a Zionist perspective, the proposed plan had another advantage: by recruiting American Jews to support immigration to Palestine, HIAS would be adding a Zionist stamp to its activity on behalf of Jewish immigrants, thus giving American Jewry a connection to Zionism. "This procedure will result in the creation of a personal relationship between the lender and the loans and will arouse the American brother's interest in the fate of the person he is helping, as well as in the general work of renewal and rebuilding in Palestine. . . . HIAS currently has an opportunity to carry out the great mission, a truly Jewish mission."[46]

This collaborative project never came to pass. HIAS concentrated the bulk of its efforts on sending Jewish immigrants to South America and focused less on immigration to Palestine. But the very idea shows that there was dialogue between the Jewish migration societies and the aliya department and Palestine Offices and that they relied on one another.

Emigration resumed immediately after World War I and soon reached its prewar dimensions. The push factors in the countries of origin had grown worse; the hardship and poverty were more extreme. Tens of thousands of refugees were wandering through Europe. The United States, fearing inundation by Europeans, closed its gates. Other immigration countries followed suit, starting to pose difficulties for prospective immigrants. Westward emigration from Europe was no longer unrestricted; various travel papers and visas were required. Whereas before World War I the admission procedure to the destination country had taken place at the end of the journey, in the 1920s it started in the country of origin, in a form resembling that familiar to us today: one visited an embassy or consulate, was interviewed by an immigration official, signed various forms, and finally received the entry visa or rejection.

The emigrants had a hard time understanding and coping with the new situation. They needed middlemen to help them cross the bureaucratic minefield created by tough postwar immigration policies. The result was the emergence of Jewish aid organizations, which worked hard on behalf of the Jewish emigrants. At first these were HIAS and the ICA, founded before World War I. Later several migration committees were set up, followed by new migration societies: Emigdirect and HICEM. These societies served as the emigrants' representatives. They negotiated with consuls for visas and with shipping companies for lower fares and better conditions; they provided reliable, up-to-date information in various languages and helped the emigrants obtain the necessary travel papers. This was a multifaceted, multidimensional, philanthropic, humanitarian project conducted by organized world Jewry and led by American Jewry.

The activity of the Aliya Department of the Zionist Executive should be viewed in this historical context, as part of a continuum of events and organizations, and not in isolation. In practice, the assistance provided by the Aliya Department to prospective immigrants to Palestine was no different from the aid offered by the non-Zionist Jewish migration societies, but despite the similarities, and although there was some collaboration, there was one fundamental difference that prevented greater collaboration. The Zionist movement only helped Jews who wanted to immigrate to Palestine, whereas the migration societies helped all Jewish emigrants, irrespective of their destination. Emigdirect and later HICEM had the welfare of the entire Jewish people in mind. They offered financial and legal assistance to all emigrants until they arrived in the destination country. In contrast, the Zionist movement in the 1920s focused on the welfare of Palestine and regarded candidates for immigration as means of achieving its national objectives. Therefore the Zionist movement adopted a selective immigration policy and preferred to assist those who could contribute to building up the land. For the Jewish migration societies, aiding Jewish emigrants was the goal for which they had been founded. They were not trying to further a particular national idea or ideology, but rather to find ways of resolving the migration difficulties of the Jewish people in view of the harsh conditions that prevailed at the time and in view of the Jews' desire to go to any country that would let them in.

2

Town on Fire

We are the segment of Jewry, incited against and despised, that has borne
the nation's troubles on its shoulders for generations. We are the ones who,
imprisoned and oppressed in the Pale of Settlement, were forced to eat each
other's flesh and breathe air that suffocates both body and soul under the
old regime of Nicholas and his predecessors. We are the ones who bore the
nation's guilt on our shoulders and were condemned by libels that threw our
honor in the dirt at the time of the Beilis trial. We are the ones who were
constantly attacked in pogroms, our lives and property forfeit and trampled
under our enemies' feet. We are the ones who, sheep to the slaughter, were
killed by the thousands, even tens of thousands, in the days of Denikin and
Petliura and their comrades, who rose up and drowned us in rivers of blood,
smashed our children and broke open our pregnant women, killed our
young men with the sword and looted our property. [We are the ones] who
moan and groan under the weight of terrible suffering in bitter, black exile,
and whose only hope, the hope of revival in our land, has consoled us in our
distress and lit up our dark lives, which are immersed in a sea of troubles and
filled with thousands of sacks of tears.[1]

This desperate cry, sent by thirty-one families from Ukraine to the Zionist Executive, expresses the main reasons for Jewish emigration from eastern Europe
in the 1920s: financial hardship, government persecution, pogroms, and Zionist
ideology. In addition, the far-reaching quota laws enacted in the United States
in 1921 and 1924 (discussed in the previous chapter) directly affected the scope
of immigration to Palestine during the Mandate period.

Zionist historiography has divided immigration in the 1920s into two waves:
the Third Aliya (1919–1923), defined as pioneering (halutzic) immigration, and

the Fourth Aliya (1924–1928), defined as bourgeois. Historians have paid little attention to the immigrants' motivations, focusing instead on their contribution to the Yishuv. The resultant dichotomy between halutzim and bourgeoisie has blurred the range of push factors that brought immigrants to Palestine in the 1920s.[2] When we examine the causes of Jewish immigration from eastern Europe at that time, we find that the prevailing historiographical division into halutzic immigration and bourgeois immigration is erroneous and fundamentally flawed. Rather, the entire decade should be viewed as a single period in which olim, immigrants, and refugees all came to Palestine.

One of the main causes of immigration in the 1920s was the Ukrainian civil war (1917–1920), whose devastating effects claimed a high price from the Jews of eastern Europe, particularly Ukrainian Jewry. These bloody events have not been given the importance they deserve in Zionist historiography; they have not been treated as a decisive, constitutive event in modern Jewish history in general and the history of immigration to Palestine in particular. These were not pogroms like those of 1881–1882, Kishinev (1903), or Odessa (1905) but rather a bloodbath on a scale and with a brutality unprecedented in Jewish history, claiming a price in blood of one hundred thousand killed and wounded.

Why, then, have the pogroms in Ukraine not topped the list of motivations for immigration to Palestine in the 1920s? The First Aliya and Second Aliya are perceived as fitting Zionist responses to the waves of violence in Russia, embodying the essence of the Zionist idea and its vindication. The Third Aliya and Fourth Aliya, in contrast, are identified with the halutzic youth movements and the ruination of the middle class of Polish Jewry but not with the pogroms in Ukraine, even though the number of casualties was immeasurably greater than in the earlier pogroms.

This chapter argues that we cannot understand immigration to Palestine without discussing the pogroms in Ukraine as a paramount push factor that sent many refugees to Palestine. The pogroms that broke out in the wake of the civil war were catastrophic for the Jews of eastern Europe. Ukraine became a mass graveyard, tens of thousands of Jews were turned into refugees, children were orphaned, and women were widowed. Another event was the October Revolution (1917), followed by the establishment of Bolshevik rule in extensive areas of the crumbling czarist empire. The Bolsheviks' brutal, merciless economic policy caused severe famine and the destruction of Russian society in general and Russian Jewish society in particular. Furthermore, in the mid-1920s, Poland—home to the largest Jewish community in eastern Europe—suffered an economic crisis that impoverished it and for the first time prompted many Jews to consider leaving the country.

Countries of Origin of Immigration to Palestine

The main countries of origin of Jewish immigration in the 1920s were the USSR and Poland. As we can see from figures 2.1 and 2.2, until 1923, most immigrants to Palestine set out from the territory of the Soviet Union (primarily Ukraine), but from 1924 on, the share from the USSR dropped and that of Poland increased.

Until 1923, about half the immigrants (46.4 percent) came from the Soviet Union and about 30 percent from Poland. In 1924–1931, the trend reversed, with 50 percent coming from Poland and only 19 percent from the USSR. Over the decade, more than 70 percent of immigrants came to Palestine from these two countries. Therefore, to understand the motivations for immigration to Palestine, we must look at what was happening in Ukraine, Bolshevik Russia, and Poland in the 1920s.

Because the statistics compiled by the Aliya Department regard Ukraine as an integral part of the Soviet Union, it is hard to estimate the number of Jews who went to Palestine due to the civil war in Ukraine. According to the book *Eretz Yisrael bi-Shnat Tarpag* (Palestine in 1922/23), between June 1922 and March 1923, 7,943 Jewish immigrants arrived in Palestine. Of these, 2,651 were from the USSR, a third of them (651) from Ukraine.[3] Presumably, during and shortly after the civil war, Jews from Ukraine constituted more than a third of those going to Palestine from the Soviet Union. Indeed, a report by the Palestine Office in Constantinople notes that in the seven months from June to December 1920, approximately three thousand people were sent to Palestine, and from December 1920 to May 1921, the aliya committee sent another twelve hundred. The statistical distribution of immigrants in the six months from December 1920 to May 1921 indicates that more than half (55%) of the Jewish immigrants to Palestine were from Ukraine; 17 percent were from Bessarabia; and smaller percentages came from the Caucasus, Lithuania, Crimea, Poland, Bulgaria, Romania, and elsewhere. Some 69 percent were male, and 31 percent were female. In the second half of 1921 (July–December), the percentage of immigrants from Ukraine rose to 80 percent; only 11 percent were from Bessarabia. During that time, 65 percent of the immigrants were male, and 35 percent were female; 11 percent were children under ten.[4] From these data, even though they are not continuous, we can assume that more than half of the immigrants who went from the USSR to Palestine between 1919 and 1923 were from Ukraine.

Rest of Europe 246
Italy 37
France 154
Netherlands 28
UK 180
Hungary 291
Czechoslovakia 112
Austria 497
Germany 469
Greece 158
Yugoslavia 145
Bulgaria 328
Romania 1404
Poland 9158
Lithuania 901
Latvia 401
USSR 14363

0   2000   4000   6000   8000   10000   12000   14000   16000

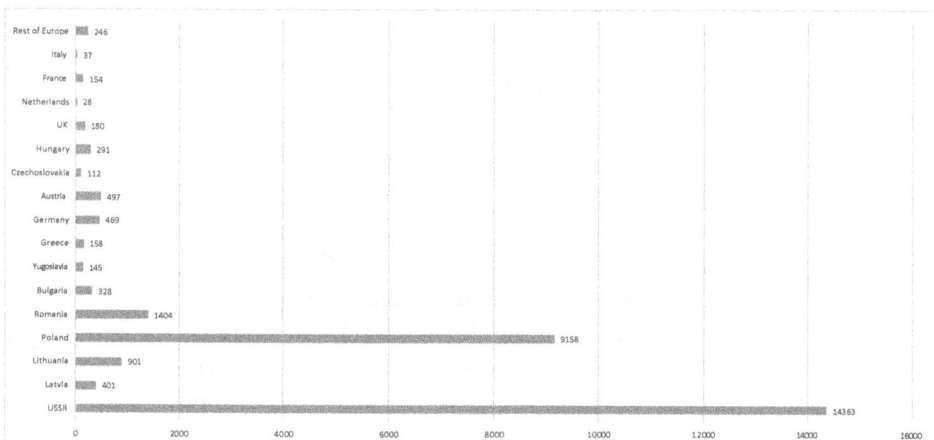

Figure 2.1. Countries of origin of Jewish immigrants to Palestine, 1919–1923.
Source: Gil, *Dappei Aliya*, 28.

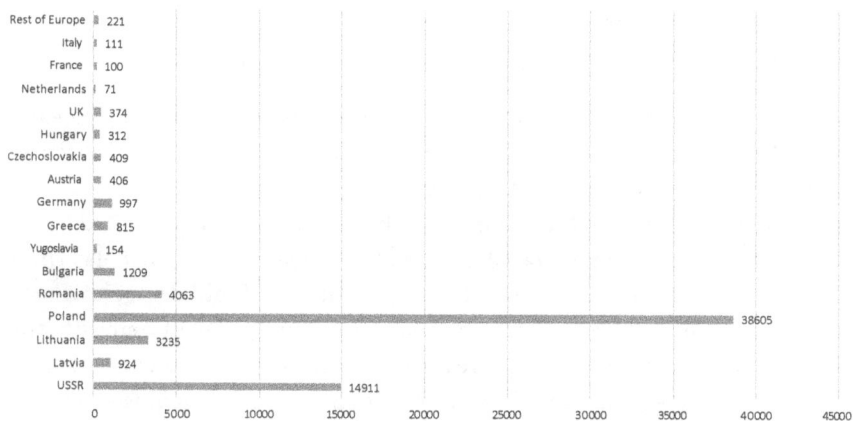

Rest of Europe 221
Italy 111
France 100
Netherlands 71
UK 374
Hungary 312
Czechoslovakia 409
Austria 406
Germany 997
Greece 815
Yugoslavia 154
Bulgaria 1209
Romania 4063
Poland 38605
Lithuania 3235
Latvia 924
USSR 14911

0   5000   10000   15000   20000   25000   30000   35000   40000   45000

Figure 2.2. Countries of origin of Jewish immigrants to Palestine, 1924–1931.
Source: Gil, *Dappei Aliya*, 28.

Ukraine

With generous largesse of freedom and deliberate lies
You sneaked Cossacks' horses into synagogues.
You raped and slaughtered my daughters before their fathers' rheumy eyes,
Mothers—hanged with their suckling babes from railway pylons.
Thus shall set the sun upon you: like a head, tumbling from the sword,
While all the victims lie in your red-dyed rivers, O daughter of Ukraine!
Broken limbs dance a-sway in macabre conflagrations: "Save us, Lord!"
Your drunkards' blades are drawn from rivers of blood and charred remains.
Your temple's incense bears the stench of Torah scrolls torched;
The sunflowers in your land have an ochre hue, like plague survivors' skin,
While the raking of your sheaves reaps bones.
The hand of fate was dealt long since.
The inferno is part of your nature innate . . .
Until your redemption comes from the heaps of defeat,
Those judging you, Shabbos goyim, over fine bread altercate . . .
Destined are all sins to come home to roost.
They will be welcome![5]

Ukraine was the main country of origin of Jewish migration during the early 1920s. It was a bloody country whose Jewish citizens were slaughtered in scores of brutal pogroms during the Ukrainian civil war from 1917 to 1920. The pogroms were the result of the chaos and political anarchy that prevailed in the territory of the crumbling czarist empire after the fall of Czar Nicholas II. In October 1917, the Bolsheviks overthrew the nine-month-old democratic provisional government headed by Alexander Kerensky. The fall of Kerensky, the dissolution of the Duma (legislative assembly), the establishment of workers' councils ("soviets") that would govern the country, and the signing of a peace accord with Germany that led to the withdrawal of Russia from World War I made the Bolsheviks many enemies. These enemies disagreed with the Bolsheviks ideologically and opposed the way they had seized power.

The political changes did not pass Ukraine by. The Central Council of Ukraine (*Rada*) was formed in April 1917. At first it made only modest national demands, but after a while it sought to secede from Russia and achieve full Ukrainian independence. The fight for independence began. In June–July 1917, the Ukrainian General Military Committee was established, headed by the nationalist Symon Petliura, and the first Ukrainian battalions were created. On November 7, the Rada proclaimed the Ukrainian People's Republic, and a few months later, it issued the First Universal (manifesto) for the Ukrainian people. "The Russian Provisional Government," said the Universal, "rejected all of our demands; it refused the outstretched hand of the Ukrainian people. ... If the Russian Provisional Government cannot introduce order in our land ... we must undertake it ourselves. ... Therefore we ... declare that from now on we shall build our own life."[6] The next day, the Rada declared Ukrainian independence and the severance of any connection with Russia. The Bolsheviks responded by invading Ukraine. On January 26, 1918, they captured Kiev and the Rada fled to Zhitomir. Ukraine—especially the three districts of Kiev, Volhynia, and Podolia—became killing fields. Cities were captured and abandoned, and the conquering and retreating troops left behind a trail of destruction and ruin.

An assortment of soldiers from various armies and with opposing interests fought each other and became integral parts of the Ukrainian landscape during the civil war: Ukrainian nationalists headed by Petliura, battalions of partisans who had formed alliances with Petliura and then joined or betrayed him, Red Army troops, Polish soldiers who had joined Petliura, Germans who were first allies and later enemies of the Ukrainians, White Army troops under the command of General Anton Denikin, and locals who joined whoever was fighting the Bolsheviks. The only thing that united all these forces was their hatred of the Jews and a desire to hurt them.[7] Forty percent of the pogroms were carried out by Petliura's forces and his allies, 25 percent by local farmers and gangs, 17 percent by Denikin's White Army, 10 percent by the Polish army and Grigoriev's troops, and 8 percent by the Soviets.[8]

Sometime in 1920, Lucien Wolf, one of the leaders of English Jewry, received a detailed, thirty-one-page report on the violence in Ukraine. According to the report, the bloodbath there was not like the familiar pogroms from the distant or recent past; the events were unprecedented in scope and intensity. "The events now taking place in Ukraine cannot in any sense be understood as mere 'pogrom excesses' which the Jewish people had to live through so often in its long history. It is necessary to open one's eyes to the fact that during the last two years the Jewish population of the Ukraine is being exterminated systematically, persistently and evidently with a firm determination of utterly destroying this branch of the Jewish people."[9]

The language the report's author chose to use leaves no doubt that they considered the violence in Ukraine unprecedented in its brutality and believed that the murderers' intent went beyond random killings of Jews. The anonymous author stressed that the aim of the pogroms was systematic, consistent liquidation of Ukrainian Jewry—an attempt to thoroughly wipe out this segment of the Jewish people. The conceptual world of the report seems to be drawn or copied from the Holocaust. Were it not for its date and historical context, one might assume it was written amid the annihilation of European Jewry during World War II.

The number of people murdered in the pogroms is a matter of historiographical controversy. As early as the 1920s, several attempts were made to estimate the number of shtetls destroyed and the number of Jews murdered, which ranges from conservative estimates of 30,000 to much higher figures of 250,000. A Red Cross report published in the early 1920s estimated that 30,500 Jews had been murdered.[10] However, Elias Heifetz, who served as chair of the All-Ukrainian Aid Committee that operated under the auspices of the Red Cross, argued in his book on the slaughter of Ukrainian Jewry that the number murdered was much greater than that. According to him, the report did not consider Jews in small villages; Jews who had fled their homes and been murdered in the forests, on the roads, and at train stations; Jews thrown overboard from ships into the rivers of Ukraine; or those who had died of starvation and illness. Heifetz estimates that 120,000 people were killed in the pogroms.[11] Eliezer David Rosenthal, author of *Megilat ha-Tevah* (Scroll of slaughter), estimated that a quarter of a million people were murdered. "Of the 124 cities and towns in the Kiev Governorate in which Jews had lived before the war, between 85 and 90 were wiped out. In the many villages where Jews had lived in the Kiev Governorate, almost the entire Jewish population has been wiped out. Of the half million Jews, 200,000 were killed by the sword of the Petliuras, the Denikins, and the various hetmans, who multiplied like truffles and mushrooms. One hundred fifty thousand were killed and slaughtered and 50,000 died of starvation, cold, and various infectious diseases."[12]

Estimates published in 1928 by the scholar Nahum Gergel were more conservative than those of Heifetz and Rosenthal. In an article titled "Di Pogromen in Ukrayne in di Yarn 1918–1921" (The pogroms in Ukraine in 1918–1921), Gergel took a different tack in estimating the number of murder victims and determining the geographical pattern of the pogroms and the identity of the murderers. His article was based on 688 cities and towns in which roughly fourteen hundred pogroms took place; according to his conservative estimates, fifty thousand to sixty thousand Jews—twice the number given in the Red Cross report—were murdered.[13] According to Gergel's research, thirty-five thousand victims had been murdered in the actual pogroms and fifteen thousand at train stations, on trains, and on roads; in addition, there were victims who had been severely wounded in the pogroms and died in the days and weeks that followed.[14] The number of people injured was around the same as the

Table 2.1. People killed in pogroms, by governorate.

Governorate	No. killed	Pct.	Pogroms in the governorate (pct.)
Kiev	16,569	53.3	33.0
Podolia	8,111	26.1	22.8
Volhynia	1,952	6.2	17.0
Kherson	2,693	8.7	10.2
Chernigov	523	1.7	5.5
Poltava	366	1.2	6.8
Yekaterinoslav	564	1.8	0.7
Taurida	20	0.1	0.7
Kharkov	24	0.1	2.0
Central Russia	249	0.8	1.3
Total	31,071	100	100

Source: Gergel, "Di Pogromen in Ukrayne," 112.

number murdered; thus, the total killed and wounded came to about one hundred thousand.[15]

Table 2.1 shows that the pogroms followed a distinctly regional pattern. In some regions of Ukraine, there were relatively few pogroms, whereas in other regions, there was a bloodbath, with tens of thousands losing their lives. More than 70 percent of the pogroms took place in the three governorates of Volhynia, Podolia, and Kiev, which passed from hand to hand in the civil war and were beset by political instability. Of the victims, 53.3 percent (16,569 Jews) were killed in the Kiev Governorate, 26.1 percent (8,111) in the Podolia Governorate, 8.7 percent (2,693) in the Kherson Governorate, and 6.2 percent (1,952) in the Volhynia Governorate.

Although the Bolsheviks, Ukrainian nationalists, farmers, partisans, and Denikin's White Army troops fought one another, they also took advantage of the prevailing chaos to plunder, attack, and slaughter the Jews. The occupying troops and those retreating from the Volhynia, Podolia, and Kiev Governorates wreaked massive destruction. The Jews were the first to pay the price of the war and anarchy. Many shtetls suffered more than one pogrom.[16]

The attackers showed no mercy; they killed whoever was in their path, young or old. Ten percent of those murdered were children, ranging from just a few months old to age fifteen; 12 percent were aged sixteen to twenty; 50 percent were aged twenty-one to fifty; and 26 percent were aged fifty and over.[17] The

Figure 2.3. The destruction in the synagogue in Khodorkov. Photo courtesy of the National Library of Israel.

mass murder of the Ukrainian Jews was preceded by sadistic acts of abuse by both the soldiers and the local population. Contemporary reports published at the time and testimonies taken from the survivors stress repeatedly that for the perpetrators it was not enough to just murder Jews and steal their property; they tortured them to death viciously and mercilessly. "What typified the acts of the volunteer troops was severe, vicious torture," wrote Joseph Schechtman. "For the rioters it was not enough to spill blood and maim; they intended especially to torture and afflict."[18] In *Megilat ha-Tevah*, Rosenthal described a long list of particularly brutal pogroms. The following are just a few examples:

In Makarov [Kiev Governorate] there were a few thousand Jews before the pogroms. The whole shtetl was wiped out. Now the entire population is Christian. I found only three Jewish families there, and even that is a wonder. The sicarii fought the Jews of Makarov "with sword and fire," annihilated the

men, smashed the women's bellies, and impaled the children on stakes. The
Petliuran Cossacks stripped the Jews of their clothes and dragged them naked
in the snow: they roasted the Jews "in their own juices": They locked them
in their homes, set fire to the houses, and posted guards to make sure the
victims would not escape. A delegation of seventeen old people were sent to
plead with the hetman for the lives of the Jewish residents of the town. The
hetman gave a signal. His companions quickly fell upon the delegates and
carved them up with their swords like cabbage. All that remained was a heap
of pieces of meat and bone.[19]

In Zhitomir there were three pogroms, each one more vicious and violent
than the last. The first two were in January and March 1919; the third was in June
1920.[20] The attackers not only destroyed and plundered the Jewish community
but first abused some four hundred Jews before murdering them:

> The Cossacks broke into the homes, barged into the basements, dragged the
> Jews who fell into their hands, and killed them mercilessly. The Cossacks took
> seven Jews out of the hospital to the Teterov River, where they shot them to
> death.... The river rocks the ... Jews in its waves.... In the cemetery, the
> room of the dead, rows and rows of chopped-up bodies are piled up. The
> victims' relatives walk past together to identify the slain. Burial must wait;
> that was the order. Meanwhile, a repulsive odor from the slaughtered corpses
> spreads through the city. The bad smell lasted eight days.... In the cemetery
> lie young women with smashed bellies, their breasts chopped off. Corpses are
> piled up on each other—columns of heads, bodies.... Next to the bodies of
> the parents lie the bodies of their small children. On a Kiev street Slibordsky
> saw a live child suckling from the breasts of his dead mother.[21]

In Dubova, eight hundred local Jews were brutally tortured and murdered.
"Before the eyes of the Jewish blacksmiths they cut off the head of pregnant
young Esther Dinstein. Her black head, combed and adorned with little combs
over the ears, rolled along the street amidst the garbage and the dust. Next to
her rolled the fetus, whom the murderers had removed from her split belly and
thrown to one another like a rubber ball."[22] In Boguslav, in the Kiev Governorate, the murderers seized a young woman "in order to violate her, and when
she gathered all her strength to save herself from them they cut her to pieces.
One old man was beaten in the head until his brain spilled out and was eaten
by dogs. There was a woman about to give birth whose husband was killed by
the Cossacks in front of her; they didn't touch her—so that she would watch
in hopeless desperation. A thirteen-year-old girl was violated by four Cossacks
one after another."[23]

In the middle of February 1919, a pogrom broke out in the city of Proskurov; fifteen hundred Jews were murdered. The Cossacks split up into small groups and spread out over the streets where the Jews lived. They broke into their homes and slaughtered everyone in their way. The attackers made no distinction between women and men or between young and old. "They cut their victims with swords and stabbed them with spears. They shot to death only those who managed to escape outside. Then they showered the fugitives with lots of bullets until they had used them up. When the Jews found out about the slaughter being perpetrated in the city by the haidamaks, they started to seek refuge, hiding in attics and basements. But the Cossacks crawled into the attics and dragged out the people hiding, and they threw bombs into the basements."[24]

One characteristic of the Ukrainian pogroms was the rape of Jewish women on a scale the Jews had never seen before. The pogroms in 1881 and 1882 had involved mainly robbery, looting, and destruction; in the Kishinev pogrom, testimonies tell about the rape of women. In the pogroms from 1904 to 1906, approximately three thousand Jews were murdered, and many Jewish women were sexually assaulted and raped.[25] But the pogroms during the Ukrainian civil war were known for their brutality. Jewish women were raped and tortured by all the armies fighting in the civil war:

> A special place in the pogroms perpetrated by the volunteer troops is occupied by rapists of women. In none of the previous pogroms were women raped in such large numbers and with such atrocious brutality. There was not a single pogrom in which the rioting volunteers did not defile Jewish women. In some towns absolutely all the women, young and old, were raped. The age of the women—whether extremely elderly or tender girls—was no barrier to the monsters. Some, turning themselves into brute animals and depraving themselves, would rape a sixty-year-old woman and on the same occasion defile a ten-year-old girl. Sometimes they raped a mother and her daughter and granddaughter side by side. They raped them right in front of their husbands, fathers, and brothers. Anyone who tried to protect the poor wretches paid with his life. There were many cases of gang rape: a few dozen soldiers and Cossacks would violate one woman, and afterwards either they would kill the unfortunate soul or she would die from the torment or go crazy.[26]

There is no way to estimate the number of women who were raped, but reports and chronicles from that period contain scores of testimonies about the subject. Alter Druyanov devoted the third volume of the journal *Reshumot* to the pogroms and included many testimonies about rape and assaults on women. The following are just a few of them:

On July 28—reports S. S., a 28-year-old widow and factory worker—Cossacks started coming into our yard and they all robbed and stole. One of the Russian neighbors had warned us Jewish women in the courtyard that the Cossacks were planning to come at night to violate [us], so all the women fled; only I couldn't leave my home because my son had German measles. A widow with a sick child, poor and downtrodden—I believed I would arouse the compassion of those brutes and I stayed home. At night three Cossacks burst into my room, broke and destroyed all my things, took the most valuable objects, and then raped me. . . . All my pleas not to hurt me were in vain. In vain I kissed their hands, cried, sobbed. . . . They violated me, tortured me, and defiled me.[27]

On October 17—recounts David Chernobelsky—the steamship *Vilna* approached the port in the city of Verkhnedneprovsk (Yekaterinoslav Governorate). At midnight six men boarded the ship and demanded a ransom of 12,000 rubles from the passengers. The passengers collected this sum and gave it to those demanding it. At two a.m. about twenty armed men boarded the ship, took all the men off the ship, lowered them to the shore, stripped them of their clothes, and left them only in underpants. While stripping them of their clothes, they beat the people they were robbing, and when they found gold teeth in their mouths they yanked them out. When they had finished their work with the men, they put the eighteen young Jewish women who were on the ship on shore and raped them all, torturing them brutally. They carried out this outrage before all our eyes. The abuse and rape continued until noon.[28]

On July 28—reports G. R. of Kremenchug—armed, mounted Cossacks entered our yard, demanded money, and took all the money that my son-in-law and I had. . . . At night eight Cossacks—including two officers—broke into our home, searched our entire house, and took everything they found. While doing so they beat me, my son-in-law, and my fifteen-year-old son with their horsewhips. They stripped my son of his clothes and took them. After they took the things, they raped my two married daughters, one nineteen years old and pregnant and the other twenty-one, holding her sick baby in her arms. When my daughters started asking the cruel rapists to have mercy on them, the Cossacks threatened to hang them. Whips at the ready, they put them in a room and locked the door. . . . They wounded me with a sword and beat my son-in-law senseless.[29]

In his article "Antishemiut u-Fera'ot" (Antisemitism and pogroms), published in *Reshumot*, Schechtman states that he has lists of women who were raped but adds that he cannot determine their number, since "most of the poor

souls hide their shame." Nevertheless, "according to the estimates in our possession, the number raped exceeds ten thousand." He continues, "The issue of
the thousands of women who were raped has become a severe, painful national
and psychological problem in Ukraine."[30]

These harsh descriptions are a shocking testimony of the hardships and tor-
ments suffered by the Jewish community during the civil war. This is a gendered
issue that has been addressed little by historians. The rape of Jewish women had
far-reaching social and ethical ramifications. Violence against women was part
of a broader strategy of harming Jews as a distinct ethnic group in Ukraine. The
perpetrators plundered, destroyed, burned, and murdered, but the harm they
caused a Jewish man became total only when they desecrated the bodies and
psyches of the women in his family. Through these horrific acts, the murderers
completed their work. They not only took the Jews' lives and wiped them out
physically but simultaneously defiled the women, thus thoroughly dispossess-
ing and dominating the Jews. Raping Jewish women was a way of not only hu-
miliating, degrading, and shaming the women but also wounding and defeating
their husbands and fathers, who were forced to watch helplessly from the side.

The pogroms had fateful consequences for Ukrainian Jewry. Jewish communities that had thrived before the war vanished without a trace. In eighteen out
of forty-seven Jewish towns examined in Ukraine, not a single Jew remained.
In fourteen others, the Jewish population shrank by 90 percent; in five, by
70 to 90 percent; and in ten, by 20 to 70 percent.[31] The damage to property
was tremendous. The demographer Jacob Lestschinsky published a series of
articles entitled "After the Pogroms in Ukraine" in the American newspaper
The Forward, which were translated into Hebrew in the newspaper *Kuntres*.
Lestschinsky wrote, "Of every hundred families, the homes of 28 were burned
. . . 79 percent of the shops were looted and only 8 percent of them were burned
along with their merchandise. The rioters knew what was in front of them and
did their work in an orderly, regimented way, first removing all the merchandise
from the shops and only afterwards setting fire to them. The same was done
with the whole house."[32] According to Lestschinsky, there was a clear distinction between the looting by Denikin's and Petliura's troops and the looting
by Ukrainian locals. "The gangs of Denikin or Petliura," wrote Lestschinsky,

> would first completely empty the Jews' homes of all their money and property
> and load it in carts. Then the farmers from the vicinity would come and set
> about their work: they would remove the windows and doors of the house,
> dismantle the roof, take apart the ovens, and transport the materials to the
> village. In many towns the following sight was seen: entire streets of roofless
> houses lacking doors and windows, like big, open holes that resemble open

Figures 2.4 and 2.4A. Survivors of the pogrom in Khodorkov. Photos courtesy of the National Library of Israel.

mouths groaning and telling of the people buried within, of the blood clotting on their walls, of the violation of the bodies of tortured sisters.[33]

In some Ukrainian cities, the Jewish population more than doubled after hundreds of refugees from the villages fled to the big cities: in Odessa the Jewish population rose by 36 percent; in Uman by 40 percent; in Kiev by 216 percent; and in Kharkov by 400 percent—from eleven thousand in 1897 to fifty-five thousand in 1920. In contrast, there were towns in which the local Jewish community shrank dramatically, sometimes even ceasing to exist. In Tetiev, hometown of poet and playwright Ya'akov Orland (whose family's story appears at the beginning of the book), not a single Jew remained. The same was true of other towns: Bulanovka, Brusilov, Germanovka, Dubova, Dzyunkov, Veselinoya, Zhivotov, and Pyatigory. The survivors, now refugees, migrated to the big cities.

For those who survived, "only one way remains: to flee wherever the wind takes them. Indeed, whoever still has strength in his legs and a desire to live abandons everything in his home and flees to the neighboring countries, Bessarabia and Poland, to save his life."[34] According to *Doar Hayom*, thirty thousand Jewish refugees reached Constantinople. "The condition of the refugees . . . is dreadful. Until October 15 the French and American Red Cross were supporting twenty thousand refugees at their expense. Now these organizations have terminated their support."[35]

The plight of the Jewish refugees was indeed terrible: with no roofs over their heads, no source of livelihood, and a lack of basic living conditions, many went hungry and could barely survive. In Tiraspol, on the east bank of the Dniester in the Kherson Governorate (currently Moldova), large numbers of refugees lived in abominable conditions: "Many children, neglected by their starving parents, wander the streets and run around the garbage bins hoping to find scraps of food."[36] Every day around forty people, mostly children, died. An outbreak of typhus in Odessa killed numerous refugees: "A rather large number of the Jews [in the city] were condemned to starve to death. . . . The entire population is dreadfully filthy. Swarming with parasites. In the absence of sanitary services and amidst constant hunger, epidemic typhus has spread, and thirty to forty people are dying daily."[37] The casualties were buried hastily and in a disorganized manner:

> Mortality in Odessa, especially among the Jews, is tremendous. . . . The dead are buried in a large mass grave in the cemetery. Such a grave is approximately 2 meters long, 10 meters wide, and 4 meters deep. . . . They simply bring the deceased to the cemetery, where they are thrown together into the graves in a

disorderly manner; [the graves] are barely covered with 50 cm of soil. Bringing the deceased to the cemetery is also very expensive, so sometimes the
dead are simply thrown into the street and from there they are later removed
to some other place.[38]

In his article "Antisemitism and Pogroms," Schechtman discussed the severe consequences of the pogroms for Ukrainian Jewry: "The result was that
after the pogroms the survivors found nowhere to return to. They couldn't
even find a place to spend the night." Those who fled their homes "were left
half-naked, with no underwear or clothes, with no pillow, blanket, or bed, no
chair to sit on, no rags to plug the holes in the walls, and no oven for heat." The
cold, filth, epidemics, and starvation ravaged the Jews

> no less than the rioters' swords had done. There was nothing to lay the sick
> on, no way of keeping the infected away from the uninfected. It was impos-
> sible to get rid of the lice. For months those who had been robbed had no way
> to wash themselves with water. There was no medicine because there were no
> Jewish hospitals (and in the shtetls all the hospitals had been run by Jews);
> they had been totally destroyed. Medical assistance was also lacking for the
> most part. If any doctor survived the pogroms, he would quickly flee to the
> cities for safety. In addition to the illnesses there was hunger. The Jews, having
> been robbed by the rioters to the point that they had nothing left, could not
> get the food they needed anywhere. The farmers in the area did not want to
> sell the necessary food to the plundered Jews, aside from which the Jews had
> nothing to buy it with.[39]

In June 1921, the British Mandatory government dispatched Major Morris, the director of the Department of Immigration and Travel, to Europe for
a close-up look at the work of the Palestine Offices there and at the profile of
the population seeking to immigrate to Palestine. Morris met with the British
consuls who issued visas, the heads of the Palestine Offices, and prospective
immigrants themselves. In a comprehensive, detailed report that he submitted
to Herbert Samuel, Morris discussed the problem of postwar refugees in Europe and the impact of the American quota laws on immigration to Palestine.
The refugees' plight, Morris maintained, might put pressure on the Zionist offices and distort the judgment of the heads of the offices, who were then liable
to send undesirable immigrants to Palestine.

> America has closed her doors to mass Immigration, which I understand is
> only the beginning of introducing a system of Immigration by selection; and
> the American Joint Distribution Committee which has done so much relief

work in Eastern Europe, is also closing down for want of funds. Thousands of refugees are pouring into Roumania and Poland from Russia. A Jew's life in either of these countries, and in the newly occupied Russian territories, is not of the happiest at any time and it is worse if he is a refugee. And so it might be that the situation in Eastern Europe, where so much suffering is endured, may have inspired the sub-offices of the Organization to find an outlet which would afford some relief, morally and spiritually as well as materially.[40]

Following conversations with many prospective immigrants, Morris stated that "a large number of those examined and rejected" only "a few persons are emigrating from the states of which they are nationals . . . that practically all the immigrants are of Russians origin." Of seventy migrants whom he interviewed in Berlin, there was not a single German citizen—only Russian prisoners of war and refugees from the war zones in Ukraine, Poland, and Russia. Morris interviewed 150 prospective immigrants in Istanbul and 900 in Vienna, and his conclusion was the same: "Jews frequently told me that the Jew who has a home, and is successful in business, is not going to emigrate except in very small numbers, though he is ready to support the cause. It may therefore be said that it is the Russian Refugee and the unsuccessful business man who is the Immigrant at present. Jews living in more settled countries will not immigrate to Palestine until the country will is given a more permanent and secure character."[41]

The refugees' plight was the main cause of immigration to Palestine in the 1920s, and it can be understood only in the eastern European context of the Ukrainian civil war. Tens of thousands of refugees were knocking on the doors of the Jewish migration societies and Palestine Offices in Europe, seeking to escape to any country that would have them. For them, Palestine became a place of refuge.

Bolshevik Russia

The Jews in Russia after the Bolshevik Revolution formed the second-largest Jewish collective in Europe, with 2.7 million people. The 1920s in Communist Russia can be divided into four periods: the civil war and anti-Jewish pogroms; war communism; Lenin's New Economic Policy (NEP); and the repeal of the NEP and Stalin's rise to power. Each of these periods had a destructive impact on the Jews of Russia, ranging from harm to their sources of livelihood and a deepening of poverty to harm to body and soul.

As soon as the Bolsheviks rose to power, while Russia was still in the midst of a civil war, Lenin instituted a socialist economy. The period that followed,

Figure 2.5. Headstone for Zissel Malcah Pearlmutter, Derazhne, Ukraine, Photo courtesy of Ilan Troen.

known as "war communism," primarily involved the nationalization of facto-ries, banks, private homes, and workshops with one or more employees; the elimination of private commerce and greater centralization of economic life; the expropriation of agricultural produce from farmers; food rationing; and an egalitarian wage policy.[42] The rapid switch to a communal economy with no period of preparation or adjustment led to a dramatic decline in Russian agricultural produce and grievous damage to the various segments of the Russian population. The shortage of food caused severe famine in the cities. In rural areas, farmers might be able to feed their families from the small plot of land they retained, but in the cities, there was hardly any food to be bought. Many factory workers moved to the country, so that by 1921 there were only about half as many of them as in 1917. For want of a policy offering them incentives to go to work, and because of the expropriation of property and political oppression, the Russian people sank into deep poverty and profound despair.

The economic crisis in Soviet Russia did not pass over the Jews either. The unique employment structure of the Jewish population was dealt a severe blow, and many families lost their livelihoods. The impoverishment of the Russian farmers affected Jewish merchants and skilled tradesmen as well because they depended on one another for their income.[43] Following the enactment of a regulation requiring the recording and nationalization of merchandise and raw materials, private commerce was banned, and this caused even greater harm. Many Jewish merchants and skilled tradesmen were left with no source of income: their businesses had been nationalized, private commerce had ceased, skilled tradesmen were left without any raw materials, housing conditions in the cities and towns were unbearable, and about 80 percent of Jewish youth were unemployed.[44] "All the classes of the Jewish community—the bourgeoisie of the shtetl, the intelligentsia, the petty shopkeepers, the skilled tradesmen, the workers . . . all of them, all are so tormented by hunger that they are getting up and abandoning everything in the shtetl, even their homes, and setting out on the road."[45] News of the severe famine in Russia reached the Jews of Palestine, where the Jewish National Council urged the people of the Yishuv to lend a hand to their starving brethren.

> Brothers! Our brothers the Jews of Russia and Ukraine. who were the first to build our land and support the Old and New Yishuv in Palestine, are in trouble. This summer the famine that broke out in the Volga governorates of Soviet Russia reached the governorates of Ukraine and Russia, where the Jewish population lives. The famine is devastating the inhabitants. Thousands of people are wandering the streets asking for bread. Thousands of orphans remain without shelter. The formerly rich are begging for alms. People are dying in the streets with no one to gather them up. . . . The picture is terrible. There are no words to depict the magnitude of the catastrophe.[46]

Zelig Horwitz, who had moved to Palestine before the crisis in Russia, wrote to the Zionist Executive, describing what had happened to his family in the Crimean Peninsula:

In 1922, my whole family set out for Palestine illegally from the city of
Yevpatoria (Crimea, Russia). Unfortunately, however, the Soviet government
arrested them and confiscated all their money. They were left "like sheep
without a shepherd," i.e., destitute. Ever since then, their economic situation
has grown worse from day to day. I started receiving horrible letters saying
that their situation was precarious. . . . In 1923 I received shocking news, news
that devastated my whole life here in our land: Due to the famine in Crimea,
Russia, my 20-year-old brother, a student at the university in Simferopol,
had died. . . . The letters that I received from home were filled with requests,
screams, and pleas for me to take at least one of them from Russia.[47]

In early 1921, Lenin adopted the NEP to repair the damage caused by war
communism and especially to appease the starving farmers who had risen up
against him. He reestablished commerce, restored the workshops, and revital-
ized industry and agriculture, making it possible to buy food and raw materials
again. Russian farmers no longer had to hand over their produce to the state;
they could sell it on the private market. Opportunities were created for private
enterprise in commerce and industry, and workers who had fled to the villages
returned to the cities. But despite the NEP, the regime retained ownership of
heavy industry and natural resources, imports and exports remained in the
hands of the state, and the war on the urban bourgeoisie continued. In mid-1923,
high taxes were imposed on merchants and skilled tradesmen, again impoverishing the Jewish population.[48]

In his book *Ha-Yehudim be-Rusya ha-Sovietit* (The Jews in Soviet Russia),
Lestschinsky describes the history of one Jewish family in Vitebsk during the
period of the NEP to understand in depth the economic crisis that befell Russian Jewry. "I encountered this eyewitness in 1924 in Riga, where he had fled
for his life, and I wrote down his story almost word for word."[49] This is the
story of a Jewish shopkeeper. "I have never been rich, but we earned enough to
live on. My wife, three sons, and I got by. Thus the days passed until 1918. Since
then we have been plagued by misfortune and calamity—calamities that will
apparently never end." From the moment the Bolsheviks started enforcing the
NEP, his family's economic status suffered:

> The Bolsheviks started instituting new rules. One fine morning, I found a
> lock on the door to my shop. All the shopkeepers found similar locks on the
> doors to their shops. They recorded the merchandise, took it, and gave me
> a "receipt." My wife still keeps this receipt sewn in her dress. . . . They took
> away all my merchandise. Others had known a few days in advance that their
> merchandise would be seized, so they had taken precautions: some buried it
> in a basement; some hid it in the attic. But I didn't regret that at all, because

after three shopkeepers were shot for hiding merchandise, all the others, embarrassed and heartbroken, quickly turned in their merchandise to the Sovnarkhoz (National Economic Council).[50]

With no income, the family lived on the food they had stored up, hoping the situation would soon improve. "After all, it can't be that everyone will die of starvation. A month passes, two months pass, three months—but it doesn't end." A black market developed, with the Jews taking part. "I hear Jews are starting to engage in commerce a bit. Chaim, the leather merchant, obtained soles somewhere and is selling them under the edges of his kapote. So-and-so goes to Moscow. He takes sugar and tobacco there and comes back with manufactured goods and locks."[51] But the Cheka—the Soviet secret police—followed the merchants and smugglers. They "stopped the Moscow train a few versts before the city and were going to shake out and search. . . . Toward evening, they brought in a large group of prisoners. They had found 'Czarist' money sewn in hidden places that would escape even the eye of the devil. . . . Plunder consisting of a few manufactured carts and other goods fell into the hands of the Cheka." Lestschinsky summed up the Vitebsk shopkeeper's story: "Unfortunately, it is impossible to recount the entire story here. . . . [He] sees terrifying sights, horrors, and miracles, stumbles and is caught a few times, and survives until he finally escapes to Riga. We wanted in particular to describe the atmosphere in which the vast majority of the Jewish community lived for a few successive years. In this atmosphere they lived and fought hard just to have bread to eat."[52]

Zionist activists and Hebrew teachers were also persecuted by the Bolshevik government by means of the Yevsektsia—the Jewish section of the Communist Party.[53] In 1919, Yevsektsia members took over the Zionist parties' headquarters, arrested their members, and shut down their newspapers. The Hebrew language was deemed reactionary and was officially banned. Publication of Hebrew periodicals and books ceased, and libraries were taken over or closed. Teachers and students of Hebrew were put on trial and imprisoned. In March 1925, Yardeni Berman (a dentist), Yechezkel Kopper (a pharmacist), and three other Jews from Palestine applied for an immigration certificate from the Aliya Department for David Rozin, thirty-five years old, and his fourteen-year-old son Zevulun. They lived in Soviet Russia, and David had been persecuted for teaching Hebrew and heading the local branch of the Zionist movement.

> The above, a Hebrew teacher by profession, was chairman of the local branch
> of the Zionist Organization in this city for many years and was known to the

people of the district for his dedicated work teaching the language and disseminating Zionism. In the past two years he has been jailed several times by the Soviet authorities; he was in prison in the cities of Starokonstantinov and Shepetovka, and recently he has been under special observation by the GPU [Soviet secret police]. In addition, according to the latest reports that we have received from the people of the aforementioned city, he is in danger of being exiled to Siberia.[54]

War communism and the NEP that followed brought about the total ruination of Russian society. Dan Pines eloquently described the bleak situation of Russian Jewry after the Bolshevik Revolution. "The economic politics of the USSR are detrimental to the Jewish masses," wrote Pines.

The development of cooperation in manufacturing, consumer affairs, and services, the high taxes in the city and countryside . . . the disenfranchisement of broad segments of the population due to their nonworking past, which brings along with it the denial of many other rights as well, the abolition of private commerce and industry, the policy for the development of heavy industry, the nationalization . . . the purging of officials, the trade unions, the parading of new people with proletarian lineage, the barring of immigration, the persecution of religion, of the national movement, and of the non-Communist labor movement, the shortage of raw materials needed by the various branches of manufacturing and industry, *all these are bringing about the atrophy and diminution of hundreds of thousands of Jews from all social classes.*[55]

Oppression and economic hardship intensified the push factors, and many people sought to emigrate. At first this meant internal migration to regions not under Bolshevik rule, but afterward they started trying to immigrate to the United States and Palestine: "Jews would risk their lives running for the borders in those years. On one side the Cheka would shoot, and on the other side Romanian soldiers or Polish soldiers would. Nevertheless, there were about seventy-three thousand Jews in Bessarabia alone who had sneaked across the border. Even greater was the number of fugitives who fled for their lives to Poland. Some two hundred thousand Jews left Russia over the course of three years (1918–1921). 'Left Russia'—now it is easy to put these words together. But it is a uniquely horrific episode in the sufferings of the Jews."[56]

As the Bolshevik regime consolidated its hold on the country, it became less possible to emigrate. Jews encountered bureaucratic and other difficulties that prevented them from leaving. Russia, the main country of origin of Jewish emigration since the 1880s, restricted emigration in the second half of the

1920s. Poland took over as the main country of origin, a position it held until the outbreak of World War II.

Poland

As in Ukraine and Bolshevik Russia, the lot of the Jews in Poland worsened in the 1920s. Polish Jewry was the largest Jewish collective in Europe following World War I and the second-largest in the world after American Jewry. Three million Jews lived there in the 1920s, accounting for about 10 percent of the total Polish population. Between the world wars, Poland was a backward agricultural country; two-thirds of its population lived in villages and worked in agriculture. Polish farmers had small plots of land that barely supported them, and the poverty of most of the rural population was a burden on the country's economy. Poland was trapped in a vicious cycle that kept it from prospering: The extreme poverty in the rural areas directly affected markets in the cities and increased unemployment countrywide. The high unemployment rate drove down wages in industry and crafts and reduced the purchasing power of workers. Consequently, prices of agricultural produce were low, harming Polish farmers.

Unemployment in Poland in the 1920s made the poverty and economic hardship worse. Many Polish farm workers were unemployed. In industry, too, the unemployment rate was high. In June 1926, for example, there were 1,302 applicants for every hundred new jobs. The number of people out of work exceeded 300,000, whereas there were only about 35,000 jobs available.[57] Like the Russian economy, the Polish economy was centralized and subject to government oversight. The state controlled 70 percent of the iron industry, 25 percent of the coal industry, and 20 percent of the gas and oil industries as well as the production of electricity and the wood industry. The government controlled most of the banks, and in the absence of private capital and enterprise, Poland was dependent on foreign capital. In 1931, Poland's debts exceeded ten billion zloty, while the annual state budget was estimated at 2.5 billion zloty.

The centralized nature of the Polish economy and the way it was run were detrimental to the Jews due to their unique occupational structure. Two-thirds of the Jews lived in cities, and their way of life was completely different from that of rural Poles. Agriculture, the mainstay of the economy for the non-Jewish population, played almost no role in Jewish society. According to 1921 census data, only 4 percent of the Jewish population worked in agriculture, 34 percent worked in industry, 41 percent worked in petty commerce, and 5 percent worked in the liberal professions. By 1931, the trend had changed, with Jews working in industry outnumbering Jews making their living from commerce.[58]

The typical skilled tradesman was a tailor or shoemaker, either self-employed or an apprentice; the typical merchant was a shopkeeper striving for financial independence. According to Latzky-Bertholdi, the high proportion of Jewish merchants and skilled tradesmen marginalized the Jews in Polish society and pushed them "to the light, less hygienic, and socioeconomically less important branches of the economy."[59] Jews played a significant role in the professions too: they accounted for about a third of the lawyers and notaries in Poland, a quarter of those employed in journalism and publishing, and more than half of the private physicians.[60]

The Jews in Poland were no poorer than Polish laborers and farmers. Those in the cities and shtetls had a higher standard of living than Polish farmers.[61] Nevertheless, in all state-controlled segments of the economy, anyone who was not "a member of the Polish people" was discriminated against. Because the Jews were concentrated in the cities, they suffered economically more than any other ethnic group in Poland: they were barred from municipal and national administrative jobs; government institutions and government-owned companies were off limits to them; they could not obtain credit from Polish banks; Jewish merchants and skilled tradesmen had difficulty obtaining work permits; universities set restrictive quotas for Jewish students and put obstacles in their way; and the Sunday Rest Law advanced by the Polish government compelled the Jews to take two days a week off work.

To resolve the economic crisis, Polish finance minister Władysław Grabski adopted a radical economic policy. As one means of halting rampant inflation, the merchant class (which included many Jews) was taxed exorbitantly. The Polish government also reduced the number of Jews working in industry and commerce relative to non-Jewish Poles. The fight against inflation was damaging to Jewish merchants and skilled tradesmen, driving many into extreme poverty.

The tobacco industry, which was mostly in Jewish hands, also suffered severely. "As is known, Poland has imposed a monopoly over the tobacco industry, which previously employed a fairly large number of Jewish workers. Now 13,000 workers are employed in this monopolistic industry, and only 441 of them are Jews." In Grodno, Jewish workers in the local tobacco factory (which had been expropriated from their Jewish owners) were required to work on the Sabbath; consequently, their numbers dropped dramatically. "If we leave the factory in Grodno out of the calculation, before the government monopoly 95 percent of the workers were Jewish and now only 45 percent are—and we have seen that out of 12,000 workers in the tobacco industry there are a total of 102 Jews."[62]

Jews suffered discrimination in other sectors of the Polish economy as well. Of the fifty-two thousand workers employed in city-run factories in Warsaw, there were only five thousand to six thousand Jews, less than 3 percent of the total. In the late 1920s, Latzky-Bertholdi reported, the Warsaw light rail had recruited fifteen hundred workers, of whom just four were Jews. One new factory in Warsaw employed thirteen hundred workers, of whom only twenty were Jews.[63] The percentage of Jews employed in oil refineries in eastern Galicia was high. In Borysław, for instance, half the workers were Jewish, as were 70 percent in Drohobycz. Beginning in 1925, the number of non-Jewish workers in the petroleum industry, including refineries, dropped by 20 percent, but among the Jews, the figure fell by 70 percent.[64] The civil service was also closed to Jews, and the Poles made a strenuous effort to reduce the number of Jews in the professions, especially medicine and law. In 1927, Poland enacted a law requiring skilled tradesmen to take a proficiency exam in the Polish language to qualify for a business license; Jews who could not meet the minimum licensing requirements thus lost their sources of livelihood.[65] Many Jews began to realize that the solution to their plight lay in migrating across the Atlantic.

Table 2.2. Emigration from Poland, 1921–1925.

Destination	Poles	Jews	Other	Total
United States	55,000	129,000	6,000	190,000
Canada	4,000	6,000	10,000	20,000
Brazil	2,000	2,000	1,000	5,000
Argentina	2,500	17,500	5,000	25,000
Palestine	–	30,000	–	30,000
Total	63,500	184,500	22,000	270,000

Source: Dijour, *Di Moderne Felker-Vanderung*, 68.

Before World War I, 55 percent of emigrants from Poland were non-Jewish Poles, 30 percent were Jews, and 15 percent were members of other nationalities. After the war the pattern changed. In the 1920s Jews accounted for 69 percent of emigrants from Poland, Poles 23 percent, and other nationalities 8 percent.[66] Although Jewish emigration from Poland was an integral part of overall emigration, the number of Jewish emigrants was disproportionately high.[67]

As the economic status of Polish Jews worsened, they became increasingly dependent on relatives who had migrated to Palestine or America. The exchange of letters from 1922 to 1939 between Wolf Lewkowicz and his family in Łódź and his nephew Sol Zissman in the United States indicates how severely the Polish government's economic policy had impacted and impoverished Polish Jewry in the 1920s and 1930s.[68] In early 1924, Wolf described to his nephew the harsh economic situation in Łódź: "The inflation here is unbelievably high, and I, as an ordinary citizen, am not in a position to provide for my hungry wife and children. In short, cold, need and hunger reign in my home."

He shared with his nephew his wishes and aspirations, which were unattainable in Poland in the 1920s:

> Devoted and most beloved Shloymele, it is hard, very hard, for me to write this to you, since I would rather cover it all up. The gift is small, but the shame is very great. I want very much to have the honor of having a home of my own and not live with my in-laws. I would yet want to earn with my own fingers [the money with which to buy] bread and salt, and not have to depend on someone else to be my breadwinner. I want very much for joy to reign in my home and for my children not to grow up [wild] as the oaks.[69]

The money that arrived from the United States helped the Lewkowiczes hold their heads up high and consider immigrating to Palestine or America. "Don't delay your help, since the need is very great." Wolf asked his nephew's advice about whether to stay in Poland and try to survive there or "whether I should go to Palestine, Argentina or America. I impatiently await your help as well as your advice. I also want to let you know that neither my wife nor my mother agrees with my [wanting to make the] journey. They are not, however, in a position to hold me back from existing, from living, etc."[70]

In July 1924, Wolf wrote to his nephew: "Things are very bad here in Poland these days, because of the problem of stabilization of money. There are many bankruptcies and suicides."[71] About half a year later, he wrote about emigration from Poland to Palestine: "The situation is not good here in Poland. This is a wretched and depressing time. There is an emigration from Poland to Palestine, but not everyone is in a position to leave. Only the privileged, the capitalists, et al., are going. What else shall I write, my devoted one?"[72] We see from his letters that his reasons for considering emigration to Palestine were pragmatic and in no way ideological or Zionist. Financial support from the nephew in the United States was a lifeline for the Lewkowiczes. Their dependence on the dollars they received made it perfectly clear to them that they had no future in Poland, that their financial situation was not about to improve, and that emigration was the only possible solution.

And with respect to your writing that you want to send me a weekly subsidy and that I should write you how much I need per week, so dear child, I have written to you several times and write again that I request nothing of you. While I know very well that you think constantly of your uncle, nevertheless, you must always have yourself in mind. I mean your wife who is closest to you, and so on. Furthermore, I'm not a person who would burden another. May G-d help me so that I can repay you what I already owe you. As of now, I don't foresee that in Poland there can be an opportunity for me to live and, nevertheless, I live . . . not because I want to live, but because I have to live. You know, surely, how a Jew lives: a little with miracles, a little with hope . . . and, in this way, one's few years pass with nothing. The children grow up, not as I once imagined. We spend our lives, not as I once imagined. And we write letters to a nephew in America, not as I once imagined.[73]

In his book *Di Ekonomishe Lage fun Yidn in Poyln* (The economic situation of Polish Jewry), Lestschinsky gives a powerful description of the hardship, desperation, and loss of hope of Polish Jewry. "The tumult of the Jewish masses on Nalewki Street in Warsaw these days gives the impression of drowning people who are treading water but can't move forward . . . a swamp with standing water that someone who falls into can't crawl out of again."[74] Despair—what Lestschinsky terms "collective depression and panic"—became the norm for the Jews of Poland, as they could not extricate themselves from their economic predicament. His impressions of the Warsaw street markets and the local Jews are depressing and poignant: "When you come to such a market on a Sunday, you are first struck by long lines of low stalls lying silent and dead as if they were hiding something underneath them. . . . You see old Jewish women wrapped in rags; young women with pale, gaunt faces . . . a hunchbacked old man sitting in a corner repairing shoes; a figure, half-woman, half-witch, asking you to taste her warm, fresh beans."[75]

When he visited the office of a small merchants' association in Lemberg, Lestschinsky made the acquaintance of a few of the "living dead": "Saturday night. The office is packed with Jewish men dressed in worn, faded Sabbath robes. Their faces are like their robes. A group of women stand separately off in a corner. They are short, dirty, and wrapped in strange scarves that hide their faces." Lestschinsky went into a side room with the chair of the merchants' association, and one after another impoverished Jews came in and presented their requests for assistance and economic support:

> A small, thin woman stands in front of us, a big scarf covering her eyes. When she launches into a long, enthusiastic speech, the scarf rises and falls and we notice that the gaunt, dried-out Jewish woman who we had thought was over

fifty is actually a young woman of thirty to thirty-five, with young, vibrant eyes. The way she speaks is a pleasure to hear. . . . She begins: Jews, compassionate children of compassionate parents! Will you allow a poor widow to fall into the abyss? Jews, a poor person like me is considered like one who is dead, but I am not yet dead, and my four children don't want to die either. They peck but there is no bread, so they eat me alive and soon I will die. Jews, put yourselves in my place. My children have no father and no one to support them. Have mercy, as a father has on his children. Be their father![76]

The widow explains that she must pay annual municipal taxes of sixty zloty for the right to have a stall in the market. Because she did not pay the tax from the beginning of the year, the city has decided to confiscate her stall unless a member of the Jewish council guarantees that she will repay the debt. Although she paid taxes for several months, the last month was particularly difficult for her, and because she did not have enough money, her debt built up. Furthermore, even before her husband died four years earlier, the burden of earning a living had fallen on her shoulders because he spent most of his time studying Torah and only from time to time earned a little from teaching.

Another person who came to meet with the chair of the merchants' association in Lemberg was a tall, thin young man wearing clean, polished shoes. He had owned a shoe store in the center of Warsaw, but during the economic crisis of 1925, he was forced to close it and rent another store. He had to close that one, too, and then he started selling shoes in a market stall. Lestschinsky described the man's foppish appearance as a sort of last remnant of better years when he had earned a living with dignity. The decline of the economy and the closure of his business had caused the overdressed man to lose hope of improving his financial status. For years he had hidden his troubles and hardships, but finally he realized that he would have to ask for assistance from the Jewish charitable organizations—the latest to join the ranks of beggars.

The three cases described above—the Lewkowicz family, the young widow, and the overdressed shoe seller—exemplify the economic hardship into which Polish Jewry sank in the second half of the 1920s. As the situation worsened, more and more people sought to migrate to Palestine and elsewhere. From 1924 to 1926, more than sixty-two thousand immigrants arrived in Palestine—more than twice as many as between 1919 and 1923.

Joshua Gordon, a high-ranking official in the Aliya Department and the first director of the Tel Aviv aliya bureau, wrote a comprehensive study in the mid-1920s entitled *Immigration Problems in Palestine*. In it he claimed, "In spite of the fact that Poland exists now as a united state de jure, it cannot be regarded as such de facto as far as the immigration material and the conditions of Jewry are concerned."[77] According to Gordon, the causes of emigration from Congress Poland (Russia), Lithuanian Poland, and Galicia (Austria) were all different. For instance, in Congress Poland "the Halutz movement in Congress Poland is quite backward." The halutzic component "is so small that it is nearly not worthwhile mentioning. Most of the members belong to the other Polish provinces and come mainly from Polish Lithuania and the adjacent district." In contrast, in Polish Lithuania "the position is quite different in this district. There also is noticeable a more or less considerable movement among the middle class and to a certain extent among the artisans." According to Gordon, however, "they are small village merchants who have a piece of land which both they and their children cultivate as a garden. The number of these people increased especially during the war. Now, they feel compelled to leave these places owing to political and economic and also to the attitude of their neighbours ... their only desire is to go to Palestine."[78] In Galicia, Gordon wrote, "social life is to a certain degree different to that of congress Poland." In the past, "Galicia furnished the bulk of the highest quality of Halutz material but at present the membership has dwindled down to a negligeable quantity.'" His conclusion was that "without doubt there is much good material for Palestine among all classes in Eastern Galicia; but as a result of the general depression and inefficient organization sufficient use is not made of the good field of work and the available hidden forces are not given a chance to develop and become active."[79]

Gordon also explained the reasons for emigration from Poland. The simple fact, he recognized, was that most of the Jews trying to migrate to Palestine were doing so because of the severe push factors in their countries of origin and not primarily because of the pull factors of the destination country. "And, daily they stream in their hundreds to the Palestine Offices to inquire about the possibilities in Palestine. What they want to know is, whether there are any possibilities of existence and doing business in Palestine. We must be clear in our minds about this point: it is not the ideal which they discovered suddenly that makes them turn to Palestine; it is not the light of Zionist idealism which they have suddenly seen; it is the Palestinian reality which they want to try."[80]

Having said "there is no intention whatever in this statement to reflect in any respect upon Polish Jewry and its ideal qualifications," Gordon clarified, "There is no degradation in it at all." In other words, "it only means that Polish Jews simply learned the Zionist lesson under the pressure of circumstances in a forced and quicker tempo and from a different aspect, consequently the results must also differ somewhat." At first, Polish Jews were skeptical about the idea of rejecting the exile and about the Zionist argument that the Jewish people had no future—neither spiritual nor economic—in the Diaspora. "But now from actual life they suddenly realized the practical truth of this fact. Now, when our propagandists came again to tell them, that now the only place where the Jewish people will find a haven of rest and a possibility to exist in Palestine; this, which formerly appeared to them as a remote dream of the Kingdom of Heaven on earth, now suddenly began to be seriously considered by them not only as a national solution of the Jewish problem, but as a business proposition to every Jew in Particular."[81]

Zionist Ideology

Alongside the government persecution, the danger of pogroms, and the economic hardship, there were those who had ideological motivations for wanting to immigrate to Palestine. Some of these Zionist Jews were young, unmarried socialists who wanted to establish a model socialist society in Palestine; others were people with families who belonged to the European bourgeoisie.

The Balfour Declaration and British conquest of Palestine breathed new hope into the Zionist movement and put the wind back into its sails. The British government kept its commitment to establish a national home for the Jewish people in Palestine. Herbert Samuel was named the first high commissioner, and Palestine was opened up to immigration. In 1921, Chaim Weizmann was elected president of the Zionist Organization and started rebuilding its institutions after a five-year moratorium due to the war. It seemed to be straight sailing for the Zionist movement, in terms of both practical settlement and political and diplomatic affairs.

While Weizmann was rebuilding the Zionist institutions, new halutzic youth movements were formed and others resumed their activity, embarking on a series of steps in preparation for immigration to Palestine. Hechalutz, the Dror Federation, Hashomer Hatzair, Tze'irei Zion, the Socialist Zionists (who had broken off from Tze'irei Zion), Blauweiss, Tekhelet Lavan, and Betar all sought to win young Jews over to the Zionist idea and encouraged them to move to Palestine. Disputes over matters of principle, sometimes fundamental and sometimes picayune, prevented the youth movements from cooperating with one another; each followed its own ideology to further its goals. Despite the disagreements and the ideological gaps, however, the youth movements had one thing in common: they all trained their members to settle and work in Palestine, taught them Hebrew, and helped them obtain the necessary travel papers for aliya. A call circulated by the Tze'irei Zion Center in Russia shortly after the Balfour Declaration expresses the innermost feelings of the Zionist youth: "Members of Tze'irei Zion! Stand ready in the ranks of the pioneers.

Now, after the worldwide emergency, what was distant will once again be near. The great call for the redemption of our people and our land will reach the ears of the entire nation, wherever they may be. When systematic work begins on the new aliya, which is unprecedented in the history of our people, we will all be ready."[82]

Unlike in the Second Aliya, when young people migrated on their own or in couples, the migration of youth movement members in the 1920s was organized and structured. The movements brought over large groups of immigrants after a training period on a farm in Europe. The Russian Hechalutz movement, whose prominent founders included Joseph Trumpeldor, occupied an important place in this effort. After the fighting in Gallipoli, Trumpeldor returned to Russia and worked tirelessly and resolutely to establish branches of his movement and training farms for young candidates for aliya. At the meeting of the Hechalutz board in Cracow in January 1918, Trumpeldor defined the movement's aims and objectives: "Hechalutz is in the vanguard of workers immigrating to Palestine to actualize the settlement issue. Its aim is to prepare the land for the people by uniting and bringing together all the forces ready to dedicate themselves to achieving this goal in Palestine."[83]

Branches of Hechalutz existed in places such as Poland, Lithuania, Romania, Latvia, Galicia, and central Europe. In 1921, the movement became the executive branch of the Zionist movement with respect to training halutzim and distributing immigration certificates. Eliyahu Dobkin, the Warsaw-based secretary-general of the World Hechalutz movement, maintained that at the height of halutzic aliya, roughly 11,500 halutzim arrived in Palestine.[84]

Another important halutzic youth movement in the 1920s was Hashomer Hatzair. This movement was founded in 1913 but only took shape during World War I. It had two centers: one in Galicia, which until the end of the war was part of the Austro-Hungarian Empire, and the other in Congress Poland, which was part of the Russian Empire. In Galicia, most Hashomer Hatzair members came from the better-off classes in Jewish society: merchants, professionals, and affluent skilled tradesmen. Many of the young people were assimilated, and the movement's activities (especially in the big cities) were conducted in Polish. World War I was the formative experience of their adolescence. They lived as refugees in Vienna, they witnessed the impoverishment of their parents and the breakup of their families when their fathers were drafted to fight the war, and they were forced to take odd jobs.[85] Hashomer Hatzair in Congress Poland, in contrast, had a more "Jewish" character and was aware of the part it played in Jewish society.[86] When the new Polish republic was established, Hashomer

Hatzair members from Galicia and Congress Poland found themselves in the same country. In practice, however, the two branches of the movement never merged and continued to coexist as fraternal twins.

The first wave of olim from Hashomer Hatzair came from Galicia; most arrived in 1920, with a smaller number immigrating in 1921. Although an estimated six hundred people arrived in this wave, most of them did not make it and left the country.[87] The newcomers, who dispersed throughout Palestine, had to adapt themselves to local working conditions. Groups of Hashomer Hatzair members settled in Beit Gan (near Yavne'el), Dilb (Kiryat Anavim), Umm al-Alaq (Shuni, not far from Binyamina), Migdal (on the Haifa-Jedda road), and Bitanya Illit. Few olim arrived from Congress Poland in those years; only after the aliya bureau regularized the aliya process did their share increase. The big wave of Hashomer Hatzair olim came from Poland in the second half of the 1920s, in the years that Zionist historiography has identified as the bourgeois Fourth Aliya.

In 1923, Hechalutz had 5,470 members in 224 branches located in nine European countries. Hashomer Hatzair had 1,400 members aged twelve to nineteen. The other pioneering movements, such as Blauweiss in Germany and Tekhelet Lavan in Czechoslovakia, were much smaller and probably had no more than a thousand members altogether. Thus, the aliya "reserves" of the halutzic movements in Europe in the 1920s, including the young members, did not exceed 7,000.[88]

The Zionist ideology promoted by the various youth movements was a major component in their members' decision to immigrate to Palestine. They were motivated first and foremost by their national worldview, which regarded the Land of Israel as the place for the revitalization of the Jewish people. The pogroms during the civil war, systemic government discrimination against the Jews, and economic hardship were not their reasons for aliya; they were merely bleak manifestations of the plight of the Jewish people in exile. For them, the appropriate solution was immigration to their one and only national home in Palestine. The pull factors of Palestine were stronger than the push factors of their countries of origin; their arrival in Palestine was the practical fulfillment of the Zionist idea. Although halutzim accounted for a small proportion of immigrants to Palestine in the 1920s, their contribution to the Zionist enterprise was tremendous.

In the following chapters, we will see the main dilemma that the Zionist movement faced with respect to the distribution of immigration certificates: Should they be given to members of the halutzic youth movements, who were young and healthy in body and soul and wanted to immigrate to Palestine for clear Zionist reasons, to build up the country and be transformed by it? Or should they be given to Jewish refugees and immigrants who had lost their families and their worldly possessions and who regarded Palestine as no more (but no less) than a land of refuge?

The geopolitical situation in Europe after World War I directly influenced immigration to Palestine in the 1920s. The Austro-Hungarian and Russian Empires had broken up; new nation-states had arisen in their place; and Jews found themselves in a new, unfamiliar, and harmful political and social order. The civil war in Ukraine left one hundred thousand Jews killed or wounded and triggered the migration of tens of thousands of Jewish refugees, who reached almost everywhere in Europe. Life in Russia after the October Revolution of 1917 was unbearable. The Bolshevik regime imposed a rigid, dogmatic way of life by violent, brutal means, causing severe shortages and famine and impoverishing the Russian people. In Poland, meanwhile, inflation was rampant, and the government adopted an economic policy that harmed the middle class, to which most Polish Jews belonged. The Jews of eastern Europe sought to flee to any country that would have them. The United States—their preferred destination—set new, restrictive quotas on immigration and thus no longer offered a solution to the plight of the eastern European Jews. After other destination countries followed suit, tightening their own immigration policies, Palestine gradually became the main destination for Jewish immigrants. While the socioeconomic situation of eastern European Jewry suffered, the Zionist movement found itself in a much better position after World War I than before the war. The British takeover of Palestine and the Balfour Declaration inspired new hope that Zionism could be realized through immigration to Palestine and settlement there.

In his study on the problems of immigration to Palestine, Joshua Gordon distinguishes between olim and immigrants and discusses the nature of Jewish migration in the 1920s: "Together with the Hechalutz movement which is developing in a normal and systematic manner in every country alongside with the general internal Zionist work there awoke at the same time a movement among the masses to emigrate to Palestine. This movement can be noticed in every country where Jews are to be found in more or less considerable numbers. Originally called to life by the Zionist ideal, it does not at present stand any more under the influence of ideals in general or under the influence of the Zionist Organisation in particular." According to Gordon, the push factors in the countries of origin and the Jews' desire to emigrate had turned the migration into a social phenomenon that had spiraled out of control.

From the symptoms which are already noticeable this is not a movement of
many individuals which are converted into a mass by the addition of the right
numbers but it is a mass movement by nature in which the will or the common sense of the individual is of no account. The individual is simply carried
along by the general stream not being able to resist the force of mass psychol-
ogy. But at the same tone the moving forces which are behind this movement
do not remain in one place but are becoming more and more powerful from
day to day; and the development of these forces is, just as much as these
forces themselves are, outside the sphere of our influence.[89]

Jewish immigration to Palestine in the 1920s, Gordon argued, was uncontrollable, and the Zionist movement was helpless to influence it, change its
direction, or determine its characteristics. "This mass movement to Palestine
has now reached especially the middle classes of the Jewish people in nearly
all the places of the Diaspora. This immigration movement I called 'Natural
Immigration' to distinguish it from the Zionist pioneer movement, because
the original causes to which it is due are the same as those of all immigration
movements." Gordon saw no difference between Jewish immigration to Palestine and to other countries. "The present natural immigration movement
to Palestine presents one phase of the many wandering of the Jewish people
during the time of its exile. We would very quickly have recognised it as such if
its aim had been Galveston, Buenos Aires or the United States, but it appears
rather strange to us when, owing to the force of a complex of circumstances
... it has chosen as its destination the Tel Aviv of Palestine instead of the East
Side of New York."[90]

3

The Gates Open

After the British conquered Palestine and the British Mandate began, the country was opened to immigration. Tens of thousands of olim, immigrants, and refugees arrived in Palestine in the 1920s—more Jews than had immigrated in the thirty-two years of the First Aliya and Second Aliya (1882–1914).

Jewish immigration in the 1920s was a continuation of prewar immigration: eastern Europe was still the Jews' main place of origin. The economic hardship on the European continent had worsened, as had the political persecution and the pogroms. Despite the similar motivations for immigration and similar push factors in the countries of origin before and after the war, the Mandate period was differentiated by one aspect that dramatically affected immigration. During this period, immigration policy to Palestine was formulated, restrictions were introduced to regulate both the number of immigrants and their demographic composition, and an aliya department was established that took on responsibility for organizing and handling immigration to Palestine.

Studying immigration to Palestine according to the immigration regulations enacted in the Mandate period and British and Zionist policy rather than the demography of the immigrant population blurs the dichotomous division into two separate waves of aliya—the Third Aliya and the Fourth Aliya—that has become a fixture of Zionist historiography. The number of immigrants, their traits, and the unique character of each wave of immigration were determined in practice by British immigration policy on the one hand and the Zionist movement's preferences on the other.

The Regulation of Immigration: First Steps

The repatriated Jews who had been deported from Palestine or simply stranded outside the country during World War I and the immigrants who arrived in 1919 found a Jewish community that was licking its war wounds. Because its organized structure had collapsed, the community had a very hard time absorbing them.[1] But the reality of thirty-eight hundred Jews entering the country in that year could not be ignored; guidance was needed to regulate and organize immigration. The leaders of the Zionist movement believed that immigration must not be left to local or spontaneous initiatives; instead, the movement had to prepare for and control it. The issue of organizing and overseeing immigration to Palestine was addressed in a postwar Zionist conference that took place in February and March 1919. There, Zionist Organization representatives who were able to reach London resolved to establish an aliya department and a network of Palestine Offices that would deal with applications for immigration throughout the Jewish world, mainly in eastern Europe but also in Palestine.[2] In June 1919, an official announcement was sent out to all Zionist organizations about the establishment of an aliya department under the auspices of the Central Zionist Office in London. According to the announcement, the department intended to open aliya bureaus in the countries of origin of Jewish immigration, establish information bureaus to provide Jews interested in going to Palestine with up-to-date information about the journey and about living conditions in Palestine, and to negotiate with the shipping and cargo transport companies regarding conditions on the voyage.[3]

The Provisional Committee for the Jews of Palestine took responsibility for organizing immigration, in cooperation with the Zionist Commission for Palestine. During the Ottoman period, no orderly records had been kept on people entering the country; immigrants had been given no guidance in advance, so the Zionist institutions had had difficulty helping them settle in and deal with the hardships. In contrast, under the British military regime, an official policy was developed for the admission of immigrants, as was customary in modern immigration countries; the policy included recordkeeping on people entering and leaving the country, ties with shipping companies, medical exams in the countries of origin and in Palestine, cargo handling procedures, immigrant houses for the newcomers to stay in initially, and dispersal around the country.

The Provisional Committee sought to establish an orderly admission procedure in Palestine resembling the one on Ellis Island in the United States. The immigration station on Ellis Island, located in the Hudson River estuary between Manhattan and New Jersey, had opened on January 1, 1892. Previously, immigrants had been processed at Castle Garden in Battery Park (Manhattan) and given permission to enter the city from there. The increase in the volume of immigration, however, was hard for immigration officials in New York to cope with and forced US immigration authorities to find another solution. Ellis Island was chosen partly for its physical proximity to Manhattan but also because it was separate from it. After passenger ships anchored in Manhattan, the first- and second-class passengers disembarked and entered the country with no inspection or processing. Third- and fourth-class passengers waited for ferries to take them to Ellis Island, where they began the procedure for entering New York. From the day Ellis Island opened until it closed in 1954, 12 million people passed through it. Immigration officials, with the help of interpreters, asked the newcomers about their family status and employment, their age, their former place of residence and their destination in the new land, their height, their physical condition, and their state of health. From 1899 they were also asked about their ethnicity. Immigrants who had not completed the entry procedure spent the night there, and those who fell ill were hospitalized and given medical treatment. Only 2 percent of immigrants were sent back to their countries of origin.[4]

When the leadership started thinking about a registration and admission procedure for people entering Palestine, their intention was to adopt the Ellis Island model. On December 21, 1918, the Provisional Committee for the Jews of Palestine convened in the auditorium of the School for Girls in Jaffa to start preparing for general elections in the Yishuv.[5] Representatives of Moshavot Yehuda, the Jaffa community board, the ICA, Hapoel Hatzair, Poalei Zion, Hashomer, and the Teachers' Center, "representatives of Hanikhei Herzliya, representatives of the national democratic clubs in Petah Tikva, Rishon Lezion, and Nes Ziona, and members of the organizing committee" took part.[6]

In their meetings, the Provisional Committee addressed various aspects of the postwar rebuilding of the Yishuv, including regulation of immigration and preparations for it. On April 24, 1919—a month after the Zionist conference in London—the Provisional Committee resolved to establish an "immigration council" (referring to it as *hagira*—"immigration"—and not *aliya*) comprising Israel Shochat (Ahdut ha-Avoda), Menashe Meirowitz (Moshavot Yehuda), Michael Erlich (Center for Skilled Tradesmen), Rachel Grazovsky (Women's Association), and Nachum Tversky (Hapoel Hatzair).[7]

About a month later, the immigration council met to discuss anticipated difficulties and ways of resolving them. Its decisions were of great importance, as they laid the foundations for immigrant absorption throughout the 1920s and 1930s. The participants specified the assistance period for newly arrived immigrants (up to seven days for singles; up to ten days for families); resolved to establish aliya bureaus in Jaffa, Haifa, and Jerusalem; considered disembarkation arrangements, including a contract with the Arab boat owners, employment terms for Jewish stevedores, and the disembarkation fee; and discussed the establishment of a shelter for immigrants' first few days, operation of a kitchen for them, and assistance with job hunting.[8]

At another meeting a few days later, the council's areas of activity were delineated. Henceforth the immigration council would be responsible for all aspects of immigration to Palestine and would convene every Tuesday afternoon.[9] Immigrants would be offered financial assistance in the form of loans (if they could be expected to repay them) or gifts (when there was no chance of repayment). The loans would be distributed from a loan fund at the discretion of two representatives of the immigration council, who would determine each immigrant's financial status and likelihood of repaying the loan. They decided to postpone discussing which immigrants were desirable until a special meeting to which the heads of the agriculture and industry departments would be invited.[10]

At one meeting of the immigration council, it was reported that a twenty-three-room house had been found near the Jaffa shore where immigrants could be housed. The council stated, "Obtaining a house for the immigrants is one of the most vital needs. When the exiles from Jaffa arrived from Egypt, there was no house to put them in, and the few homes obtained were expensive."[11] Opening the immigrants' house in Jaffa was the first step taken in the 1920s toward offering newcomers decent, spacious housing; additional buildings were subsequently found in Jaffa, Haifa, and Jerusalem. These houses were managed meticulously and in an orderly manner during the Mandate period: immigrants were registered, loans were issued, and efforts were made to help the immigrants settle in and find jobs in the cities and villages.

The meeting that would address the desirability of certain categories of immigrants was scheduled for the middle of June 1919. By then a significant number of immigrants had already arrived, and the immigration council was asked its opinion on what sort of immigrants the Yishuv needed. No dramatic decisions were made at this meeting; from the discussion it seems that this was a highly sensitive topic and that the council was not equipped to take a position on the matter. "We discussed what type of immigrant is desirable for the country. This question is currently important because certain answers are needed to questions being asked abroad in this regard. It is therefore essential to determine what lines of work new immigrants can be employed in. On the other hand, it is impossible to give a clear-cut answer. Moreover, the present conditions—both political and economic—are not permanent, so it is not yet possible to determine the country's true needs and to draw conclusions based on current wages and needs in Palestine. Certain decisions were not made."[12]

This discussion was one of the first held after World War I on this sensitive topic, which continued to occupy the Zionist movement and the State of Israel for many years. Although nothing was decided at the meeting, it was clear to the council members that mass immigration should not be allowed and that immigration should be guided by the absorptive capacity of the country and the needs of the Yishuv. It should be noted that the immigration council did not have the authority to decide such a sensitive issue, but its members were certain of the need for a decisive, official immigration policy that would encourage able-bodied people to settle in Palestine. A few months later, the Zionist Executive would claim full authority over immigration to Palestine and would set immigration policy.

The uncertainty regarding the type of immigrant needed to build up the land was nothing new for the Zionist movement. Between 1882 and 1914, approximately sixty thousand Jews arrived in Palestine; only a small minority were Zionists who chose to come for reasons other than being pushed out of their countries of origin. Due to the objective limitations on mass absorption of immigrants, the leaders of the Zionist movement and immigration policymakers were compelled to decide what sort of Jewish immigrants were desirable.[13] In his article "Derekh La'avor Golim" (The path of exiles), written in the early days of the First Aliya, Moshe Leib Lilienblum wrote, "When rousing people to settle the country, we think only of the wealthy, who can pay in full for property and prepare all the instruments at their own expense. The poor, however, have no place in Palestine."[14] Menachem Sheinkin, head of the Hovevei Zion information bureau in Jaffa in the early 1920s, and Arthur Ruppin, director of the Palestine Office, begged Jews not to come to Palestine unless they had the means to support themselves.

This dilemma led to a selective immigration policy that gave preference to people with capital and young, able-bodied olim over older, destitute immigrants. The country's inability to take in every Jew who wanted to come evoked a moral debate in the Zionist movement on the good of the people versus the good of the country. Those who gave precedence to the good of the people advocated mass immigration to Palestine in order to save the Jews physically and spiritually. In contrast, those who favored the good of the country maintained that Palestine could not, within a short time, absorb the masses of Jews who wanted to go there, and therefore they preferred people with capital or the young and able-bodied over poor or disabled immigrants who would contribute little to the Yishuv.

Sheinkin's involvement in immigration affairs and the information bureau were the main reasons for his appointment as head of the Zionist Commission's aliya bureau in Tel Aviv.[15] During World War I, Sheinkin had been deported from Palestine and had gone to the United States. When the war ended, he returned to Palestine. There was no better candidate to head the aliya bureau at the time. Sheinkin understood not only the importance of ensuring orderly, organized immigration but also the need to determine what sort of immigrants were needed for settling Palestine.

In early February 1920, Sheinkin was officially appointed head of the Tel Aviv aliya bureau. In a letter to the Zionist Organization, he announced, "The Central Bureau of Immigrant Affairs has been established here in Jaffa by the Zionist Commission for Palestine, and I am honored to head it. We have branches in Jerusalem, Haifa, Tiberias, Safed, and Beirut."[16] He said he would send out his bureau's detailed plans soon. In addition, he asked the Zionist Organization for up-to-date, accurate information about the number of people setting out for Palestine and whether they were poor or wealthy. Along with precise recordkeeping on people leaving and entering the country, Sheinkin tried to institute an orderly procedure for the entry of immigrants.

> In the near future we will send you [the following items] for those traveling to Palestine:
>
> 1. Slips of paper to paste onto the belongings in order to distinguish between hand luggage that the passenger must take with him . . . when leaving the ship and bring to the hotel (these parcels will generally not be inspected in the customs house unless some passengers abuse this and embarrass us), and large items of baggage, which we will take from the ship to our storerooms on shore in special boats, and which the passengers can receive once they have rested a bit from the journey.
> 2. Lists of immigrants on which each passenger will write the number and sort of packages that he has with him on the ship, [and] what is in the packages: clothing, underwear, housewares, merchandise, and so on. . . . This will be very helpful in facilitating and expediting the arrival of passengers and belongings in an orderly, dignified manner befitting *returnees to Zion rather than panic-stricken immigrants*.[17]

For the first time in the history of immigration to Palestine, the disembarkation procedure would be regulated, with the newcomers being informed what baggage they could take with them and what they should leave on the ship for the stevedores. The order and discipline at the entrance to Palestine had additional significance as well, aside from merely increasing efficiency. For Sheinkin, they were a means of giving their arrival an ideological, national character and turning the panic-stricken immigrants into olim. Meanwhile, Sheinkin started establishing aliya bureaus in the port cities where the ships docked on the way: Beirut, Alexandria, Port Said, and Sidon. These bureaus were of great importance because many immigrants who headed for Palestine were forced to travel via those cities and arrange for travel documents with the British consuls there: "Here those who have no visa from the British consul are not permitted to enter," Sheinkin wrote to the Zionist Organization. "They disembark in Beirut and after extensive efforts they obtain permits to come to Haifa or the Upper Galilee overland. We have now arranged for an aliya committee in Beirut with a paid official. The official is Mr. Trifon, a hard-working young man who is acceptable to the French and English authorities there."[18]

The purpose of the aliya committee in Beirut was to help with arrangements for the Jews who were arriving en masse in the port cities of Egypt and Lebanon. These people had become a burden on the local Jewish communities, which were trying with great difficulty to assist them and resolve their problems. "During this time I have managed to see and observe the disorder in the aliya committees in Sidon and Beirut," Trifon wrote to Sheinkin. "People come to Sidon and spend weeks staying on the synagogue floors, suffering from cold and hunger. The carters take however much they want for transporting them to Haifa or bringing them from Beirut. There is no one to take care of this and get involved. The same is true in Beirut. People come and the boat owners rob them, steal their belongings, and take them wherever they want."[19]

Trifon reported to Sheinkin that while in Sidon and Beirut, he had sent Jewish immigrants to Palestine "by various means: on horseback over the mountains, via Tyre, and many by ship."[20] His reports strongly reinforce the argument that the number of immigrants who arrived in Palestine during the period of the military regime was much greater than reported by the Zionist Commission's information bureau because many entered the country by land and were not counted or included in the records.

Due to the immigrants' hardship and the need to help them out, the Jewish community board in Beirut established an aliya committee: "We are hereby honored to inform you [Sheinkin] that, at its last meeting, the board in the city of Beirut discussed the aliya plan proposed in your aforementioned letter and decided to appoint a special committee to handle the affairs of immigrants in our city.... This committee, composed of people who are dedicated to the idea, will be in touch with you directly on all matters concerning aliya."[21] To help immigrants who had reached Beirut and Sidon, Trifon suggested to Sheinkin three essential steps: finding a house for the immigrants "furnished for at least 25 people"; appointing a representative of the Zionist Commission to board ships anchored in Sidon and Beirut, "put [the passengers] in boats with their belongings, transport them to the house, and try to send them on right away by any means"; and renting a permanent office in the city so that "those passing through know where to go and do not spend days at the doors of the members of the city board."[22]

In addition to the information bureau in Beirut, the Zionist Organization made sure to establish one in Alexandria, an important port and way station for Jewish immigrants en route to Palestine from the port of Trieste. In early June 1920, the Zionist Commission wrote to Zionist Organization headquarters, announcing the establishment of a combination information and aliya bureau. The monthly budget that the Zionist Organization made available to the bureaus in Egypt was very small—not enough for the Alexandria bureau to take care of the immigrants efficiently and quickly. Zionist Commission chair Menachem Ussishkin therefore proposed that the wealthy Jewish community of Alexandria help out: "Regarding your letter in which you ask us to allocate 15 Egyptian pounds a month to support this bureau, attached is a comment by Mr. Ussishkin saying that in his opinion the Alexandria community is wealthy enough to provide for the needs of the bureau and that for now we should just maintain the Cairo bureau at our expense."[23]

After the Arab riots of 1921 and the temporary suspension of immigration to Palestine, Alexandria became a bottleneck, as hundreds of immigrants arrived there and were unable to continue on to Palestine. The information bureau had no choice but to find a shelter for those stranded in the city. The bureau secretary wrote to the Zionist Commission asking for its consent to establish a "pioneers' home," where immigrants would stay until they could sail for Palestine.

We hereby confirm receipt of your letter of June 19, 1921, regarding the pioneers' home in our city. The halutzim here are costing us a lot. We are paying 6 pounds a day per person for a hotel and tea, and this does not include food, which is still not organized for want of a pioneers' home. In our previous letter we therefore advised you to look into this matter. We have found a two-story house in Miharem Bey; it has eight large rooms and open space around the house. This house can hold 150–200 halutzim and will cost us 180 pounds a year in rent. We hereby advise you to arrange for a pioneers' home in our city because, as we know, it is currently impossible to send large groups of halutzim to Palestine. . . . Most of them will have to wait here a while for a ship in order to continue on to Palestine. In order to minimize the high cost, we advise you to look into this matter and arrange for a pioneers' home in our city as soon as possible.[24]

We do not know how the Zionist Commission responded to the initiative, but the idea of establishing a "pioneers' home" in Alexandria was just one of the ideas for assistance suggested during the period of the military regime (some of which were put into practice). By the time Herbert Samuel arrived in the summer of 1920 to assume the office of high commissioner, there was an organized system of aliya bureaus in Palestine and the nearby coastal cities to welcome the immigrants and help them settle in. Within a relatively short time—from the end of the war until the establishment of the civil administration—the Provisional Committee's immigration council managed, despite the many difficulties, to create a modern system suited to receiving the immigrants; this system was further developed and improved in the 1920s and 1930s, as we shall see in the coming chapters.

Immigration to Palestine during the Period of the Military Regime

Under the military regime (1919–June 1920), both Jews and non-Jews immigrated to Palestine. We do not have complete data on the entry of non-Jews, but from the limited documentation available, it seems that Arabs who had left Palestine due to the war returned when this became possible. In this sense the Arab exiles were no different from the Jews who had been deported from Palestine and returned at the first opportunity.

Concerned about the return of the Arab exiles, the Zionist Executive in London asked the Zionist Commission for accurate data: "Recently (in late August of this year [1919]) you started to send us, at our request, a list of non-Jewish immigrants as well. We are exceedingly grateful to you for this, because these lists are now especially essential to us."[25] It is not clear what was "especially essential" about them; however, the letter gives the impression that the Zionist Executive was concerned that mass Arab immigration to Palestine might hinder realization of the Balfour Declaration and wanted to prepare for this possibility: "The evidence from the lists that you obtained, according to which 80–90 percent of all non-Jewish immigrants are exiles who have now returned to their homeland, seems somewhat dubious to us. The proofs of this detail leave a great deal of room for seeing the applicants for entry permits. We would like to know your opinion on this matter."[26] To provide the Zionist Executive with the desired information, an official working on behalf of the Zionist Commission sat in the port of Jaffa and kept records of people entering Palestine.

According to estimates, fifty-four hundred Jews and Arabs entered Palestine from the beginning of the military regime period until High Commissioner Herbert Samuel arrived. Presumably, the true numbers are much higher because the available data is for Jaffa only, whereas people also entered the country through Haifa port and overland; however, the Zionist Commission did not record those people.

As stated, most of the non-Jews who entered Palestine were Arabs who had been abroad and returned when the war was over. They were mostly merchants, some of them petty merchants, who had spent the war years in the United States, South America, or Europe. Only 10 percent of the 420 Arabs who arrived at Jaffa port between March and July were immigrants; the others were returnees.[27] Half were young and about 8 percent were children. Between August 17 and 19, 1919, sixty-four immigrants arrived by ship from Beirut and Alexandria, half of them merchants coming from South America (Argentina, Brazil, and Chile). According to the records, all were Palestine residents who had lived in villages near Jaffa and Jerusalem before the war.[28] On August 28 and 29, another 151 Arab exiles arrived in Jaffa port. Ninety percent of them had spent the war in America working in commerce and skilled trades. In September and October 1919, about 80 percent of the Arabs who entered Palestine via Jaffa port were petty merchants from Bethlehem returning from America. All the others were women and children coming from Beirut and Egypt for short visits.[29]

The extraordinary story of one halutz, Shlomo Zacharin, offers additional evidence regarding the return of the Arab exiles to Palestine. In his memoirs, Zacharin recounts that when he reached the age of military service in 1913, he was unsure whether to move to Palestine or visit his brother in one of Baron Hirsch's colonies in Argentina. He arrived in Argentina a few months before the outbreak of World War I and was stranded there until the end of the war. To obtain an immigration certificate to Palestine, he posed as a Palestine-born Arab, paid the membership fee for a Muslim association in Argentina, and received a document attesting that he was a returning exile. In February 1919, Zacharin sailed from La Plata to France, but due to a shortage of ships in Marseilles, he roamed around the port city with nothing to do. "After we had wandered the streets of Marseilles for about two weeks, it occurred to one of our men, an Arabic speaker, to take advantage of our Arab brothers who had found themselves in Marseilles during and before the war and had been stranded there with no hope of returning to Syria. There were about 80 of them, most of them out of work and destitute."[30] Zacharin and his friends organized a demonstration together with Arabs who wanted to return home; together, they tried to exert pressure on the municipality to find them a solution to their plight. "Their job was to shout and make as much noise as possible in the offices at Marseilles city hall, a job they did perfectly. After a few such demonstrations, which prevented the municipal officials from being able to work, the city of Marseilles decided to get rid of them no matter what."[31] Finally, the city obtained permission for them to leave for Beirut, and Zacharin was able to immigrate to Palestine along with the Arabs. Some of them disembarked in Beirut—others, like him, in Jaffa.

Studies of immigration to Palestine at the beginning of the Mandate period do not give reliable immigration figures for 1919. In the *Statistical Abstract of Palestine*, David Gurevich, the statistician of the Zionist Executive, writes that 806 people arrived in the country in 1919, 670 of them on the ship *Ruslan*.[32] The demographer Moshe Sicron, in contrast, states that immigration that year totaled 1,806.[33] Baruch Ben-Avram and Henry Near maintain that Sicron's figure originates in a misprint, since Gurevich's figure of 806 immigrants is based on monthly immigration rates.[34] Gurevich explains that the aliya figures from September 1919 until the end of 1934 are based on records from the aliya bureaus in Haifa, Tel Aviv, and Jerusalem, where all Jews entering the country were recorded on cards containing their particulars: sex, age, family status, nationality, last country of residence, and occupation.[35] Because some immigrants arrived before the aliya bureaus opened in September 1919, however, Gurevich's statistics are incomplete and therefore inaccurate.

Table 3.1 shows that the number of Jews who entered Palestine in 1919 and the first six months of 1920 is estimated at 3,815—at least twice that of Arabs. Most of the non-Jewish arrivals were Arab exiles returning to their villages. In contrast, only 1,200 of the Jews were exiles; the others were all immigrants and refugees. "The following numbers refer mainly to the immigration of Jews via the coast of Jaffa, as well as some of those who disembarked in Haifa (about 60 people)," reported the Zionist Commission's Department of Statistics and Information, "and 1,220 returning exiles who came from Egypt by train (740 to Jaffa and 480 to Jerusalem). But we have no figures on those who entered the country by train via Egypt or via the shores of Beirut."[36] Moreover, Jewish immigration to Palestine in 1919 exceeded not only Arab immigration to Palestine but even Jewish immigration to the United States.

The demographics of immigrants entering Palestine during the period of the military regime suggests that they were not halutzim: 58 percent were men and 42 percent were women; 31 percent were children up to age fourteen; 61 percent were aged fifteen to fifty-nine; and 8 percent were aged sixty or over. More than

Table 3.1. Entry of non-Jews and Jews into Palestine via Jaffa port.

Month and year	Non-Jews	Jews
February 1919	Unknown	284
March 1919	90	122
April 1919	50	152
May 1919	80	44
June 1919	100	1,039
July 1919	100	91
August 1919	385	174
September 1919	158	195
October 1919	204	94
November 1919	115	51
December 1919	32	708
January 1920	136	91
February 1920	12	206
March 1920	84	213
April 1920	79	204
May 1920	28	147
Total	1,653	3,815

Source: CZA, L2, file 231; Yediot ha-Mahlaka le-Statistika ule-Informatsia [News of the Department of Statistics and Information], July 30, 1920.

72 percent were married, 17 percent were single, and the rest were widowed, divorced, or orphans.[37] The descriptions of the newcomers in the press at the time confirm the conclusions that emerge from the statistical analyses. Many of them did not conform to the definition of halutzim; instead, they were ordinary immigrants, who sometimes arrived without prior planning and may have gone to Palestine as a default. Yitzhak Lufban, editor of the newspaper *Hapoel Hatzair,* described immigration to Palestine after the British "cannon fire" had augured "a new political era for the country and Zionism":

> This we know and the olim also know: they have been called on to be
> pioneers, to immigrate under poor conditions and with no guarantees. They
> have been called on to be volunteers, doing hard work that pays little and
> whose yields are not particularly noticeable, but whose national principal
> is unequaled and enduring and whose cost is outweighed by the gain. This
> was the aim of this aliya, which began in dire straits. But it was not always
> possible to achieve this aim in full; it was not always possible to select the

Figure 3.1. The *Ruslan*. Photo courtesy of CZA.

human material with precision. Non-halutzic elements were swept along by the current—refugees from the Polish draft and ordinary people fleeing economic hardship in eastern Europe, who basically don't care whether they go to Palestine, America, or some other *land of refuge*. Obviously these people are not ineligible to be in the country; but under the present conditions of volunteer work that requires immigrants to make sacrifices and make do with little, they cannot cope.[38]

The *Ruslan*

The historiography of the Yishuv and aliya regards the *Ruslan* as the ship that heralded the onset of immigration to Palestine after World War I. The ship anchored in Jaffa on December 19, 1919, with roughly 670 passengers on board. Most were refugees from the civil war in Ukraine or Jews who had been deported from Palestine. Some were halutzim and Zionist activists coming to build up Palestine; they included prominent public figures such as Dr. Joseph Klausner, Moshe Glueckson, the poet Rachel Bluwstein, Rosa "Red Rosa"

Cohen, and Dr. Baruch Nissenbaum. The impending arrival of these well-known Zionists evoked excitement and interest in the Yishuv.

On November 27, 1919, at the height of the civil war in Ukraine, the *Ruslan* sailed from Odessa for Palestine. News of the ship's imminent departure made waves among Russian Jewry: "From all over the country, many families started streaming to Odessa, having heard the rumor about mass immigration to Palestine. The Zionist activists were faced with the difficult, tragic duty of explaining to those hoping to emigrate that the *Ruslan* was just the first swallow and was not yet bringing spring in its wings."[39]

The migration of the ship's passengers was made possible thanks to residents of Palestine who had settled in the Black Sea port city of Odessa during World War I. Some of them were merchants who had gone there on business and had been stranded by the war and the closure of maritime routes; others were refugees—primarily from Safed and Tiberias—fleeing persecution by the Ottoman regime and the grave economic situation in Palestine. Approximately 150 refugees from Palestine had arrived in Odessa in the winter of 1918 after an arduous journey from the Galilee to Syria, then by train to Constantinople, and from there on a collier to Odessa. Because no one knew of their arrival, they had nowhere suitable to stay, and they spent several nights on the shore before local Zionist activists offered assistance. The Zionists housed them in a warehouse in the suburbs and even established the "Committee to Send the Refugees from Palestine Back Home." Thus was born the idea of aliya on the *Ruslan*.

The committee, headed by David Hachamovich and his deputy Moshe Goldin-Zehavi, decided to take advantage of the refugees' return to Palestine to send other Jews along, posing as refugees. The people pretending to be refugees had to learn the geography of Palestine and "various details such as the streets of Tel Aviv, Jaffa, Haifa, Petah Tikva, Rishon Lezion, etc., Yishuv activists, etc."[40] The committee provided each of the refugees—the original ones and the impostors—with a certificate written in Russian, Hebrew, and French identifying the person as a refugee from Palestine who was entitled to reenter the country. "The journey from Odessa to Jaffa lasted about a month. The captain had promised it would take only about ten days, but because the ship visited various shores that they had not originally intended to go to, its arrival in Jaffa was delayed for another two weeks or so."[41] A shortage of water, poor sanitary conditions, and extreme crowding on board made the voyage even harder for the passengers. On December 19, 1919, the third night of Hanukkah, the *Ruslan* reached the coast of Jaffa.

Jaffa had no deep-water port for anchoring safely, so ships would anchor about a kilometer from the shore. Sometimes passengers had to wait a long time on board during a storm until the sea quieted and rowboats could approach

Figure 3.2. The refugee certificate of a *Ruslan* passenger. Photo courtesy of CZA.

to pick them up. At other times, when it proved impossible to reach the shore, ships even sailed back to Beirut or Port Said, returning to Jaffa a few days later. This was what happened with the *Ruslan*. The passengers were greeted by a storm, and even before they could all disembark and their belongings could be unloaded, the anchor came loose. The *Ruslan* sailed to Egypt and returned to Jaffa a few days later. Despite the stormy weather, the passengers received a warm welcome. Their arrival had stirred up tremendous excitement. Zionist Commission chair Menachem Ussishkin gave a speech, and refreshments were served. In all the hubbub and excitement, one passenger collapsed and died—the first casualty of the *Ruslan* aliya.

The arrival of the *Ruslan* triggered rumors in Jaffa that the "Third Aliya" was imminent and that the ship was just "the first convoy to Palestine."[42] Indeed, the *Ruslan* and its passengers went down in history as the harbinger of the Third Aliya—"the Palestinian *Mayflower* that opened the country's gates after World War I."[43] Its immigrants "breathed life into the Yishuv and their part was evident in all areas of life and activity."[44]

The number of immigrants who arrived in Palestine on the *Ruslan* far exceeded that on any other ship in 1919: 670 people, 520 of them actual immigrants and 150 returning exiles.[45] The impressive number of immigrants, olim, and refugees arriving on one ship was one of the reasons why the *Ruslan* was etched in the minds of its contemporaries as a symbol of the start of postwar aliya to Palestine. One ship bringing hundreds of olim was considered a major turning point, more significant than the scores of ships that routinely reached the country with no more than a few dozen olim on board. Moreover, the *Ruslan* brought community leaders, Zionist activists, and well-known public figures; thus, the impression was that the *Ruslan* was different from the ships that had preceded it not only in the number of immigrants but in their identity as well.

However, the *Ruslan* was one of the last ships to arrive in Palestine under the military regime, and it did not carry halutzim only. Of the sixty-eight ships that brought immigrants to Palestine in 1919 and early 1920, hardly any came after the *Ruslan*.[46] The *Carinthia*, for example, brought 124 people to Jaffa port in September 1919; the *Galicia*, which preceded the *Ruslan* by five days, brought 62 new immigrants who "mostly belong to the General Zionist Organization and have come to settle in the country."[47]

A comparison of the immigrants on the *Ruslan* with overall immigration in 1919 by sex, age, and occupation (see tab. 3.2 below) shows that *Ruslan* passengers were no more pioneering than the rest. The percentage of women and

Table 3.2. Comparison of the *Ruslan* immigrants and overall immigrants, 1919.

Ships	Distribution by sex		Distribution by age				Distribution by household size		
	Men	Women	0–14	15–20	21–40	41+	1	2–5	5+
All ships (1,363 immigrants)	61.0	39.0	23.8	17.3	40.9	18.0	68.2	27.8	4.0
Ruslan (554 immigrants)	55.0	45.0	26.8	19.7	37.7	15.8	57.4	34.3	8.3

Source: CZA, L2, file 231.

children on the *Ruslan* was greater than the overall percentage on ships that arrived that year. Although the percentage of laborers on the *Ruslan* far exceeded that on earlier ships, that is not necessarily indicative of a ship carrying halutzim, as the number of immigrants traveling on their own (rather than through a Zionist youth movement, for instance) on the *Ruslan* was over 10 percent less than on other ships. Not everyone who described himself as a laborer was necessarily a halutz.

Contemporary testimonies confirm and reinforce the statistics. In *Doar Hayom*, Esther Slonim gave a bleak description of the ship's passengers, whom she called "refugees":

> In the flow of speech, some call them "immigrants." Others use more precise, prettier language, affectionately and caressingly calling them "olim," "returnees to Zion." The truth is that they are refugees, refugees from the vale of killing. Six hundred fifty came, a drop in the ocean, a tiny grain that can do nothing to save Russian Jewry. But in our small, narrow world, it was an event. The Russian refugees are a microcosm of the whole terrible situation there.... Do you see the thin, gaunt Jew over there, moving slowly like a weakling? He is all of thirty-five years old, but he has already managed to die four times. No joking! He's a dead man who has come back to life for the fourth time. He's from a little shtetl in the Poltava area. When "the action" started in his town he was beaten, wounded, and left for dead. Only when he was about to be buried did he open his eyes. Through hard work and many metamorphoses, he carried himself to Odessa.[48]

A similar description of the *Ruslan* immigrants appeared in *Hapoel Hatzair*: "On a gloomy ship rocking on murky waves, after long, extensive wanderings, they reached their destination. Some of them were despondent and grieving, shadows of human beings, the frightful reflections of the life of terror in Russia and Ukraine still visible in their faces and eyes; widows and orphans, half-families and remnants of families, uttering the dreadful news, first-hand, of the tremendous wrath that was poured out onto the masses of our wretched people."[49]

In *Doar Hayom*, Itamar Ben-Avi wrote, "I don't know the nature of many of the immigrants who arrived on last week's ship.... I have grounds for suspecting that some of them—and not a small portion—will not settle in this country, even if they find work here by which they can earn a living."[50]

Irrespective of the gap between those who viewed the *Ruslan* as the harbinger of the Third Aliya and those who regarded it as a "pathetic cargo ship, the most pathetic of cargo ships" that had rescued its passengers from a "life of terror in Russia and Ukraine," the ship served as a meeting place between the immigrants and olim on board. Speaking to the passengers when they arrived at Jaffa port, Menachem Sheinkin asked them not to consider themselves "immigrants, like people who are just wandering aimlessly from place to place," but rather "olim [literally, "people ascending"] to their ancestral land." True, Sheinkin maintained, "in the recent aliyot there have also been negative, exilic factors operating, but we have to assume—even if you are unaware of this— that even now most of the olim from Russia have a national spark and love for the Land of Israel entrenched deeply in their hearts." Thus, Sheinkin took the "immigrant" label away from the *Ruslan* passengers and relabeled them "olim"—"so that they [would] appreciate the magnitude of what they have done by coming here."[51] Klausner added, "You are not 'immigrants' and you are not 'olim'; you are children who have returned to their mother's bosom. Until now you had been banished from your father's table, but you have returned to your parents' home. This elevated feeling should accompany you in everything you do in this country. With the help of this feeling you will adjust to conditions in this country and settle in it."[52]

In this encounter with the *Ruslan* immigrants at Beit Ha'am in Jaffa, a distinction was drawn between Jewish immigration to Palestine and to other countries. In other countries, the Jewish immigrants did all they could to integrate in the surrounding society, to prosper economically, and to become citizens with equal rights. But in Palestine—alongside the natural aspiration of all immigrants to better their living conditions—they were exposed, then and even more so in the years that followed, to the national ideology. This ideology, initially the domain of a small group, was instilled in the newcomers and their offspring in encounters and events like the meeting with Sheinkin at Beit Ha'am.

British Immigration Policy

British immigration policy in the 1920s can be divided into two periods: The first started with the issuance of the first immigration regulations in late September 1920 and ended on July 3, 1921, with the enactment of new regulations following the riots of May 1921. This was a period of unrestricted immigration to Palestine, under the full responsibility of the Zionist Executive. The second period started in June 1921 and lasted throughout the 1920s, until the publication of the White Paper in October 1930 following the bloody riots of 1929.

In July 1920, the military regime was replaced by a civil administration headed by High Commissioner Herbert Samuel, and in September of that year, the first immigration ordinance was issued. According to the ordinance, the high commissioner was to permit entry into Palestine, whether for permanent or temporary residence, according to the conditions and needs of the country. Immigrants had to have an entry visa and prove that they had the necessary means to support themselves and their dependents or that they were able to obtain them. Permanent residents of Palestine who had left the country during the war or after the British occupation started were allowed free entry. Immigrants were required to show passports or other form of identification, and they had to satisfy all the requirements of the director of the government immigration department. According to Aviva Halamish, admission to Palestine in the 1920s was based on the country's economic absorptive capacity and the state of the Jewish economy, not on British political considerations. In the 1930s, however, things changed. Political considerations were given increased weight in British immigration policy, and the influence of the Zionist institutions was reduced.[53]

The vague phrase "according to the conditions and needs of the country" left the British and Zionists a great deal of leeway and was subject to changing interpretations. The ordinance divided the immigrants into two categories: Category A included those who had been issued immigration permits by the Zionist Organization because they were needed to build up the country and could be beneficial to it. The Zionist Organization was to give the Mandatory government a guarantee for housing in Palestine for one year. Immigrants in this category could obtain a visa from the British consul in their place of residence after presenting authorization from an official Zionist Organization representative. The number of immigration permits was determined by the government with the consent of the Zionist Organization, in accordance with the country's absorptive capacity. From October 1920 until September 1921, they agreed on 16,500 households—that is, about 85,000 immigrants per year. The Zionist Executive did not take full advantage of the quota, however; by the beginning of March, only 1,250 immigration certificates had been issued. Category B consisted of people of means who could support themselves in their first year in the country. The minimum sum needed was estimated at 120 pounds per person.

The immigrants who arrived in Palestine in the period of the first immigration ordinance had a hard time finding work and housing. Their integration was slow and took longer than anticipated. Consequently, the Zionist movement faced a dilemma: Should it admit the legally permitted number of immigrants, or should it restrict immigration? In his book *Palestine Immigration Policy under Sir Herbert Samuel*, Moshe Mossek states that the movement decided to limit immigration. The Zionist Commission reported to the Zionist Executive in

London on the problems the immigrants were having and asked it to temporarily delay the influx of immigration. After serious vacillations, the Zionist Executive decided to request assistance from the British Foreign Office in regulating the flow of immigrants, to admit no more than one thousand immigrants a year and to give preference to young and unmarried people.[54]

A wave of violence that broke out in Palestine in May 1921 put an end to free immigration. The Mandatory government issued an order to turn back those who were already in the ports of Palestine and Egypt or on ships en route to Palestine and to delay the departure of those waiting their turn in the ports of origin and Palestine Offices. Although the Zionist Executive managed to persuade the Mandatory government to issue entry permits for the people on board the ships, it was stripped of most of its powers, which were taken over by the government. On June 3, 1921, Herbert Samuel announced changes in the immigration regulations. The new regulations, issued in September, limited the authority of the Zionist Executive and divided the immigrants into three groups: those sponsored and guaranteed by the Zionist Organization; those not sponsored by the Zionist Organization but who possessed assets and would be able to find employment and means of subsistence in Palestine; and family members of Palestine residents with sufficient means.[55] The three groups were then further divided into seven categories:

A–Travelers coming for a period of no more than three months
B–Persons of independent means who could support themselves in Palestine
C–Members of professions who intended to work in their professions
D–Wives, children, and others who were wholly dependent on residents of Palestine
E–Persons with a definite prospect of employment with a specific employer
F–Persons coming for religious reasons who could show that they had adequate means of subsistence
G–Returning residents

The most conspicuous, fundamental change in the new immigration policy was the elimination of category A of the immigration regulations of September 1920, which recognized immigrants sponsored and guaranteed by the Zionist Organization. Henceforth, able-bodied immigrants capable of building up the country were included in category E. Such people were entitled to an immigration certificate only if they worked in a specific occupation and had a definite prospect of employment with a specific employer.[56] Family members of applicants for immigration wrote to the Aliya Department requesting authorization for their relatives and asserting that they could guarantee them employment in Palestine. The Aliya Department sent the requests on to the relevant Palestine Office, noting the applicant's name and requesting authorization for immigration in accordance with the quota for each country of origin.

Below are a few examples of the many hundreds of letters sent to the heads of the Aliya Department.

> [1.] I, the undersigned, request that the Aliya Department . . . issue an entry permit for Palestine to my brother Avraham Weissmann and his family, who are in the city of Novograd-Volynskiy, Ukraine. My brother has a trade; he knows how to make candy and pastries. . . . Moreover, his wife knows photography and photographic enlargement and can manage on her work. Thus, when they arrive they will not have to be a burden on anyone. Allowing them to enter the country will save a family that is being destroyed there. I think writing about the situation there is superfluous because our city is known for the pogroms that it has experienced.[57]

> [2.] I hereby appeal to you with the following request. I have been in this country for about three years. Although when I arrived I was dependent on my brother, who works here in printing, I have been employed the entire time in the workers' kitchen and have earned an ample living the whole time. I already applied to the government more than three months ago through the community board for a permit for my sister in Ukraine, who has a trade and will not be a burden on anyone. In any case I am always willing to take responsibility for her subsistence. Despite my frequent efforts for more than three months, however, they have not agreed. . . . I now cry out and vehemently request: let me bring my sister here.[58]

A new immigration ordinance issued in August 1925 resembled the ordinance of June 1921 but included precise definitions of the categories as well as the rights and responsibilities of the Zionist Organization. The aim of the ordinance was to minimize the Zionist movement's leeway for interpretation and to make the rules clearer and more understandable. It set forth three main categories of immigrants: persons of independent means, laborers, and dependents of Palestine residents. The "persons of independent means" category, which included all those who could support themselves, was divided into subcategories: businesspeople with at least 500 pounds; skilled artisans with at least 250 pounds; people with an assured income and at least 60 pounds; people in religious occupations whose maintenance was assured; and students whose maintenance was assured. The Mandatory government allocated very few entry permits to artisans and the other subcategories, and immigrants with an assured income needed a bank guarantee valid for an unlimited period.[59]

The new ordinance tightened the requirements for obtaining visas for dependents of Palestine residents and hamstrung the Zionist Executive. Because visas now had to be authorized in Jerusalem by the British, they took much longer to obtain. The authorization was valid for only a limited time, so prospective immigrants had to close their businesses and leave more quickly than anticipated, sometimes losing a lot of money as a result. Furthermore, the permits were sent directly to the applicant and not to the Palestine Office; because of this, many valuable permits were lost. The Zionist Executive, for its part, was required to submit a proposal every six months for increasing the number of immigrants, to state the likelihood of their finding work, and to pledge to support them for a period of one year of unemployment. Following a recommendation by the Zionist Executive, the Mandatory government decided on quotas for laborers, stating the maximum number of laborers to be admitted and their division by occupations. After the high commissioner approved the quotas, certificates were sent to people who had applied directly to the government, to employers who had listed the workers' names, and to the Zionist Organization.[60]

The Volume and Social Composition of Jewish Immigration in the 1920s

Between 1919 and 1929, more than one hundred thousand Jews arrived in Palestine. Of them, 27 percent arrived between 1919 and 1923; 73 percent between 1924 and 1929. About half of the immigrants to Palestine in the 1920s arrived in 1924 and 1925. The year 1925 was an important turning point because for the first time more Jewish immigrants arrived in Palestine than in the United States.

The standard assumption among scholars is that the halutzim who arrived as part of the Third Aliya came mainly between 1919 and 1921.[61] An analysis of the immigrant population of 1919, based on reports by the Zionist Commission, refutes this claim and shows that even in its first years, the Third Aliya was not particularly halutzic.

The Statistics Department of the Zionist Executive did not keep orderly records of people entering the country at the time, so we do not have complete demographic data about the immigrant population. The historian and economist Jacob Metzer tried—in a trailblazing study—to decipher the demography

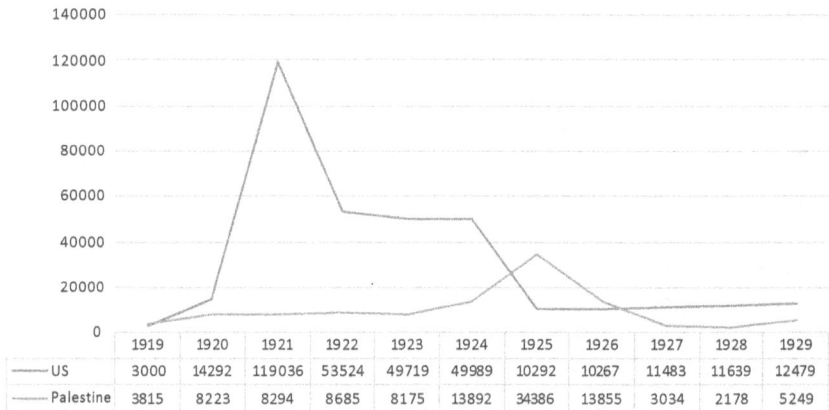

	1919	1920	1921	1922	1923	1924	1925	1926	1927	1928	1929
US	3000	14292	119036	53524	49719	49989	10292	10267	11483	11639	12479
Palestine	3815	8223	8294	8685	8175	13892	34386	13855	3034	2178	5249

Figure 3.3. Immigration to Palestine and the United States, 1919–1929. Source: Linfield, *Jewish Migration*, 40; Gurevich, *Statistical Abstract of Palestine*, 50.

of immigrants to Palestine in the 1920s. His conclusions are based on a special database containing the personal records of applicants for aliya, some of whom ended up going to Palestine and others who didn't. The 53,191 names in the database represent about 42 percent of the number of people who entered Palestine in the 1920s.[62]

We do not have complete data on immigration in the first decade of the Mandate. In addition to Metzer's study, we have reliable, accurate statistics on immigration during the period of the military regime in 1919 from a June 1920 bulletin of the Zionist Commission Statistics Department.[63] A comparison of Metzer's data on immigration in the first decade of the Mandate with the profile of the population of immigrants to Palestine in the period of the military regime (until the first immigration ordinance) reveals real differences between the periods. The profile of immigrants from 1919 until September 1920—the period of free immigration to Palestine—was not the same as the average profile of immigrants from 1919 to 1932. The graphs shown here present Metzer's data for 1919–1932 alongside the data of the Zionist Commission Statistics Department for 1919–1920.

As figure 3.4 shows, the two periods were similar in terms of gender. However, in terms of age and family status, there was a significant difference between the decade as a whole and the years of the Ukrainian civil war.

In figure 3.5, we see that 15 percent of people entering Palestine between 1919 and 1932 were aged fourteen or under, compared to 31 percent in 1919–1920; 68 percent were aged fifteen to forty, compared to 51 percent in 1919–1920; and

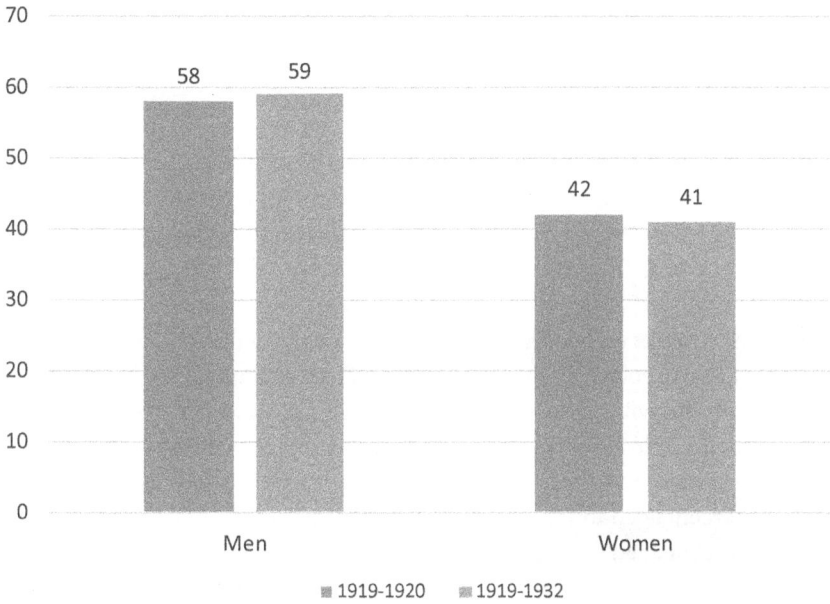

Figure 3.4. Distribution of immigrants to Palestine by sex, 1919–1920 and 1919–1932. Source: Metzer, *Jewish Immigration to Palestine; Yediot ha-Mahlaka.*

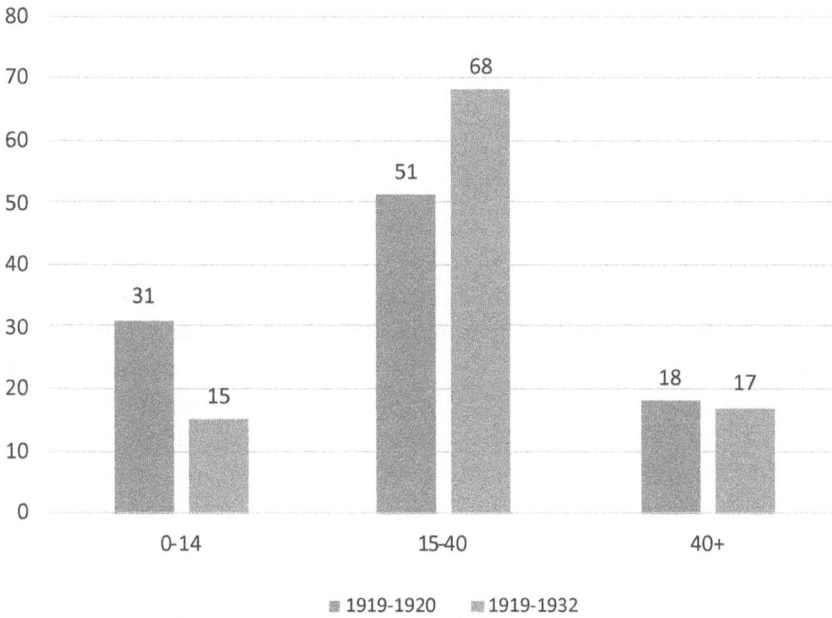

Figure 3.5. Distribution of immigrants to Palestine by age, 1919–1920 and 1919–1932. Source: Metzer, *Jewish Immigration to Palestine; Yediot ha-Mahlaka.*

17 percent were aged forty and up, versus 18 percent in 1919–1920. Under the military regime, the rate of children who arrived in Palestine was twice that for the entire period of the Third Aliya and Fourth Aliya.

The immigrants who arrived in Palestine during the period of the military regime differed demographically from the immigrants in the 1920s overall for two main reasons:

1. The return of exiles: The people who had been deported during World War I returned to Palestine in 1919, and they included a high proportion of families with children. However, this is not enough to explain the demographic difference because only 32 percent of people entering Palestine were exiles. The other 68 percent were distributed as follows: 25 percent aged fourteen or under; 57 percent aged fifteen to forty , and 18 percent aged forty or over.
2. The pogroms in Ukraine: Until the 1921 riots, Palestine was fully open to immigration with no restrictions. Refugees from the bloodbath in Ukraine took advantage of the liberal immigration policy before the introduction of a selective policy that gave preference to the young and healthy and to persons of independent means over the elderly, sick, and destitute. Many of the people entering Palestine in that period were refugees from the civil war in Ukraine, and they included orphans, widows, and families with members of various ages.

The case of the *Khokhlinets* is representative of many ships that sailed for Palestine during the civil war and can explain the demographic differences between the immigrants in the early 1920s and in the decade as a whole. In mid-December 1919, the *Khokhlinets* sailed from Sebastopol in the Crimean Peninsula, with some two hundred Jewish refugees on board. Most were between the ages of twenty and thirty and had received permission from the Sebastopol authorities to leave Ukraine in exchange for renouncing their Russian citizenship. "The ship sailed, but for where? Even the sailors and the captain [didn't] know." When the ship anchored in Constantinople, the refugees were not permitted to disembark. According to the Hapoel Hatzair representative in the city, when he was informed "of the refugee ship I loaded a boat with bread and went out to search for it. I found it anchored far from shore. . . . When I approached the ship I saw the faces of frightened Jews. All were on deck shivering with cold. Many of them were sick and most had gone hungry for a few days." The representative asked them where they were headed. They replied that they intended to immigrate to Palestine and asked him to try to put them

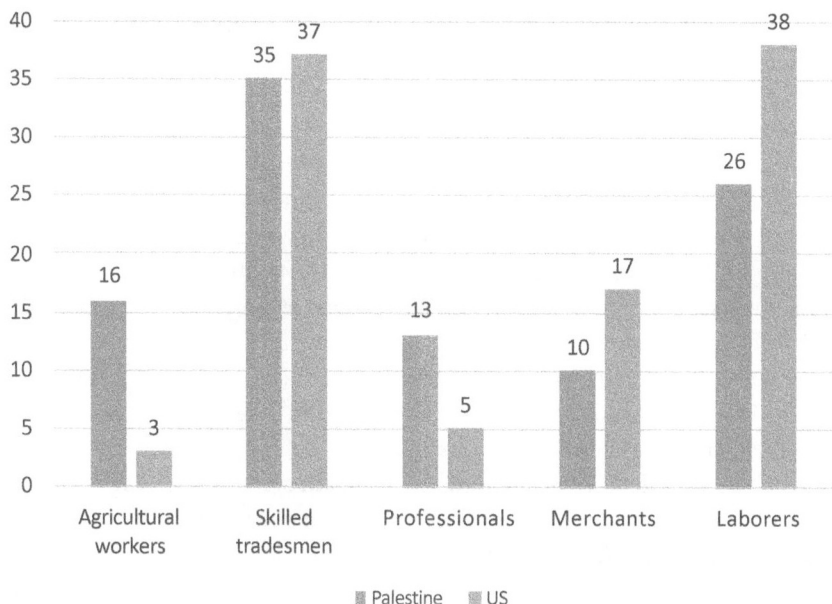

Figure 3.6. Occupational distribution of immigrants to Palestine (1924–1927) and the United States (1921–1924). Source: Memo on immigration to Palestine, CZA, S81, file 37; Hersch, "Jewish Migrations," 424–26.

on the *Ruslan*, but their request was turned down. "There was a shocking scene when the two ships—the *Khokhlinets* and the *Ruslan*—neared each other. The refugees on the small ship lifted their eyes enviously to their fortunate brethren and called out to them: 'Let us on board! Aren't we Jews?'"[64] The *Ruslan* continued on to Palestine, while the refugees on the *Khokhlinets* waited for days for permission to disembark. Because they were stateless, no country or consulate would agree to take them. Only after persuasive efforts by the Zionist representative in Constantinople were the refugees finally allowed to enter the city temporarily, mainly because they threatened to "first throw their children and then themselves into the sea" if they were sent back to Russia.[65]

The occupational distribution of immigrants to Palestine and the United States in the 1920s shows both similarities and differences between the two groups. As we can see in figure 3.6, 35 percent of the immigrants to Palestine were skilled tradesmen, approximately the same as among those entering the United States. The internal breakdown among skilled tradesmen who immigrated to Palestine shows that 32 percent of them worked in the garment industry, 20 percent in the wood industry, 16 percent in construction, 11 percent in the metal industry, and small percentages in the leather, weaving, printing, and other industries. In the United States, the percentage of workers in the garment industry was twice as high: 60 percent. Another 15 percent worked in construction, 9 percent in the metal industry, 7 percent in the food industry, and 2 percent in leather and paper. Another interesting statistic is that 42 percent of those going to Palestine were unskilled workers: 26 percent simple laborers and 16 percent agricultural workers. In the United States, the proportion of unskilled workers was 41 percent: 38 percent simple laborers and only 3 percent agricultural workers. Of those entering Palestine, 13 percent were members of the liberal professions, compared to only 5 percent of those entering the United States. Ten percent of immigrants to Palestine were merchants versus 17 percent in the United States.

Analyzing the data on the immigrants' occupations, we find that agricultural workers and professionals immigrated to Palestine more than to the United States. The proportions of skilled tradesmen and unskilled workers were similar in the two countries.

Redemption or Rescue? Zionist Immigration Policy

The annual conference of Hapoel Hatzair was held on December 25–27, 1919, about a week after the *Ruslan* arrived in Palestine. The participants were given an overview of "the terrible plight of the Jews of Russia and Ukraine" and expressed their sorrow "about the fact that aside from protests and expressions of opinion, the Jewish world is apathetic to the dreadful, unprecedented tragedy and to the fate of tens of thousands of our tormented brothers and sisters."[66] The conference participants passed several resolutions regarding the Jews of eastern Europe in general and Ukrainian Jewry in particular. They urged the leaders of the Zionist Organization to act quickly and decisively to open up Palestine to immigration "and to start extensive settlement work immediately so that some of the flow of migration of Russian Jewry can be diverted to Palestine." They also called on the Zionist Organization to do "all it can so the young halutzim can be moved from Russia to Palestine as soon as possible in order to prepare the country for mass immigration." In addition, they resolved to establish a special committee that would collect "the material about the events in Russia, organize it, and publish it appropriately."[67]

A month after the conference of Hapoel Hatzair, the executive board of the Provisional Committee for the Jews of Palestine met in Jaffa. The participants called for Palestine to be opened up to immigration and for Ukrainian Jewry to be saved from annihilation. They were aware of the urgency and the magnitude of the emergency and regarded the Zionist movement as a rescue movement destined to save eastern European Jewry:

> The recent pogroms in southern Russia, which have wiped out tens of thousands of Jews and put the survival of all the Jews in those lands in jeopardy, mandate that the entire Jewish people not only attempt to secure protection for some of those Jews (the success of which is doubtful), but try to extricate them completely from all the regions where the Jews' lives are in danger. Their last remaining hope is to be saved in Palestine, which the Jews of southern Russia hold in their hearts. The anguished cries and calls for help that have reached us from there require all the Jewish people today, the Zionist Organization foremost, and us, the residents of Palestine, in particular, to come to the aid of our brethren. The only truly necessary action is to try to take the Jews in southern Russia away from their enemies and move them to Palestine. We regard immigration from the lands of southern Russia as the rescue of thousands, even tens of thousands of Jews from annihilation.[68]

Shmuel Yavnieli's exhortation to open Palestine to immigration and rescue "thousands, even tens of thousands of Jews from annihilation" reflects a dilemma noted by the historian Hagit Lavsky. According to Lavsky, the limit on the number of immigrants was not only a decision imposed by the Mandatory government but an objective necessity that the Zionist Executive had no choice but to accept. Weizmann could not completely abolish the quantitative restriction because he was concerned that without any objective economic absorption policy, an economic crisis would ensue, ultimately leading to return emigration from Palestine and a loss of trust among Jewish immigrants in the country's ability to absorb them.[69] The Zionist Executive's dilemma should be considered not only in relation to the country's economic absorptive capacity and the crisis that was liable to result from the uncontrolled arrival of tens of thousands of immigrants, but also in relation to the annihilation of Ukrainian Jewry.

The historian Meir Margalit has identified three fundamental approaches in the public debate over the refugees from Ukraine: Some people maintained that priority should be given to saving survivors of the pogroms and that the Yishuv was duty bound to rescue those in danger of annihilation. Others held that there was no contradiction between saving Jewish lives and building up the Yishuv; all Jews should be allowed to immigrate to Palestine, whether their motivations were ideological or material/physical. According to a third group, immigration to Palestine had to be selective because the welfare of the country took precedence over the welfare of the nation; therefore, only the needs of the Yishuv should be considered.[70]

The Zionist Executive, headed by Chaim Weizmann and others who dealt routinely with the implementation of settlement policy, advocated the third approach. Requests from within the Yishuv to allow mass immigration and rescue Ukrainian Jewry fell on deaf ears.[71] Arthur Ruppin, for instance, warned that the people likely to come to Palestine would endanger the Yishuv. The Zionist Organization's immigration policy, he insisted, had to be selective and had to further Zionist objectives: "The higher the level of the immigrant, the more easily the objective can be reached. And the level will be raised if, by sifting our immigrants as far as possible, we shall help bring into the country such elements as by education, occupation and character come closest to our ultimate aims. As stated, thus far the selection of human material has not fulfilled any function."[72]

The first Zionist conference after World War I took place in London in early 1919, with the participation of Zionist Organization representatives from various countries. The conference participants decided to establish an aliya department that would operate out of the Zionist office in London as well as a network of Palestine Offices that would handle aliya requests throughout the Jewish world, especially in eastern Europe.[73] Shortly after the conference, Nahum Sokolow and Chaim Weizmann warned against mass immigration and called for minimizing immigration as much as possible: "The hour of immigration to Palestine has not yet arrived. Such immigration will be impossible until systematic settlement programs are in place that address the financial and economic elements and all the other issues—programs that require a solution to the political questions that our country is known to have. Until then not a single immigrant should enter Palestine. We consider it essential to emphasize this warning as vehemently as possible to all societies and individuals so that they do not do anything hasty with respect to continual immigration to Palestine."[74]

The main consideration behind the desire to limit immigration to Palestine or to stop it completely was not fear of mass aliya but fear of the arrival of hordes of refugees from the pogroms and immigrants unfit to build the country. On several occasions in late 1919 and early 1920, Weizmann said he was concerned not about the country's economic absorptive capacity but about who would enter the country. Weizmann was afraid of a rabble of unfit refugees and immigrants; he was willing to accept only olim who were physically and mentally healthy.[75]

In a speech on December 17, 1919, shortly before the arrival of the *Ruslan* and his departure from Palestine for the Zionist conference in London, Weizmann stated explicitly that Palestine could absorb thousands of olim each year, but that those seeking to go there were unsuited to the "great Zionist program" whose objective was the establishment of the national home in Palestine. The speech, given at the Laemel School in Jerusalem, was attended by prominent public figures, Yishuv activists, teachers, doctors, and writers.

> Immigration arrangements must also be in our hands. We have made this demand and it is essential, but I don't believe in unorganized aliya. Though it pains the heart, we must always insist that Zionism cannot be the solution to a catastrophe. I admit to you that when we spoke at the peace conference about tens of thousands of immigrants annually, I felt pangs of conscience, not because it was impossible—*the country can absorb this number year after year*—but because I don't see in the terrible destruction that we have today the tremendous constructive force required for this great program.[76]

Weizmann regretted having announced at the Paris peace conference that he anticipated tens of thousands of immigrants a year. Although Palestine could absorb the masses of Jews who wanted to go there, the catastrophe experienced by eastern European Jewry had brought to Palestine undesirable elements unsuited to building up the country. Weizmann therefore asked for patience so as not to repeat the mistake of permitting indiscriminate immigration.

> Perhaps in ten years we will be able to accept larger numbers. We have to understand all this so as to avoid despair. There are no grounds for despair. We have not strayed from the path; we are moving forward slowly. Hyperbole has understandably put us in a pessimistic mood. Remember all the exaggerated rumors that circulated after Herzl's meeting with Wilhelm, remember all the flights of Jewish fancy in the Diaspora regarding the imminent redemption, and you will understand how exhilarated the Jewish imagination has been in this time of affliction and anguish to hear the proclamation read through to the end in a single breath. The excitement is understandable and the despair is understandable, if after the rumors of a Jewish republic in Palestine people come and find a military government.[77]

Weizmann said something similar, albeit in different words, at a meeting of the Zionist General Council in London on February 23, 1920. He argued that the Jewish settlement in Palestine had to contend not only with the issue of British permission for immigration but most importantly with the composition of the immigration. Weizmann believed that the revitalization of the Jewish People depended on the nature and quality of the immigrants, and he compared the rebuilding of Palestine to General Herbert Kitchener's organization

Figure 3.7. "Necessity breaks iron! Open the gate or they will break it open!" *Der Groyser Kunds*, September 12, 1919.

of the British army: Kitchener first established a volunteer corps within the Royal Army during World War I, and eventually the entire British army was based on it. "The question of the Jewish state, not just concessions by the British government but an actual Jewish state, is in my opinion just a matter of the first 400,000 Jews in Palestine. What we want now is exactly what Lord Kitchener wanted when he started recruiting the British army. The British army of millions grew out of 'the first hundred thousand.'"[78] Weizmann's statements make it clear that he was afraid of indiscriminate immigration bringing undesirable elements to Palestine. Although his comments furthered the policy of the Zionist movement and the Yishuv, they certainly did not benefit eastern European Jewry. If we consider his remarks in the context of the pogroms in Ukraine and the annihilation of Ukrainian Jewry, he was clearly saying that Zionism was not the solution to the catastrophe in eastern Europe and that Palestine was not the solution for the tens of thousands of refugees from the civil war.

Weizmann preferred productive olim over needy refugees. Applications for immigration permits by Jews who did not fit Weizmann's model were turned down by the Palestine Offices in eastern Europe on the grounds that the time was not yet ripe. Weizmann was aware of the bloodbath taking place in Ukraine and the plight of the Jews there, but he nevertheless opposed mass immigration: "The Zionist Organization is taking into consideration the dreadful plight that currently plagues the masses of our people almost everywhere in eastern Europe," Hapoel Hatzair wrote. "It is also aware of how eagerly all segments of the nation hope to immigrate to Palestine." Only through well-organized, orderly immigration, however, "will we achieve fulfillment of our national ideal—to erect our national home, the Land of Israel."[79]

The fear of uncontrolled mass immigration stemmed, as stated, from the large number of applicants thronging the Palestine Offices in Europe. "The situation is extremely grave here," wrote Ze'ev Tiomkin, director of the aliya committee in Constantinople, to the Zionist Commission in Jerusalem. Immigrants were coming from countries "where the economy has suffered massive destruction. Most of them are destitute from the day they arrive here and need continual assistance."[80] This highly problematic situation put the aliya offices between a rock and a hard place: on the one hand, they were under tremendous pressure from the masses who wanted to go to Palestine, but on the other hand, the selective immigration policy limited their discretion.[81] The Zionist Commission's instructions were clear and left no room for interpretation: undesirable elements—particularly refugees from the pogroms—who would not be able to participate in building up Palestine were not permitted to immigrate. "You should therefore alert all the Zionist bureaus with which you are in contact regarding aliya that each and every immigrant must be examined thoroughly. Attention must be paid to the immigrants' state of health, both physical and mental. We hope you can influence these bureaus to work patiently and with moderation and not make matters worse by being rash and rushing things."[82]

Eyal Katvan and Nadav Davidovitch have shown that the doctors who examined the migrants before they set out for Palestine were instructed to hold back anyone in poor health who could not contribute to building up the land.[83] As we shall see in chapter 4, the medical exams conducted for immigrants and prospective immigrants were part of a medical policy that was not limited to health matters. The policy was intended to serve Zionism rather than the ordinary Jew who wanted to immigrate to Palestine.[84]

The horrific slaughter of Jews in Ukraine—including acts of abuse, rape, and sadism by soldiers and the local populace—and the plight of the tens of thousands of refugees did not trigger the opening of Palestine to free immigration by all. On the contrary, it resulted in restrictions on the number of Jews admitted and the adoption of a selective immigration policy that reflected, at root, a preference for halutzim over refugees, for the strong over the weak.

By the time of the second Zionist conference in London (July 1920), the military regime in Palestine had been replaced by a civil administration headed by High Commissioner Herbert Samuel. As noted, the first immigration regulations were issued in September 1920. These were liberal regulations that permitted the entry of anyone who was physically and mentally healthy, had a guaranteed livelihood, and did not pose a danger to society from a criminal or political standpoint. Although the regulations officially went into effect on September 1, it took another few months to complete the bureaucratic arrangements needed to implement them fully. In the six months between the abolition of the military regime and the enforcement of the regulations, immigration to Palestine was free and unrestricted. In that half year, approximately seven thousand immigrants arrived in Palestine, many of them Jewish refugees from eastern Europe. Because such a population was inconsistent with the immigration policy set by Weizmann and Sokolow, the Zionist movement sought to reduce the cap on immigration from eighty thousand to just one thousand.[85]

The decision to limit immigration during such a fateful period for eastern European Jewry is one of the most controversial decisions in the history of Zionism, and it is surprising that historians have paid little attention to it. Scholars and historians of the Yishuv in Palestine have treated the catastrophe suffered by Ukrainian Jewry as something incidental and for the most part have merely mentioned the events that caused one hundred thousand casualties laconically and in passing. Zionist historiography has tended to look at Zionist immigration policy in the context of contacts with the British government, the economic absorptive capacity of Palestine, the type of immigrants needed to build the country, the contribution of the Third Aliya to the development of the Yishuv, and so on. These issues have not been examined as independent events against the backdrop of the bloody pogroms in Ukraine. This was not just another wave of eastern European pogroms. It was of such crucial significance that without addressing it, one cannot possibly understand and analyze the Yishuv in the 1920s and Zionist policy concerning immigration to Palestine.

The Zionist movement was confronted with a harsh reality when it had to decide between rescue immigration and selective immigration. On the one hand were the desire, the need, and the obligation to help fellow Jews who had survived the pogroms; on the other was genuine fear that Palestine was not capable of absorbing the thousands of refugees and immigrants who wanted to enter the country. Of these two mutually exclusive options, the Zionist leaders

Figure 3.8. "Open, open!! Let there be trachoma, let there be malaria, let there be cholera. It's all better than the 'guarantees' of justice in Poland and Ukraine." *Der Groyser Kunds*, October 3, 1919.

and policymakers chose selective immigration. Zionism, Weizmann and So-kolow argued, could not solve the pressing problems caused by the calamity in Ukraine. Palestine needed healthy, resilient immigrants, not refugees weak in body and soul. The Zionist leadership chose not to lend a hand to the survivors of the massacres and not to put the economic absorptive capacity of the Yishuv to the test. Weizmann and Sokolow preferred one thousand halutzim over eighty thousand "despondent and grieving [people], shadows of human beings, the frightful reflections of the life of terror in Russia and Ukraine still visible in their faces and eyes."

The selective aliya policy that prioritized the select few and the gradual building of the country over mass immigration was not viewed favorably by certain circles within the Zionist Organization. For instance, at the London conference, Max Nordau proposed bringing half a million immigrants into Palestine. His proposal was not even discussed, however, partly because it was deemed unrealistic and partly due to the "lack of emotional preparation" among the Zionist leadership.[86] Nordau was one of the most prominent opponents of Weizmann's policy, which he lambasted in his writings and speeches: "I furiously protest against the craven cowards who constantly insist that everything must be done with extreme caution, that Jewish immigration to Palestine must proceed extremely slowly and in a very sober, gradual manner, and that the number of immigrants to Palestine must not exceed two thousand a year if we want to avoid mishaps. In this way—or so they tell us—we can hope to have a few hundred thousand Jews in our ancestral land after fifty years."[87]

Given the race against time in the wake of the slaughter of Ukrainian Jewry, Nordau believed that mass immigration to Palestine should be permitted. He recognized the importance of the halutzim and their contribution to the development of the Yishuv but believed that under the circumstances, thousands of people should be brought in. Small-scale immigration and gradual building, he maintained, were wrong:

> No. This will not happen and will not be! The present times require that we look at this matter from another standpoint entirely. We must ensure that the business is done on a large scale. We must take wide-ranging action. Our masses in the lands of the pogroms want to shake the blood-soaked dust of those lands off their feet—not in fifty years, not tomorrow, but today! They fought heroically during the years of the inferno of the world war. From now on they want to live as a free people, as a dignified nation with full human and national rights.[88]

Nordau utterly rejected the Zionist immigration policy of tailoring the volume of immigration to the economic absorptive capacity of the country. He believed that despite the grim, complicated economic situation, it would be possible to take in all the Jews who wanted to come. In an article entitled "Tseva'a la-Tsiyonit" (A will for Zionism), he presented his views and countered the arguments of Weizmann and Sokolow regarding the country's economic absorptive capacity:

> We have no houses for them to live in. No houses? So put them in tents. It's better to live in a tent than to be murdered in a pogrom. They won't have food to eat. So feed them with the first crop that comes in. After all, 22 million recruits were fed during the four years of the war, when no one was planting or harvesting. It would cost billions. No, but it would cost many millions, and this must be found. The Jewish people will give it when they are certain that it will be used in a way that is likely to lead to lasting results. And what will the millions of immigrants do to earn a living . . . ? They will work the land, at first not assiduously and in a primitive manner, until they get used to the work and switch to more scientific methods.[89]

The mayor of Tel Aviv, Meir Dizengoff, basically agreed with Nordau; he believed that Palestine could and should take in the refugees: "Palestine must be a *land of refuge* for us, the place where our national home is built, and we must make all the preparations and do all the training necessary so that the immigrants from Russia can be absorbed in our land." Dizengoff stressed the feeling of solidarity of the Jews of Palestine with their brethren in Ukraine. "We now all feel the anguish of our brethren in Russia, and we are prepared to meet, as brothers, all the survivors from that vale of killing coming to our land. The entire Jewish community of Palestine has opened its arms and is waiting to welcome gladly their brethren coming from Russia."[90]

Weizmann, as stated, disagreed with Nordau and Dizengoff. He was more cautious, opposed mass immigration, and was convinced that only the gradual admission of immigrants could lead to the establishment of the national home. One person who expressed Weizmann's worldview well, coming out against Nordau, was Itamar Ben-Avi; in his newspaper *Doar Hayom*, he set forth his fundamental position on the refugees seeking to come to Palestine: "Because despite all the thundering of Dr. Nordau and like-minded people, Prof. Weizmann and his colleagues were absolutely correct in declaring that for now Palestine is not the answer to the huge crisis affecting a large portion of our people in the Russian exile. . . . The entire fate of our activity here depends on our insisting on this foundation without budging by even a hair's breadth. *This national enterprise cannot be based on compassion and mercy.* Where the downfall of the nation's revival on its ancestral land is at stake, compassion cannot be factored in."[91]

The selective immigration policy of the 1920s has not been considered according to the same criteria as the immigration policies of the 1930s and post–World War II—even though then, too, not only was a sword hanging over the Jews' heads but it was being wielded against them. Historical research on Zionist immigration policy in the early 1920s has been conducted in isolation from the so-called mini-Holocaust in Ukraine. The dialogue with the British, the country's limited absorptive capacity, and the riots of 1920–1921, which influenced the scope of immigration, have been overemphasized, and too little attention has been given to the plight of the refugees who had survived the slaughter in Ukraine and were trying to reach Palestine in those years.

The disagreement between Weizmann and Nordau over Zionist immigration policy is considered part of a fundamental dispute within the Zionist movement that began with the Uganda debate and was pointed up by the pogroms in Ukraine. It was a dispute between Zionists with a catastrophic worldview, who were pressing for an immediate, rushed solution, and Zionists who believed in a cautious, gradual immigration policy. This conflict came to the fore at the 12th Zionist Congress in Carlsbad, Czechoslovakia, in 1921—the first Zionist Congress after World War I and the civil war. Sokolow, the newly elected chair of the Zionist Executive, opened the Congress, speaking about the bloody pogroms in Ukraine and the helplessness of European nations.

Nahum Sokolow's speech at the Zionist Congress is important to understanding the Zionist response to the pogroms because it was made around the time the events occurred and included an assessment of the postwar situation of the Jewish people and the Zionist movement. Sokolow devoted much of his long, comprehensive speech to the subject of the pogroms, expressing the official Zionist position on the matter. "Horrors, unspeakable horrors took place in Ukraine," Sokolow began.

> In hundreds of Jewish communities there were bloodbaths; the Jewish masses were like dung upon the fields, as a wicked mob sliced them with swords and knives and split them in pieces. They cracked their bones and chopped up their skulls; brains poured out onto the ground. They dragged the wounded with the slain, those wallowing in their blood with organs diluted in lakes of mire and pipes of effluent. . . . Murder, rape, torture, beating, robbery, and destruction were the order of the day. The wild mob knew no mercy. . . . They slaughtered the Jews as if they were sheep.[92]

After describing what the Ukrainians had done, Sokolow denounced Europe for having watched the bloodshed from the side and done nothing to help the Jews: "Europe watched this slaughter with folded arms: no heartwarming protest, no demonstration or simple disclosure of facts, not a word of solace rang in the wretches' ears."[93] But despite all this, Sokolow stressed to the Congress delegates: "Our people lives!" World Jewry had mobilized to help the Jews of Ukraine; Sokolow particularly praised American Jewry: "Our brethren in America took the moral high ground. They set up a large array of societies and saved what they could. It would be insulting to say that our American brethren 'gave donations.' In our nation we have no 'givers and takers,' only members of one people who know their duty to help themselves."[94] It was a time when the Jewish people shone, Sokolow believed, "an episode full of lofty splendor" that showed the strength, and especially the morality, of the people.

Sokolow took the opportunity, at the podium of the Zionist Congress, to call on world Jewry: "Rescue the Jews of Ukraine! Save the children! We are sure this voice will be heard. Such a nation cannot vanish from the world stage! But it is duty bound to prepare itself for free, natural living conditions." In calling for the rescue of Ukrainian Jewry, Sokolow linked the act of rescue to the Zionist movement and its aspiration for free, natural life in Palestine. He maintained that Zionism had warned the Jews of the imminent catastrophe, but some had refused to listen and opposed Zionism. The result of not having a national home, he said, was the slaughter of the Jews:

> Theodor Herzl, whose great shadow precedes us to this day, guiding us like the pillar of cloud, warned a quarter-century ago of the growing dangers of the lack of a national home. Wisely and in good faith, Herzl disclosed the source of the evil. For that they fell upon him and us with the libel that we see in the clouds. The outcry of the offended humanity within us, which burst out bitterly, insisting that this situation must not continue, that outright annihilation would be better than living through a conflagration and suffering these troubles, the call for redemption that burst from our hearts back at the First Zionist Congress, was not addressed seriously. . . . If the Jewish people had devoted all its strength then to fulfilling our ideal, we would already have had the national home.[95]

In his speech, Sokolow stressed the correctness of the Zionist idea and denounced its opponents. According to him, if only the Jewish people had cooperated with the Zionist movement from the start, if only they hadn't been so skeptical about its intentions, if they had taken its pessimistic predictions seriously and heeded its warnings about the anticipated dangers for the Jewish

people, the national home would already exist. According to Sokolow's depic-
tion, the Zionist movement had foreseen the catastrophe and had sought to save
the Jewish people before it was too late.

Sokolow's claims require us to reexamine Zionist thought and activity from
the day the Zionist Organization was founded until the Zionist Congress convened in Carlsbad in August 1921. It was not the Jews' skepticism or opposition
to the Zionist idea that had delayed the building of the national home. The
reasons for the delay were mainly prosaic, along with the Zionist policy that
preferred the good of the country over the good of the people. Herzl, in his
diplomatic activity and Zionist doctrine, had indeed "of the growing dangers
of the lack of a national home." Without international and legal recognition,
he foresaw a bleak future for the Jewish people; as he saw it, a Jewish state was
the only possible solution to the Jewish problem. However, it was not the "libel
[against the Zionists] that we see in the clouds" that had prevented the diplo-
macy from achieving its aim and had caused the failure to receive a charter for
large-scale settlement of Palestine.[96] On the contrary, it was voices within the
Zionist movement—including those of Sokolow and Weizmann—that had
disagreed with Herzl and opposed his diplomatic policy.

The bloodbath in Ukraine was the first test for the Zionist movement after
the Kishinev pogrom and the pogroms of 1904–1905. It was the first time since
Herzl had introduced the proposal to settle in East Africa at the Zionist Congress that the Zionist movement was forced to decide between saving Jews
and building up the country; between bringing over and absorbing tens of
thousands of Jewish refugees from the killing fields in Ukraine and bringing
physically and mentally healthy halutzim; and between selective immigration
and indiscriminate immigration. In each of these dilemmas, the Zionist leadership chose the good of the country over the good of the people, the halutz
over the refugee, and a selective immigration policy that met the needs of only
a specific, limited group within the Jewish people.

The policy of selective immigration to Palestine that Weizmann and Sokolow formulated in 1919–1920 was a continuation of the selective immigration policy developed by Arthur Ruppin during the Second Aliya. That, too,
favored people of independent means over destitute immigrants. In Ruppin's
opinion, Palestine was not a land of refuge and was not capable of absorbing
everyone who wanted to come. He called for giving preference to immigrants
with money, who would not be a burden on the Zionist movement and who
would lay the foundation for the absorption of the masses who would follow.
To those fleeing Russia, he recommended going to the United States.[97]

There were two fundamental and essential differences between Ruppin's
immigration policy and that of Weizmann and Sokolow. The first is that Ruppin

had no power to enforce his proposed policy; he was merely making recommendations. Weizmann and Sokolow, in contrast, had a real influence on immigration quotas, at least until May 1921; they had the power to open or close Palestine to newcomers. The second difference had to do with the chaotic situation in eastern Europe before and after World War I. Pogroms had taken place in eastern Europe even before the civil war. Between 1903 and 1906, roughly three thousand Jews were murdered in the Pale of Settlement. The next eight years were relatively quiet. Jewish refugees were not thronging the Zionist information bureaus, and the hardship was mainly economic. But after the world war, in 1919–1920, approximately sixty thousand Ukrainian Jews were murdered in one of the most horrific periods the Jewish people experienced before the Holocaust.

Few of the Congress delegates knew that Sokolow and Weizmann, in conjunction with the British, had reduced the quota for Jewish immigration to Palestine from eighty thousand to just one thousand. The delegates thought the restrictions on immigration had been imposed in the wake of the riots of 1920 and 1921 following Arab pressure on the high commissioner. In this context, Sokolow's call to rescue Ukrainian Jewry and his complaints about the Jewish people's failure to cooperate with the Zionist movement took on different meaning. The Zionist *rhetoric* was inconsistent with the Zionist *policy*. Weizmann and Sokolow were aware of the dimensions of the catastrophe in Ukraine, but they were more concerned about the limited absorptive capacity of Palestine than about the tens of thousands of Jewish refugees seeking in vain to escape eastern Europe.

The publicist and author Moshe Smilansky came out against the selective Weizmann-Sokolow immigration policy. According to Smilansky, the purpose of immigration to Palestine was not just to build up and settle the country but also to rescue the survivors of the pogrom in Ukraine. The Zionist movement was obligated to lend a hand to the needy; otherwise, it would be a miserable failure from a moral standpoint and would be irrelevant to the Jewish people. On the question of the "good of the country" (selective immigration) versus "the good of the people" (mass immigration), Smilansky chose the people and called for free immigration to Palestine:

> What should the immigration be like? Limited, selective, and blocked, or
> large-scale, free, and unlimited? Large-scale and free! We must understand
> immigration as a means of saving at least some of the refugees from the
> Russian hell and as a means of building up our land. . . . Yes, for many years
> we have been saying that Zionism is not here to resolve the question of the
> survival of individual Jews. And that was true in ordinary years. It is not the

case now during these emergency years. If Zionism cannot provide at least
a partial solution now for the question of the survival of individual Jews,
then it is bankrupt—and it can never become a popular movement with the
potential to resolve the question of the Jewish people.[98]

Menachem Sheinkin felt similarly. He opposed an immigration policy that
preferred young, idealistic halutzim over a rabble of destitute immigrants:

> Nevertheless, we must point out here the injustice in the fact that *the young
> elements have obtained a monopoly on the name "halutzim," which they have
> taken from all the other Jews.* And we must especially note the unforgivable er-
> ror of the Zionist Organization and the Zionist Executive, which have put all
> their moral weight and the bulk of their strength on the side of these halutzim
> exclusively; all the other thousands of Jews who yearn for the land and come
> to it have been left in the shadows as stepchildren of the movement, as less
> worthy immigrants and lower-class citizens in Palestine itself.[99]

In an article titled " Me-Eizeh Sug Mehagrim Netuna Eretz Yisrael" (In
what kind of immigrants does the hope of Palestine lie), printed in the US-
based newspaper *Der Tog* in early June 1922, Sheinkin claimed, "Of the more
than twenty thousand Jews who have entered Palestine in the last two years,
over five thousand have been of the pioneering type—in other words, youths
who, either back in the Diaspora or when they came to Palestine, were organized in groups with a work plan." The rest, "approximately three-quarters,
are mostly ordinary Jews with families who came at their own expense and
on their own responsibility."[100] This group, Sheinkin believed, could make
a real contribution to building up Palestine, and the Zionist movement must
not give up on them. "They have settled quietly and peacefully and have found
themselves sources of income naturally by means of their crafts and skills and
by their ability to adapt to local conditions, something in which the Jews excel
in every country they go to." Moreover, Sheinkin argued that the immigrants
who went to Palestine were different from those who went to the United States
and elsewhere: "In Palestine the Jew does not engage in peddling or trade in
old clothes. The Jew tries to earn his bread honestly [and] he does so because
of national honor. This is a very good sign of our spiritual redemption."[101] He
termed such people *folk pioneers* and believed it was a mistake not to bring them
to Palestine. Instead, the Zionist movement should once again issue "the great
call to the Jewish people: 'House of Jacob, come and let us go.' Come, Jews, let
us go build the Jewish home. From all classes of our people those with a strong
will and tremendous energy will appear and become pioneers." Although many

of those coming would not share the Zionist ideology, "let us not panic about the exilic mindset that prevails among extensive segments of our people." Just as among the halutzim "all that glitters is not gold," so, too, "not all the people are flotsam. Many precious souls are rolling in the muck at the bottom of the middle and 'lower' classes. . . . This is correct Jewish democracy; it is very hard work, but we must do it or the nation cannot be revived."[102]

Immigration to Palestine resumed soon after World War I. The first ships arrived in January 1919 and more came throughout that year. Over thirty-eight hundred immigrants entered the country under the military regime, and more than one hundred thousand came throughout the 1920s. The main countries of origin were Russia in the first half of the decade and Poland in the second half. At the start of the period, in addition to members of the Hechalutz movement, the newcomers included survivors of the pogroms in Ukraine and returning exiles. For this reason, the proportion of children and married people in the first two years of this period far exceeded the multiyear average for the entire decade. The occupational distribution of immigrants from 1924 to 1927 bears some similarity to that of immigrants to the United States before it was closed to immigration: specifically, there was a high proportion of skilled tradesmen and unskilled workers. However, the proportion of agricultural workers and professionals was higher among immigrants to Palestine than among immigrants to the United States.

The resumption of immigration led to a series of debates in the Jewish National Council, the Zionist General Council, and the Zionist Commission and to the fundamental decision that the Zionist movement had to take responsibility for regulating and organizing immigration. With the arrival of High Commissioner Herbert Samuel, an immigration policy was introduced that changed with political circumstances in Palestine. The first immigration ordinance gave the Zionist movement extensive authority over immigration, but this was taken away after the bloody riots in Jaffa in May 1921. Herbert Samuel suspended immigration for one month, after which he issued a new immigration ordinance that divided the newcomers into categories, with rigid quotas for each.

We see from the Zionist immigration policy in the 1920s that the Zionist movement was opposed to indiscriminate immigration and during part of the time even tried to minimize it. In the debate between Max Nordau, who advocated mass immigration and came up with the idea of bringing in half a million Jews, and Zionist Organization president Chaim Weizmann, who favored controlled, selective immigration, Weizmann won out. The Zionist Commission, and in later years the aliya bureau, sent clear instructions to the Palestine Offices about what sort of immigrants the country needed. The Palestine Offices were asked to send only those who would be able to actualize the Zionist idea, not only by immigrating but also by settling in Palestine and building up the country. It seems that when it was a choice between "the good of the people" (physical rescue and survival) and "the good of the country" (settlement and building), the Zionist leadership in the 1920s preferred the good of the land.

The Zionist policy was intended first and foremost to strengthen the Yishuv rather than to help the Jews of eastern Europe or relieve their distress. The needs of the Yishuv took precedence over saving the nation; there was no room in Palestine for anyone who did not serve the Zionist ideology and did not contribute to the settlement effort. The Zionist policy had an internal logic that was inconsistent with Zionist rhetoric. Fear that the Yishuv was incapable of absorbing masses of refugees overcame solidarity and concern for their plight. The primary mission of the Zionist leadership in the years that followed the Balfour Declaration was to build the national home in Palestine, and this required an immigration policy that would place the national interests of redeeming the land above the moral considerations of saving the people.

In the next chapter, we will see that the Palestine Offices developed a selective procedure for sending only the physically and mentally fit to Palestine. Nevertheless, to the displeasure of the Zionist leadership, some of the immigrants and refugees who arrived were motivated not by Zionist ideology but by personal and other considerations.

4

Over Troubled Water

Once the future immigrants had made their final decision to go to Palestine, they had to start planning the journey. Scholars studying migration in general and immigration to Palestine in particular have paid little attention to the journey to the destination country. They have not considered it a major stage in the immigration process, one that is important enough in its own right to be worth researching. English and other languages distinguish between emigrants and immigrants—that is, they address the direction of the migrant's movement. In Hebrew, the distinction is different. Someone who goes to the Land of Israel is termed an *oleh* (pl. *olim*), while *mehager* is the general term for anyone who relocates from one country to another. In the historiography of the Yishuv and of immigration to Palestine, the *olim* came by sea, but their journey, rife with obstacles and challenges, has been marginalized by scholars.

In this chapter, we will look at migration in practice from the perspectives of immigration officials and Jewish immigrants, from the moment the decision was made to immigrate until they arrived on the coast of Palestine: the bureaucratic difficulties in obtaining travel papers, medical exams, the journey to the port and the wait before sailing, the cost of the journey, the role and function of shipping companies in immigration to Palestine, and conditions on the voyage. By focusing on administrative and "technical" issues, we can get a different perspective on more fundamental questions relating to Zionist immigration policy and the procedure for selecting candidates for immigration.

Palestine Offices

After World War I, immigration offices were established in various parts of Europe to handle the large numbers of Jews who were considering immigration to Palestine or were applying to immigrate. These offices continued the work of the information bureaus that had been established in the early twentieth century throughout the Pale of Settlement to help Jews immigrate to various destination countries. The Jewish Colonization Association (ICA) was the first to establish an information bureau in St. Petersburg; this bureau was responsible for hundreds of information bureaus throughout the Russian Empire. In 1905, the Hibbat Zion movement established an information bureau in Odessa that helped Jews reach Palestine. A year later, it also founded information bureaus along the route that ships followed to Palestine—in Trieste, Constantinople, Beirut, Alexandria, Jaffa, and Haifa.[1]

When immigration to Palestine resumed after World War I, it once again became necessary to provide relevant information about the country and to assist Jews in going there. From 1919 to 1921, the Zionist General Council and the Zionist Congress discussed the subject, and the decision was made to establish Palestine Offices in every country that had potential immigrants. Although the Palestine Offices were known by the name of the country in which they were located, they were subordinate to the Zionist Organization and received instructions from the Aliya Department.[2] The Palestine Offices were divided into several categories: a central office covered several countries; a national office handled immigration affairs in a single country; a district office was a branch of the central or national office and dealt with one district; and coastal offices were established in major coastal cities from which Jews sailed for Palestine. The territorial boundaries of the offices' activity were determined by the Aliya Department; if a country had more than two offices, one of them was defined as a central office.[3]

Europe had the highest concentration of Palestine Offices, but there were also offices in North and South America (New York, Ottawa, and Buenos Aires), Africa (Egypt, Tunisia, and Johannesburg), and Asia (Yokohama and Baghdad).[4] Their role was to provide information to Jews interested in immigrating to Palestine, to identify and select "suitable" immigrants based on the employment situation in Palestine and the instructions of the Zionist Executive, to keep orderly records on the applicants, to help them obtain the necessary travel papers, to represent the immigrants vis-à-vis the local British consul, to help ship the immigrants' belongings to Palestine, to arrange lodging for the immigrants at the ports of departure, and to assist them until they boarded the ship.[5]

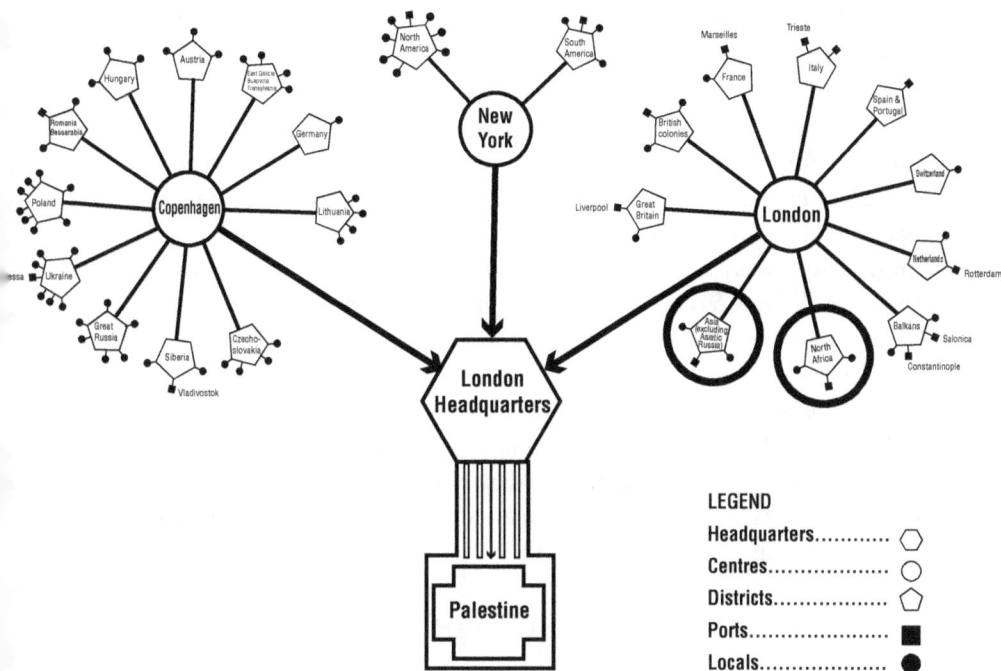

Figure 4.1. Geographical distribution of Palestine Offices.

The procedure in the Palestine Office included registration, a medical exam, obtaining a visa and other documents, medical inspection, and follow-up with the immigrants from the moment they left their country of origin until they reached Palestine. Prospective immigrants would fill out a questionnaire with details including age, family status, occupation, property, and whether they had relatives in Palestine. Applicants also had to be examined twice by a doctor from the office before receiving authorization to immigrate. The first exam took place before they obtained their passports; the second was before they set out. The Palestine Office was responsible for obtaining the visa from the British consul and other travel papers needed to pass through European countries. For protection from travel agents and scoundrels of various sorts who might exploit their dependence, the immigrants paid the Palestine Office for their visas, tickets for the train and ship, and shipment of their belongings to Palestine.[6] The Palestine Office assigned the immigrants to ships sailing to Palestine, sent them on a special railroad car to the port of departure, made sure their belongings were sent on time, and sometimes even had a representative escort them and make sure they reached their destination safely.[7]

The hardest part for the Palestine Offices was to select the most suitable candidates for settlement in Palestine. Because the number of applicants exceeded the number of immigration certificates issued by the Mandatory government, the Palestine Office workers had to decide who could go and who could not. These workers were stuck in the middle: on the one hand, they were being pressured by the Zionist movement to send able-bodied candidates who could take part in building the Yishuv; on the other, large numbers of Jews were asking to immigrate. It was a time of political persecution, pogroms, and economic hardship, and all these factors increased the pressure on the Palestine Offices. They found themselves in a tight spot: they wanted to satisfy the Zionist Executive but also approve the requests of prospective immigrants.

The most prominent and most important of the Palestine Offices established in Europe in the 1920s were in Vienna, Trieste, Warsaw, and Constantinople. Each office faced unique challenges, depending on circumstances of time and place, but they all tried to help Jewish migrants while complying with the decisions of the Aliya Department and the Mandatory government.

Vienna and Trieste

The first two Palestine Offices established were in Vienna and Trieste. These cities were major way stations for thousands of Jews en route to Palestine: Vienna was a central crossroads for Jews on their way to Trieste, and Trieste was the main port of departure for Jewish immigrants to Palestine in the 1920s (in some years, the sole port).

The offices in Vienna and Trieste opened in November 1918 and helped Jews seeking to reach Palestine after the war.[8] The Vienna office rented three houses near the city as temporary lodging for Jews on their way to Trieste. There, prospective immigrants spent twelve days in quarantine and then underwent disinfection and medical exams before they were permitted to continue on to Trieste to board the ship that would take them to Palestine. Those who did not undergo disinfection and exams in Vienna did so in Trieste, but because conditions in Vienna were more pleasant, many preferred to wait there for authorization to immigrate. At the end of the quarantine period, they were examined again, and only afterward did they take the train to Trieste.

The Palestine Office in Vienna was one of the most active, busiest offices in Europe, with twenty people working there. From 1920 to 1922, some twelve thousand people passed through it.[9] The office helped destitute immigrants and provided them with kosher meals in public kitchens. Some immigrants were given clothing, travel expenses, and assistance in obtaining entry visas for

Palestine. Candidates were asked not to apply directly to the British consulate; their applications were handled by Palestine Office employees, who filled out the consulate's questionnaires on their behalf and collected the fee for the visa from them. The Vienna office also dealt with sick people who had been sent back from Palestine to Europe after having been refused entry or who had fallen ill in Palestine and needed medical treatment.

The diverse population that went through the Vienna office gives us an idea of the profile of prospective and actual immigrants to Palestine and returnees from there in the 1920s. A survey of immigration via Vienna divided the Palestine Office's clientele into three categories. The first category consisted of people from Vienna—those who had been born in Vienna or who had gone there before or during World War I and settled there. Some of them believed in Zionist ideals; others were "passive regarding the [Zionist] movement but were quiet, dedicated working people with a healthy national consciousness."[10] Most of the people in this category were able-bodied and had recognized occupations, and they would fit in well in Palestine. The second category consisted of so-called pilgrims—people who had gone to Vienna illegally in order to reach the port of Trieste. According to the survey, not all of them contacted the Palestine Office and officially applied to immigrate. They tried to change money and exchange information, and only sometimes did they ask to lodge in one of the office's homes. The third category, refugees, was subdivided into two groups. The first comprised young people who had left Poland, Galicia, and Hungary "under pressure from various external factors (usually the army)." The second consisted of Hechalutz members who had official papers and authorization for aliya. "Some of them have a trade and have had a halutzic education; others are young men who were forced to flee only by fear of the army. They include people with various qualities, and not always bad ones."[11]

The protracted wait in Vienna for documents and aliya authorization gave the workers in the office a chance to determine the caliber of the prospective immigrants and to filter out problematic ones who would be unsuited for aliya.

These are the faces of the immigrants who have filled the Hechalutz homes in Vienna for more than two years. They all clustered around the Palestine Office and Hechalutz Federation, did all sorts of hard, dirty work in villages nearby and in the city, and lived under conditions of hardship and strain for many months. That life revealed the face of each and every one of them—both their human and social attitudes in general and their attitude toward Palestine in particular. In some cases the Viennese filth swept up laggards who, whether by force or willingly, became pimps and idlers in the course of their long stay.

The small group of olim—"the Association of Olim in Vienna"—spewed them out of the Hechalutz house and sent them away scornfully. Those who remained were the ones who had enough desire to keep waiting for aliya.[12]

The heterogeneity of the prospective immigrants led to intraorganizational disagreements on a matter of principle: whether to approve all applications to the Palestine Office or only those from Zionists: "Regarding those from abroad [the pilgrims and refugees] there was a difference of opinion. One extreme opinion insisted on the principle of absolute centralization and total opposition to the wild migration that has muddled the work of the aliya offices."[13] Some Palestine Office workers favored rejecting everyone "who came from abroad without a letter from the office in their country, not giving them any moral or material assistance, and therefore not admitting them to the Hechalutz house." The workers' circles felt differently, maintaining that they had to take care of everyone. Reality, they argued, superseded bureaucracy: "Fleeing and migrating are natural phenomena originating in other factors and not in the availability of a visa in Vienna, Trieste, or Galați." Hechalutz members also argued, "One army call-up notice in Poland or Galicia will bring hundreds of young Jewish men across the border despite all the Palestine Offices in the world and without any letters or authorization from them. We will not be able to lock the door to them because the torrent will be stronger than we are. . . . We must therefore regard all those in Vienna as one immigrant camp from lots of origins and native lands."[14]

The Vienna office chose a middle way. It issued warnings in the Jewish press in the countries of origin—"Let no one dare come to Vienna from there because [they] will not be sent to Palestine"—and acted heavy-handedly with Jews who arrived without authorization. However, it opened its homes to them and made efforts to find them work, teach them a trade, and—if it became possible in the future—send them to Palestine: "We did this if someone was found to be qualified and if there was no explicit objection to him from the Palestine Office in his country or the Hechalutz Federation in his country." The Vienna office came under criticism for sending to Palestine Jews who had not gone through the Palestine Offices in their countries of origin; the workers were accused of sending undesirable elements.

> The outcry and the dust of controversy stirred up by certain offices against
> the Palestine Office in Vienna, [with the claim] that we will destroy discipline
> in the Zionist camp by sending to Palestine people who were rejected in
> their own countries, and their demand for a monopoly on these grounds
> over people from their countries everywhere in the world, this is all mere

self-righteousness. . . . Regarding the selection of "human material" for immigration, we have no less expertise than the people in the office that is complaining about us. The fact is that we have never sent to Palestine people who were rejected in their country.[15]

Poet Isaac Lamdan, too, got a bad impression of the prospective immigrants in the summer of 1920 when he was waiting for travel papers to immigrate to Palestine. During his stay in the city, he was seized by despair in view of "the human material now immigrating to our land." In his diary he wrote, "Most of the immigrants are destroying and not building. This is a herd of people with twisted brains and no feeling, the buds of ugly exile. Will they build us?"[16]

The workers' parties were also preoccupied by the "undesirable element." Due to the difficulty the Vienna office was having regulating immigration and filtering out unsuitable candidates, Hapoel Hatzair established an aliya committee to take care of halutzim before their aliya, providing material assistance, arranging lodging, supplying food, and most importantly, selecting the appropriate "human material." "You comrades must remember that our job is not to send exiles/refugees but to arrange for human material willing to take part in building up the country through work."[17] The Hapoel Hatzair aliya committee also came under pressure from Palestine not to send halutzim who were unfit (whether mentally or physically) for work: "There is no doubt that the grumbling stems from the same reason, namely, that those complaining were not aware of the true situation when they moved to Palestine, and in their first experience of work, their hopes and illusions were dashed on the rock of harsh reality. Aside from these immigrants, who were not prepared materially and spiritually for their great, difficult destiny, we see here and there a hodge-podge of immigrants who are having a hard time adjusting to conditions in Palestine."[18]

The Trieste office cooperated with the office in Vienna and generally only accepted immigrants who had already undergone disinfection and received the travel papers needed to enter Palestine. The office arranged for lodging and meals for immigrants who could not afford them, handled the transfer of their belongings to the ships, provided financial and consular assistance, negotiated with the Italian government to ensure the rights of immigrants passing through Italy, and served as point of contact with the shipping companies.[19]

More than four thousand immigrants per year passed through the Trieste office in the 1920s. Half of them went to Palestine in the summer months (June–September), the busiest time of year.[20] The large number of immigrants using the Trieste office's services were a financial burden on the office, making it

Figure 4.2. Palestine Office in Trieste. Photo courtesy of CZA, PHG\1006662.

difficult to provide assistance, especially to those not permitted to board the ships. "As you know, there is a terrible shortage of lodgings here, but we are sure we can eliminate this problem through our efforts. What we cannot do is cover the cost of supporting those who are kept back."[21] Despite the financial hardship, the office provided the immigrants with lodging, kosher food, and sometimes even the fare for the voyage "from Trieste to Jaffa-Haifa for deserving yet destitute halutzim." Immigrants who fell ill received medical care from a special doctor "who treats the needy for free. We have counted eleven cases of serious illness among olim who have received our assistance, both in the immigrants' house and in the hospital. Unfortunately, we must note the deaths of two patients from cardiac arrest. They passed away upon arrival in Trieste."[22]

In Trieste, as in Vienna, Zionist aliya officials were asked to send to Palestine only those who could contribute to building the Yishuv. Because the immigrants were aware that they would have to undergo an approval procedure at the Palestine Office, some simply avoided the office and went directly to the ship: "Unfortunately . . . there are also many who deliberately avoid coming to our office while they are here—knowing in advance that we would try to keep them here since the terms of their travel are not in accordance with your orders."[23]

Figure 4.3. Palestine Office in Trieste. Photo courtesy of CZA, PHG\1006676.

Due to the large number of Jewish migrants in the port city, the high costs, and the difficulty of making all the arrangements for immigration to Palestine, the heads of the Palestine Office in Trieste asked the Zionist Commission and the Zionist Executive in London for the authority to regulate immigration via Trieste to Palestine. "Only we know the conditions on the voyage, the local government regulations, [and] the local absorption capacity. It is unreasonable for national Palestine Offices to send as many olim as is convenient for them without checking with us regarding possibilities for lodging and sailing and prevention of an unreasonably long wait in Trieste. The Palestine Offices should therefore be required to be in touch with Trieste before arranging to transport olim to there."[24]

Warsaw

The third Palestine Office, after the ones in Vienna and Trieste, was established in Warsaw in 1920 and soon became one of the biggest and most active offices in Europe. By 1925, approximately twenty-five thousand migrants had passed through it, and it oversaw fifty-four local offices throughout Poland.[25] The office handled all the necessary arrangements for leaving Poland and entering

Palestine and answered the questions of Jews seeking preliminary information about immigration procedures and conditions in Palestine.

The Warsaw office also handled transit permits for passing through Austria on the way to Trieste. The immigrants had to present permits and travel papers when crossing the border en route. Without these documents, they could not set out, and there was constant concern that their entry visas would expire. A report by the Warsaw office stated, "It is worth paying attention to the various impediments to aliya aside from approval of the British visa. The matter of authorizations from Vienna, which were essential in order to obtain a visa to pass through Austria, has always been an obstacle for us."[26] According to the report, the immigrants paid large sums for the long stay in Warsaw, awaiting permission to board the ship in Trieste. "Sometimes it took around six weeks or more until we received the authorizations for the immigrants, which took hard work to obtain. In Vienna the immigrants had to wait twenty-one days in free quarantine and they had to pay the Ma'avirim company here for their stay in Vienna. Payment would be accepted in Austrian or Italian currency and they would have to buy the currency from speculators and scalpers, losing a lot of money in the process."[27]

The initial years of the Palestine Offices—and particularly the office in Warsaw—were hard ones. The Zionist Organization had difficulty financing their activity, and without money, it was hard for them to assist the immigrants. One solution to the immigrants' empty pockets was to appeal to American Jewish aid organizations. The Warsaw office signed an agreement with HIAS, which sent money from "American Jews for their relatives in Poland who wanted to immigrate to Palestine. It was kept in the office for the immigrants until they set out for Palestine." In addition, the office negotiated with the Zionist Organization in the United States "regarding arrangements for sending money . . . for their relatives in the emigration countries so that they can go to Palestine."[28]

The main difficulty for workers in the Palestine Office involved filtering out unsuitable candidates. The heads of the office were subjected to incessant heavy pressure to send only the physically and mentally fit, not to compromise on the caliber of the immigrants, and to avoid sending Jews who were liable to end up not settling in Palestine. Menachem Ussishkin, for example, pleaded again and again with the directors of the Warsaw office to send young people and, as much as possible, to avoid sending immigrants who were unfit for physical labor in Palestine:

> Nevertheless, Heaven forbid we should stop immigration by the young
> people. You simply have to keep a closer eye than you have until now on the
> element that is going to make sure they are physically healthy in the full sense

of the word. We are getting weak people with nervous ailments, consumption, and so on. The catastrophe that such miserable people inflict on the Yishuv goes without saying. Examine the halutzim over and over again before you give them permits to go. Those going also have to be spiritually healthy; in other words, they should know what they are going to Palestine for. . . . *The fearful and faint of heart should stay home.*[29]

The director of the Haifa aliya bureau, Levi Shvueli, also complained about the low caliber of the immigrants arriving in Palestine. In a letter to the Zionist Executive's Aliya Department, he wrote that some problematic immigrants who had arrived in Haifa had caused problems for the bureau: "Z. H. of Kharkov, 37, a metalworker, came from Berlin on May 25 on the *Gastin* with a certificate from us. Almost the entire time he was here he was physically and mentally ill, creating scandals in our office, demanding that we send him back abroad or bring his wife and children here." Of N. S. from Białystok, aged fifty-two, Shvueli wrote, "a blacksmith, sickly and weak. . . . He and his wife are sick most of the time. They don't want to leave their lodgings unless we give them 15 Egyptian pounds." And Y. N., a mechanic from Poland, "is a very coarse person. There is no limit to his demands of us. He says he is weak and cannot work."[30] Shvueli placed the blame for the selection of undesirable immigrants on the Palestine Offices:

We accuse the Palestine Offices abroad of not paying attention to the quality of the people they are sending to Palestine or to their state of health. The matter has already reached the ears of high-ranking government officials. In a recent conversation with the local governor, the undersigned stressed the great responsibility that the Zionist Executive is taking upon itself with respect to immigrants coming with certificates issued to it by the government. I particularly criticized the Palestine Office in Warsaw, which according to reports that I have received is not at all picky about the human material that it sends to Palestine.[31]

The Palestine Office in Warsaw had a hard time implementing the Zionist Executive's policy but did try to send to Palestine only those who could adjust to conditions and strike roots there. Tables 4.1 and 4.2 summarize the office's activity in November and December 1921.

Table 4.1 shows that 40 percent of people who contacted the office registered as candidates for aliya, and 80 percent of those registered were approved by the Palestine Office. Of 1,015 visa applications received by the consul, 88 percent were approved. A total of 1,266 people left Poland—that is, more than the number of applications approved by the consul. Apparently, these people

Figure 4.4. Palestine Office in Warsaw. Photo courtesy of CZA.

had been approved earlier in the year but only left for Palestine in November or December.

The distribution by sex and age in table 4.2 shows that the Palestine Office carefully chose candidates in an effort to implement the Zionist and British immigration policies and to send young people to Palestine. Roughly 80 percent of the visa recipients were male, and 70 percent were aged thirty or under. The preference for men made it harder for women to receive visas. The reasons for the gender preference included a rash of preconceived notions about the difficulty women had adjusting to the new country, compared with men's good ability to adjust. "For the most part, women who immigrate imagine that the country is prepared to employ them as soon as they arrive in Palestine; many women come to Palestine in order to help their families by sending back money." But their initial encounter with the country was harsh and disappointing. "As soon as they arrive [they] encounter the unique conditions of our country. They are driven to despair in their very first days in Palestine and come close to a state of physical and mental decline."[32]

Table 4.1. Emigration from Poland, November–December 1921.

Month	Contacted the office	Registered	Approved by the office	Inspected by the consul*	Received visas	Left Poland**
November	1,522	750	635	582	518	718
December	1,342	440	311	433	374	548
Total	2,864	1,190	946	1,015	892	1,266

Source: CZA, S6, file 338/2.
* Including some applicants approved by the Warsaw office in previous months.
** Including some who received visas in previous months.

Table 4.2. Distribution of visa recipients by sex and age, November–December 1921.

Month	Sex			Age			
	Male	Female	Total	–30	31–50	51+	Total
November	410	108	518	335	102	81	518
December	301	73	374	285	65	24	374
	711	181	892	620	167	105	892

Source: CZA, S6, file 338/2.

The case of Yona Shapiro of Jerusalem illustrates the difficulty women had getting travel papers and the preference for men in the issuance of aliya authorizations. Shapiro had received permission for her mother to come and wanted her sister's daughter to accompany the woman on the arduous journey, but she knew her niece had little chance of being approved for aliya. "Please pay more attention to my request this time and try to fulfill it as quickly as possible. The matter is as follows: I received a government permit for my mother a while back and sent it to her, but she cannot set out on what would be such a long, difficult journey for her. For this reason I wanted my sister's daughter to travel with her, but ... what can I do? It is harder for young women to get permits as the number of certificates for them is much more limited than for young men."[33]

Shapiro therefore asked for a certificate for her brother, "who wants to come with my mother. I wrote to the department asking them to help me and my

Figure 4.5. Palestine Office in Warsaw. Photo courtesy of CZA.

mother by sending my brother a certificate, if possible before Purim, so she can come here for Passover when the sea voyage is not difficult. . . . I would be very grateful if my mother could travel together with my brother and come to Palestine for Passover."[34]

In 1922, a total of 3,053 people immigrated to Palestine from Poland: 2,577 adults and 476 children. Of these, 46 percent were female and 54 percent were male. Ten percent of the immigrants were between the ages of fifteen and twenty; 49 percent were between sixteen and thirty; 17 percent were between thirty-one and fifty; and 24 percent were under fifteen or over fifty. Altogether, 2,532 applicants to the Palestine Office (83%) received visas "on the basis of invitations (request documents) from relatives," and 322 (11%) had "entry certificates from the Zionist Executive." The remainder were persons of means, professionals, tourists, and returning residents. Approximately 84 percent of the immigrants sailed to Palestine via Vienna and Trieste on ships belonging to the Lloyd Triestino company; the other 16 percent sailed via Romania. A total of 1,001 were Russian nationals, and 2,052 were Polish nationals.[35] A representative of the Palestine Office summed up his considerations for selecting the "human material" as follows:

> A glance at these lists proves that, with the restrictions on aliya, immigrants dependent on others for their livelihood in Palestine outnumber those with

a trade and workers seeking to build up the country through their work, although the latter are the most desirable immigrants from our Palestinian perspective. Our information work gave us a basis for registering only those prospective immigrants who had a chance of managing in Palestine and of obtaining an immigration permit, whether by invitation from relatives in Palestine or with a certificate from the Zionist Executive. We used these certificates without exception to approve expert tradesmen who, based on our knowledge, will be able to get by in Palestine.[36]

According to the Palestine Office in Warsaw, the office also handled immigration arrangements for Jews from Russia: "In the past half year three hundred halutzim have come here from Russia and Ukraine on the instructions of Hechalutz in order to immigrate to Palestine."[37] The Russian nationals reached Warsaw when Palestine was still open to immigration and the directors of the office thought they would be able to continue on to Palestine. The British immigration ordinance enacted after the riots of 1921 made it hard for those halutzim to obtain entry visas, and the Warsaw office had to take care of them. "We managed, with great difficulty, to set them up in the area of Poland and find them short-term jobs. Now the situation has become worse: the Polish government is starting to take practical measures against letting in people from Russia and even against allowing those who arrived here as much as half a year ago to stay." The Palestine Office took care of those halutzim and helped them for fear that they would be sent back to Russia. There, "without a doubt severe punishment awaits them for fleeing here, because they are all young and most of them had jobs and responsible work that they left when they fled for their lives."[38] The directors of the office asked the Zionist Executive to help obtain visas for the three hundred halutzim from Russia who were stuck in Warsaw.

An immigrant shelter was established in Warsaw with funds from the Joint Distribution Committee (JDC). It had eleven large, spacious rooms and sixty beds. The shelter was run according to clear, strict rules, and residents were expected to comply with its schedule: the maximum stay in the shelter was two weeks; residents were responsible for the items in the house; they were expected to make their beds by eight o'clock, after which they were not allowed in the bedrooms until eight in the evening except during lunchtime; the residents in each room had to choose a supervisor who would be in charge of tidying, cleaning, opening, and closing the room, and in the end would return the key to shelter management. Breakfast was served from eight thirty to ten, lunch from two to four, and supper from seven to nine. Eating was permitted in the dining room only, and lights-out was at eleven o'clock.[39]

Constantinople

The Constantinople office was the most complicated of all the Palestine Offices. Unlike the others, it handled hardly any local applicants for immigration. The city's proximity to the port of Odessa brought (along with halutzim and olim) thousands of Jewish refugees from the terror of the Ukrainian civil war seeking to go to Palestine and elsewhere, including the United States, Canada, and Argentina. Many of the refugees needed material and emotional assistance while waiting for entry permits, and often they became a burden on the local Jewish community. The initiative to establish a local office that would help the refugees was taken by Russian Zionists living in Constantinople who had seen the plight of their fellow countrymen in the city.

In June 1920, Russian Zionists in Constantinople founded the aliya committee, headed by Ze'ev Tiomkin. "Immigration to Palestine via Constantinople is increasing from day to day and taking on the form of real migration," Tiomkin wrote to the Zionist Commission. He noted that hundreds of halutzim were thronging Constantinople from Crimea, Bessarabia, Bulgaria, Romania, and even Iran, and there was no one to help them overcome the bureaucratic obstacles to leaving Constantinople and entering Palestine:

> Regarding Palestine, there was no institution here dealing with immigration, supporting them initially, and making it easier for them to continue on their way. . . . Consequently, the Russian Zionists living in Constantinople decided, together with local elements, to quickly rectify this urgent situation. At a general meeting to which representatives of various organizations were invited, the decision was made to form an aliya committee in Constantinople. Its aims would be to establish a migration station, offer material and moral support, provide medical assistance, arrange visas and fares for the journey, make arrangements for lodging, and offer reading and Arabic lessons.[40]

The establishment of the aliya committee was a welcome gesture of goodwill on the part of public figures to help the olim, immigrants, and refugees in the city. However, the committee had a hard time helping them due to a dearth of material and financial means. Tiomkin hung his hopes on the Zionist Commission and appealed several times to Ussishkin for assistance, but the money did not arrive: "For about two months now, we have been fighting for our existence here under the worst conditions. For several days the halutzim who have been suffering here for half a year have had no bread to put in their mouths. And now that we have received visas for some of them, we have no way to send them because we have no [money] to pay for the ticket."[41]

The aliya committee's work in its first year was rife with difficulties, including that of fulfilling the requests of the Jews who had come to Constantinople
en route to Palestine. Many letters and memos were sent to the Zionist Commission complaining about the dysfunction of the aliya committee and its inability to help: "We know of cases in which immigrants slept on the beach, in
the open air, because no home had yet been found for them."[42] After a home was
found, it turned out to be unlivable and too small to hold its residents. "Single
immigrants are being put up in general hotels. Dormitories of a Jewish school
in a Constantinople suburb are now being used as such a hotel. There are about
250 people in four rooms. In addition to singles they have put . . . a few families
with small children there as well." The wait in the apartments the committee
rented was unpleasant: "It is hard to describe the unsanitary conditions in this
apartment: There is no sign of any furniture in the house, such as beds, tables, or
chairs. They sleep, eat, and work on the filthiest floor." Moreover, the rent that
the committee charged turned out to be much higher than the going rate and
wiped out the immigrants' funds: "It goes without saying that the apartments
rented with the help of aliya committee workers should cost the immigrants
less than if the immigrants living in them, who are not familiar with the city
and its language, rented them on their own."[43]

Complaints were heard about the storage of the immigrants' belongings in
a special warehouse rented by the committee, but the main complaints were
directed against Tiomkin and the obstacles he placed in the way of people seeking to go to Palestine. "The director of the aliya committee, Dr. Ze'ev Tiomkin,
has a preconceived notion that each and every immigrant, without exception,
is a cheat and a schnorrer. Often he doesn't let the immigrants express what
they want, interrupts them, and orders them to get out." The complainers were
also astonished by Tiomkin's attitude toward Zionism, which they described as
"very strange." They stated, "He asks almost every one of the immigrants why
he is traveling to Palestine; it would be better to go to America; what will you
do there in Palestine?"[44]

Placing obstacles in the way of the immigrants in Constantinople was part
of the Zionist movement's immigration policy, and Tiomkin was acting in
accordance with his instructions from Menachem Ussishkin. In early October, Ussishkin asked Tiomkin to be sure to send only physically and mentally
healthy immigrants to Palestine and to prevent the weak and unfit from going.
According to Ussishkin, the Jews in Constantinople were unsuited for settling
Palestine and had become a burden on the Yishuv institutions: "When you send
immigrants here, check over and over again that those coming to Palestine are
mentally and physically healthy enough. Because the recent arrivals include

some who are very defective and not at all capable of settling in Palestine. Even one percent who aren't good are enough to ruin many good ones."[45] Tiomkin agreed. He replied, "The aliya committee in Constantinople gives due attention to examining the immigrants to Palestine. Since its very first day it has examined the immigrants thoroughly both physically and mentally before they are sent to Palestine."[46] Indeed, the letter of complaint to the Zionist Commission gives the impression that Tiomkin questioned, examined, and interrogated prospective immigrants and was careful to send only those who fit the required profile.

The issue of suitable candidates for immigration was of paramount concern to the Palestine Offices, which found themselves between a rock and a hard place. On the one hand, the aliya bureau expected them to conduct thorough, meticulous examinations of the immigrants, but on the other, they were subjected to incessant pressure from the applicants to authorize their immigration. Although the offices generally complied with the aliya bureau's demands, they could not always withstand the pressure and sometimes sent people who did not fit the preferred Zionist profile.

The cooperation between the aliya committee and the Jerusalem aliya bureau with respect to the desirability of certain immigrants caused tension with the JDC in Constantinople. Because the aliya committee lacked the necessary financial means and because Tiomkin was not getting financial assistance from the Zionist Executive, he asked the JDC for assistance. The JDC agreed and did indeed fund the committee's work, but sending only healthy young people to Palestine ran counter to JDC policy, which sought a solution for all Jewish refugees in the city.[47]

The Constantinople aliya committee was officially designated a coastal Palestine Office in late 1920. In March 1921, after Tiomkin's visit to London, it was declared a central Palestine Office. In 1921, Dr. Kalb, director of the local JDC office at the time, took over from Tiomkin. Jewish refugees who had fled to Odessa had arrived in nearby Constantinople during and after the pogroms in Ukraine and told Dr. Kalb what was happening in their country. On June 13, 1919, he published his impressions in *Hapoel Hatzair*, based on the testimonies he had heard. "In brutality and terror, the recent pogroms in Ukraine have surpassed the pogroms in the days of the Czarist government in Russia," Dr. Kalb wrote. "Men and old people, children and women, were slaughtered; no one was left alive. Not content with mere robbery, the murderers perpetrated a general massacre. Their aim was to annihilate Jewish communities wherever they went. Tens of thousands were wounded or killed. The slaughter was conspicuous for its unheard-of brutality and unbelievable tortures."[48]

Refugees thronged the aliya bureau, seeking to go to Palestine, though many did not even want to go there at all; they were hoping to go to the United States, Canada, or Argentina. They only chose Palestine when it became clear to them that they had no chance of going to America: "It often happens that people cannot go to America because of the quota, because they lack sufficient means, or due to someone sick in the family, etc. On the other hand the ICA does not consider them suitable for Argentinian colonization and so does not give them its full support, or (as I was told by the director of the ICA) the Canadian government makes certain demands regarding immigrants' fitness for working the land. In such a case, the person concludes that the only place for him is Palestine."[49]

Because Constantinople had become a temporary place of refuge for many Jews who had fled the terror of the pogroms in Ukraine, the Palestine Office had no choice but to deal with the refugees. For these people, Palestine was a default on which their lives depended. The Palestine Office workers found themselves in constant tension between a growing stream of refugees longing to reach Palestine and the Aliya Department's demand that only halutzim who worked in agriculture be sent there. Many "peddlers, restaurant owners, and owners of soda fountains" were sent from Constantinople to Palestine, while the "productive element" sent was smaller than anticipated, to the displeasure of the Aliya Department.[50]

The large refugee population in the city dictated the Palestine Office's working methods, which differed from those of the offices in Europe. Most migrants arrived in Constantinople without aliya permits, stayed in the city for a long time, and were a heavy burden on the local Jewish community. The office obtained entry visas for Palestine, negotiated with the British consul, arranged for medical exams, and purchased tickets for the voyage on the immigrants' behalf.[51] It even found them jobs and trained them to work the land in Palestine.

In 1911, the ICA purchased a large tract of land about twenty kilometers from Constantinople to house Jews. The colony, known as Mesila Hadasha ("new track"), was just one of several Jewish agricultural colonies founded by the ICA; others were in North and South America.[52] In 1919, Yosef Trumpeldor of Hechalutz signed a contract with ICA management to train halutzim at the colony before they moved to Palestine.[53] In the 1920s, Mesila Hadasha took in young halutzim, who worked there in agriculture and prepared for life in Palestine. "In recent years the Mesila Hadasha colony has been the place where the halutzim cluster during their stay in Constantinople. Now the halutzim are working in the forest there and pulling up roots. The Palestine Office and the Hechalutz office are currently busy with a broad, systematic work plan for the halutzim in this colony. They have already started implementing the plan for setting up a mixed farm that can employ a number of halutzim; they will train there to work in Palestine and will earn their livelihood there during the time they have to stay in Constantinople."[54]

Halutzim who underwent agricultural training in the colony were sent to Palestine, but many of the thousands of refugees and migrants in Constantinople had no solution to their plight. Aside from the inherent difficulties of aiding the masses who thronged the Palestine Office, political instability in Turkey hampered orderly work vis-à-vis the authorities. The years after World War I were marked by political upheaval and governmental instability; this directly affected the work of the office, which had to deal with several government authorities rather than just one. Only in October 1923, after Mustafa Kemal Atatürk deposed the sultan and declared the establishment of the Turkish republic, was political stability restored, after which the issue of refugees seeking to immigrate to Palestine was gradually resolved.

The Palestine Offices in Warsaw, Vienna, Trieste, and Constantinople bore the burden of immigration to Palestine and formed a crucial link in such migration in the 1920s. For this reason, the Zionist movement invested great effort in creating a multibranched, hierarchical immigration apparatus capable of implementing an effective, selective policy that would serve the strategic goals of the Zionist movement. Their primary task was to carry out the immigration policy of the aliya bureau and Mandatory government while assisting Jewish migrants. Because these two needs did not always overlap, the Palestine Offices were constantly in crisis. The difficulty of maneuvering between the migrants' expectations and demands and those of the Zionist Executive created tension for the directors of the aliya bureaus in Jaffa and Haifa and for the heads of the Palestine Offices.

In March 1925, a conference of Palestine Offices was held in Jerusalem, with the participation of eleven representatives of the central offices in Europe; one representative of World Hechalutz; and the directors of the aliya bureaus in Jaffa, Haifa, and Jerusalem. These officials working in Palestine and abroad discussed the difficulties and challenges of making arrangements for immigration and sending Jews to Palestine. At the end of the conference several fundamental decisions were made that affected the work of the offices. The most important of them concerned British policy on immigration to Palestine. "The conference expresses its distress that the present immigration laws are preventing the Palestine Offices from bringing to Palestine those agricultural elements and tradesmen capable of increasing the productivity of the developing Yishuv in Palestine. The conference unanimously calls on the Zionist Executive to take measures to immediately repeal the present immigration rules that were introduced after the events of May 1921."[55]

The conference participants declared that the immigration regulations "hinder the Palestine Offices in the fulfillment of their duty to organize immigration, cause resentment of the Mandatory government and the Jewish Agency within Jewish society, and undermine the foundations of trust in the Zionist movement and its operator in Palestine."[56] A motion was introduced urging the Zionist Executive to "pay as much attention as possible in distributing certificates to the Jewish refugees who remain on European shores to how well they meet the country's needs."[57] Another resolution made at the conference was as follows: "In approving certificates, special attention shall be paid to those trained by Hechalutz and to others educated in the spirit of productive work."[58]

The Palestine Offices also had to contend with distrust on the part of the consuls and their repeated allegations that the heads of the offices were not complying with the immigration laws enacted by the Mandatory government. At a meeting held in the Palestine Office in Warsaw, Joshua Gordon stated that "an atmosphere of distrust" had developed. The Mandatory government, he said, "has informed us that some intolerable things are being done in the offices. If we do not set things to rights, the Palestine Offices will be stripped of their privileges."[59] Gordon provided a few examples that he claimed had embarrassed the Zionist Executive. For instance, a Persian family had gone from Constantinople to Warsaw and applied for immigration permits for Palestine, but the supposed family members included a Yiddish-speaking Polish girl. In another case, a "daughter" was just five years younger than her "mother." Some Jews tried to blackmail the Palestine Office, threatening that if they didn't get what they deserved, they would inform the consul of the widespread forgery of travel papers in Warsaw, Constantinople, and other Palestine Offices. This triangle of forces, whose vertices were the Zionist Executive, the consuls, and the immigrants, made the offices' work highly sensitive and complex and directly influenced immigration to Palestine in the 1920s.

The Bureaucracy of Immigration

The bureaucratic procedures that Jewish applicants went through to obtain the necessary travel papers for immigration, as described in the following pages, relates to the activity of the Palestine Office in Warsaw in 1925. The Warsaw office was one of the most important and busiest offices in Europe, with thousands of Jewish migrants passing through. The procedures instituted there, which were implemented in all the Palestine Offices in Europe, give us an indication of the complexity of the procedure for obtaining travel documents and entry permits for Palestine.

Prospective immigrants seeking the papers and authorizations needed to leave their countries of origin and enter Palestine had to meet criteria set both by the Mandatory government and by the Zionist movement. The bureaucratic procedure took a long time and cost money, and at the end of it their applications were either accepted or rejected. The procedure for obtaining the travel documents and entry permit can be divided into two parts: meeting the Mandatory government's requirements and meeting the requirements of the Aliya Department of the Zionist Executive.

The first step was to ask the Palestine Office to determine whether one qualified to immigrate. Office workers started the process of obtaining an entry visa to Palestine only after having ascertained that the candidate had a good chance of getting it. Anyone who had capital of £500 was asked to show it in cash or property. Machinery, work tools, merchandise, and other valuables were considered, but only as a certain percentage of the total capital, and for no more than £100. Those in category E, who had written invitations from people already in Palestine, could receive a visa without delay, but the visa was valid for only a year; in order to extend it, they had to contact the immigration office of the Mandatory government in Palestine.[60] Women whose fiancés were in Palestine were asked to bring "for inspection . . . the most recent letters (with the envelopes from Palestine) that they had received from their fiancés. Without this they will not be given the visa."[61]

Immigrating to Palestine with a certificate was a complicated process. Twice a year the Zionist Executive gave the central Palestine Offices a certain number of these certificates:

> On the basis of these entry permits and in accordance with the instructions received from time to time in this regard from the Zionist Executive in Palestine, the Aliya Office approves workers with a trade who are well developed physically, and can manage in Palestine and adjust to all the harsh living conditions of workers there. Visas based on certificates are issued only to those aged 18 to 35, [or] in special cases, with authorization from the government of Palestine, up to 45 years of age. The passports of certificate holders must state the trade on the basis of which their immigration certificate is approved. Those authorized to immigrate based on certificates can bring their families with them (wives, sons under age 18, and daughters). Sons aged 18 and over and parents are not included in the immigrant's family for a certificate.[62]

משרד ארץ ישראל לעליה

הסוכנות היהודית לארץ ישראל

מחלקת-העליה והעבודה

ירושלים

משרד ארץ-ישראלי

כתבות של מוסדות העליה:

Warszawa, Krolewska 18.
Misrad, Warszawa.
Wien I, Kärntnerstr. 28.

I משרדי חוץ בחו"ל
Ufficio Palestinese
TRIESTE, Via del Monte 7.
Misrad, Trieste
Oficiul Palestinian
CONSTANTA, Strada Tache Ionescu 6,
Oficiul Palestinean, Constanta

II לשכות-העליה בא"י:
לשכת-הדעליה של הסוכנות היהודית
תל-אביב, רחוב' העליה
Jewagency, Tel-Aviv
תחנת-העליה של הסוכנות היהודית
יפו, בחוף
לשכת-העליה של הסוכנות היהודית
חיפה בת גלים
Jewagency, Haifa

29800

משרד ארץ-ישראלי ב

Palestine Office

תעודת-עליה
Palestine Immigrant Certificate

השם
Name

Presas Sara

אזהרה

העולה הנוסע בלי תעודה כזאת לא יקבל
שום סיוע חמרי או מוסרי מהמוסדות הציוניים
בארץ-ישראל ובגולה.
התעודה הזאת צריכה להמצא בידי העולה
במשך כל ימי נסיעתו ולהמסר ללשכת העליה
הציונית מיד אחרי בואו לארץ-ישראל.

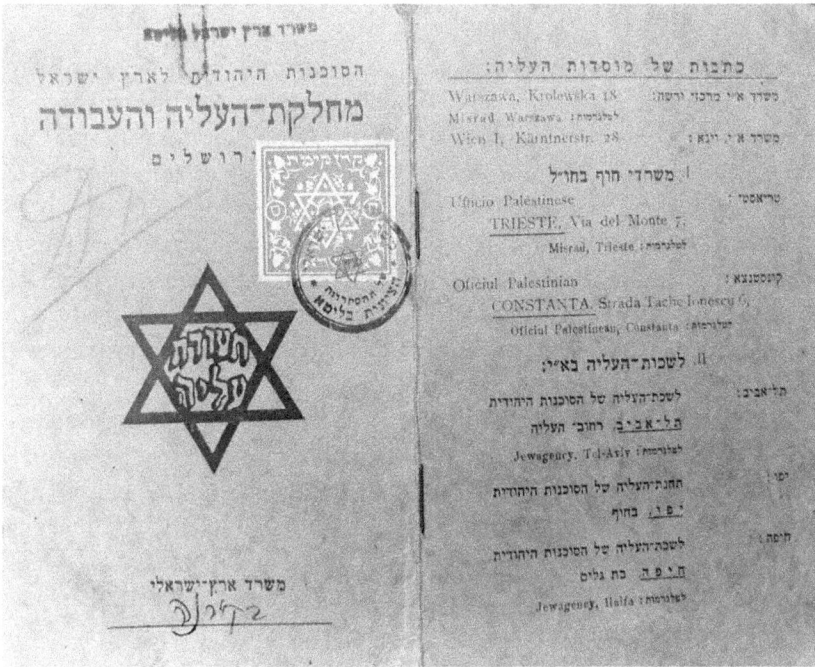

Figures 4.6 and 4.6A. Immigrant certificate of Sara Presas, 1932.

To qualify for travel papers from the Palestine Office (in Warsaw) under any of the categories, a candidate had to submit a questionnaire that had been approved by the local office, along with a photograph and Jewish National Fund stamp. Questionnaires of prospective immigrants from eastern Galicia were handled by the Palestine Office in Lwów, those from western Galicia by the Cracow office, and those from Lithuania by the office in Vilna. Applications for an immigrant certificate were discussed at meetings of the office in the order in which the questionnaires were received. Applications submitted directly to the central Palestine Office and not sent via the district office in accordance with the rules were not accepted.

Those whose applications for immigration certificates were approved were asked to apply to the government office in their district for a Polish passport. Each also had to get a certificate of good conduct from the police, approval from the tax authorities, and a document from the army. Young men of military age needed a special exit permit from the Polish district headquarters for conscription and reserve duty (Powiatowa Komenda Uzupełnień, or PKU). Passports were free to applicants who had a special permit to migrate to Palestine from the government emigration office in Warsaw. To obtain such a permit, the candidate had to show the central Palestine Office "a certificate stating that he earns his living by manual labor in a certain trade (*zaświadczenie pracy*), a certificate of poverty (*zaświadczenie ubostwa*), or a document proving that he does not work and has no income but rather is dependent on support from relatives."[63] The passport application form was signed by all members of the family seeking to emigrate. By law, children aged sixteen and over needed their own passports.

Palestine residents who had gone to Poland on a British passport containing a Polish visa could return to Palestine without a British visa; instead, they needed a transit visa issued at the central Palestine Office in Warsaw. If the person wanted to return to Palestine after the passport had expired, he or she would be issued a new visa, but only after the British consul in Warsaw had received authorization from the Mandatory government in Palestine. Residents of Palestine who had gone to Poland on a Polish passport containing a Palestine government stamp reading "has permission to remain in Palestine in perpetuity" or "good for returning before the expiry date of this document" could return to Palestine without a British visa. Tourists could enter Palestine only with Polish (or other foreign) passports. They had to present a sum of money sufficient for the trip to Palestine and back and their itinerary in Palestine. The visas were issued for a period of three months.

After obtaining a passport, the candidate had to undergo inspection by the Mandatory government of Palestine. The inspections took place at the Palestine Office in Warsaw on Tuesdays and Thursdays, and applicants had to come on the day and at the time assigned to them. "Immigrants must come for inspection together with their wives and children who are traveling with them and must bring the proper papers."[64] In some cases a married couple was asked to bring a *ketuba* or official marriage certificate. In order to get a visa, each candidate (which included children up to age sixteen) had to bring to the Palestine Office a passport, medical certification of good health, three passport photographs, and about two and a half pounds sterling for the visa and entry tax to be paid to the Mandatory government (children up to sixteen paid an entry tax of ten shillings).[65] On inspection days, the central office in Warsaw was extremely busy, with prospective migrants from throughout Poland waiting their turn.

A wonderful historical source that gives us an idea of how crowded and busy the Palestine Offices were is a children's story titled "He-Halutz ha-Katan" (The little pioneer). The story, published in installments in the youth newspaper *Shibolim*, which came out in Warsaw in the 1920s, is told from the point of view of David'l, an immigrant boy. David'l sends letters to the editor, each of which describes another stage of the immigration process: deciding to emigrate, waiting one's turn at the local aliya office, traveling to Trieste, boarding the ship, and sailing to Palestine. David'l's exuberance and optimism are reminiscent of Mottel the cantor's son in the novel by Sholem Aleichem.

This is how David'l describes his parents' decision to go to Palestine for Zionist reasons: "Well, we are going to Palestine. All of us: my parents, my two little brothers, Shmuel Yona and Naftalke, and the youngest of us all, my sister Rochele. In addition to our family, a big group of halutzim are going. These are young men and women going to Palestine to work the land, build roads, drain swamps—in short, to do all the extensive work that the Jewish people has to do in Palestine."

The journey begins with waiting for the clerk at the crowded district Palestine Office in a small Polish city. "Meanwhile we go every day to the Palestine Office, where the clerks prepare the paperwork for the visas. The office is Jewish and all the clerks there are Jews, and they occasionally even speak Hebrew. But it is hard to get up to the clerks because the entire building is packed with such a huge crowd that there is no room. Everyone is pushed and shoved to where the clerk sits, because everyone wants to be among the first to get the necessary information. We all crowd together from nine in the morning until lunchtime."[66] This was the applicants' experience: long lines; tiring waits; and prying, draining interviews.

Although the immigration arrangements were supposed to be made through the Palestine Offices, some people set out without the necessary paperwork or with the wrong papers. These people became a burden on the coastal offices, which were expected to help them straighten out their status. "We note favorably the excellent attitude of the Polish consul in Trieste, who, thanks to our intervention, has put order in disordered passports." In exceptional cases the consul even waived the consular fees. There were also cases of immigrants with forged visas. The office workers helped "those wretches who had fallen victim to exploiters of immigrants to return to their country. In a few cases we were able to straighten things out and obtain legal visas for the immigrants."[67]

Once the visa had been issued, all the bureaucratic preparations were complete, and the immigrants were told to start getting ready for the trip: purchasing tickets for the ship and arranging transport of their belongings to the port in Palestine.

Medical Examinations

Jews seeking to immigrate to Palestine underwent thorough medical exams at the Palestine Offices in Europe before a decision was made as to their future; they were also examined on the way and when they arrived in Palestine. These exams became a standard, familiar procedure. Before World War I, immigrants to the United States had undergone three medical exams: the first was done at one of the border stations between Germany and the Russian Empire; the second was done by the shipping company in the port city before they sailed; and the third was conducted when they arrived at Ellis Island. Most Jews crossed the Russian border illegally and were therefore only examined twice. The medical exam done in the port city on behalf of the shipping company was strict because immigrants found to be sick were not permitted to enter the United States and had to return to the port of departure at the shipping company's expense. To avoid unnecessary expenses, the companies tried to take only immigrants whose chances of being admitted to the United States were high.

The medical exam at Ellis Island started as soon as the new arrivals entered the immigration station, after they had placed their belongings in the entrance hall and walked up the steps to the registration hall. Doctors stood next to the long lines and on the peripheral balcony above them, observing the people waiting in line, watching their behavior and how they conducted themselves, and looking for signs of illness or other physical or mental problems. Each immigrant's eyelids were raised to check for trachoma. Boys and men were examined by male doctors; the exam included looking at the sex organ and crotch area in search of signs of sexually transmitted diseases and to rule out a hernia. Girls and women were examined by female doctors; their exams were not as invasive as those of the men, unless they were suspected of having a sexually transmitted disease. Immigrants who were found to be sick or problematic in some way had a chalk mark placed on their lapels and were taken for an additional physical or mental exam in a side room before it was decided whether to send them back to their country of origin or let them stay in America.[68]

Like immigrants to the United States, those to Palestine also underwent thorough medical exams as a condition for obtaining travel papers and entering the country. Because the Zionist Executive was looking for a specific type of immigrant, the doctors were given clear criteria for deciding who was fit to immigrate and who was condemned to stay behind. An essential criterion in addition to good physical and mental health was the immigrant's suitability for living conditions in Palestine. "The harsh conditions in Palestine demand tremendous effort from all new immigrants during their acclimation. Even those trained to withstand the many dangers anticipated to the immigrants' health suffer somewhat from the change in climate and endemic diseases." Therefore, a candidate for immigration whose "state of health cannot withstand the special hardships in Palestine and [who cannot] earn a living under these conditions necessarily becomes a heavy burden on the Zionist Organization and the general public."[69]

The doctors were asked to conduct thorough medical exams and get an impression of the applicants' physical and mental condition in order to spot the weak, disabled, and ill in advance. The Zionist Executive held the doctors responsible for the caliber of Jews arriving in Palestine. The instructions to the doctors were clear: "*The exam must be practical, thorough, and free of all sentimentality. The Palestine Office doctors bear a tough moral responsibility for the tremendous loss caused, both to the country and to the immigrants themselves, if they neglect this requirement.*"[70]

Prospective immigrants were divided into three medical categories: Category A comprised healthy people with no physical defect "or affliction, who are fit to do the hardest work under poor conditions, and who are not under 18 years of age or over 45." Candidates in category B were not in perfect health but, as "master workers (in a craft or spiritual work)," were classified as skilled tradesmen who would not endanger the health of those around them, and they had a chance of finding permanent work in Palestine. This category included wives and children, provided they were in good health. Candidates in category

C were rejected immediately and were not allowed to immigrate on medical or psychological grounds; these included tuberculosis, heart or kidney disease, a tendency to "diarrhea and chronic intestinal inflammation," and "the mentally disturbed, especially cases of melancholia and mental illness, epilepsy and dimwittedness." The doctors were instructed to identify not only the ill but also those who were "weak with no conspicuous organic defect." Those who appeared to be unable to cope with the conditions of the country were rejected out of hand. "One must always pay attention to the constant physical strain required of workers under the conditions of the country and the little resistance of the weak to malaria, typhus, dysentery, and other illnesses of the stomach and intestines."[71]

Although the Palestine Office doctors followed the instructions they had received from the Zionist Executive, sometimes immigrants who did not meet the criteria were sent to Palestine. "Many times we drew the Palestine Offices' attention to the fact that the medical exam had not been performed by the Palestine Office doctor with the most elementary precision. Various chronically ill immigrants and even complete invalids have managed to get consent from the Palestine Office to immigrate to Palestine."[72]

The Zionist Executive in Palestine was outraged about sick and unfit immigrants being sent there: "We have a list of hundreds of immigrants who came to Palestine while sick and cannot manage at work by any means due to their state of health."[73] S. R., for example, arrived on the *Campidoglio* in February 1922 with an advanced case of tuberculosis. He was hospitalized in Haifa for a few weeks until he passed away. R. D., age twenty-two, arrived in January 1923 from Ukraine; she, too, was hospitalized: "She lies there all the time and there is no hope of her being able to do physical labor in the coming months. Her subsistence in Palestine will always be a burden on the public institutions. She has no relatives in Palestine."[74]

When Tiomkin took over as head of the Palestine Office in Constantinople, he was aware of the problems with medical exams and the absence of a clear, straightforward policy regarding fitness for immigration. "One of the most important questions regarding aliya, which until today has not received special attention from the offices dealing with immigration, is the matter of the immigrants' health and their examination before they go to Palestine." Tiomkin claimed, "To this day there is no permanent language on this subject and there are no fixed rules governing the functioning of all the offices dealing with aliya." He called for order and logic "with respect to the medical exams for the immigrants and having the same order and the same language in all the immigration centers. . . . We have to try to ensure that the few who do immigrate to Palestine are at least physically and mentally healthy so that they can bring benefit and blessing to the land. The Palestine Offices should pay attention to this question and adopt measures to regularize the examinations of the immigrants in the future."[75]

The medical exam was a crucial step in immigration to Palestine, and the Palestine Office doctors had tremendous power in that they could prevent people from going. Six Jewish doctors worked in the Palestine Office in Warsaw. Most of them were from religious families and had acquired their education and medical training in Europe.[76] An interesting biographical detail that emerges from Katvan and Davidovitch's studies is that the Zionist doctors had been army doctors during World War I; that experience had shaped their professional identities. They had worked in a system that selected candidates for military service and had to decide on the conscripts' fitness for combat. According to Katvan and Davidovitch, a close connection is discernible between the doctors' work for the Palestine Office and their experience in the military. The examinations of prospective soldiers and of prospective immigrants were similar: the Palestine Office doctors were asked to assess candidates' fitness for immigration in terms of their physical strength and their suitability for settlement in Palestine and not only to determine whether they were carrying any infectious diseases.[77]

The medical exams were a fundamental issue in immigration, reflecting the complex dilemmas faced by Zionist immigration policymakers and the practical and utilitarian impacts of these dilemmas. The doctors came under incessant, heavy pressure from everyone involved in immigration: the British government pressured them to implement the policy stipulated in the law; the aliya bureau oversaw their work out of concern about the entry of undesirable elements; the heads of the Palestine Offices in Europe, who were directly responsible for sending people to Palestine, watched them from up close; and the applicants themselves contended with them in various ways and sometimes even tried to deceive them.

Dr. Mordechai Lansky at the Palestine Office in Warsaw felt the pressure firsthand on a daily basis: "Everyone will understand that a huge responsibility has been placed on the Palestine Office doctors abroad—to keep back those immigrants whose health would prevent them from fulfilling their difficult task in Palestine properly."[78] Lansky, himself a Zionist, understood the importance of the medical exam and considered it an essential condition for the success of the Zionist enterprise: "Anyone who cares about Palestine will acknowledge that the country's development depends to a large extent on the caliber of the human material entering. If the new immigrants whom history has charged with the lofty task and burden of building the country with their own hands are truly prepared for their destiny, both spiritually and in terms of their health, we can hope that their efforts will be blessed. But woe to us if we ignore this aspect and let admission to Palestine be like a ball played with by random fate."[79]

The doctors not only served as gatekeepers for public health; they also filtered out candidates who were "unfit" in terms of employability or even politics and were influenced by the intervention of the aliya bureau in Jerusalem.[80] Because most of the doctors were Zionists, there was tension between their ideological and political views and the medical ethics they had sworn to uphold. On more than one occasion, doctors were accused of succumbing to partisan pressures and giving medical approval to applicants who belonged to the right party or taking advantage of their work in the Palestine Office to make some money on the side. Such allegations led to the dismissal of two doctors in the 1920s: Dr. Meir Pecker, who was fired after having been accused of corruption (even though an investigation found him not guilty), and his replacement Dr. Mordechai Lansky, mentioned above, who was accused of not being meticulous enough in his medical exams and sending sick immigrants to Palestine.[81]

Once official arrangements had been completed and tickets for the sea voyage had been purchased, immigrants were sent a telegram telling them when to go to Warsaw to pick up their travel papers and tickets. Each needed a passport, immigration certificate from the British government or invitation from relatives in Palestine, immigration certificate and payment vouchers from the Palestine Office, tickets for the train and ship, British government form 39, a voucher for the entry tax, an application to the immigrant houses in Palestine (if the person was destitute or had no family there), medical authorization, two photographs, and a declaration that the person was going to Palestine on his or her own responsibility.[82]

Next, they had to make their way to the port of Constanţa or Trieste. The Palestine Office reserved one railroad car for the immigrants and another for their belongings. A representative of the office escorted them to the Romanian or Austrian border. At the Romanian border another escort waited for them from the Palestine Office in Cernăuţi; at the Austrian border they were awaited by an escort from the Vienna office. The new escorts took over responsibility for the group after being given the immigrants' passports, and they accompanied them to the port of departure. Immigrants traveling on their own handled their own arrangements for taking the train to the port of departure.[83]

The heads of the Palestine Offices not only had to deal with the medical and psychological problems of candidates who were deemed unfit for life in Palestine; they also had to contend with Jews with dubious moral

Figures 4.7 and 4.7A. Immigrants and their baggage at the Trieste train station. Photos courtesy of CZA, PHG\1078896.

backgrounds—criminals and scoundrels—who wanted to go there. Their arrival in Palestine caused tension between Mandatory officials and the aliya bureau directors; moreover, future problems that might be caused by such immigrants were liable to cast aspersions on the Zionist enterprise, jeopardizing its success. When the immigration ordinance took effect, Sheinkin demanded that the aliya bureaus in Vienna, Trieste, Constantinople, Kishinev, Warsaw, and Crimea be especially careful in selecting immigrants for Palestine.

> Along with the groups of halutzim—who excel in their dedication to our cause in general and to our land and working the land in particular—and along with ordinary, honest families, a number of people who are not decent people—thugs, rowdies, and layabouts—have come to Palestine with your assistance. Such people steal from their fellows while still en route and then in the immigrant houses here. Some of them get drunk here on wine and look for all sorts of excuses not to go to work, instead boldly demanding blankets from the community funds with the use of threats. Please, please do not do anything to help make the journey possible or facilitate it for people who have not brought you a certificate of loyalty and good conduct from the Zionist committee in their place of residence or from the committee of the organization to which they belong. We must not be lenient in this regard because our lives depend on it.[84]

The director of the Haifa aliya bureau also complained about two young "pioneers" who went to Palestine and were subsequently found to be prostitutes. On March 23, 1926, the sisters, Malka and Chana, arrived from Danzig on the *Britannia*. At passport control in Jaffa port, they claimed that they had been accused of forging Polish banknotes and that their father had therefore smuggled them to Danzig so that they could move to Palestine. After disembarking in Haifa, they "went to Tel Aviv, where they wanted to be—according to them—and from there they went to Haifa, where they managed on their own. Now they are prostitutes and give themselves to Arabs for money. . . . I think such 'pioneers' should be deported, and if you approve this action I will contact the police on the matter."[85]

The Cost of Immigration to Palestine

Immigration to Palestine, as to any other destination, involved numerous expenses: a fee to the Palestine Office for handling the application; train fare (usually third class); the cost of food and lodging while waiting for the ship to sail; fees for loading the baggage onto the ship and unloading it in Palestine; the fare for the sea voyage (usually fourth class); the cost of food for the six-day sea voyage to Palestine; entry taxes in Palestine; and unanticipated expenses along the way.[86] In addition, the immigrants had to pay for entry visas to the countries they passed through on their way to the port of departure. The Yugoslavian visa, for instance, was generally issued on the train to Trieste, but in addition, there was a fee for simply crossing the country. To pass through Italy, the immigrants had to pay a border-crossing tax and an additional fee for an Italian visa.[87]

The estimation is that the cost of the journey to the immigrant was 190,000 Polish *marka*, equivalent to £73 in the 1920s (£4,200 today).[88] A family of six would have had to pay an estimated 1.1 million Polish marka, equal to £426 (£25,000 today). Due to high inflation in Poland and the decline in the value of the currency (which grew weaker by the day), it is hard to estimate the purchasing power of the Polish currency, but few prospective immigrants had the money needed for the journey. Many needed loans, which they requested from relatives or the Palestine Offices. The candidates from the youth movements were destitute, and their travel to Palestine had to be financed almost in full.

Immigration in the imperial era, before World War I, was easier and less expensive. The Jews of the Russian Empire sailed for Palestine from Odessa, whereas the Jews of Galicia and the Austro-Hungarian Empire sailed from Trieste. It was relatively simple to reach the ports of departure, and there was no need to cross international borders. After World War I, the process became much more expensive. Crossing the European continent between the two world wars involved passing through new nation-states, and about a quarter of the cost of immigration went to paying for visas, border crossings, and the various travel papers.[89]

The Palestine Offices helped the immigrants obtain the necessary documents and even covered some of the expenses of their journey. At a conference of Palestine Offices held in Jerusalem in March 1925, the heads of the offices complained that the entry tax and the British visa fee accounted for a sizable portion of the immigrants' travel expenses and that it was a heavy burden on the halutzim, the workers, and the aliya budget. They called on the Zionist Executive to reduce the fees and help create sources of income to support halutzim from various countries.[90]

In some cases, immigrants set out without sufficient funds and appealed to the Palestine Office for assistance. These requests, too, were a burden on the office. "Recently there have been numerous cases in which immigrants to Palestine left Poland without enough money to cover the costs of their journey, ignoring our warnings and requirements in this regard." They asked the Palestine Office in Vienna to help. "We hereby announce that any such request to the

Palestine Office in Vienna will be rejected and immigrants who leave Poland without sufficient money for the costs of the journey will have to remain in Vienna and not continue on their way. It should be noted that there have even been cases in which immigrants stated before setting out that they had the necessary sum and they signed this statement, and then when they reached Vienna they denied it."[91]

A calculation of the cost of immigration to Palestine and conversion of this cost into present-day sums indicates that it was an expensive undertaking and that ordinary immigrants had genuine difficulty raising the money. Most immigrants in category A (certificate recipients) had limited or no means. In the absence of financial assistance, many applicants had no choice but to give up on going to Palestine, despite having received aliya certificates and completed all the bureaucratic arrangements for the journey. These delays and cancellations caused great suffering to the applicants and were a source of tremendous discomfiture to the Zionist Executive, which had obtained the certificates but was unable to use them.

The Voyage to Palestine

As the sky turned gray, the ship neared the shores of Haifa. Shortly thereafter, a pink wreath appeared on the eastern fringes. Ahead of us we saw Mt. Carmel, adorned here and there with green groves, and with white houses in the middle. The sea devoured the golden sand dunes, with the bunches of tall palm trees jutting out from them. . . . The ship sailed along the coast. On the horizon, mountains turned black. Clusters of lights sparkled from towns. As we neared Jaffa, the wind brought with it the fragrant scent of orange blossoms.[92]

The big, old, dirty ship that had become filthy during the voyage, with its three hundred fifty passengers, dropped anchor in the sea of Jaffa. It was the beginning of winter. The sea lay quiet and still, as if oil had been poured on it, and lots of boats, big and small alike, with oars and with sails, plied its waters. None of them touched the ship or even came near it. As if it were defiled, as if they were ostracizing it. This was an immigrant ship. . . . The three hundred fifty immigrants, gaunt, hungry, and dirty, with skinny faces, wearing wrinkled, worn-out, filthy clothing and loaded down with parcels, burst forth out of the black arms of the ship's cabins below.[93]

This is how the arrival on the shores of Palestine is described in the memoirs of people of the Third Aliya and in a 1925 children's story by Moshe Smilansky.

According to the memoirs, written many years later, the newcomers, who had not yet entered the country, were captivated by the coastline of Jaffa and Haifa as seen from the deck of the ship. Standing on the deck, they smelled the citrus blossoms (even though the ships anchored about a kilometer from land) and they looked out at the Carmel range and the Hadar neighborhood of Haifa. They saw the mosques and homes of Jaffa, with their Muslim architectural style that differed so greatly from the familiar European landscape. In the memoirs of Ya'akov Midrashi and his fellows, they were lost children returning to their ancestral homeland. By returning to the land and embarking on a life of farming, they sought to re-create themselves as new, healthy Jews coming to build Palestine and to be transformed by it. Their journey to Palestine was a modern version of the return to Zion by a nation that had been exiled and returned home, been exiled again, and was now returning a second time after two thousand years.

In Moshe Smilansky's children's story, there is no coastline or scent of citrus blossoms. The immigrants were crammed into the belly of a stifling, rickety ship. They were dirty, hungry, and dressed in patched-up rags. When they went onto the deck, they "looked at the city that lay on the shore, stretched out their hands to it, prayed, and begged to be redeemed from captivity."[94] For them the voyage was not a return to Zion but an escape from economic hardship, persecution, and pogroms to a land of refuge.

The Jews' return to agriculture and to working the land, and in later years to the sea as well, was one of the cornerstones of Zionist ideology. At the inception of the Zionist movement, the sea was not perceived as having any inherent national significance. Beginning in the 1930s, however, a change occurred in the Zionist movement's attitude toward the sea: it gradually became a "Jewish sea," as various national projects and experiences imprinted it with Zionist meaning. The historian Maoz Azaryahu has shown how the sea became an integral part of everyday life for the people of Tel Aviv during the Mandate period and how their attitude toward it changed over time.[95]

As Tel Aviv grew during the 1920s, its homes and streets reached the shore, which became an attraction and a place for leisure activities and amusement. For eastern European Jews who were experiencing the Mediterranean climate for the first time, the beach was something special, refreshing, and completely new. Bathing in the sea became an integral part of how the eastern European immigrants spent their free time, especially on the Sabbath and festivals.[96] According to Azaryahu, the beach embodied the tension between secularism and tradition and between the New Yishuv and the Old Yishuv. Going to the beach on the Sabbath (rather than to the synagogue) was not just fun; it was a statement of principle that the emerging society in Palestine was new and different from that in Europe.[97]

Azaryahu has additional examples of the nationalization of the sea, both commercial and ideological, on behalf of Zionism. In 1924, an American Jewish group established the American Palestine Line, which operated a fixed route between New York and Palestine and brought a ship flying a Zionist flag to Haifa for the first time; that same year, a Sea Scouts youth movement was founded for Palestinian Jews. The General Federation of Jewish Labour inaugurated water sports competitions in 1928. Private entrepreneurs—aware of the sea's economic potential—bought ships and fishing boats.[98] A significant milestone in turning the sea into an integral part of the Zionist space was the opening of the port of Tel Aviv in 1936. Though small and of limited capacity, the port was "Hebrew" (i.e., Jewish run) and was a proud symbol of the integration of the sea into the geography of national revival.[99]

The historian Joachim Schlör saw the sea as a tool with which to track the migration experience of Jews from Germany in the 1930s. Based on diaries, memoirs, and photographs, Schlör reconstructed the voyage to Palestine from the point of view of the Jews fleeing Nazi Germany and their encounter with the local population in Palestine.[100] When they arrived in Tel Aviv, they changed the face of the city, detaching it from Arab Jaffa and turning it into a Jewish coastal city with a vibrant promenade and a bustling shoreline. The sea was a place to bathe and have fun but also a symbolic boundary separating the Jewish and Arab populations.

Kobi Cohen-Hattab's comprehensive book *Ha-Mahpekha ha-Yamit* (Maritime revolution) reinforces the distinctions made earlier by Azaryahu and Schlör. Cohen-Hattab argues that the Yishuv's conquest of the sea was not just part of an economic and occupational conflict between groups with common interests but also part of the national struggle for Palestine. The ports, Jewish seafaring, fishing communities, and maritime training strengthened the Yishuv and, along with labor and security, became integral parts of the formation of the new Jew, the "man of the land and sea," that the Zionist movement wanted to create in its image.[101]

Whereas Azaryahu, Schlör, and Cohen-Hattab address the various aspects of the sea in the emerging Zionist ideology and outlook, for most ordinary Jewish immigrants the sea had a single, prosaic meaning: it was an obstacle to be crossed as safely and quickly as possible. Many were preoccupied with day-to-day problems, the hardships of the journey, and fears regarding the future.

For them, the ship was merely an efficient though uncomfortable vehicle taking them from one port to another one at the far end of the Mediterranean Basin.

The voyage from the European ports to Palestine lasted about a week. During this time, an interesting dynamic developed among the passengers who had come together, completely at random, on board the ship. They included families and single people, women and men, religious and secular Jews, ardent Zionists, and refugees fleeing Europe to the only country that would take them. They all shared a space where they slept, ate, prayed, talked, and argued before arriving in Palestine and going their separate ways. The gap between the heroic image of the return to Zion and the rough, taxing journey by land and by sea demonstrates the complexity of migration in general and immigration to Palestine in particular.

Before boarding the ship, the immigrants had to go through inspections and an identification process. "Before sailing, the olim receive tickets from us for the ship, which we obtain from Lloyd Triestino in exchange for the appropriate vouchers."[102] Their particulars were recorded in an orderly, precise manner at the Palestine Office at the request of the Zionist Executive so that information could be provided to family members asking about them while they were en route. The passengers underwent another medical exam on the ship, while the Palestine Office obtained exit permits for them from the local police.

Dealing with the immigrants' belongings was one of the most complicated issues of all for the coastal Palestine Offices. Each person was permitted to send three items weighing one hundred kilograms each. They were supposed to pack their belongings in such a way that they could be opened by border-control officials. Each item had a tag with the immigrant's name and address and the city from which he or she was sailing to Palestine.[103] When they reached Palestine, immigrants picked up their belongings from the aliya bureau in Jaffa or Haifa.

In their first few years, the Palestine Offices were not set up to handle the immigrants' baggage. This service was provided by the Jewish Company for Travel and Cargo Transport to Palestine—Ma'avirim. The company, which had branches in the major Jewish centers, acted as a broker between the Palestine Office and both the railway offices in Europe and the shipping companies whose vessels plied the Mediterranean. Its representatives were in contact with the Palestine Offices, and they negotiated with the management of the European railroads and the shipping companies over fares and cargo transport costs. Ma'avirim ran into financial difficulties in its first year and asked the American Jewish judge Louis Marshall to help it find an investor in the United States. "Although less than a year has passed since we embarked on our activity, we can state that we have achieved a lot with respect to the technical management of immigration to Palestine, and this has given us a good name. All the more so, as we are motivated by Zionism and are working in cooperation with the Palestine Office in Vienna and the other offices in the various cities where we have branches."[104]

Despite describing its motivations as Zionist, Ma'avirim was a private company that worked with but not under the Zionist Organization. Therefore, the company sought financing from wealthy Jewish investors. "Due to our poor financial situation, our Jewish brethren outside Palestine must fortify us. We stress explicitly that this is not a donation but an interest-bearing financial investment with full securities. Capital may be placed at our disposal either through a loan or through membership in the company. As far as we are concerned, the minimum participation is 1,000 Krone, but we leave it to you to suggest a minimum."[105]

There were many complaints about Ma'avirim; these were passed on to the Zionist Executive in Jerusalem and to the Palestine Offices. Passengers complained that they were being overcharged for sending their belongings to Palestine. They complained about lost property, about being given incorrect information, and about costs that turned out to be higher than necessary. Ma'avirim was, as stated, a private company whose owners were aware of the economic potential of immigration. But in its dealings with the immigrants, it created the impression that it was an integral part of the aliya bureau. On numerous occasions, immigrants' complaints were directed to the Palestine Offices even though these offices had no commercial relationship with the company. "We would like to draw your attention to a stumbling block in the way of immigrants bound for Palestine in the form of the Ma'avirim transport and travel company," the director of the Mizrachi labor bureau in Palestine wrote to the Zionist Commission. "According to what people abroad are hearing, this company declares itself a Zionist company whose stated goal is to facilitate the journey and the transport of cargo to Palestine. The immigrants hand over their parcels to Ma'avirim with complete trust, and when they arrive in Palestine most of the immigrants complain bitterly about the Ma'avirim management. Obtaining their belongings from the company usually involves shouting, quarrels, and legal action."[106]

The aliya bureaus in Palestine received many letters of complaint about the company, and an investigation they conducted found that the complaints were justified: the company was exploiting their dependence in the name of the Zionist idea and was stealing their money. It was therefore decided that the Palestine Offices would take over cargo transport arrangements as an integral part of their work with the immigrants:

Figure 4.8. Luggage in the port of Trieste. Photo courtesy of CZA, PHG\1078857.

The resolutions adopted by Zionist congresses against the private Jewish cargo transport companies were worded especially sharply in 1924. We must admit that there were grounds to all the allegations against these companies, as the facts have proven in the course of time. As a result of these resolutions, all the Palestine Offices have taken on the task of transporting the immigrants and their belongings. The job is always done devotedly and accurately, so the immigrants put their complete trust in the Palestine Offices to transport them and their belongings. This has put an end to all the immigrants' complaints about late, poor-quality, irresponsible shipments—complaints that in previous years marked a dismal chapter in the history of Jewish immigration to Palestine.[107]

From then on, the aliya process was in the hands of the Zionist Executive and under the watchful eye of the aliya bureau in Jerusalem from start to finish. From the moment people decided to emigrate until they arrived in Palestine, they received advice and assistance from sources authorized by the Zionist Executive. Private and foreign individuals and companies had no access to them, and every stage of migration was overseen and monitored.

Figure 4.9. Immigrants' belongings watched over by Italian customs officials. Photo courtesy of CZA, PHG\1006656.

The immigrants traveled to Palestine to settle there, and they brought with them everything they could to help them in their new lives in the new land. The letters of complaint to the Aliya Department in Jerusalem from passengers who had lost their luggage give us a glimpse into the contents of their cargo. Immigrants were asked to sew onto each piece of luggage a piece of white fabric stating their names and parcel numbers. After depositing their belongings at the port of departure, they would receive vouchers. The belongings of immigrants who sailed on the deck of the ship were usually packed in baskets rather than suitcases. Yisrael Keller arrived in Palestine with three parcels: "2 big baskets sewn with a piece of cloth and tied with ropes, 1 small box with iron bands. Around it is written the name." Michael Gartenberg arrived with a package of pillows and a bicycle. Nota Goloboti brought three parcels: the first containing pillows, the second underwear, and the third various tools. His name was written on each of them, and "all are bound with iron bands." Batya Gurwitz brought a sewing machine wrapped in fabric and a box with her name written on a piece of white fabric near the top. Yehuda Stab brought three parcels: one big basket, a package of pillows and duvets, and a box containing tools.[108] The most common items among their belongings seem to have been pillows and duvets, which may have been better suited to the European winter than to the hot Middle Eastern climate.

But the significance of the bedding went deeper than their simple function. In the late nineteenth century, the Russian economist Andrei Pavlovich Subbotin published his book *V cherte evreiskoi osedlosti* (*In the Jewish Pale of Settlement*). The first part of the book came out in 1888, and the second in 1890. Subbotin crossed the Pale of Settlement from north to south. He stopped in cities and towns, visited Jewish neighborhoods, entered the homes of Jews, and described them and their lives without embellishment and without sparing his readers any detail. Among other things, Subbotin described the furniture and the bedding: "But the height of glory is the bed, with a big feather duvet and a pile of pillows. As a rule, the Jews love to have lots of junk (*bebekhes*) and glory in abundant bedding."[109] Subbotin added that when Jews married off their daughters, pillows and bedding were important components of their dowries. "And those pillows, being the main luxuries, are what is confiscated in other towns from those who fail to make their regular payments to the community, and they are kept as a guarantee until payment is made."[110] Thus, it comes as no surprise that the immigrants brought with them to Palestine the pillows, duvets, and other bedding that attested to their financial status and were a major component of the young women's dowries.

Some people brought housewares and valuables. Ida Levin, whom we will meet again in the next chapter, brought gold jewelry, but it was stolen from her while she was undergoing disinfection. Chaim Lederman brought silverware and kitchen items: "Dear Sir, I am writing to you with a request. On Tuesday, August 4, I arrived on the *Romania* and I lost one parcel containing the following items: two small silver spoons, three phials with medicaments, cups and bowls, and other food and objects that I will not specify. The parcel is made of straw and tied with a thick rope. Please inform the Jerusalem aliya bureau if this parcel is found and send it to the Jerusalem aliya bureau for me."[111]

In the 1920s, ships from fourteen companies visited the shores of Palestine each week. The ten main ones were Lloyd Triestino, Società Italiana di Servizi Marittimi (SITMAR), Serviciul Maritim Român (SMR), Messageries Maritimes, Deutsche Orient-Linie, the Khedivial Mail Line, the National Greek Line, Les Affrêtteurs Réunis, Lloyd Royal Belge, and the Fabre Line.[112]

The two most active companies, and those preferred by the Jewish migrants, were Lloyd Triestino, which sailed from Trieste to Palestine every Friday at one o'clock in the afternoon, and SMR, which sailed from Constanţa on Fridays at five o'clock in the evening once every three weeks.[113] Conditions on both companies' ships in the first half of the 1920s were dreadful: "There is no place to sleep, there is no place to bathe, and the lavatories are unspeakably bad, not meeting the minimal laws of any country."[114] In many respects conditions were particularly bad for women, who had to share the bathrooms and sleeping quarters with men.[115] In the absence of suitable living quarters, passengers spent most of their days on deck. "It should be added that there is nowhere for people to sleep, and the passengers spend entire nights sitting in rented chairs. They cannot change their clothes for days and nights on end."[116] Another problem concerned the provision of food during the voyage. The shipping companies did not provide meals; passengers had to buy provisions for the voyage at the port of departure and wherever the ship anchored on the way to Palestine. Those who did not stock up or whose provisions ran out or spoiled went hungry and needed the assistance of their fellow passengers. In the children's story published in *Shibolim*, David'l the immigrant describes to his friends back in Warsaw (the children reading the newspaper) the conditions on the sea voyage to Palestine:

> A day after we left Venice, our ship started wobbling a bit because the sea was much stormier than it had been until then. Many of the people who were with us became sick at that point; their heads were spinning like wheels and all their insides felt as though they were turning over. My father gave them a few of the lemons that we had brought with us from Trieste, on my mother's instructions. Although we weren't affected by this sickness, we were cold at night while lying on the bedding that we spread out for ourselves on the deck of the ship. Reb Baruch-Noach the Caucasian, who had promised to prepare us for the heat in Palestine, almost froze one night when there was a constant drizzle and he was lying on the thin blanket that he had spread out as bedding at one edge of the ship. So we started going down into the belly of the ship at night, to the engine room, where the clattering engines emitted tremendous heat. The sailors and the ship's officers didn't stop us from warming ourselves up by the machines; they knew that we passengers were miserable and couldn't afford to pay a lot of money for the warm ship's cabins where the rich passengers stayed.[117]

There were two reasons for the terrible conditions. The first was the quality of the ships. Some were cargo ships that had been hastily converted into passenger ships after World War I and were unsuitable for carrying people. The second reason was that the shipping companies tried to maximize profits by selling too many tickets, despite the shortage of space on board: "One of the main reasons seems to be that tickets are being sold to halutzim in numbers that exceed the ships' capacity. We must use all possible means to prevent . . . such

Figure 4.10. Immigrants' baggage. Photo courtesy of CZA, PHG\1006678.

crowding of the halutzim traveling on Lloyd ships. We have been informed by [the people in] Palestine that many of the halutzim coming from Trieste are arriving in Palestine broken and ill, and this seems to be mainly because of conditions during their voyage on the Lloyd ships."[118]

The passengers' poor physical condition due to the terrible hygiene on board was of grave concern to the heads of the aliya bureau. They were worried that the immigrants would not be in good enough health after the six-day voyage to pass the medical exams conducted by the Mandatory government and that the British doctors would not let them into the country:

> The laws regarding disinfection on the shores of Palestine, which the immigrants find so annoying, are based on conditions during the voyage. Because of these unsanitary conditions, Jewish immigrants to Palestine have acquired a reputation for being unclean. This is the basis for the attitude of the authorities and the ship's officers toward them. Because in practice there is no fourth class, and instead they set up the deck as a place to sleep, the passengers in the other classes have complained about the Jewish passengers. Hence the shipping company's attitude towards these passengers, which is by no means respectful.[119]

Figure 4.11. Boarding the ship. Photo courtesy of CZA, PHG\1006680.

Zionist officials were worried about Mandatory government officials even seeing the immigrants on the ships. Their concern was that the passengers' appearance—exhausted and dirty from the voyage—might cast the Zionist enterprise in an undignified light and be detrimental to national pride. "On multiple occasions I have heard from people coming to escort the olim to the shore that the disembarkation process degrades us and the Jewish people." While waiting for British officials after the ship dropped anchor off the shores of Palestine, passengers pushed one another, "and sometimes even [pushed] women and hapless infants, without looking to see whom they were shoving. The screams reached the high heavens. Of course, this did not induce the sailors on the ship to treat the Jewish immigrants politely and respectfully."[120] The newcomers to the country were often a source of embarrassment and worry for Zionist officials.

However, Lloyd Triestino also had complaints about the Zionist Executive representatives and the Jewish immigrants. Letters of complaint from the shipping company indicate that the reality was complex and not one sided: some passengers dishonestly obtained discounts to which they were not entitled, broke the rules, and bribed sailors. The "customer" that the Palestine Offices had promised the shipping companies was not necessarily a quiet, pleasant passenger but rather a demanding, stubborn, undisciplined one.

> Since last year Lloyd Triestino has been showing signs of extreme annoyance with us. . . . They continue to complain that affluent people are using the immigrant discount [and] that tourists are using the discount as well. Our passengers buy tickets for the deck and then think to obtain good cabins by bribing sailors on the ship. We heard these complaints all the time, but especially when our Trieste office had to renew the contract. Everyone heard that Lloyd Triestino was considering not renewing our contract [unless] we agreed to exclude categories A and B from the discount recipients.[121]

To improve conditions, the Palestine Offices negotiated with the shipping companies and signed contracts with them requiring certain changes. Lloyd Triestino (and other shipping companies), aware of the economic potential of immigration to Palestine, tried to compromise with them. There was an American precedent of which the Zionist Organization was aware, and it sought to reach a contractual agreement with the shipping companies with similar terms.

In the second half of the nineteenth century, the US Congress had enacted a series of laws requiring shipping companies to provide passengers with decent, more humane conditions. The purpose of these laws was to protect immigrants from the high-handedness of the shipping companies during the long voyage from Europe to America. The laws limited the number of immigrants on the ships and required the shipping companies to provide passengers with suitable food and reasonable living conditions. Because the companies did not always obey the laws and sometimes violated passengers' rights, the American immigration authorities sent undercover agents posing as immigrants to inspect conditions on board.[122]

The Zionist movement, too, sought to require the shipping companies to improve conditions, but it was aware of its limitations. "We have to remember that conditions on the voyage to America also evolved somewhat. At first they were completely inhumane, and only by exerting its power was the American government able to bring conditions up to a level that met minimum standards."[123] Unlike the US Congress, which had the power to enforce its laws, the Zionist Executive had no means of pressuring the companies. The volume of immigration to Palestine was much smaller than that of transatlantic migration. "Unfortunately, we do not even have the power to influence the ships' sailing schedule, much less conditions on the voyage. We can achieve this only through successful commercial tactics that will empower us to make demands of the companies."[124]

Despite the problems and limitations, on April 28, 1921, the Zionist Executive signed a contract with Lloyd Triestino, with rules for the voyage to Palestine that included improved conditions. The company agreed to have a Jewish ship's doctor and undertook to enforce the rules of the emigration authorities in Trieste regarding sanitary conditions. The company also agreed to provide each passenger with a bed and blanket (two blankets during the cold months), and no passenger was to be placed below the water line. A telegraph system was to be installed on board and arrangements made for kosher food to be sold at affordable prices. Furthermore, the contract stated that if a ship did not sail on schedule, the shipping company would assume responsibility for meeting all the passengers' needs until the next voyage. The duration of the voyage, according to the contract, was to be 144 hours (six days), except in cases of delays due to bad weather, force majeure, or any other factor not dependent on the company's goodwill. In addition, Lloyd Triestino agreed to give the heads of the Zionist movement or someone of their choice a free cabin for every twenty cabins booked and three free tickets for every hundred tickets purchased by the Zionist Organization. Zionist representatives would be allowed to inspect conditions on board, speak with passengers, and make sure that the company was abiding by its commitments.[125]

In September 1923, as the expiration date of its contract with the Zionist Organization drew near, Lloyd Triestino sent a representative to a meeting of Palestine Office representatives in Carlsbad to renew the contract.[126] Dramatic changes were taking place in Jewish migration routes, and the Italian shipping company was concerned about a drop in profits. The increased flow of emigration from Poland (and neighboring countries) had gradually turned Constanța into the Zionist Organization's main port of departure, and the Palestine Offices in Warsaw and Romania had signed contracts with the Romanian shipping company SMR and with the Fabre Line. The renewal of the contract with Lloyd Triestino was a good opportunity to demand further improvements in conditions on the voyage. To maintain its position as a leading shipping company, Lloyd Triestino offered perks and discounted fares and substantially improved conditions on board its ships. The company also made three ships—the *Carniolia,* the *Gianicolo,* and the *Trento*—available exclusively to the Zionist Organization and for the first time inaugurated a direct route between Trieste and Palestine without a stop at Alexandria on the way; that stop had been a source of tremendous hardship for the passengers.

Ships bound for Palestine played host to a fascinating six-day encounter that replicated the life that passengers could expect in Palestine: tensions between religious and secular passengers and between ideological Zionists (olim and halutzim) and ordinary immigrants and refugees migrating due to physical distress; social solidarity and shared fate but also apathy and selfishness; political awareness and ad hoc aid committees established during the voyage for the immigrants; and even a newspaper that documented the voyage to Palestine for reasons of historical consciousness. Life together on board the ship, with the intense relationships among the passengers, was thus a microcosm of Jewish life in Palestine.

The voyage of the *Ruslan* is an interesting test case of the social dynamic that developed en route from Odessa to Palestine. The encounter between the halutzim and Zionist activists and the refugees is particularly interesting considering the different motivations that brought the two groups to Palestine. The first group was migrating for ideological reasons; the second group included survivors of the pogroms who were fleeing Ukraine. The prolonged voyage, which lasted about a month, was a golden opportunity for the Zionists to win over their fellow passengers to the Zionist ideology and to prepare them mentally for their arrival in Palestine. No longer a mere passenger ship taking olim, immigrants, exiles, and refugees to Palestine, the *Ruslan* became a center for Zionist indoctrination. The Zionist passengers created a humor publication entitled *Tevat Noah* (Noah's ark), devoted to "affairs of the 'prisoners' on board the *Ruslan*." Its editor, the journalist and humorist Chaim Katznelson, set out its goals in the introduction:

> The ship's committee, in view of its great concern for making the voyage pleasant for the passengers—the same committee that will be making all the nice, pleasing arrangements on our ship, the same committee that made sure that each and every passenger would have a special place to sit and lie down and that no one would suffer "thirst for water and hunger for bread," the same committee that has worked hard to ensure that we do not spend even one extra hour en route—has also arranged for the publication of a newspaper on board, so that the refugees know what is happening in our world and so that the Jews know what the committee has done for them. Let us, then, be grateful to the committee for all the good and the kindness that it is doing for us.[127]

By drawing a parallel with Noah's ark, Katznelson associated the *Ruslan* with the biblical account of salvation from the flood as well as the return to Zion, Cyrus's declaration, and the Exodus from Egypt. "In the year one thousand eight hundred fifty since the destruction, the Lord caused it to be proclaimed throughout the camp.... The heavens are the heavens of the Lord, but the earth He gave to men, and He has commanded us to build Him a house in Jerusalem, which is in Judah. Whosoever there is among you of all His people, a survivor and refugee—may the Lord his God be with him—let him go up to build the house of the Lord God of Israel."[128] Katznelson also tried to spark a discussion about the renewal of Jewish immigration to Palestine and to explain to the refugees and immigrants the historic importance of the event in which they were taking part. "In order for things to be more or less clear to every reader, we find it necessary to explain the history of this aliya in brief." He coined the phrase "Third Aliya" and explained its history succinctly:

> During the war a certain number of Palestine residents were in Russia and could not return to Palestine. Once it became known that the British had conquered Palestine, these people started trying to get permission to return home. This was very difficult vis-à-vis both the British authorities and the Russian authorities.... Along with these people came large numbers of those who yearned for the Land. It was as hard as the parting of the Red Sea. They spent almost an entire year looking for a suitable ship until they finally found the *Ruslan*. The ship's owners undertook to transport six hundred fifty people, although there was really only room on board for half that. The crowding on the ship was inestimable and led to many complaints. In addition, the ship spent twice as long [as it was supposed to] en route.... As a result the provisions that the passengers had prepared for themselves ran out and they anticipated that they would go hungry.[129]

Despite the terrible conditions during the voyage and "all the trials and tribulations that the passengers suffered, for the most part an elevated mood prevailed and they spent most of their time on singing and dancing, lectures and speeches."[130] The newspaper, written during the voyage in late 1919 in the middle of the civil war, is a fascinating document that shows how immigrants and refugees could be converted to Zionism even before they reached Palestine. However, this was an exceptional voyage, with a group of passengers who belonged to the Zionist aristocracy. On most voyages, no satirical newspapers were published, and passengers did not rub elbows with Zionists who had such a well-developed historical consciousness. For most ordinary immigrants, the voyage was one more hurdle to be crossed on their way to the new land.

On one voyage of the Lloyd Triestino ship *Trento*, a group of passengers organized to protest the poor conditions on board. The hunger and crowding during the six-day voyage had brought them together and given them common

Figure 4.12. The Lloyd Triestino ship *Trento*. Photo courtesy of CZA, PHAL\1600040.

cause. The *Trento* passengers decided to form a committee that would present their claims and would thereby help future passengers as well. They chose a chair, a deputy chair, a secretary, and committee members to represent all the passengers. This committee organized the immigrants' complaints in a memorandum, which they sent to the heads of the aliya bureau in Jerusalem after arriving in Palestine. "The ship's committee . . . in submitting this memorandum, has set itself the goal of highlighting the negative aspects of the institutions and companies involved in aliya and demanding that the top authorities of the Zionist Organization use the necessary financial means to remove, as soon as possible, all obstacles in the way of the masses immigrating to Palestine, who are encountering various stumbling blocks every step of the way."[131]

The passengers criticized the terrible service provided by Ma'avirim and protested the Palestine Offices' dependence on the company. "This company must do its important job. It is providing both the halutzim and the immigrants to Palestine with incorrect, untrue information in order to exploit them as they cross borders and travel by rail, as well as while transporting their cargo and belongings by land and by sea."[132] The ship's passengers shared their stories and hardships with the committee, including examples of how Ma'avirim had deceived them and stolen their money. But the dreadful conditions on board the *Trento* were the passengers' greatest hardship. This ship, built in 1901, had been used as a hospital ship during World War I and had never been converted properly into a passenger ship. "On our ship, the *Trento*, there are 250 people crowded into the lower part of the ship, which has a maximum capacity of 100 people." The belly of the ship was dark, the "atmosphere suffocating," and there were "coal remnants" present. Passengers who wanted to go up on deck to breathe fresh air were turned back by the sailors. "In addition, there is our prickly relationship with the ship's officers, who regard us hostilely and bar us from various parts of the deck."[133] Given all these factors, the committee asked the Jerusalem aliya bureau to make the following changes in the immigration procedure:

1. Having all institutions and companies involved in aliya provide correct information;
2. [Obtaining] a report on the spending of money paid to Ma'avirim;
3. Giving groups immigrating to Palestine special railroad cars to send cargoes directly from place to place together with their owners;
4. Sending an escort and having Ma'avirim fulfill all of its commitments;
5. Setting a maximum number of passengers for the ship in accordance with feasibility and the ship's normal capacity;
6. Providing the most basic hygienic conditions on board the ship;
7. Resolving the dispute between the Palestine Office and Ma'avirim in Trieste.[134]

The memorandum from the *Trento* ship's committee is interesting not only for the description of the voyage from the immigrants' perspective but also because of the initiative to organize and establish an actual committee. Even before they arrived in Palestine and became immersed in political activity and life there, they had already formed a committee to protect the interests of a group of Jews who had come together by chance on a ship bound for Palestine. The immigrants' expectation that the Zionist institutions would take care of them made immigration to Palestine different from immigration to any of the Jews' other destinations. Jews bound for Palestine relied on the Zionist institutions to handle all arrangements for the voyage. Whenever problems arose (even if they were entirely the immigrants' responsibility), the address for their complaints was the Zionist Executive and the people in charge of it. These expectations, which had developed in Europe or during the sea voyage to Palestine, would remain with the immigrants throughout their lives in Palestine.

The ship was also a place for activism for the religious olim in the Mizrachi movement. They regarded the voyage as an excellent opportunity to spread their religious-Zionist ideology and especially to promote Sabbath observance, both on the ship and afterward in Palestine. "While still on the ship, every member of our movement should feel this great event in his life: He has a privilege that Moses and Aaron did not have. He has the privilege of seeing the wonderful, longed-for land."[135] Like Chaim Katznelson, the Mizrachi olim associated aliya with biblical accounts and extolled the great privilege they had of settling in the Land of Israel. They were tasked with uniting and organizing during the voyage, demonstrating their presence and conducting political activities: "From the very first steps of the journey, we must all call attention to our organization. All of our members traveling on the ship must join together in one group as the Mizrachi convoy ... and conduct conversations and lectures about the doings and developments in the world of Mizrachi."[136]

Beyond politics, however, Mizrachi members saw it as their responsibility to make the voyage more Jewish and more religiously meaningful for the other passengers as well. "Our members crossing the sea en route to our land are duty bound to take action, get others active, and influence others as well." To this end, they were asked to act in several ways:

Public prayer: "Our members must make sure that public prayer services are held three times a day in the designated place." Mizrachi members were requested not "to pray by themselves but rather to fulfill the mitzvah of public prayer, thereby setting an example for others." **Torah study**: "There is no better place for public Torah study than the ship. There are no annoying interruptions, and the entire day is at your disposal. Between the heavens and the sea, the sound of Torah must be heard every day while the ship sails." **Kosher food**: Members were to make sure there was kosher food available because the passengers included "many of our brethren who are repulsed by nonkosher foods that dull body and soul alike." Because "traveling to our land should uplift the soul so as to elevate and sanctify life," Mizrachi members were duty bound "to exert widespread influence on the passengers, suitably and appropriately, to eat only in a kosher kitchen." **Sabbath observance**: "Promoting the cause of the sanctity of the Sabbath, the nation's queen and its glory, should begin during the voyage, while on the ship, before our brethren set foot onto our holy land." Mizrachi asked its members to turn the voyage into a public-relations campaign among the passengers on behalf of the Sabbath, emphasizing its importance both on the ship and in life in Palestine. "Our members must be the influencers and must explain what the Sabbath was for us in exile: the mother who sustained us throughout the generations and in all times. . . . Many of the Sabbath desecrators in Palestine lack knowledge about how valuable the Sabbath is to our national existence, and it is important, while still on board the ship, for every Jew to hear about the essence and value of the Sabbath. To this end, on the Sabbath our members who are traveling should organize a Sabbath party that will sanctify the Sabbath among the Jews."[137]

The issue of kosher food on Palestine-bound ships was of great concern to Mizrachi. The organization put a great deal of effort into convincing the aliya bureau of the importance of the matter and even negotiated on its own with the shipping companies to make the ships' kitchens kosher. Representatives of the movement were sent to the ports of departure, visited the ships, and inspected the kashrut arrangements. The difficulties they encountered were twofold: stocking the ship with kosher food in the port of departure and arranging for workers who would run a kosher kitchen on the voyage itself. "We reiterate again and again that so long as we have not ensured the quality of the slaughtering, inspection, and porging of the meat in Trieste and the kashrut arrangements on the ship itself . . . we will not take any responsibility and in any case will not provide support to the cooks and inspectors."[138] The insistence on kashrut on the ships was not only intended to make the voyage to Palestine easier for the religious passengers; it was also a matter of principle that reflected the Mizrachi movement's desire to give life in Palestine a religious character in accordance with its beliefs. Achieving this aim began with making the ships' kitchens kosher and ensuring mitzvah observance during the voyage: "Let it be clear to you: The Mizrachi Federation is an organization of Orthodox Jews that sees to it that the building of the country and the life of the Jewish people in general are consistent with the spirit of the Torah. Based on this outlook, we have agreed to take on kashrut supervision on the ships and assume the expenses this entails."[139]

The Zionist Organization recognized the importance of kashrut on board the ships, but it could not afford to pay for a kashrut supervisor and staff of Jewish cooks. Therefore, Mizrachi informed the Zionist Organization in late August 1926 of its decision, passed at the movement's world conference in Antwerp at the beginning of the month, to support kashrut supervisors, cooks, and other workers for the kosher kitchens on the Lloyd Triestino ships and the *Dacia* (belonging to SMR).[140] Mizrachi chose to send Rabbi Yehuda Leib Fishman, a member of the Mizrachi World Center who was in Romania at the time, on the *Dacia* to study conditions on the voyage up close. To this end they asked to "immediately telegraph their representative in Constanța with instructions to try to obtain a ticket for the *Dacia* for Rabbi Fishman, who, as the representative of Mizrachi, will be able to investigate kashrut matters there and on the ship."[141]

In December 1926, the Mizrachi movement sent out a notice to all immigrants, the Hebrew-language press, and the Yiddish press in Europe about the state of kashrut on the ships:

> The aliya department of the Mizrachi World Center in Jerusalem hereby announces that of the three ships *Trento, Carniolia,* and *Gianicolo,* belonging to Lloyd Triestino and sailing directly from Trieste to the shores of Palestine, only two, the *Trento* and the *Carniolia,* have kosher kitchens under the supervision of Mizrachi. The third ship, the *Gianicolo,* has no kosher kitchen. The Mizrachi aliya department considers itself duty bound to declare and warn that none of the Fabre Line ships that come to Palestine or the fast Lloyd Triestino ships on the Trieste-Alexandria route have absolutely kosher kitchens. On the SMR ship *Dacia,* too, which sails from Constanța to Palestine, the kitchen is not considered kosher. Negotiations over the appointment of a kashrut supervisor and arrangements for a kosher kitchen on that ship are still in progress, being conducted through the Zionist Executive in Palestine.[142]

When World War I ended, Jewish immigration to Palestine resumed, and tens of thousands of olim, immigrants, and refugees attempted to go there. The Zionist movement prepared for the new arrivals and assumed responsibility for organizing migration, both in Palestine and in Europe. Within a short time, the movement had established a well-ordered hierarchy of Palestine Offices that implemented the Zionist and British immigration policy and helped Jews reach Palestine. The establishment of these offices in almost every place in the world from which Jews were immigrating to Palestine can give us an idea of the impressive organizational ability of the Zionist leadership, which succeeded in implementing the resolutions adopted at the various Zionist conferences and congresses and served as the leading player in building up the country.

The Palestine Offices handled all aspects of immigration: obtaining entry visas to Palestine and preparing travel papers, scheduling interviews with the British consuls, conducting medical exams for prospective immigrants, sending their belongings to Palestine, escorting them to the ports of departure and solving problems that arose on the way, negotiating with the shipping companies over conditions on the voyage, and purchasing tickets for the trains and

Figure 4.13. En route to Palestine. Photo courtesy of CZA, PHG\1006687.

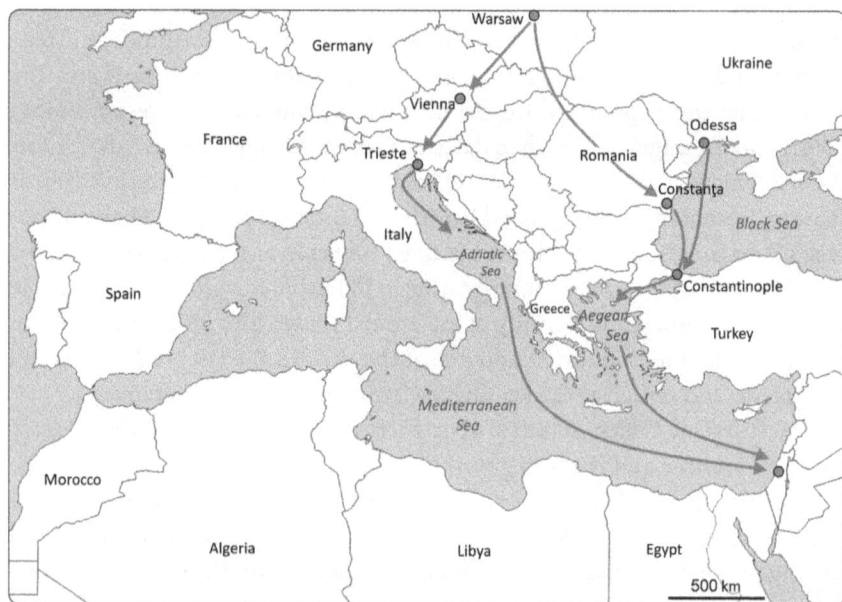

Map 4.1. Routes from Europe to Palestine.

ships. Were it not for the Palestine Offices, it is doubtful whether one hundred thousand Jewish immigrants would have reached Palestine in the first decade of the Mandate. These offices enabled the Zionist movement to oversee the immigration process fully and closely from start to finish. The aliya bureau ensured compliance with the Zionist and British immigration policy. In addition, through direct, close contact with the heads of the Palestine Offices, it learned about the difficulties and challenges they had to deal with following the changes in the immigration laws and the political and social changes in Europe.

From the bureaucracy of immigration, organization and management of immigration, its costs, and the actual bringing of immigrants, an effort was made (sometimes overtly and sometimes behind the scenes) to lend the journey an ideological Zionist hue. In almost every stage of the journey, the Zionist Executive attempted to influence the composition of the immigrant population, both by giving preference in the distribution of entry permits to certain applicants over others and by inculcating Zionist principles in the immigrants while they waited to make the journey and on the ships themselves. Its aim in all this was to prepare them for life in Palestine and ensure that they would build up the country and be transformed by it.

5

Reaching the Shore

Until the outbreak of World War I, there was no orderly entry procedure into Palestine for immigrants. Passenger ships would anchor about a kilometer from the shore and wait for the Arab boatmen to row out to them. Using rope ladders, the boatmen would then take the passengers and their belongings into their small boats, which rocked on the waves, and row them to shore. When the sea was stormy, it was an unpleasant and even dangerous experience. On the shore, the immigrants underwent a brief classification process: they were asked to declare their property and deposit their passports (if they had them), and they were given a red slip of paper allowing them to stay in Palestine for three months. When the Ottoman authorities forbade an immigrant to enter the country, the consul or his representative would intervene on the person's behalf and force the Ottoman official to provide an entry permit. Most immigrants spent their first days in the country in a hotel in Jaffa.

When immigration to Palestine resumed after World War I, the admission procedure took place in accordance with the regulations stipulated in the Mandatory government ordinances and the aliya bureau procedures. Orderly records were kept, the immigrants were disinfected and given medical examinations, and sick immigrants were sent to a quarantine camp. Immigrant homes were established in Jaffa, Haifa, and Jerusalem; there, immigrants received hot meals, a place to sleep, and information about job options in Palestine. The stay in these homes eased the immigrants' first days in the country and prevented exploitation and cheating of newcomers not yet familiar with the mores of the land and its various characters. These immigrant homes were in many ways a microcosm of the life that awaited them in Palestine. During their brief stays in them, the newcomers met Palestine residents, both Jews and Arabs; learned a little about the situation in the country and about economic prospects; and were visited by representatives of the various political movements, which viewed them as potential supporters and recruits.

This chapter traces the Jewish immigrants from the moment they disembarked until their arrival at the immigrant homes: the disembarkation itself, the bureaucratic procedures they underwent upon arrival, the medical exams, and their daily routines in the immigrant homes.

Jewish Immigrants and Arab Boatmen

In Moshe Smilansky's children's story "Al ha-Saf" (On the threshold), mentioned in previous chapters, ten-year-old Shaul, an orphan whose parents were killed in a pogrom in Ukraine, is not permitted to enter Palestine because he does not have travel papers and an entry visa. The heads of the aliya bureau in Tel Aviv try to get him a special entry permit, despite British opposition, and attempt to prevent his ship from sailing back to Europe. It is the chief boatman in Jaffa, Abu Ali, who comes to the orphan boy's aid. Abu Ali is "a head taller than all his fellows. Over two meters. His two legs were like two marble pillars, his chest was broad and prominent, and his two hands were like two iron bars." After he helps the other passengers off the ship, Abu Ali goes back to the ship with his boatmen, climbs aboard by means of a rope ladder, and smuggles the boy off in his wide trousers without anyone seeing or knowing.

> Abu Ali ordered his men to tie a rope from the boat to the railing of the ship. He leaped onto the ladder and, quick as lightning, climbed up to the third-class deck. His eyes rested on a boy standing next to the railing, his gaze fixed on the boat and on the sailors who were climbing and tying a rope to the railing. Abu Ali touched his hand to his back. When the boy saw the "Ishmaelite," his face lit up. Abu Ali did not delay even a moment. He motioned to the boy to follow him down to one of the ship's cabins. The boy went after him, his heart full of trust. When they reached a hidden corner, Abu Ali stood and, in one quick motion, untied his wide trousers and dropped them. The boy saw before him two long, powerful, hairy legs. Come! The boy approached him and Abu Ali tied him securely to one of his legs. The boy watched everything being done to him in astonishment, but fearlessly and without worry. Abu Ali pulled his trousers back up and tied them. The boy was swallowed up in the trousers and no one knew he was inside.[1]

Figure 5.1. A chief boatman. Photo courtesy of CZA, PHO\1350249.

The story, published in the children's newspaper *Ben Artzi*, was intended to improve young Jews' image of the Arab inhabitants of the country. Smilansky was a member of the First Aliya, a farmer and author who wrote extensively about the lives of Arabs in Palestine. He was affiliated with Brit Shalom, an organization that promoted the idea of binational autonomy in Palestine. In his

1926 story, there is no tension between Jews and Arabs but rather a shared fate and mutual responsibility, represented by the smuggling of a Jewish boy into the country. Not only did Jewish immigration to Palestine pose no threat to the Arab majority, but the two peoples could live together in peace and brotherhood. However, this children's story was a far cry from reality. Disembarkation of the Jewish passengers by Arab boatmen was accompanied by extreme tension and sometimes confrontations with the passengers and the Mandatory immigration authorities. Ismain Nasrat, the chief boatman in Haifa, was—as we shall see in this chapter—the diametric opposite of Abu Ali from Smilansky's innocent children's story.

Disembarking in Haifa was easier than in Jaffa. Although the Haifa port had not yet been built, the natural conditions of Haifa Bay allowed for safe anchoring. Mount Carmel blocked the east winds, and the bay was not rocky, as it was at Jaffa's port, so ships could anchor close to shore. After the ship dropped anchor, the passengers transferred to rowboats or lighters that were towed to the Turkish pier. From there, they proceeded on foot to where they underwent disinfection and medical exams.[2] Each lighter could carry about two hundred passengers; in pleasant weather, two lighters could be attached to a tugboat and all the ship's passengers could disembark together with the cargo. In Jaffa, disembarkation was more complicated, as the ships had to anchor far from shore and the many rocks endangered the rowboats.

Third-class passengers were sent straight to quarantine, whereas first- and second-class passengers disembarked at the customs house: "When the sea is not calm, which is approximately eight months of the year, they let all the immigrants out at the customs house." Then the third-class passengers "go in automobiles to the quarantine house at our expense. The immigrants' belongings—their heavy cargo and small parcels—all enter our warehouses, which are the customs warehouses."[3] In contrast, first- and second-class passengers received their belongings without delay when they arrived in the country.

The process of reaching the shore of Jaffa or Haifa in many ways reflected the complexity of Jewish-Arab coexistence in Palestine. The Arab leadership understood the dangers inherent in the mass immigration of Jews to Palestine and was opposed to it. Disembarking Jews, in the knowledge that they were coming to settle in Palestine, was perceived as active participation by Arabs in Jewish immigration and as a direct threat to the national interests of Palestinian Arab society. When Palestinian Arabs met with Winston Churchill, secretary of state for the colonies, they presented their concerns regarding the entry of Jews to Palestine and the fulfillment of the Balfour Declaration: "It is also a fact that there has been and still is, against our will, a great influx of Zionist immigration largely composed of those least likely to make good citizens. The policy of the British Government may be, in intention, as benevolent to the Arab population as you claim, but all its outward manifestations and results (by which alone the people of Palestine can judge) show that policy will, in fact, develop into the displacement of the Palestine Arab from the control, and even from the occupation, of his own country in favour of foreign Jews."[4]

As the number of Jewish immigrants to Palestine increased, concern grew among the Arabs. The leaders of the Arab national movement in Haifa exerted heavy pressure in the form of boycotts, strikes, and violence against the ports administration and even more so against Arab boatmen who agreed to disembark Jewish passengers onto the shores of Palestine. The attempt to prevent Arab boatmen from doing their jobs hurt their livelihood and interfered with the routine operation of the port. The administration was compelled to intervene and break the strike.

On June 28, 1921, the *Galicia* anchored in Haifa with twenty-eight Jews aboard. "The local Arabs were aware of the impending arrival of these immigrants about a week before they arrived. No stirring was noticed among them. The boatman Ahmed Rino, who would disembark the immigrants, planned to disembark them this time, too. He waited impatiently for the ship, because disembarking immigrants was his sole source of income."[5] The day before the ship arrived, Ismain Nasrat called a meeting to prevent the disembarkation of the Jewish passengers. When word of the meeting became known, "representatives of the boatmen, including Ismain Nasrat, were called into the port director's office. . . . The meeting was held behind closed doors. The quarantine doctor (an Arab) also took part. According to one of the boatmen, they promised the port director that they would not organize any strikes and would disembark the immigrants." But promises can be broken. The boatmen refused to send their boats.

> Meanwhile, the boatmen held another meeting, and they notified the government that they would not provide their boats to disembark Jewish immigrants. A mob of Arabs with sticks started forming at the shore. . . . The police chief and the deputy governor immediately came to the shore and ordered that the immigrants be disembarked in government boats. At 10 a.m. the port director rode out to the ship in the government boats (two [unpowered] boats and a motorboat). The quarantine officer gathered his policemen and started dispersing the crowd. . . . Police came from the other side and dispersed the mob armed with sticks that had gathered at the shore. At twelve o'clock the disembarkation of the immigrants was completed. They were sent

from the shore in small groups under police supervision—some to private hotels and others to the lodgings of the Zionist Commission.[6]

The British circumvented the Arab boatmen's strike by using government boats, but what they really wanted was to calm down the strikers and get them back to work. The next day, the *Umbria* arrived with ninety-five Jewish immigrants on board, and again the boatmen refused to disembark the passengers. "The situation this time was clear. The Arabs were no longer even promising to disembark immigrants. . . . An order was received . . . to have all the shore police ready and to order Ahmed Nasrat to prepare his two boats [presumably to disembark the immigrants] alongside the *Umbria*."[7] Nasrat refused, and the British, wanting to speed up the disembarkation and avoid demonstrations, took out the government boats again. The disembarkation was quick. "At precisely twelve o'clock the ship reached Haifa. All the formalities were concluded with extreme haste. Three secretaries and two other Haifaites were dispatched to the quarantine office. An order was also issued not to make up a smallpox [vaccine] for the Jewish immigrants so that they would not have to spend much time in the port."[8]

The disembarkation of the Jews in government boats caused a financial loss to the boatmen, and they started cooperating with the port administration despite their fear of the local Arabs' reaction. On July 10, the *Campidoglio* arrived from Trieste carrying twenty-eight immigrants. Ahmed Rino agreed to disembark them, but only if the government promised protection.

> The government agreed to this condition. At 6 a.m. the police chief came
> to the shore and announced that all was quiet in the city. His officers were
> prepared for anything, and the disembarkation of the immigrants could
> begin. The disembarkation took half an hour. At 7 a.m. Ahmed Rino's boat
> with the immigrants aboard arrived at the shore, escorted by a government
> boat. No attempt was made to create disorder. No stirring was noticed among
> the Arabs. Ahmed Rino's fear was in vain. No threats were even made against
> him by the other boatmen.[9]

In Jaffa, too, there was tension between the Arab population and the coastal aliya bureau and Mandatory government. At times, the Arab boatmen refused to disembark Jewish passengers; when the ships arrived, the boatmen simply disappeared. Passengers were delayed on board and the ship could not set out again. "Al-Hamis and Ahmed Buda left [i.e., disappeared]. People were sent to find them, and eventually they brought Al-Hamis to me and the director of the government immigration office." When asked why they were not disembarking

Facing, **Figures 5.2 and 5.2A.** Entering Jaffa port. Photos courtesy of CZA, PHG\1012837 and NKH\406882.

passengers, one of them replied "that he had no boat. . . . Afterwards he said he had no boatmen . . . and when they brought him boatmen who were prepared to go with him and demonstrated that he was lying about not having a boat, he still did not want to disembark the Americans [i.e., the Jewish passengers], saying that he was afraid."[10]

The Arab boatmen's fear was understandable. A month earlier, riots had broken out in Jaffa as the local Arabs protested the entry of Jews into the country. Arab demonstrations against Jewish immigration continued even after the wave of violence in May. Chaim Ridnik, an employee of the Jaffa aliya bureau, described the Arab demonstrations when immigrants arrived at the port:

> A few moments later, Arabs started to gather with sticks and shouts (as on the days of the riots). They climbed up on the rocks in the port and, with ferocious screams, wielded the sticks threateningly alongside the sea where they saw the boat carrying the people. I shut myself up in our office on shore, immediately phoned the governor, and told him what was happening at the port. The customs house was locked from the inside. Around two or three hundred Arabs armed with sticks (as far as I could see from the window) had gathered. About three-quarters of an hour after I notified the governor, English soldiers came with an officer. One of them fired in the air and they started to disperse the Arabs. Reluctantly, the Arabs slowly left the port.[11]

The Arab boatmen realized that their livelihood came from disembarking Jewish immigrants on the shores of Palestine. Despite the national tension and the pressure exerted on them by the Arab national movement, they chose livelihood over struggle. In May 1929, a rumor spread that the government had "given an order to disembark no more than fifty third-class passengers from each ship at Jaffa; if there were any more the ship would go to Haifa." The rumor caused "great bitterness among the Arabs, too," because their income was liable to suffer.[12] *Ha'aretz* reported that in an effort to reverse the decision, Sa'id Jaber (apparently the chief boatman in Jaffa) wrote an open letter "to the mayors of Jaffa and Tel Aviv, the Sarona local council, chambers of commerce, property owners and merchants, and the sailors of Jaffa," warning them against turning Haifa into the main entry point into Palestine.

> He [Jaber] complains about this decision. He offers proof that the Jaffa quarantine house has room for three hundred immigrants and that the decision is detrimental to the shipping agency and the revenues of the city of Jaffa. The

writer points out to Mr. Dizengoff that if the government's decision goes into effect and the commercial center of Palestine moves to Haifa, the new [city of] Tel Aviv will become the "paradise" of Palestine, a primeval place. . . . Arab sailors in Jaffa went to the offices of *Falastin* and protested this decision. One sailor said: "We are just as entitled to a livelihood as the residents of Haifa are. It is unreasonable to deprive us in order to give others a livelihood."[13]

The Arab demonstrations for and against Arab boatmen disembarking Jewish immigrants are interesting not only in the context of the procedure for disembarkation and reaching the port but also because they were some Jewish passengers' first encounter with the inhabitants of Palestine. Their reception from the Arab boatmen and the local populace foreshadowed subsequent Jewish-Arab relations in Palestine. Even before they set foot in the country, the Jewish immigrants were exposed to the tension and polarization that characterized the two ethnic groups living in the country. Presumably, the Arab demonstrations at the entrance to the port, the wielding of sticks, and the loud denunciation of their entry into the country turned the Jewish newcomers off from the local Arab population and made it harder in later years to establish Jewish-Arab trust and dialogue in Palestine.

Despite the tension, strikes, and demonstrations, the disembarkation of passengers in the port took place peacefully during most of the year. The aliya bureaus in Tel Aviv and Haifa paid the Arab boatmen for each immigrant they disembarked onto the rowboats. Zvi Livneh (Lieberman), a Hapoel Hatzair representative in Jaffa port, describes in his memoirs how the accounting took place with the chief boatman: "All the boats in the port were organized and subject to the authority of the chief boatman Ahmed Buda, a tall, fat Arab who always had a smile on his broad, red face. On his head was a pressed red tarboush." Once a week, an aliya bureau employee met with the chief boatman and paid him for the disembarkation of immigrants. "Each of us holds a pencil and paper and we both do the calculations. The calculation was smooth and round: one pound per person. If 74 people disembarked from a particular ship, 17 from another ship, and 97 immigrants from a third, then in the course of the week 188 immigrants had disembarked. In other words, he was owed 188 pounds. I would count out the money into Ahmed Buda's hands, and then we would have another sip and part with a handshake."[14]

Passport Control

In the 1920s, passports and entry permits were checked on board the ships when they reached the shores of Palestine. "As soon as the ship reached the

Figure 5.3. Aliya bureau in Tel Aviv. Joshua Gordon, director of the bureau, is fourth from the right. Photo courtesy of CZA, PHG\1015344.

coast of Jaffa (or Haifa), aliya bureau officials would board the ship, help the immigrants through passport control, organize their luggage, and disembark them in boats to the customs house."[15] Until the immigration ordinance of June 1921, the immigrant absorption procedure was in the hands of the Zionist movement; the British administration did not intervene. After the immigration ordinance took effect, the British enforced it strictly. From then on there was a great deal of tension between the British officials and the immigrants and aliya bureau workers and between the aliya bureau representatives and the Jewish immigrants. Passengers were not permitted onto the shores of Palestine until British government officials had inspected their papers. These officials placed a table on the deck of the ship and summoned passengers for inspection. Because the aliya bureau representatives were not allowed to take part in the registration procedure, they had to set up their own inspection desk on the deck, and the immigrants were asked to register there as well and answer the questions a second time. The British officials and aliya bureau representatives were joined

Figure 5.4. Document inspection on deck. Photo courtesy of CZA, PHG\1078895.

by a Health Ministry worker, who got an impression of the immigrants' physical state and could exempt them from the medical exam in quarantine. "The Health Ministry official always forms his impression on the ship together with our impression and the government's, and the immigrants do not all enter quarantine." If the Health Ministry representative did not show up, all the immigrants were examined in the port, and their entry into the country was delayed.[16]

The immigration officials questioned passengers based on their visas. Those who had visas of skilled tradesmen were asked about their occupations and their expertise; those with invitations from relatives were asked to provide information about their relatives; and those entitled to immigrate as persons of means were asked to present proof of their means. Passengers who were given authorization to enter Palestine then went over to the inspection desk of the Zionist immigration workers and registered again: "We also do another inspection on the ship regarding the immigrants' means. We distinguish between immigrants who have no means and need our assistance—a hotel or immigrant home—and immigrants who don't need any assistance from us at all. We derive all this information from the immigrants' aliya certificates, as well as from the questions that we generally ask the immigrants, since in this sense the ship is the surest source, where the immigrants think these questions are required and they are obligated to answer them."[17]

The director of the Haifa aliya bureau stated that the passengers looked on the Zionist aliya bureau workers as a welcome relief. "From the moment our workers board the ship together with the government immigration and quarantine officials, the immigrants sense that there is someone taking care of things and seeing to their property."[18] Passengers who were rejected and were waiting for resolution of their cases were the focal point of tension between the British and Zionist immigration workers. For example, a passenger by the name of Sheinfeld told the British officials that he had handed his passport over in Alexandria "in order to send it by post to Jerusalem. He had no other documents. The matter is slightly suspicious," the Zionist representative reported. Indeed, Sheinfeld's explanations were not deemed adequate, and he was not permitted to disembark.[19] Fourteen-year-old Lazer Leifer and sixteen-year-old Ya'akov Brzeski, both orphans, had arrived without papers and "sneaked on board without tickets together with a group of halutzim. Now they want to disembark here."[20] Such cases and others created bureaucratic complications that the Zionist representatives had to work out vis-à-vis both the British authorities and the passengers.

In some cases, passengers lacking visas were permitted to enter quarantine and wait there until their cases had been resolved. However, it was clear to the passengers and the aliya bureau representatives "that disembarking in quarantine . . . does not mean an entry permit, just that he gets out of there and is considered to have disembarked. It's like Ellis Island."[21] The British officials made things difficult for the passengers. They sometimes concluded that, based on their responses, immigrants did not qualify for the kind of visa they had or that their state of health was problematic:

Shmuel Shimonovitz. 15 months in Constantinople. He is with his family, a wife and two sons: Moshe, 25, Nechemia, 22—a shoemaker. His sons work with him. They have no money. They came at the invitation of a man named Berel Genkes. A while back he had an invitation from someone else. He doesn't know the man who issued the invitation. When asked what the man does he replied [that he is] a guard in an orchard. The immigration official's opinion is that an orchard guard cannot support a family of four. . . . Aharon Kranker. His visa is fine, but he is suspected of having a sexually transmitted disease. Perhaps syphilis. Therefore a blood test is needed. The blood was sent to a government bacteriological laboratory in Haifa for testing and so far there has been no reply.[22]

Because aliya bureau representatives often came to the passengers' aid, the British immigration officials sought to prevent them from being involved in the inspection of the travel papers. The directors of the aliya bureaus warned against attempts to exclude their representatives, regarding them as a dangerous precedent: "Here it has long been the privilege of the Zionist Commission, and now of the Zionist Executive, to board the ship in an official capacity. . . . True, government officials have objected to this on numerous occasions. The reasons were varied . . . but we always fought for our right." Aliya bureau representatives' involvement in passport control was routine: "Sometimes the government officials even wait for us on the boat until we come. For the boatmen it is already an inviolable law."[23]

Some passengers managed to enter Palestine on forged visas, without the knowledge of the aliya bureau:

> Recently there was an unpleasant incident here that is worth noting. On the last ship from Constantinople (the *Umbria*) there were nineteen people whose papers were not in order: no visa and no papers. The ship's committee informed us that eight of them are honest people and only by chance did not receive visas, but that eleven are known thieves and the committee has requested that they not be disembarked. Guarantees were not given for the nineteen people and they went to Egypt. A few days later, about ten of them returned (including seven of the suspicious characters), some with visas from Egypt and some without visas. By some means unknown to us they almost all disembarked onto the shore.[24]

Zvi Livneh describes in his memoirs how immigrants with forged travel papers were brought into Palestine without the knowledge of the British. Zvi Yehuda, a member of Hapoel Hatzair, sailed to Europe to expedite the arrival of the halutzim in Palestine. In Vienna, he met with the head of the Palestine Office and was surprised to find that the office, far from encouraging the arrival of the halutzim, was holding them back. On one of his visits to the Palestine Office, he overheard a conversation between a worker there and a Sephardic Jew who wanted to return to Palestine. The Jew "held out a Turkish passport attesting to his Palestinian citizenship from before the world war and asked for a visa to return to Palestine." Yehuda, realizing that this passport entitled the man to an entry permit to Palestine, asked if he could hold onto it for a few days so that he could forge it for those halutzim who were not being allowed to go. He "carefully put the crumpled paper in his pocket and left with a feeling of relief and hope. Not a few days passed before experts produced Turkish passports from crumpled paper. Halutzim from Galicia, Czechoslovakia, and

Poland started thronging the Palestine Office with crumpled passports in their hands, requesting British visas."[25]

Another way of entering Palestine illegally was to bribe the Jewish secretary who worked for the British in the port. This secretary was extremely strict about the admission of immigrants into Palestine. He "was a Levantine clerk type for the British—a native of one of the Baron's colonies who had been educated in Egypt, was careful about the crease in his trousers, was punctilious about shaving his mustache and about his hairdo, and looked down on the lowly clerks. When police officers were hired, he did not insist that the candidate be a Jew, and one of our Jews."[26] Zvi Livneh sent one of the members of his party to the village where the secretary lived to check "the situation of the port secretary's family in great detail—who his parents were, what their occupation was, whether they had an income, who his brothers and sisters were, what kind of work they did, and so on." Livneh found out that the official had a big family, that his parents lived in poverty, and that his brothers "had no trade and [were] unemployed." Having discovered the secretary's weak spot, they made him a tempting offer: "I heard you have a few brothers, older unmarried fellows. If you're interested, I can get them a budget to study English for a few months and then they'll get jobs on the railroad or in the government."[27] Indeed, this was an offer the "Levantine secretary" could not refuse. Before the bribery, there were fourteen police officers and one sergeant in the port, most of them Arabs. Afterward, the secretary made sure that the police force was made up "of seven Arab and seven Jewish officers. The sergeant was also a Jew."[28] From then on it was easier for the aliya bureau workers to deal with the British, to resolve bureaucratic difficulties, and to disembark passengers without visas.

> I considered myself duty bound to board every ship as soon as it anchored, and when there was a particular need I would board even before the doctor—which was absolutely forbidden. . . . How would we disembark the illegal immigrants? When I boarded the ship my first question was: How many don't have visas? When I found out the number I would gather the young men in a corner and instruct them: Don't take any suitcases. Shave, comb your hair, put on nice clothes, and act like Palestinian [Jews] who boarded the ship to meet their relatives. When you go out through the gate of the port don't go with the visa holders to the inspection office. Instead mix in immediately with the people watching. I would give each of them a red slip of paper—a signal to the police officer to let him pass.[29]

So as not to put the Jewish guards in an awkward position, Zvi Livneh asked the Jewish sergeant to post Arab police officers; these men turned a blind eye and accepted a bribe from the chief boatman in the port, Ahmed Buda: "An immigrant with a passport and visa would show the official papers to the police standing at the entrances, whereas those without visas would show my slips of paper and the Arab police officers would let them out. These slips were taken from the immigrants at the first gate and handed to Ahmed Buda, who would bring them to me and get one pound in exchange for each slip."[30] In Livneh's estimation, "many hundreds of 'illegal' immigrants entered Palestine by the port gates in full view of the police and officials." Thus, through bribery and deception and by giving gifts and perks to port officials, many immigrants who arrived without papers were let into the country.

Immigrants were also smuggled into Palestine through the port of Beirut. In his memoirs, Zvi Livneh describes Jewish immigrants arriving in Beirut and contacting the local representative of Hapoel Hatzair, who helped them cross the northern border to the Galilee villages, and from there to central Palestine. "At first just a few individuals came to the country in this way, but when it became known abroad, large groups started to come."[31] The son of the Hakham Bashi—the chief rabbi of Beirut—helped smuggle the Jews into Palestine. He greeted them at the port of Beirut, saw to all their needs, and sent them on to Palestine. The smuggling route was shut down after the Hakham Bashi innocently mentioned to the French governor of Syria and Lebanon, at a festive reception in his honor, how the French government was indirectly helping Jews enter Palestine.

> Look at the difference between the enlightened French government and the British government. The latter pledged to help establish a national home for the Jews in Palestine but is essentially restricting immigration, limiting it to zero and often even sending back Jews who have arrived in their homeland through tremendous effort. Whereas glorious France—despite having made no commitment to the Jews—lets Jews disembark freely on its shores. When the guests at the reception were in high spirits from wine, one French general approached the Hakham Bashi and seemingly entered into a friendly conversation with him about the immigration. The Hakham Bashi, enjoying the conversation with the exalted individual, spared no details about the aliya via Beirut.[32]

The Aliya Department considered it important for aliya bureau representatives to board the ship with the government officials for several reasons. First, they had to draw up orderly lists of immigrants and prepare for the passengers' entry and absorption in Palestine. Because the Palestine Offices did not send up-to-date passenger lists, neither the aliya bureaus nor the immigrants' relatives knew when they were expected. "Furthermore, accompanying the immigration official on the ship step by step during the inspection of the olim enables us to draw up a list of immigrants on the spot. By the time the immigration official disembarks we already have a detailed list of everyone disembarking, along with the names of their relatives, as well as a list of all those who were rejected or whose visas require looking into. Thus we can always inform the relatives in time that they need to take action."[33]

Another important reason for the aliya bureau representatives to board the ship together with the British government officials was the possibility of influencing the latter's decisions in real time and thereby to help the immigrants. Once the officials and the doctor had decided who could enter the country and who was to be turned back, the aliya bureau representatives no longer had any influence and could not reverse the decisions. For those who had made the long, exhausting journey from Europe to Palestine, being prevented from entering the country was a real tragedy; they needed assistance from someone who had their welfare at heart. "After all, it is important to be there when the immigration official questions each immigrant and requests his visa," wrote Joshua Gordon to Professor Hermann Pick, director of the Aliya Department, "and not afterwards, when he has already formed his opinion of the immigrant and the visa."[34] In certain senses, the assistance provided by aliya bureau workers on board the ships resembled the help provided by consuls to Jewish immigrants turned back by Ottoman officials before World War I, whereas the aid of the aliya bureau representatives resembled the aid activities of the HIAS representatives on Ellis Island, who mediated between the Jewish immigrants and the American immigration officials.

At times, government officials displayed hostility toward the immigrants, asking them antagonistic, objectionable questions. At a meeting of the aliya bureau held in Jerusalem in late 1921, Joshua Gordon claimed, "The questions that the officials ask the immigrants when they encounter them on the ships exhaust the immigrants and sometimes cause resentment. Among the questions they are asked are why they came to Palestine, what they will do here, and why they left [where they came from]. The immigrants see this as an insult to their national feelings and this sometimes results in an undesirable attitude."[35]

One of the reasons for interrogating the immigrants on the ship was the British desire to keep Communists and other undesirable elements out of Palestine. In the 1920s and 1930s, Communists were considered the sworn enemies of Western countries, and these countries persecuted, imprisoned, deported, and sometimes even assassinated them. In the United States, for instance, immigration officials on Ellis Island interrogated newcomers suspected of having radical Bolshevik views. Revolutionaries who managed to deceive the immigration authorities and enter the United States became agitators who used strikes and demonstrations to undermine the existing political order. American politicians, regarding them as a genuine danger to American society, took steps to deport them and advance the quota bill that would restrict the entry of immigrants from eastern Europe.[36] The case of the Jewish anarchist Emma Goldman is the best known, but she was just one of many immigrants deported from the United States.

The British had similar concerns.[37] One of the reasons for the outbreak of the bloody riots on May 1, 1921, was a march, approved by the governor of Jaffa, by workers belonging to Ahdut Ha-Avoda. Another group from the Socialist Workers Party (SWP, or Mapas—a Communist group) also came out to demonstrate despite not having a permit, and a violent quarrel erupted between the two groups. The Haycraft Commission, formed to investigate the causes of the riots, found that in the wake of the initial violence on May 1, rumors had spread that the Jews had attacked Arabs and that the Jewish Communists had incited the Arabs against the Zionist imperialists and the British.[38] The commission took testimony from survivors of the riots and met with David Eder, acting head of the Zionist Commission, and with Joshua Gordon, director of the Jaffa aliya bureau.

Eder and Gordon were questioned about the Zionist movement's policy regarding the admission of Communists into Palestine. They explained that efforts were being made to prevent the entry of undesirable elements such as Communists. Eder claimed, "Regarding the level of Jews who arrived, it was said that they were all Bolsheviks. I would like to narrow down the definition of the term Bolshevik. The Bolshevik is, as I understand it, a member of the organization committed to the Socialist International. Many Englishmen from the Labor Party belong to the Second International. The number of people who arrived in this sense is very small in Palestine. As far as I know, they were under a hundred last May. They do not come as workers. Sometimes they come with money in their pockets." Gordon, on the other hand, as the director of the Jaffa aliya bureau for the past five months, maintained, "I take care of the immigrants getting off the ship and check that their visas are in order, that is, the Zionist approval, allow them to enter, and take care of their livelihood for the first week." He expounded on the procedure for obtaining an entry visa to Palestine and said, "The visa is British, given by the consuls in the countries of origin, and in addition they have a permit issued by the Zionist office in London that receives the consular permit. The Zionist representative confirms that the immigrant is suitable for immigration to Palestine and that he is not a Bolshevik."[39]

Entry into Palestine was difficult not only for Communist enemies of British imperialism; even ordinary immigrants encountered discrimination and hostility. In Haifa, the quarantine doctor Kamil Eid was accused of deliberately harassing the Jewish passengers. Dr. Eid was described as someone who hated Jews and who "utters poisonous words about them."[40] Another report quotes Eid as saying, "No matter, let the Jews come to Palestine en masse. There is plenty of room here for graves for them." Levi Shvueli, director of the Haifa aliya bureau, noted the Arab doctor's discriminatory attitude toward the Jewish immigrants: "On several occasions . . . I had the opportunity to bring to . . . the attention . . . the troubles suffered by the new immigrants because of the management of the quarantine camp in Haifa, headed by Dr. Kamil Eid." The Haifa aliya bureau asked the doctor to change his treatment of the immigrants, but to no avail.

> Once or twice we saw changes for the better, but these were just temporary. We armed ourselves with patience and made friendly attempts to sway Dr. Eid not to hurt the people, but in the end we realized that it was impossible for us and perhaps also for Dr. Eid himself to overcome his personal inclinations against the Jews. This man tries to harm and harass the new immigrants every way he can. He interprets the laws and ordinances in such a way as to harm the Jews and on the basis of his understanding issues decisions that cause trouble for the immigrants.[41]

The inspection of passports, travel papers, and entry visas to Palestine was part of a fateful, momentous procedure for the immigrants, relatives awaiting their arrival, and the Zionist Executive, which was trying to bring as many Jews as possible into the country. One of the issues of greatest concern to all the heads of the Aliya Department was sending immigrants who had been refused entry back to Europe. This was a sensitive issue for everyone involved. For British officials to keep Jews out of Palestine was perceived as a terrible act of injustice vis-à-vis the Zionist movement and the Jewish people. According to the Aliya Department's annual report, "We are referring here to the matter overall, which we think is the greatest wrong done to the Jewish people in recent years. We have fought this injustice by all possible means. We have sent letters and memoranda, and we have made verbal protests and efforts in various places."[42]

We do not have complete data for the entire decade on the number of Jews sent back to the ports of departure, but the numbers were not negligible. British officials sent eighty-four passengers back to Europe in the space of just four months: twelve in February 1921, eighteen in March, forty-three in April, and eleven in May.[43] In most cases, they were denied entry because they had the wrong travel papers or illegal visas: "On January 15 [1922], they started send-ing back immigrants from the shores of Palestine if the government official found that the consul had issued a visa in contravention of the law. . . . We have records of more than six hundred cases in which immigrants who came with British visas were not permitted to disembark in Palestine. Among those sent back were people of means who had come as tourists, not with a national pass-port [but] with a laissez-passer. For this they were sent back from the shores of Palestine."[44]

Some immigrants came on forged passports. The *Carnaro*, which anchored in Haifa in September 1925, brought twenty immigrants, four of whom were not permitted to disembark "because the immigration official found that their passports were forged." On the cover of the passport "within the crown on the eagle's head, there is supposed to be a small circle. The forged ones have only a line." Furthermore, there were spelling mistakes in the French.[45] Other pas-sengers were not admitted into Palestine because their answers did not satisfy the immigration officials: "Salt Moshe, six persons" belonged to "no category and he has no relatives and no money." Topek Alexander, Weiss Andrei, Rosa Gustav, and Roma Yosef arrived on tourist visas, but they had no money, which tourists were expected to have. They were detained in quarantine, but they escaped under cover of darkness and were swallowed up in Palestine.[46] Other immigrants were sent back because they were carrying diseases, and the quar-antine camp doctor refused to let them disembark.

> Recently there has been an increase in cases of immigrants being sent back. Most of them were sent to Vienna, some to Romania and Poland. Most of them were sick people who could not help themselves. A minority were sent home to their parents. Even in this case the halutz who volunteered for the country—sometimes against his parents' will—and returns to his parents stricken with a malady and completely destitute, is nevertheless better off than the one sent back to Vienna, a place that is totally foreign to him, where he has no friends or acquaintances but only a letter of recommendation from our office. . . . Those sent [back] in order to recover not only don't get the necessary treatment but actually die of disease on the streets and contract new illnesses.[47]

Sending immigrants back to their place of origin was dramatic and trau-matic, not only from the Zionist and economic perspectives but first and foremost from the personal and family perspectives. The rejected immigrants could see the shores of Palestine before their eyes but could not reach them. The knowledge that their relatives were so near yet so far caused tremendous frustration and anger at everyone involved in immigration: the British officials, the representatives of the coastal bureaus, and the Palestine Office workers.

The Quarantine Camp and Disinfection Room

The immigrants who arrived in Palestine before World War I did not undergo medical exams, and most of them entered the country without any difficulty. When the British army conquered Palestine and new rules were drawn up, immigrants were required to undergo medical exams both in the Palestine Offices in their countries of origin and upon arrival in Palestine. The Quarantine Ordinance was one of the first ordinances enacted by the British in Palestine. It required examination of passengers by the quarantine camp doctor, a stay in an isolation facility when necessary, and repeated exams by the district doctor if suspicion arose that an individual was carrying a disease.[48] According to Eyal Katvan, a scholar of the history of medicine in Palestine, the first passengers were examined in April 1919. These passengers were Arabs traveling from Tripoli to Alexandria, whose ship apparently anchored in Haifa.[49]

After disembarking, the immigrants were sent with their belongings for disinfection and immunization. Those found to be ill remained in quarantine pending the results of blood tests, after which a decision was made regarding their future. The medical exams were the responsibility of the Mandatory government health department, and the aliya bureau representatives could not intervene. This was the only time the immigrants found themselves facing the authorities alone, without the accompaniment and assistance of their representatives. "Our workers are barred from entering there," the director of the Haifa aliya bureau wrote to the Zionist Executive. "The exhausted immigrants can get enraged by every little thing and they clash with the Arab guards, who don't understand their language. The result is an undesirable situation."[50]

A doctor from the quarantine camp or a Mandatory Health Ministry official conducted the first medical exam on the ship and gave the signal to start document inspection. If someone was found to be carrying an infectious disease and there was concern that fellow passengers had become infected, all the passengers and crew were quarantined. After completing a survey on board the ship, the doctor returned to the quarantine camp and the disinfection building and started examining each immigrant individually. "The doctor in charge of quarantine affairs, in addition to the regular work of inspecting the ships—which takes up most of his time—also works in the quarantine house: inspecting the immigrants' state of health, making up the smallpox [vaccine], and giving injections, which according to the new law could be done only by him."[51] Making up the vaccine took a long time, and sometimes the doctors had to leave their work in the quarantine camp and go out to receive another ship that had anchored. These absences delayed the passengers, who became angry and resentful over the cumbersome, exhausting procedure.[52]

After the medical exam, or sometimes at the same time, the immigrants were disinfected. This procedure exacerbated their anger and frustration: "There are many justified complaints in the quarantine camp. They do two disinfections . . . of the immigrants' clothing . . . and of their belongings. The disinfection of the immigrants' clothing is done very badly in a way that ruins the clothing. All the clothes are dumped into one big sack and after the disinfection is finished everyone has to pick out their clothing."[53] *Davar* described the disinfection as a totally illogical procedure that infuriated the passengers: "There are surely those who think the quarantine house in Palestine serves just one purpose: to protect the country from the introduction of infectious disease. The facts, however, prove otherwise." After the passengers were disinfected, going through "all the circles of disinfection," they returned to the same room "where they had sat for two hours before disinfection."[54] It was chaos. Disorder, confusion, and embarrassment prevailed, with dozens of half-naked immigrants searching for their clothes in the big sack that had been put into a steam disinfection machine:

> And as if this were not enough, then came the disinfection of the belongings. Between six and eight low-level officials were put in charge of taking underwear showing signs of use out of the hundreds of suitcases. This was done viciously . . . for the sake of speed; afterwards the immigrants, especially families with children, had to spend hours organizing the belongings that had been taken out. Because of the speed people lost objects and money. . . . Obviously, after spending two or three days with pleasures like these, the immigrants come out in a black mood and furious at the whole world. You will hear vehement cursing of the land of Ishmael here. This inquisition must be stopped. If [there must be] quarantine—then let it be quarantine and not a hellhole. Let them build quarantine houses for the hundreds of immigrants per day and not stuff those hundreds into a building intended for five passengers a month.[55]

To make things easier for the immigrants, the head of the Tel Aviv aliya bureau suggested buying them personal bags. Each immigrant would have a "small parcel of clean underwear and a clean suit in his hand so that he can wear them when he comes for disinfection while handing over his clothes for disinfection."[56] Shvueli, director of the Haifa aliya bureau, appealed to the

Figure 5.5. Quarantine camp office in Jaffa. Photo courtesy of CZA, PHG\1012838.

district governor to intervene in the quarantine procedures: "Despite Dr. Lit-vori (P.M.O. Haifa) telling me that the disinfection was set up here in such a way that it takes only a minute per person to complete, we see that people are spending half a day and sometimes entire days there. And Dr. Eid always finds all sorts of excuses for delaying the work."[57] On December 19, 1921, Shvueli wrote that 234 immigrants had arrived in Haifa. One hundred of them dis-embarked at 11:00 a.m., but the disinfection only started at 3:15 p.m., and the passengers reached the immigrant home at 7:30 p.m. The second group, 134 people, disembarked at 2:30 p.m. All had to spend the night in the quarantine camp, causing the aliya bureau unnecessary expenses. At 9:00 a.m. they left the camp, but the disinfection only started at 11:00 a.m., and they reached the immigrant home at 4:30 p.m.[58]

Aside from the disorder surrounding the medical exam and disinfection, the Aliya Department had to contend with three other disturbing problems: theft, the location of the quarantine camp in Haifa, and sick immigrants. While the immigrants were being examined by the doctor, their belongings were left unguarded in the disinfection camp or customs house. "Not a week goes by without grievances from the new immigrants about thefts discovered from their luggage, especially of valuable items," wrote Beiteli, Shvueli's successor as director of the Haifa aliya bureau, to the head of the Zionist Organization political department, Colonel Frederick Kisch. He continued, "The immigrants claim that the theft occurred in the disinfection house because the belongings were there without their watching over them. However, in the absence of any proof of this we have no one to accuse, and the immigrants are suing us in the Jewish district court and accusing us."[59] An investigation by aliya bureau workers found that the thieves were guards at the disinfection camp and customs house: "In order to save time and to prevent the belongings from being moved to the customs house, it was arranged that the customs officials would come to the disinfection [place] and examine the belongings there. The eyes of some of them alight on valuables, and while the immigrants are completing the injections and bathing and leaving their belongings there for disinfection, which is generally done the next day, various things are stolen. (It should be noted that the immigrants' belongings are not opened in our workers' presence because our workers are barred from the disinfection house)."[60]

Ida Levin arrived in Haifa in March 1925 aboard the *Barga*. In a letter of complaint to the aliya bureau, she wrote that her jewelry and other valuables had been stolen from her luggage: "I disembarked that day at 6 p.m. with my belongings. . . . When I reached the shore they separated me from my belongings. They told me that everything would be all right and that I should go. I wanted to take the small suitcase with the silver and gold but they wouldn't let me. They said everything would be all right." She claimed that when she returned from quarantine, her suitcase was closed "in a special way, not the way I had closed it. . . . I saw that all the gold and silver were missing, as well as the kerchief that they had been in. I started screaming and complaining." The quarantine official, "who was wearing a white apron and had a whistle in his mouth, told me to go away because everything would be all right, even though I had told him that my things were missing."[61] Six gold rings were stolen from Ida, "two simple ones, two with stones, and two with stones that had fallen out, a woman's gold watch with a gold chain" and three wristwatches, one of them with a leather strap and two with chains. Some Russian money was also stolen.[62]

Often luggage was lost because the passengers disembarked in Jaffa but their cargo was sent on to Haifa, or vice versa. Sometimes luggage simply got lost en route. Scores of complaints were sent to the Aliya Department, demanding that lost luggage be found. "Dear Sir, I came to Palestine on the *Barga* on June 16. Because they wouldn't let me disembark in Jaffa I was forced to disembark in Haifa, but my belongings remained in Jaffa. I am therefore asking you to send my belongings to me here, as I came on a certificate and can't pay for the trip

Figure 5.6. Arab guard and immigrants in Haifa port waiting for the customs house to open. Photo courtesy of CZA, PHG\1006763.

to come get them. I hope you will be considerate of a new immigrant with no means and accede to my request. Thank you in advance. . . . Note: The baggage is in one sack, numbered 25486."[63]

Shmuel Rosenbaum lost his suitcases and sued the Zionist Executive for compensation. He stated that the suitcases had been taken off the ship with him; what happened next is described in his claim: "And when he reached the shore the plaintiff wanted to take his parcels from the boat, but they wouldn't let him [because] he was being taken to quarantine. The next day the plaintiff came for his belongings but found only one parcel. The second parcel was lost." The court recognized the Zionist Executive's moral responsibility for the integrity of the belongings and stressed the need to put some order in this branch of the Aliya Department's work. Nevertheless, the court had no choice but to reject the plaintiff's monetary claim.[64]

The location of the Haifa quarantine camp on an estuary of the Kishon River, right near swamps and the Shemen and Atid factories, was a source of concern for the Aliya Department. In 1919, the Mandatory government health department established the camp in a place that was malaria-stricken due to pollution in the Kishon. The camp occupied 1.8 hectares that the British had rented from Mustafa Amr. After Amr died in 1927, his heirs demanded the land back. Although the quarantine camp was supposed to be temporary, it became permanent in the 1920s and 1930s because the replacement camp had to await the creation of a new port. The British did not want to invest £30,000 in building a new quarantine camp before the new port was built.[65]

According to the Immigration Ordinance, immigrants were to be quarantined if they had come from a port where cholera or some other epidemic had been discovered or if there had been an outbreak of disease on their ship; if they arrived in such large numbers that they could not all undergo disinfection on the day of arrival; if they arrived too late in the day to have time for disinfection; or while waiting for disinfection.[66] They had to walk to the quarantine camp. The tiring walk on what wasn't even a proper road caused anger, resentment, and especially disappointment with their initial encounter with the country. This was not how they had imagined their arrival in Palestine. After passing through document inspection, they marched to the quarantine camp—"a twenty-minute walk on loose sand, escorted by police on all sides. This is the most painful impression that the immigrants get in their first moments in the country. The singing of 'Hatikvah' is immediately silenced by this reception, [and] they complain about walking on sand with children in their arms, about the escort by the Arab police." Their belongings were brought "to the quarantine field in small dinghies. Dozens of Arabs stand in the water in a long line, almost naked, and carry the parcels on their shoulders to the disinfection house."[67]

When immigration via Haifa was minimal and only a few immigrants were sent to the quarantine camp, the location of the camp posed no problem. But the difficulties mounted in the years when immigration via Haifa increased and many more passengers were quarantined. Doctors from Hadassah, and afterward other doctors as well, drew attention to the fact that many of the passengers were contracting malaria while in the quarantine camp.[68] Aside from the danger, living conditions in the camp were harsh and sometimes unbearable: "The entire vicinity of the quarantine camp is full of all sorts of mosquitoes, and aside from causing disease, they definitely steal the people's rest, especially at night. Some time ago, the health department gave the quarantine camp a small number of mosquito nets, but first of all, there are not enough for everyone in the camp, and second, even most of the ones that are there are ruined and torn and don't provide the necessary protection against the mosquitoes."[69]

A doctor from the Haifa quarantine camp initially denied the claims of the aliya bureau director, but when the latter showed him proof of malaria among immigrants who had spent a few days in quarantine, he became convinced that the quarantine camp should be moved elsewhere. A report on conditions in the quarantine camp, ordered by the second British high commissioner in Palestine, Herbert Plumer, indicates that the Mandatory government was aware of the poor conditions.

The quarantine camp was divided into four compounds separated by barbed-wire fences. According to the report, the fences were in poor condition and needed maintenance every month or two. "Each compound contains wooden huts with concrete floor" and was divided into three sections by class and financial means. "The first class hut consist of single rooms furnished with all requirements but not luxuriously." In the second-class compound, the shacks were similar, but there were two beds per room. The compounds for the first two classes had a comfortably furnished dining room for the use of the people staying in the camp. "The third class, originally Army huts, are furnished only with mattresses and blankets, tables and forms, and matting on the floors." Beds were not provided "because of the extreme difficulty of keeping them free from bugs and lice which so commonly accompany the third class passengers and secondly because the Arab or Egyptian or Indian pilgrim or passenger, who has so frequently to be accommodated in quarantine, is unaccustomed to a bed, and is more likely to sleep under it than upon it if it is provided for him." The report on the state of the quarantine camp indicates that the Jewish immigrants were considered Europeans, so the attitude toward them was different. "In the meantime I have ordered the completion of the fencing round the lazarat at a cost of £500. I had intended to postpone this item of expenditure for inclusion in the budget of 1927. The director of the Department of Health has been awaiting the completion of this fencing before installing certain improved equipment to meet Jewish requirements by fitting up some of the third class sections of the lazaret with European equipment including beds, linen and furniture on what was previously the second scale."[70]

Men and women were housed in separate shacks in the same compound, but the showers and lavatories with wooden seats were merely separated by iron partitions. Meals were the responsibility of Jews who had been awarded the concession by the Mandatory government, and the separation between the classes was retained. In the first two classes, Arab waiters served the immigrants. For the third-class passengers, one of the shacks was used as a dining room, and the meals, mostly prepared from cans, were served by various people according to a rota.[71]

The stay in the disinfection room and quarantine camp made a poor impression on the immigrants and tainted their experience of arriving in Palestine.

They frequently complained about the conditions and the officials' attitude. The board of the Society of Polish Jews in Haifa sent the Zionist Executive a letter of protest signed by thirty Polish immigrants who described their terrible experiences with disinfection and quarantine. Regarding the disinfection rooms, they wrote, "We were taken off the ship weak and tired from the agonies of the journey and seasickness and were taken under guard to empty barracks without even benches to sit on. . . . The barracks were too small to hold us all and we were so crammed that there wasn't even air to breathe. . . . While we were incarcerated, the officials treated us like a gang of robbers or murderers."

Conditions in the quarantine camp were no better. "The way they treated us in the quarantine camp was so rough, immoral, and inhumane. . . . We were ordered to strip, and while we were standing around naked the order came that we should go eat. We were so outraged and resentful that we refused to go eat despite our tremendous hunger." The immigrants waited naked for hours, and after a quick shower, "we men were forced to stand, still naked, for a few hours, waiting for them to release the women and children who were in the other room getting shots."[72] The letter added,

> After all, you know as well as we do that from time to time when immigrants come they have to undergo quarantine and disinfection with all sorts of torments like the seven circles of hell. They complain and scream, but no one hears or lifts a finger to make things better in the future. And the bad conditions and irregularities in the quarantine camp multiply from day to day to the point that the five hundred people, entire families, who came on the *Barga* were treated this way. . . . We therefore appeal to you, dear sirs, as the managers responsible for immigration to Palestine, to put all available means into improving the situation, easing matters for the immigrants in every way possible starting today, not to embitter their lives with totally unnecessary agonies, and especially to admonish the officials to treat the immigrants politely and civilly.[73]

The thorniest problem for British immigration officials and the Zionist Executive was the arrival of sick immigrants who became a burden on the aliya bureaus and medical clinics. The Aliya Department took care of the immigrants—finding them employment and housing and providing medical care—during their first year in the country. Therefore, if immigrants fell ill or turned out to be carrying chronic or infectious illnesses, the aliya bureaus were responsible for their treatment. US immigration authorities tended to send immigrants suspected of being ill or unfit for work back to their countries of origin. In Palestine, however, this would have been problematic, both due to budgetary limitations and because aliya was perceived as a value, an integral part of the implementation of the Zionist idea. Sending Jews back to Europe instead of letting them into Palestine (even if they were not able-bodied and would be a burden on the Zionist institutions) were weighty issues of great concern that were no simple matter to decide:

> In general we must stress that we are encountering cases of people who were already weak or sick upon arrival; clearly there is no room for these under the prevailing conditions. Sick or even weak people who manage to start working are affected by the maladies endemic to Palestine, spend most of their time in hospitals, and after all that are sent back, having suffered terribly and cost significant sums of money. (Perhaps some of them need the air of Palestine for their health, but only if they have the necessary means of subsistence.) We must alert all the comrades in the places that the immigrants pass through and warn them how much of a burden such elements are for them and [that they should] examine the passengers well.[74]

Among the Aliya Department files in the Central Zionist Archives are several dealing with medical issues pertaining to Jewish immigrants who arrived in Palestine in the 1920s. The Mandatory government and British Health Ministry issued special orders concerning immigrants carrying infectious diseases. Anyone with an infectious disease was to be hospitalized immediately and was not to encounter healthy immigrants. The coastal bureaus were required to set up special tents (a sort of temporary quarantine camp) for immigrants found to be ill following the government medical exam. These people were to remain under the supervision of the doctor of the immigrant home until they were moved to the government hospital.[75]

We see from the medical files that a significant number of mentally ill and emotionally frail people arrived in Palestine, and constant bureaucratic and medical efforts were made to find solutions. Conventional medical treatment or rest in an immigrant home did not help such patients; they had to be hospitalized in special institutions. Below are several examples, with the patients' names omitted for reasons of privacy.

1. Mr. L. K., twenty-four, arrived on the *Prinkipo* on September 11, 1921, and was in the camp. "Last night he showed signs of insanity and the camp doctor who examined him immediately informed us that he had to be under supervision and in the care of a home for the mentally ill."[76] L. K. had been found to be healthy in the medical examinations on the ship and in the quarantine camp; his illness only appeared in the

immigrant home run by the Jaffa aliya bureau. Three weeks later, the aliya bureau sent L. K. back to France, "to the place he misses."

2. According to a letter sent to a home for the mentally ill and incurable in Jerusalem: "One young man among the new immigrants in Jaffa suffers from frequent attacks of mental illness. His condition is very serious and he needs treatment in a home for the mentally ill. Because he is hard-pressed financially, it would be impossible to pay you for his maintenance. It would be appropriate if you could take this case into consideration and admit him to your institution for free." The institution replied, "Regarding the sick young immigrant in Jaffa, we hereby inform you that the institution's situation . . . does not allow us to admit patients without payment."[77]

3. M. A. arrived in Jaffa on the *Sardinia* in October 1921 with his wife and five children. Because he had no money, he received "assistance with the disembarkation expenses, i.e., the government tax, boat, boatmen, customs, and so on." It turned out that one of his daughters, "age six, has a mental illness that is manifested in the form of kleptomania. The doctors have instructed that she must receive treatment in a hospital for the mentally ill. The father of the family works in construction and can barely support his family. Please try to have the ill daughter admitted for treatment for free."[78]

4. "M. G. of Riga, who arrived as a halutz on Nov. 6, 1924, is insane. M. P., who came from Cernăuți on June 3, 1924, tried to commit suicide the day after she arrived. N. W., a family of three that came from Warsaw on Jan. 1, 1925, with no money and no relatives . . . Mr. N. W. suffers from heart disease and cannot work."[79]

5. According to Dr. Dorian Feigenbaum, a psychiatrist and the first director of the Ezrat Nashim psychiatric hospital, the halutz P. G. suffered from a nervous malady and it was unclear how he had passed the medical exams conducted by the Palestine Office doctors:

> Permit me in this case to make a few comments that I feel I owe it to myself to make. I am very surprised at how the Zionist Organization brought this man to Palestine, despite the fact that his illness, which is unfortunately untreatable incurable, was already noticed in Constantinople. He will only be a burden on you here. Treating him will take a great deal of work and be expensive. My opinion is that the medical exam in the countries of origin and on the coast needs improvement, as it is apparently badly flawed if such a sick person can pass.[80]

Dr. Feigenbaum tried to have the man admitted to Rothschild Hospital, but they refused to accept him due to his medical condition. "My advice is to admit him today to Bikur Holim Hospital and after a while to send him back abroad."[81] But it turned out that the psychiatrist's suggested solution was complicated. Two years after his arrival in Palestine, the aliya bureau was still taking care of P. G.'s needs. In January 1924, Levi Shvueli wrote to the Aliya Department in Jerusalem that all efforts to send him back to Europe had been to no avail. "We did everything we could to convince the patient to leave Palestine at our bureau's expense," but he refused and threatened to commit suicide: "By no means will I leave Palestine voluntarily. If you decide to do something against my will, I will throw myself into the sea." Shvueli added, "The workers in our bureau have discussed this matter seriously and decided that we must not do anything against the patient's will, as it could have dismal consequences."[82]

6. "Z. W. arrived via Jaffa in September 1921. A doctor's certificate is attached. He has a nervous malady. I must draw your attention to the type of patients. This is the second of this sort. The first was L. K.—a mental patient—whom we sent to Jerusalem in accordance with your instructions. According to the director of the Jaffa aliya bureau, there are more and more patients with nervous and mental illnesses due to the lack of permanent employment. Waiting for a job brings them to the point of despair, and also has a terrible effect on those who come after them."[83]

The heads of the Aliya Department in Jerusalem were also concerned about the arrival of mentally ill immigrants, and they asked the heads of the aliya bureaus in Tel Aviv, Haifa, and Jerusalem for up-to-date reports on the scope of the problem:

The frequent cases of nervous and mental illness, especially among young women, that have been brought to our attention by the bureaus are very worrisome to us. Aside from our concern for the fate of the individuals suffering from these illnesses, we are particularly frightened by the frequency of the phenomenon, which may be an indication of some mass, or at least group, psychosis. Therefore, we call your most serious attention to this phenomenon and ask that you take a special interest in all these cases that have already occurred or are about to occur. Each and every case must be investigated as thoroughly as possible, with an eye to its causes and effects. In addition, please ask the aliya doctors to gather all the material pertaining to these cases in the fullest manner. When the material is ready, we will call for a consultation with the aliya doctors, with the participation of experts on the matter, to clarify the problem and find means of combating it.[84]

The aliya bureau workers also had to contend with immigrants with syphilis. The concern was that they might infect the local population after leaving the immigrant home. "I hereby confirm my conversation yesterday with Mr. Unterman in this regard. He arrived on the *Semiramis* on April 16, 1922. He was not permitted to leave quarantine but instead was taken straight to the government hospital for a blood test out of concern that he had syphilis. Yesterday (May 4 [1922]), an immigration official informed me in the name of the government doctor that the immigrant had to leave the country because the test . . . had come out positive."[85]

M. K. had a similar problem: "The aforementioned has the venereal disease syphilis in the secondary stage, i.e., the most infectious," and according to the Immigration Ordinance, he was to be deported. The Aliya Department had no objection to his deportation from Palestine so long as he would not be a financial burden on it. However, because the British government and the shipping company refused to take responsibility for him, the Aliya Department had to find the funds to send him back. In a letter to Professor Pick, Joshua Gordon commented that there was no reason why Palestine should be different from other immigration countries in handling immigrants who were turned back: "In all countries deportation is at the government's expense. . . . If there is a law barring certain immigrants from entering the country, then the shipping company has to know and make sure not to take such immigrants. But until it knows the law, the government itself is responsible. Here suddenly the government is requiring us to cover the cost of deporting immigrants."[86]

The doctors in the Palestine Offices in Europe did not send people with sexually transmitted diseases to Palestine. They knew they would be denied entry, and this would cost the aliya bureau a valuable certificate. Presumably, these immigrants fell ill while waiting in the European port cities before sailing for Palestine. In Trieste and Vienna, immigrants tended to wait about twelve days before boarding the ship. During this time, some of the men visited local brothels and contracted syphilis. The illness incubated in their bodies while they waited to sail and while on the voyage and broke out when they entered Palestine at a problematic and even fateful time.

The coastal bureaus also dealt with sick Jewish immigrants who had arrived overland and had not undergone a government medical exam. These people went straight to the immigrant camp, where they sought medical treatment. In some cases, Zionist immigration officials were uncertain whether to treat them or to hand them over to the British. M. G. reached Beirut on a French visa and reportedly crossed illegally into Palestine. He went to the Haifa aliya bureau and then to Jaffa. Joshua Gordon, director of the Jaffa aliya bureau, reported to the Aliya Department, "He has the venereal disease syphilis [and] is absolutely unwilling to leave the country. He says he wants to recover and not die of his illness."[87] Gordon was caught in a dilemma between maintaining public health and handing over a Jewish immigrant to the British; the latter would lead to his deportation, not only because he was ill but because he had entered the country illegally: "If I turn to the government for assistance, they will jail him and sentence him to prison. Then afterwards they won't send him away as a sick person; they will deport him as someone who entered without permission."[88] The opinion of Dr. Seinfeld, the doctor at the immigrant home, was that he should be deported immediately because he might not recover and because he needed close medical supervision to prevent a relapse of the disease. The doctor added, "Healing takes a long time (during which time he will be a burden on the public). It is impossible to ensure that the patient will recover completely, and there is always a risk to the comrades whom he will have to live with. Our opinion is: deport him."[89]

The above examples shed new light on the period of the Third Aliya and Fourth Aliya. Alongside the healthy, idealistic halutzim, sick immigrants and halutzim also arrived in Palestine, infected with sexually transmitted diseases and mental illnesses of various kinds. The workers in the coastal bureaus had a hard time coping with the complicated situation forced on them; often, they found themselves lacking the appropriate tools or budgets needed to solve complex, sensitive problems of these sorts. Moreover, mentally and physically ill people had a direct impact on the healthy immigrants with whom they shared rooms—and sometimes even beds—in the immigrant homes. The Jews who had arrived in Palestine to start new lives did not expect to encounter violent, emotionally disturbed people or carriers of infectious diseases. Such a greeting no doubt never entered their minds.

The treatment of the ill and the financial cost of finding solutions to their plight elicited a discussion in principle about the ideal immigrant needed to build up the country. "Our criterion must be bringing productive elements to the country," Gordon wrote to Pick. Gordon complained about government immigration officials who not only would not let in immigrants unfit for work but also barred the entry of young people carrying infectious diseases, who would be able to enter the workforce after recovering. The inconsistency was

Figure 5.7. Aliya bureau in Haifa port. Photo courtesy of CZA, PHG\1006766.

problematic, and Gordon believed that the Zionist Executive had to come out against the arbitrary practices of British officialdom.

> Thus, for example, heart disease. From our perspective, such an element should by no means come here. In the doctors' opinion, conditions in this country are very hard on their health and they need to live in special conditions. Moreover, such patients are hardly capable of doing any work other than selected jobs that are almost impossible to obtain in Palestine. And if we have to bar immigrants like these, or even send them back, nevertheless the government—justifiably—does not say such immigrants can enter. But completely inconsistently, it says that epileptic immigrants—an element that is also not desirable for us, exactly like heart patients—can enter. For example, in the case of syphilis, obviously this element is undesirable to us, but I see no reason why the government should bar them for no reason. If it is only on condition that they don't become a public burden . . . from a health perspective there is no reason to bar them from entering. They are not bringing the disease to the country. There is enough syphilis without that, for instance in Ramle, Hebron, and elsewhere.[90]

Gordon expressed succinctly and in brief the Zionist movement's desired immigration policy: reject or deport immigrants who were sick or unfit for work and were liable to be a burden on the Aliya Department, and select strong, healthy immigrants who could cope with conditions in Palestine. Medical care for sick immigrants posed a heavy burden on the staff of the Jaffa and Haifa aliya bureaus, but it was very difficult, and sometimes even impossible, to deport these individuals. The representatives of the coastal aliya bureaus lacked the authority and ability to deport those who refused to leave, and turning them in to the government was out of the question.

After disinfection and release from quarantine, the immigrants were asked to register with the aliya bureau workers and answer their questions. They were then given information about the country. "Each immigrant receives tea, bread, and jam and sets out for the city or the immigrant home. Their belongings are transferred after disinfection as per the immigrants' wishes or to our bureau's warehouse."[91] Immigrants who had starting capital or relatives in Palestine simply entered the country and started their new lives. Those who were destitute and alone in the country were sent to immigrant homes.

Immigrant Homes

In the wake of increased immigration and absorption difficulties, the heads of the aliya bureau concluded that immigrant homes were needed to ensure the newcomers' well-being. These homes were not intended for everyone entering the country; they were specifically for destitute immigrants who had no one to greet them and see to all their initial needs in the new land. In the immigrant home, they received shelter, food, information about Palestine, and assistance in finding work.

Between 1919 and 1927, more than 106,000 Jews arrived in Palestine. About 15 percent of them stayed in the immigrant homes—58.4 percent in Haifa and 41.6 percent in Jaffa.[92] As we can see from table 5.1, the proportion who stayed in the immigrant homes decreased from year to year, from 36 percent in 1922 to just 9 percent in 1927.

The call for establishing temporary lodgings for immigrants came from High Commissioner Herbert Samuel. In a letter to the Zionist Commission in July 1920, immediately after the introduction of civil rule and the opening of the country to immigration, Samuel demanded that the Zionist Organization take responsibility for absorbing the newcomers and helping them find jobs and housing in their first year in the country. He asked the Zionist Organization to provide facilities for the initial housing of the immigrants and suggested that it purchase shacks and tents from the British army for this purpose.[93]

Table 5.1. Immigrants passing through immigrant homes, 1919–1927.

Year	Jaffa		Haifa		Total	Pct. of all immigrants
	Pct.	No.	Pct.	No.		
1919	—	—	—	—	—	
1920	—	—	—	—	—	
1921	—	—	—	—	—	
1922	36.1	1,218	63.9	2,166	3,384	36.8
1923	45.3	1,120	54.7	1,351	2,471	25.5
1924	47.9	1,063	52.1	1,158	2,221	13.7
1925	38.2	2,057	61.8	3,329	5,386	14.6
1926	43.3	1,200	56.7	1,571	2,771	17.7
1927	91.2	166	8.8	16	182	9.0
Total	—	6,824	—	9,591	16,415	
Total (pct.)		41.6		58.4	100	

Source: "Tazkir al Devar ha-Aliya le-Eretz Yisrael" [Memorandum on immigration to Palestine], CZA, S81, file 37, 10.

Until designated immigrant homes had been arranged, the aliya bureau rented four boarding houses in Jaffa: Beit Zariffa, Beit Roch, Beit Kandinof, and Beit Salant. In addition, the General Federation of Jewish Labour had a boarding house known as Beit Hechalutz that housed halutzim in their first days in the country. When more immigrants arrived (especially around Passover), the aliya bureau set up a tent camp on land it had near the beach in Tel Aviv.[94] Altogether the five houses had room for five hundred to six hundred people. They provided roofs over their heads and support in their first days in Palestine. Menachem Sheinkin described how the immigrant homes functioned in the early years:

> In Jaffa five immigrant homes were set up in rented buildings in various parts of the city. . . . When necessary, tents would be pitched for a few hundred more people. The immigrant homes had beds, mattresses, sheets, and blankets. In the immigrant homes themselves or very close by, kitchens were set up where they received fresh, cooked food three times a day. In the main immigrant home a reading room and infirmary were set up. In the big courtyard was a disinfection department that had showers with cold and hot water. These immigrant homes were under the supervision of a special doctor, who also kept the physical statistics on the immigrants.[95]

But even these facilities were insufficient; there were not nearly enough beds for the people who needed them. In times of recession and high unemployment, people were in no rush to leave the immigrant homes until they found work. They had no reason to leave: they were given a place to sleep, food, reliable information about the situation in Palestine, and help in finding jobs. Their long stay in the immigrant homes was a problem for the aliya bureaus because it meant they could not accommodate newly arrived immigrants. Furthermore, it reinforced the Mandatory government's position that the volume of immigration was exceeding the country's absorptive capacity. There were times when the immigrant homes were overcrowded, and sometimes even unfit for inhabiting. Ya'akov Efter, head of the agriculture committee of Hapoel Hatzair, complained to Arthur Ruppin, "Sir! The situation is very grave. In Jaffa there are currently more than 400 immigrants in need of work who are causing terrible crowding in all the lodgings and hotels. Some of them have been in Jaffa for more than ten days already. Today a ship is arriving with 110 new immigrants and by the end of the week another 300 or so [will come]. If appropriate action is not taken immediately to arrange for work, we will very soon have a catastrophe on our hands."[96]

The immigrant homes in Jaffa were moved to Tel Aviv after violence broke out on May 1, 1921.[97] An Arab mob broke into Beit Hechalutz, wreaked destruction, and murdered residents. Rachel Kaufman was one of the survivors. From her testimony to the British police, we learn of the panic that gripped the immigrants during the riots and the circumstances surrounding her arrival in the immigrant home.

> I come from Ukraine. I am not married. On Sunday, May 1, I went to the immigrant home from Sarafand, where I was working. I arrived in Palestine about seven weeks ago, shortly before Passover. I heard that a few people from my native town were in the immigrant home and I went to see them. I arrived in the middle of the day. When lunch was over, a hubbub started and the gates [of the immigrant home] were closed all at once. The Arabs started banging on them. At that moment, all the women in the room ran to Mrs. Cherkassy's room to hide. . . . After the door and windows were broken, we fled to the dining room. As we were fleeing, we heard a police officer shouting, "I am a Jew." After that the police officer who had shouted tried to rape Shoshana Sandek. He was unsuccessful and then went over to another woman named Mrs. Meller. When Mrs. Meller resisted, he hit her in the head and said that if she didn't let him rape her he would shoot everyone. Then he fired and we all lay flat on the floor. The whole time he kept threatening that he was about to shoot. . . . We escaped from the immigrant home in different directions. As I

passed through the gate, an Arab hit me in the head. I lay wounded that entire time and they stole my gold watch from me.[98]

Eleven people were killed and twenty-eight wounded at Beit Hechalutz. During the week of bloodshed, 46 Jews were murdered and 134 were wounded.[99] It was clear to the heads of the aliya bureau that the immigrant homes had to be removed from Arab neighborhoods immediately and an alternative location found for them in a better protected area. Such a place was found at the end of Allenby Street, near the shore.

When the violence died down, the aliya bureau started relocating the residents of the immigrant homes in Jaffa, the survivors of the bloodshed, and new immigrants to the new location—a camp this time, rather than a building. The haste with which the new camp was established caused numerous problems. In early July 1921, due to poor sanitation in the new immigrant camp and the Hapoel Hatzair lodgings, Gordon informed the director of Hadassah's American Zionist Medical Unit for Palestine (AZMU), Dr. Isaac Max Rubinow, of the severity of the situation and warned him of the danger to the immigrants' health.

Rubinow was a doctor who in the late nineteenth and early twentieth centuries had treated Jewish immigrants living on the Lower East Side of Manhattan. In those days hundreds of thousands of eastern European Jews were arriving in the cities of the East Coast of the United States. They settled in poor neighborhoods and lived in crowded, filthy conditions. Due to poor sanitation conditions and poor nutrition, there were high rates of illness and many of the immigrants contracted diphtheria, dysentery, and tuberculosis. Dr. Rubinow helped the Jews of the Lower East Side and promoted social legislation in the United States to improve conditions for the immigrants.[100]

Rubinow's experience as an American Jewish doctor served him well in Palestine. On June 11, 1918, Hadassah sent over the AZMU. This unit had dermatologists; ophthalmologists; gynecologists; orthopedists; pathologists; and ear, nose, and throat specialists as well as nurses, pharmacists, medics, administrators, and medical equipment. After arriving in Palestine in March 1919, Rubinow was named the medical administrator and chief of activity of the AZMU in Palestine.[101] He worked hard to create a medical system like that on Ellis Island, which required all immigrants to undergo medical inspection before entering the country. The idea was to establish medical oversight of the immigrants to protect the country's population from infectious disease and to instill proper hygienic and nutrition habits in the newcomers.

In a letter to Rubinow, British quarantine camp officials described the terrible conditions in the new camp in Tel Aviv and warned against the spread of disease among the city's population. The wooden barracks were rife with bedbugs; they needed to be disinfected and their walls had to be plastered to make them fit to live in. The latrine pits and drainage system had been dug hastily and were liable to pollute the drinking water of Tel Aviv.[102] Conditions in the Hapoel Hatzair lodgings were no better. The report notes a series of severe sanitation problems. Crowding, bedbugs, and filth were rampant in the aliya bureau camp. Sewage flowed over the ground, and residents would cover their excrement with sand. They did their laundry outside the tents, and pools of water collected. The tents, bedding, and clothes were dirty and attested to a lack of hygiene among camp residents. Flies swarmed all over the food that was scattered around the camp, and there was a real danger of pollution and disease.[103]

In September and October 1921, steps were taken to start improving the aliya bureau camp at the end of Allenby Street. With about one hundred tents, the camp had a capacity of three hundred people at peak occupancy. But even after the improvements, problems were discovered due to a shortage of funds and a surplus of immigrants. Security problems cropped up in the new location, too, and the Zionist Commission was asked to protect the residents. "The immigrant camp . . . is on the edge of Tel Aviv near the shore, very far from the settlement," Joshua Gordon, director of the Jaffa aliya bureau, wrote to the Zionist Commission. "It is bordered by two roads, both leading to places populated by Arabs. Recently many shots have been heard in this area, and the case of the Arab who was killed a while back was near the camp." Due to the location of the new camp and out of concern for the residents' security, Gordon applied for permits for the camp guards to bear arms.[104] The immigrants themselves also requested security, complaining to the camp directors that they did not feel safe in the new, isolated location on the edge of Tel Aviv.

Other problems were discovered with the sanitation, hygiene, and living conditions in the camp, especially in winter. The camp doctor, Dr. Seinfeld, had complained that "he can't possibly receive a patient in a tent that is half-collapsed and half-torn and where the rain gets in." Gordon complained that living conditions in the camp were terrible and unsuitable for housing the immigrants and that as the director of the Jaffa aliya bureau, he was personally ashamed of the conditions he was offering the camp residents.

> It is our fault that a camp of 350 people has no library where someone can go in and sit. Ultimately, the immigrants have no place to hide from the rain, even in Tel Aviv itself. They are in a camp where the tents have no lighting; they do not even have anywhere to write a letter or sit and read a newspaper. The tent is torn and the water gets in. It is dark there even in the daytime, and I simply confess that I am ashamed to face the immigrants. . . . The blanket

storeroom leaks. The blankets, sheets, and pillows are wet, and this leads to
more colds than anything else.[105]

Complaints were also heard from Tel Aviv residents about the proximity
of the camp latrines to their homes: "We have received strongly worded complaints from the residents and owners of the new homes built nearby about the
lavatories that you placed a while back by the lodgings, on the hill in Tel Aviv."
The Tel Aviv municipality and the government doctor asked the aliya bureau
to move the latrines "from where they are . . . so that they are hygienic. And we
must insist that this be done no later than a week from today. Otherwise we will
be forced to order municipal workers to remove the said latrines."[106]

But conditions in the camp did not improve. In October 1923, Tel Aviv mayor
Meir Dizengoff wrote to the director of the Tel Aviv aliya bureau that he had
found, during a visit in which he was accompanied by the governor and several
doctors, "that these places have not been set up in accordance with the requirements of hygiene. It has been decided to set up a new tent camp facility for all
the inhabitants of the tents that are scattered in various parts of Tel Aviv."[107]

The first immigrant home in Haifa was open from 1920 to 1924, but we know
very little about it. It was in the center of town, apparently on Jaffa Street, in an
Arab-populated area. A hospital was also opened there to serve the residents,
in addition to a Hadassah clinic.[108] After the violence in May 1921, the heads
of the aliya bureau decided that it was dangerous to house the immigrants in
Arab neighborhoods, so they decided to move the immigrant home in Haifa
too. "The vital need to remove the immigrant camp from where it is now is
rather clear. Time after time we have drawn your attention to the danger to our
relations with the Arabs caused by our concentrating hundreds of unemployed
people in the center of an Arab population and in the centers of town. The
district governor, Colonel Symes, has hinted to us more than once about the
need to remove the camp from there."[109] Aside from the tension and friction
with the Arabs, Shvueli cited the dreadful living conditions for the immigrants.
Two-thirds of the rooms in the rented building were used as lodgings for the
immigrants, while the rest of the building consisted of apartments occupied by
Jewish and Arab neighbors, a small private hotel, and shops. The area around
the building was in poor condition, and there was no evidence that basic cleaning was being done.

In the immigrant home in Haifa, it was particularly hard to treat sick people
in their rooms. The place housed up to four hundred people in overly crowded
conditions. Shvueli told the Aliya Department in Jerusalem that there was only
one infirmary room in the home, even though hundreds of immigrants were

staying there. Moreover, because there was no Jewish hospital in the city, Jewish residents of Haifa—dissatisfied with the medical care in the government hospital, which was run by a mostly Arab staff—also came to the immigrant home when they were ill. Due to the increasing difficulty of taking in the immigrants who were coming to Haifa in growing numbers, Shvueli suggested moving the immigrant home to a cleaner location. The place that seemed most suitable to him was in the Bat Galim neighborhood, near the shore. The location would ensure the immigrants fresh air and the opportunity to bathe in the sea in the hot summer months. The possibility of building the new immigrant home in the Shadaliya area (near the Hadar Hacarmel neighborhood) was also considered, but the idea was quickly dropped.[110] In late May 1922, the Bat Galim neighborhood committee wrote to the Jerusalem aliya bureau, requesting that the future immigrant home be established in their neighborhood:

> Because we have heard that the Governor has insisted on moving the immigrant home from an Arab area to a Jewish area, and because we already expressed interest in the matter a few months ago, we hereby propose the following. On the edge of our land, located on the coast near the Cave of Elijah, are 14 dunams [1.4 hectares] of government-owned land. When the Governor made his demand that the immigrant home be moved, your representative, Mr. Shvueli, suggested to the Governor that this land be handed over to build the immigrant home. The Governor liked the idea. He dispatched a government commission to determine whether the place is suitable for this purpose, and it also expressed its consent.[111]

In December 1923, a building contract was signed and the cornerstone was laid for the immigrant home in Bat Galim. The event was reported in *Doar Hayom*:

> In the middle of the day, a lot of traffic was already seen on the road leading from the city up to Bat Galim—some by vehicle, some on foot. All, young and old, flocked to the place near Bat Galim where the celebrations are to be held. In front of the field, a gate of honor was set up with a Jewish flag and a British flag. The members of the aliya committee stood at the gate to greet the guests. In a wooden shack . . . that will apparently be used as an office for the time being, is a table with refreshments. The tents that the immigrants are in were pitched in the middle of the field. In addition, a stage has been set up for speakers and important guests. Next to the stage is an orchestra led by Mr. Grinspon; around it, in a semicircle, are students from all the Jewish schools in Haifa with their teachers and inspectors. The crowd is growing. I don't know if Haifa has ever had such a huge crowd.[112]

Figures 5.8 and 5.8A. Photograph and sketch of the immigrant home in Bat Galim. Photos courtesy of CZA, PHG\1054242 and PHG\1054245.

In late 1924, Shvueli reported that the construction of four buildings in the immigrant home compound had been completed and noted the amount of money still needed to complete the sanitation arrangements. The kitchen building had three rooms: a cooking room, where meals were prepared and dishes were washed; a dining room, where meals were served to a hundred people; and a smaller room that served as a storeroom and pantry. The second building had four dormitory rooms for men: two enormous rooms with thirty-two beds and two small rooms with eight beds. The third building in the compound consisted of two stories. The bottom floor housed the aliya bureau office and had three rooms: a room for receiving the public, the secretary's office, and the administration room. On the second floor were two dormitory rooms for women containing twelve beds. The fourth building contained the lavatories and showers for men and women. Scattered throughout the camp were tents to house more immigrants.

In 1926, the camp doctor complained to the Aliya Department about the poor sanitary conditions there. The tents were so overcrowded, he said, that

HOME of IMMIGRANTS

IN HAIFA. Bath-Galim.

בית העולים

בת-גלים, חיפה.

9. מטבח.
8. חדר אוכל וקריאה.
7. מעונות לעובדים עברים.
6. בית עולים.
5. מעונות לעובדות עבריות.
4. מעונות לעולים עברים.
3. בית עולים.
2. מעונות בתים לעולים.
1. חדר הנהלה.

מבט כללי מצפון.

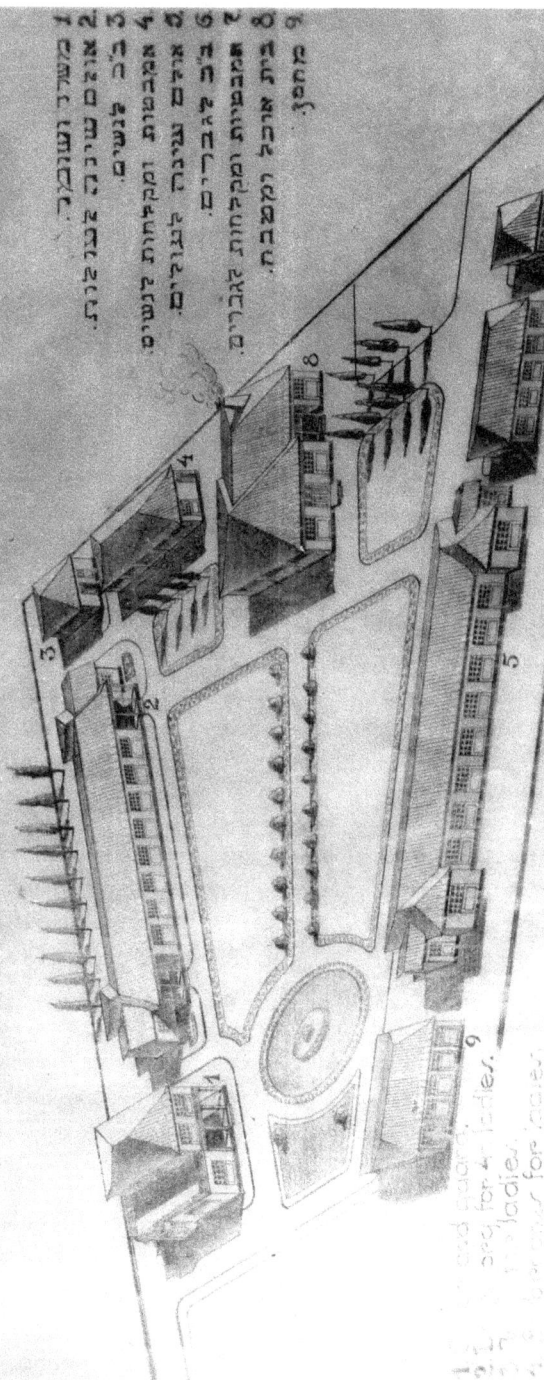

Haifa. Nov 1923

... and ...
... seg. for ... ladies.
... ladies.
... for men.
... to gentlemen.
... gentlemen.
... for de ...
... room and kitchen.

1. ...
2. ...
3. ...
4. ...
5. ...
6. ...
7. ...
8. ...
9. ...

the residents were forced to share beds. The crowding was causing illness, especially as some of the residents did not maintain adequate personal hygiene. He was not happy with the meals served either; he believed they should be modified so as to strengthen the immigrants and improve their physical condition. A doctor from Hadassah who visited also saw problems: "Nowhere in the immigrant home are there warnings or rules of hygiene informing the new immigrants how to eat or drink, how to protect against the sun's rays, etc." Furthermore, there was no dedicated infirmary room, bathhouse, or "lavatories meeting hygienic requirements"; there were no laundry facilities; "and towels are not given to each and every individual."[113] According to another report, the lavatories had "only two cubicles, one for men and one for women. This is too little. It is essential for another two cubicles to be set up." The lavatory was "arranged in a primitive fashion," with jugs under the seat. "An Arab comes every day, removes the full jugs, and pours them out 'far away.' But where is this faraway place? I couldn't get an answer to this, neither from the doctor nor from the young man who gave me the explanations." The author of the report was surprised "that when beautiful, comfortable buildings were built, there was no supervision by the doctor or else he wasn't consulted, and for that reason they didn't make sure to follow the rules for a proper lavatory."[114]

The overcrowding in the immigrant homes in Haifa and Jaffa sometimes led to clashes and violence. For example, Gordon described a fight between immigrants from Russia and Poland over the language spoken in the immigrant home:

> Moreover, there is no room for all these immigrants and nowhere to meet. As a result, the cultural campaign for languages and familiarization with the country is not feasible. I speak from experience when I say that here in Jaffa there have been fights between Polish and Russian immigrants over the Poles' hatred of the "Muscovites" and the Russians' [hatred] of the Poles. And that was just because these spoke only Russian whereas those [spoke] only Polish. Furthermore, people came to my office complaining about the behavior of many young people in the streets. . . . There are a lot of different elements whom we don't even know and who don't belong to any group or any party or any association.[115]

Battalion for the Defence of the Language was upset by all the languages spoken in the immigrant homes and asked the Aliya Department for permission to offer the newcomers evening classes in Hebrew.[116] The haredi community in Haifa wrote to Shvueli noting that haredi families were coming to Palestine and requesting permission "to post notices in the lodgings about our institutions here, since a large proportion of these immigrants have children."[117] But the haredim and the Battalion for the Defence of the Language were not the only ones who recognized the potential inherent in the immigrant homes as closed, bounded places where efforts could be made to shape and influence the immigrants' worldview; the Communists also sought to add them to their ranks.

During a visit to the local immigrant home, the director of the Haifa aliya bureau found in its yard "gangs of immigrants having a heated argument on various issues. Emissaries of the SWP are the most vocal." In a letter to the Aliya Department, he wrote, "We cannot prevent outsiders from entering the courtyard as long as there is no gate to the courtyard and anyone can enter freely. . . . Regrettably, good young people are falling into the SWP's trap because they are getting a description of the country and living conditions from only one source—the SWP."[118] He suggested having representatives of the General Federation of Jewish Labour's Culture Committee and others address the immigrants on various topics. "However, neither the Labor Department nor the Culture Committee has responded to my letters. Meanwhile, 194 immigrants in the immigrant home in Haifa are spending their evenings idle and bored."[119]

The managers of the immigrant homes faced additional difficulties as well. In some cases, troublesome, undisciplined residents refused to leave the homes, and people who had received loans from the Aliya Department to help them start out in their new country either disappeared or left the country without repaying the debt. "I hereby draw your attention," the director of the Haifa aliya bureau wrote to the Aliya Department in Jerusalem, "to the fact that recently halutzim have come into the immigrant home with exceptionally rude, strange, and wild behavior." They refused to obey the rules and caused difficulties for the staff. "From their very first day in the immigrant home, they tried to provoke all sorts of scandals by not submitting to the fixed schedules in the immigrant home. . . . And they started waging a campaign in the immigrant home not to go out to work as part of the group, not to submit to schedules, and not to make their beds (they insisted that the workers who get paid a salary should do this)."[120]

These uncontrollable halutzim simply refused to go to work. In their opinion, the work was not suited to their skills, so they stirred up the other halutzim against the immigrant home staff. "It should be noted that a representative of the Shimron group in Hadera came here wanting to take ten people to work, but out of 120 people neither he nor a representative of the aliya center could obtain the consent of more than two people." They gave various original excuses for refusing to go to work: they had not been offered suitable jobs; "Keren Hayesod [had] enough money" to support them "for a while longer until [they] were able to make arrangements as [they] wished"; and the wages being offered were not enough for them to send money back home. The fact that the immigrant home was not emptying out caused crowding and hindered the absorption of more recent immigrants. Since forcible evictions were not an option, the director of the Haifa aliya bureau had no choice but to threaten "that they would not be accepted as members of the General Federation of Labour if they continued their strange behavior."[121] The solution found in the end was "to give those engaged in scandalous behavior a loan of 250 Egyptian *grush* each and expel them from the immigrant home." The SWP was suspected of having incited them against Zionism.

Another problem had to do with the repayment of loans immigrants received from the aliya bureau to help them in their new lives in Palestine. Many borrowers had their own means but lied about their finances in order to qualify for loans and then used the money to pay for passage on a ship leaving the country. "Many people, as soon as they set foot in Palestine, want to enjoy the people's money." As soon as they received the money, they would disappear or purchase tickets to return to their countries of origin. The proposed solution was to insist that borrowers' deposit their passports; however, it turned out "that a person's passport is a personal document under the basic laws of countries with an enlightened political regime" and could not be confiscated.[122]

From these descriptions it seems that the aliya bureau directors and staffs had to contend with troublesome immigrants, even among those described as "halutzim." Some were aggressive and violent; others were exploitative liars. People with various agendas also intervened in the routine in the immigrant homes, taking advantage of the closed compound to influence the residents ideologically. On the one hand, the Battalion for the Defence of the Language sought to offer evening courses in Hebrew; on the other, the Communists tried to enroll them in their party's struggle against the British and Zionism.

The immigrant homes were also criticized by certain circles in the Yishuv who believed that the costs were too high and that renting houses would suffice. "The extent to which there is no real concern for the public purse is attested to in part by the creation of the 'camp,'" wrote *Hapoel Hatzair* editor Yosef Aharonovich:

> This "genius idea," too, seems to have been conceived mainly because it was necessary to occupy some office workers who were bored with nothing to do. And then on August 1, that is, when it was almost winter, they started establishing a tent camp for the immigrants on the shore, despite what they could have known in advance but no one mentioned: that this "camp" would

be unusable in the winter. The "camp" building was completed in the middle of September and cost close to 2000 pounds.... But can the creators of this camp please state honestly: Did they have nothing else to do than spend 2000 pounds on a camp for a few months, when for much of this time the tents would stand empty with no one to live in them? Was it impossible to find apartments for less, even at Tel Aviv prices?[123]

But the criticism of the immigrant homes was unjustified. It was not good for the immigrants to stay in hotels and rented apartments in Jaffa and Tel Aviv, and the service they received there was poor. Zvi Livneh described it in his memoirs: "Gradually it became clear that housing the immigrants in hotels was not a satisfactory arrangement." He stated that the hotel owners were eager "to make as much money as possible. They crowded people in and even set up beds in the corridors, and they were not careful about clean bedding and food provisions." He added that not all the hotels "lived up to their commitment to provide complete, tasty meals" and that, most importantly, "scattering the immigrants in several places had a detrimental effect." Livneh also reported that the newcomers had been placed in various hotels in Neve Shalom and Tel Aviv and that on several occasions "SWP people and simply bitter people in the hotels have slandered the Yishuv institutions and what has been created in Palestine to the new immigrants." This had "motivated the aliya activists to think about independent institutions for room and board that would be less expensive and cleaner, and would create an intimate, encouraging atmosphere among the immigrants."[124]

A *Doar Hayom* reporter who visited the aliya bureau summed up the work of the aliya bureaus and immigrant homes in Jaffa and Haifa and their contribution to immigrant absorption in Palestine. He recognized the importance and impact of the staff's dedication:

Altogether, this bureau contains a director and five workers, including a janitor and a yardman. The work they do is as follows: meeting the immigrants on every ship, [assisting] with document inspection, disembarking the people and their belongings and taking them to the city, taking them through customs and disinfection, keeping precise records of the individuals who come (single immigrants, people with families, and tourists as well); paying all the expenses entailed by this as well as the government tax, settling accounts with each immigrant, and, in order to expedite matters, helping with the government registration; handling the removal of the belongings from the disinfection house and handing them over to their owners under proper supervision; setting up some of the newcomers in hotels where the bureau oversees cleaning and ensures that prices aren't raised. Those who come without means are taken to the lodgings, where they stay until they find work; until then they provide them with room and board.[125]

But helping the immigrants on their first day in the country was not the only job of the immigrant homes. They were intended to "control" the traffic of immigrants, keeping them there and then releasing them gradually to strike roots in the new land only after they had found places to live and jobs. The directors of the aliya bureaus were afraid that the job market would be flooded with new jobseekers and that British government officials would voice criticism regarding the country's limited economic absorptive capacity and refuse to admit large numbers of Jews. "Thus maintenance in the camps is considered a means of diluting, albeit artificially, the arrival of new workers. Otherwise they would necessarily affect the daily job market in such a way that the arrival of each ship would be noticeable outside by a sudden, unnatural, and therefore catastrophic increase in unemployed persons."[126]

In the early 1920s, new work procedures began to take shape in preparation for integration of the immigrants arriving in Palestine after World War I. At first the Provisional Committee for the Jews of Palestine assumed responsibility for handling immigration issues and even established a special subcommittee for it. An aliya bureau was established in Jaffa, headed by Menachem Sheinkin, and more aliya bureaus were established in coastal cities near Palestine. After the Zionist Congress in Carlsbad, it was decided that the Zionist Organization would take over the handling of immigration, and the organization established the Aliya Department headed by Professor Hermann Pick. Everything to do with immigration to Palestine was the bureau's responsibility. The three Palestine aliya bureaus—in Jaffa, Haifa, and Jerusalem—were subordinate to the Aliya Department, and their directors—Joshua Gordon, Levi Shvueli, and Ze'ev Leibowitz, respectively—were put in charge of implementing the Zionist immigration policy and taking care of the immigrants.

Entering Palestine, from the inspection of travel papers until disinfection and the stay in the immigrant home, gave the newcomers a glimpse of the life that awaited them in their new country: confrontations with British immigration officials; criticism of the aliya bureaus for not doing enough for them and the feeling that they deserved better because they had come to Palestine; complaints about disinfection, quarantine, long queues, and the long, exhausting, frustrating admission procedure; and finally, the highly charged encounter with local Arabs who were incensed by their arrival. This is how the Jewish immigrants began their lives in their new land.

One of the main difficulties for the aliya bureau was dealing with those immigrants who had become a burden on the Zionist institutions. Not everyone who came was an ideological pioneer spreading the Zionist creed, draining swamps, and making the wilderness bloom. Among the tens of thousands of newcomers were also immigrants who could do nothing to build up the country: frail old people, disabled people, physically or mentally ill people and carriers of disease (including sexually transmitted diseases), thugs, criminals, and others who regarded Palestine as no more than a default option and who in many cases wanted to go back to their native lands. The heads of the aliya bureau vacillated and fought frequently over whether to send back to Europe Jews whose contribution to the Zionist enterprise was marginal or even negative or whether to let them stay in Palestine and cope with the difficulties of their absorption.

Often the encounter with the Arab population turned out to be traumatic for the Jewish newcomers. Arab boatmen helped them off the ships into rowboats, watched over their belongings during the disinfection and medical examinations, and were part of the medical staff in the quarantine camp and hospitals. The immigrants had lots of complaints against the Arabs: irresponsible and unprofessional handling of their luggage, which often fell into the sea and sank into the depths; theft of belongings from luggage that had been left unattended; inappropriate treatment by Arab medical staff; and more. The local Arabs often demonstrated on the shores of Haifa and Jaffa against the entry of Jews into Palestine. It was a frigid welcome for the exhausted Jewish immigrants, who heard invective and curses in Arabic denouncing their arrival even before they set foot on the country's shores.

Although the aliya bureau helped the immigrants enter the country and even took care of them in their first days after arrival, the Mandatory government oversaw the entry procedure and had the power to approve or reject people. Immigration regulations were issued, travel papers were inspected by British immigration officials on board the ship, medical examinations were conducted, a quarantine camp for the sick was set up, and the passengers' luggage and clothes were disinfected. For the first time in history, entry into the country was orderly and organized.

The shapers of the immigration and entry procedure took Ellis Island as a successful model to be emulated: a meticulous medical examination, appropriate travel papers, and registration of those entering and leaving the country.

Nevertheless, despite the similarities between the procedures for entering the United States and Palestine, there was one fundamental, conspicuous difference: in Palestine, there was someone offering intensive assistance to immigrants and taking care of their problems. In a lecture on arrangements for immigration to Palestine, Joshua Gordon stated, "Every passenger, upon arrival in an unfamiliar country, needs assistance and advice . . . especially if the country to which the person is coming is totally different in its customs and institutions from most of the countries with which he is familiar."[127] To help newcomers integrate in the society around them, numerous private organizations had been established that took care of them and offered them a hand. In general, these organizations were founded by people who had immigrated earlier and were thoroughly familiar with the new country.

In the context of Palestine, Gordon said in his lecture, the situation is different due to the expectations Jewish immigrants had of the Zionist movement and Palestine. They regarded the new country as their home and themselves as the homeowners; as soon as they arrived, they made demands and filed complaints if they didn't get what they wanted. "In all countries, whether they are immigration countries or not, there are therefore institutions to help foreigners coming to the country. In addition, residents or immigrants who came before establish special societies to protect the new immigrants' interests, and if necessary even to protect them from the government." In Palestine, in contrast, the Ashkenazi Jewish community was not taking part in the absorption of their countrymen at all. Responsibility for immigrant absorption fell on the shoulders of the Zionist Executive, and the local Jewish society was not doing its share: "It suffices to cross the Egyptian border and see that in Alexandria, Cairo, and Port Said there are special societies from the communities that take care of immigrants to Egypt and even those going to Palestine. Even in our country, all the ethnic groups other than the Ashkenazim—the Persians, the Yemenites, the Maghrebis, and so on—take care of immigrants from their community more or less by themselves. *The Ashkenazi community is almost the only one that has thrown off this burden and left it entirely to the Zionist Executive.*"[128]

Just as American Jewish aid organizations (some of them discussed in the first chapter) helped immigrants to the United States and local Jewish communities did likewise in other countries, Gordon believed it was the Yishuv's duty and not just the Zionist Executive's responsibility to help with immigrant absorption in Palestine. This was the main difference between immigration to Palestine and to other countries, including the United States. Those who went to Palestine expected the Zionist movement to help them settle in. It would help them find a place to live, earn a living, recover their health, and even leave the country if they decided they no longer wanted to stay. When the immigrants' expectations were dashed, even partially, they felt frustrated and betrayed and complained to the aliya bureau and the settlement institutions. The Zionist movement, for its part, tried to safeguard their journey to Palestine from the initial stage of decision-making at the Palestine Offices in Europe to their arrival on the shores of Palestine, but it could not satisfy all their expectations. The resultant tension and unpleasantness between the immigrants and the institutions in Palestine would be manifested throughout the rest of their lives in the country.

6

Invisible Immigration

"The third wave of aliya was almost entirely of a certain hue—not refugees, not immigrants, not tourists, but a vanguard of pioneers. Most of the olim received prior training through Hechalutz and came in organized groups to live communal lives, lives of labor and nature. Even those few who were unable to form a group aspired to agriculture and a life of equality and justice."[1] This is how Zvi Livneh (Lieberman) described the members of the Third Aliya in his book *Pirkei ha-Aliya ha-Shelishit* (Chapters of the Third Aliya), published in 1957/58. The olim were socialist pioneers who had been trained by Hechalutz and had come to Palestine to live lives of communalism and labor. Seven years after the publication of Livneh's book, on the forty-fifth anniversary of the resumption of immigration after World War I, *Sefer ha-Aliya ha-Shelishit* (The book of the Third Aliya) came out in two volumes, edited by Yehuda Erez. This book told the story of the Third Aliya from the perspective of those who had arrived between 1919 and 1923. About a thousand pages of memoirs describe the experience of the journey to Palestine and the initial encounter with the country, life in the Labor Battalion, the building of roads and draining of swamps, and the settlement groups in the villages and cities. "The generation of the Third Aliya, which had felt the horrors of World War I," wrote Erez, "was called on to do great deeds in accordance with the needs of the times, which were more extensive and comprehensive than the exigencies that had faced the generation of the Second Aliya."[2]

The stories of Jews who arrived in the Third Aliya and the Fourth Aliya but did not belong to the labor movement are not told—in Livneh's book or in Erez's extensive work. Livneh was a member of the Second Aliya, and Erez was a member of the Third Aliya; both were among the authors and writers who fixed the halutzic image of the Third Aliya in Zionist historiography and excluded from it anyone who did not fit the mold.[3] Baruch Ben-Avram and Henry Near, in *Iyunim ba-Aliya ha-Shelishit* (Studies in the Third Aliyah), undermine the image created by Livneh and Erez and present a different version of the history of the Third Aliya. But even they ignore the non-Sephardic, non-Yemenite Jews who arrived from Islamic countries. True, Ben-Avram and Near state that no natives of Palestine or of Asian and African countries were members of the Zionist Executive and that their representation on the Jewish National Council was 11.5 percent and 5.6 percent, respectively, but there is no mention in their book of the Jews who immigrated in the 1920s from Islamic countries. Thus, they continue the tradition of excluding North African and Asian Jews from historical scholarship on immigration to Palestine during the British Mandate.[4]

Books on the Fourth Aliya have not described it in glowing terms. Even though large numbers of halutzim, particularly members of Hashomer Hatzair, arrived in Palestine at the beginning of the Fourth Aliya period, this aliya—unlike the previous ones—consisted mainly of the petty bourgeoisie. When it was just beginning, Arlosoroff noted its identifying characteristics: "In the last year and a half the economic character of the Yishuv has changed in two ways: by initial attempts to establish modern industry, and by 'the immigration of the middle class,' customarily known as the 'Fourth Aliya.'"[5] Despite the impressive historiography on the socialist Third Aliya in contrast to the weaker coverage of the bourgeois Fourth Aliya, what these two periods had in common was the eastern European perspective on their history. True, most immigrants during the Mandate period came from Europe, but there were also Jewish immigrants from North Africa and Asia, and they should be included in the chronicles of the waves of aliya.

This last chapter focuses on immigration to Palestine from Asia and North Africa in the 1920s. From the correspondence between the Palestine Offices in North Africa and Iraq and the Zionist Executive in Jerusalem and London, we can discover the motivations for this immigration and learn about the Zionist Executive's policy regarding candidates for aliya. The study of immigration to Palestine from Islamic countries points to similar motivations and even a similar profile of the immigrant population.

The Scope of Immigration to Palestine from
Asia and Africa, 1919–1931

Between 1919 and 1931, approximately 117,000 Jews immigrated to Palestine. Of these, 11,000 (10%) were natives of Africa and Asia, according to the following distribution:

Figure 6.1 shows that 92 percent of the immigrants came from Asia (Turkey, Iraq, Iran, Yemen, Syria, Lebanon, and Afghanistan) and only 8 percent from the Maghreb (Egypt, Morocco, Algeria, Tunisia, and Libya) and South Africa. Far fewer Jews arrived in Palestine from Asia and North Africa in the 1920s than from Europe; as stated, they represented only about 10 percent of the total immigrant population. However, the proportion of Jews from Islamic countries who immigrated to Palestine exceeded the proportion of world Jewry immigrating. At the beginning of the twentieth century, there were about ten million Jews in the world, of whom 340,000 (3.4%) lived in Islamic countries.[6] The Jews' rate of immigration to Palestine from Asia and North Africa was four times that of the Jewish people as a whole. For comparison's sake, 90 percent of Jewish people lived in eastern Europe, and barely 1 percent of them came to Palestine.

Jews from Yemen and Iraq generally entered Palestine by land, and most of them continued on to Jerusalem. Some crossed the border at Rosh Hanikra and went to the aliya bureau in Haifa. There they were registered and had to pay the entry tax to Palestine. In some cases, immigrants refused to pay the tax; they were then detained in quarantine or in the disinfection shack, and there was concern that they might be sent back to Baghdad. "On December 17, 1925, seven families of Sephardic immigrants arrived in Haifa by car from Baghdad. The people left their belongings in a garage and went to the coastal office to register there."[7] The Palestine Office representative in Baghdad had not informed them that they would have to pay an entry tax, and they refused to pay. The Haifa aliya bureau refused to pay on their behalf without authorization from the Aliya Department in Jerusalem. The detention of the Iraqi immigrants in Haifa and the concern that they might be deported caused tension between the aliya bureau and the Sephardic community of Haifa, which was outraged by the discrimination against the Jews from Iraq. "As you instructed, we did not agree to pay for them, and after they were handed over to the police to be sent back, we contacted you again in this regard. (Meanwhile, the Sephardic community intervened in the matter with the intent to turn it into a scandal.) We informed you that it had been decided that they had agreed to return to Baghdad and were refusing to pay. And then you authorized us to pay for them and try to collect the money."[8]

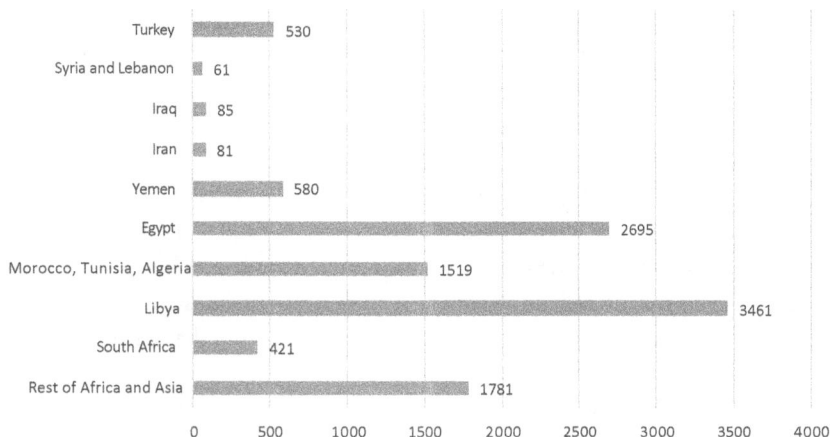

Figure 6.1. Immigrants to Palestine by country of origin in Asia and Africa, 1919–1931. Source: Gil, *Dappei Aliya*, 28.

The Haifa aliya bureau ultimately paid the taxes but did not get its money back because the Iraqi families fled Haifa in the dead of night: "If these immigrants had not gone (or more correctly, fled) that night, we would have tried to collect the money. . . . Presumably, they fled to Jerusalem because they had not been informed that we would pay on their behalf as per our request."[9]

The Jerusalem aliya bureau dealt with the immigrants from Islamic countries, assisted them in their first days in the country, and helped them settle in. According to reports sent to the Executive Committee of the General Federation of Jewish Labour, most of them seem to have managed well, without any special difficulties. "It should be noted that until the crisis erupted in full force, Jerusalem excelled in its absorption capacity; the Eastern immigrants demonstrated especially good adjustment here due to their knowledge of the Arabic language and their ways of life, which are well suited to this country. They came up with ways of earning a living by work, trades, and petty peddling. These met their needs, which did not far exceed the general Eastern standard of living."[10]

Despite the orientalist generalizations about Eastern Jewish communities making do with little, they did settle in well and fairly smoothly. A report by the Jerusalem aliya bureau for 1925–1926 indicates that 27 percent of the applicants to the bureau were from Iraq, 26 percent were from Kurdistan, and 14 percent were from Iran. Only 5 percent were from Yemen because the Yemenite Jews mostly went to Moshavot Yehuda and Tel Aviv. "So far twenty-seven certificate holders have come to Palestine from Yemen—eighty-four people including their families. Only three of them are single. Most of the immigrants have already settled in the villages: Rishon Lezion, Rehovot, and Kefar Sava. The Kefar Sava agricultural committee has issued wooden shacks on half-dunam fields to ten families and pledged to employ all family members of working age."[11]

Substantial differences became evident in the motivations for migration from Africa and Asia. Migration from Iraq, Yemen, Turkey, and Iran resembled migration from Europe in general and Ukraine in particular. There was a great deal of similarity between the Jewish refugees from Ukraine who crowded into Odessa and Constantinople and sought to immigrate to Palestine and the Jewish refugees from the Iranian-Turkish border who fled from the Armenians and waited in Baghdad for aliya authorization that didn't come. In contrast, Jews from the Maghreb region immigrated for completely different reasons. The Balfour Declaration and rumors of the resumption of immigration to Palestine led to a Zionist awakening in Morocco, Tunisia, Algeria, and Libya. The Jews there started considering the possibility of aliya and requested information from the Zionist Executive in Jerusalem via the local Palestine Offices.

Orumiyeh (Iranian Azerbaijan) and Iraq

Nuri wanted to know more about this Aghassi, who is called Agassi here. Why did he immigrate in the 1920s? One night, after studying a page of Talmud, he told him that he had been born in a small village in Kurdistan and fled to Baghdad, where he found refuge in a synagogue. He worked as a carpenter's apprentice and studied in a yeshiva. The *shamash* arranged a match for him with Nona. She didn't want to be separated from her family and preferred life in the city of sinners over the holy city, but Agassi was impatient to leave and he decided to go.[12]

World War I wreaked destruction and havoc not only in the Jewish communities of eastern Europe but also among the Jews south of the Caucasus. In the mountainous region between Lake Van and Lake Orumiyeh, the Russian and Ottoman armies fought several battles. The city of Orumiyeh, located at the intersection of three powers, was occupied and destroyed during World War I by the Russians, Turks, Kurds, and Assyrians, and its residents suffered from murder, looting, and destruction.[13] The Jewish community included Jews of various nationalities: Turkish, Russian, and a few Iranians. Each time Orumiyeh was occupied by another country, the citizens of the other countries were in danger. The Jews tried to help one another: when the Turks entered the city, Turkish Jews hid Russian Jews, and vice versa when the Russians invaded. The

Russian army's victory and its establishment of a presence in the region led to the displacement of residents, Muslims and Jews alike, who fled in fear for their lives.[14] When the Bolshevik Revolution broke out, the Russian troops withdrew and handed over control to the Armenians, who attacked the local populace. The residents' lives were turned upside down, as they found themselves under incessant attack by the Armenians.[15]

In 1918, Orumiyeh was under Armenian rule for about nine months, during which time there were vicious riots against the local Jews. The Armenians robbed and murdered the community's dignitaries, and many Jews escaped to Baghdad or Baku (the capital of Azerbaijan). By the late 1920s, only about three hundred Jewish families remained.[16] Ovadia Yedidya arrived in Palestine in the early 1920s after fleeing from the Armenians. In his testimony, he recounted the massacre of the Jews of Orumiyeh:

> Meanwhile the revolution broke out in Russia. The Russians abandoned the front and left their weapons with the Armenians. The French also supplied them with weapons. The Persians and Armenians fought wars over control of Orumiyeh. After three days of fighting the Persians surrendered. A gang of Armenians murdered and robbed the Jews and Muslims but didn't touch the Kurds. The Kurds' leader invited Mr. Shimon, the Assyrian leader, to be his guest in Salmas, and when they had sated themselves with food and drink he shot him and his fellows, some 150 Assyrian Christians who served as his bodyguards. The next day the Christians and Armenians attacked Kurdistan in an all-out war. The Kurds began to flee and many of them were killed. The Jews, about eighty families, gathered in the synagogue in Salmas. The Armenians and Christians surrounded them, searched them, and then set fire to the synagogue with all the men, women, and children inside. The Assyrian leaders rescued the Jews who weren't in the synagogue. The riots continued for about nine months. When Father came to Uremiyeh we decided to leave the area. This was in 1919. Meanwhile we started hearing news of Palestine and rumors that there was a Jewish government with a Jewish king by the name of Herbert Samuel.[17]

Alongside the riots and violence, the Jews also suffered from starvation and disease. Maston Ya'akobi recounted in his memoirs, "In 1918–1919, there were typhus and typhoid epidemics in the region. Whoever wasn't killed in the violence and didn't starve to death was afflicted by the severe illnesses that spread rapidly, especially in the Christian villages. The villages emptied out, no one was left in them alive, and they remained abandoned for years."[18] A group of young people from Uremiyeh described their harsh living conditions, which in many ways resembled the lives of the survivors of the Ukrainian pogroms.

We, the young people of the Uremiyeh Jewish community, Little Persia, were beset by terrible troubles. The frightful events and the vicissitudes of the times led to high prices. Some men, women, and children died due to the severe famine. Some Jews were so hungry that they swallowed poison and died . . . so as not to see the death of their children. Children were fainting in the streets from hunger; small children begged for bread but there was none. . . . Trouble followed trouble. Our hands were dry and our lips were too mute to talk about the second trouble. An Ishmaelite sheikh rose up against the king of Persia, made war against him, conquered all of Little Persia, and killed and destroyed the two towns of Little Persia—more than five hundred Jews. Several synagogues were burned with their Torah scrolls. And then an Ishmaelite sheikh attacked our city of Uremiyeh. We were under siege for two months. From the outside the Ishmaelite sheikh oppressed us; on the inside Persians slandered us, plundered and robbed us, and killed several Jews every day. Persians are seizing us, attacking us with swords and spears, and taking terrible vengeance on us.[19]

Starvation and need were rampant in other Iranian cities as well. Ezra Ben-Eliahu recounts in his memoirs that due to the terrible situation in the city of Hamadan, his father was forced to work as a rabbi and ritual slaughterer in the city of Khorramabad—"a distance of almost 40 days' travel by donkey." The money that his father sent didn't reach the family, so Ezra had to support the household. When they heard the news of the Balfour Declaration and rumors that Palestine was opening up to immigration, they decided to migrate. Five families set out from Iran and reached Baghdad, but were expelled from there to Bombay, India. Finally, after extensive difficulties and repeated efforts at persuasion, the British allowed them to sail to Palestine.[20] The story of the Ben-Eliahu family represents that of many Jewish families from Iran and the Uremiyeh region. Many Jews became refugees, fleeing to Kirkuk, Basra, and Baghdad. Most of them made their way to Baghdad and found themselves suffering from a precarious financial situation and emotional hardship. They became a burden on the local Jewish community, which tried to help them in part by sending them to Palestine. The British, concerned about an increase in the influx of refugees, sent many of them to India, where they tried to get visas and tickets for ships sailing for Aden and from there, via Egypt, to Palestine.

Zalman Shazar wrote further testimony about the refugees from Uremiyeh following the murder of the Jews there and about immigration to Palestine; it was printed in the newspaper *Davar*. When Shazar was a patient in Beilinson Hospital, a Jew from Uremiyeh named Shlomo Ben-Agajan had the bed next to his. His neighbor told him about the riots and his family's journey to Palestine: "When the riots broke out in 1918 and Jewish blood was spilled in Uremiyeh like water, when news of the redemption arrived and the aliya of the people of Uremiyeh began—all eyes were lifted to Jerusalem. The roads were dangerous and they had no money, but the Jewish communities in the transit countries supported them and made arrangements for their journey." They traveled "from Uremiyeh to Shushan, from Shushan to Baghdad, from Baghdad to Bombay, India, from Bombay to Muscat, from Muscat to Aden, from Aden to Qantara, and from Qantara to Jerusalem. This took two years and many people fell ill during the arduous journey; some even died."[21]

In early September 1921, the heads of the Mesopotamian Zionist Association—also known as the Zionist Office in Baghdad—wrote to the Zionist Executive in London and expressed interest in sending the refugees from Uremiyeh to Palestine. They requested the help of the central office: "Please do everything you can to obtain certificates for one thousand people in Mesopotamia.... The lives of some of them are in danger aside from the danger of starvation. Have mercy on them.... Most of them are capable of doing any work, especially working the land and raising livestock. Many of them speak fluent Hebrew."[22] At the time the letter was sent, it was not possible for the Jerusalem aliya bureau to accede to the request. The country had been closed to immigration due to the bloody riots in Jaffa, and the new immigration policy restricted the number of Jews allowed to enter the country. Two months later, the Zionist Office in Baghdad sent another letter, this time asking that the refugees from Iran and Kurdistan who were in Baghdad be brought over: "As we have already informed you, there are close to a thousand people in Mesopotamia waiting every day to immigrate to Palestine. They have escaped from Kurdistan and the villages of Persia, from the oppressor's sword. And we have heard that many of those who remained there have been killed. If these people were to immigrate, then those would come, too, and not fall victim to the people who are after their money and their lives. We therefore look forward to hearing good news."[23]

In February 1922, the Zionists in Baghdad sent a third letter, this time via the Baghdad-based Aziz Ala Na'im, honorary president of the Zionist Organization in Iran. He appealed directly to the Zionist Executive in Jerusalem, pleading for assistance for the Iranian and Kurdish refugees in Baghdad:

Due to the incidents in Jaffa in the past year, the migrants were not permitted to go to Palestine. They have decided to stay in Baghdad until the situation changes [and] they can go to the place they hope and yearn for. While here—due to the high cost of living—they have spent much of what they had at their disposal. The immigrants are now few in number and they have travel papers (visas from the British envoy). They are waiting impatiently to know their fate. But the refugees apparently left behind much of their property and fled for their lives. Many of the refugees . . . became laborers and are currently working in construction to earn a living. By day they do their jobs but at night they are in terrible distress because they have no homes where they can rest and be protected from the cold. Until now they have all been living in the *beit midrash* . . . but more than a week ago they were evicted from there—reportedly by the Hakham Bashi . . . who is expressing anger and bitterness against Zionism and its adherents. . . . They all want to go to Palestine to work there. Many of them are strong, healthy people who can tolerate hard work and make do with little.[24]

A January 1922 list of "Persian Jewish immigrants and refugees in Baghdad" confirms the accuracy of Aziz Ala Na'im's letter to the aliya bureau regarding the profile of the refugees seeking to go to Palestine. Most of these people were between eighteen and thirty-five, were married, and had children. They were listed as farmers and middlemen, with some skilled tradesmen and silversmiths as well. They had been in Baghdad for anywhere from a few months to years. Siman Tov Ben-Yitzhak, for instance, had spent just two months in Baghdad, whereas Amram Ben-Nuriel had been there for four years.[25]

The aliya bureau's answer was short and to the point: "Unfortunately, it is impossible to send entry certificates to Palestine for those people who are in Baghdad in view of the current immigration law, which requires that each person have £500 or have been offered a particular job."[26]

The Mesopotamian Zionist Association's appeals to the Zionist Executive for help for refugees from Iran and Kurdistan were similar to the appeals to the Palestine Offices in Europe (especially in Warsaw and Constantinople) for aid for the refugees of the Ukrainian civil war. In both cases the large number of refugees in the city made the Palestine Offices' work difficult, and their directors needed to find a solution. The answers from the aliya bureaus were also similar: they were unable to accede to the requests, whether the prospective immigrants were from Europe or Asia. The Zionist immigration policy in this case was uniform, preferring physically and mentally healthy halutzim over refugees, whoever they might be.

The appeals to the Zionist Executive on behalf of the refugees from Uremiyeh led to the establishment of a Palestine Office in Baghdad. This office was

subordinate to the central aliya bureau in London, which was moved after the
war to Jerusalem. The office's representative in Baghdad reported directly to the
central aliya bureau. His name was passed on to the British as the official Zionist representative in Baghdad, and he received instructions and information
about the immigration procedure: "We have informed the British government
that we have appointed you our official representative in Baghdad for matters
of immigration to Palestine. No doubt the British government has already
notified its representative in Baghdad of your appointment."[27] In addition, the
aliya bureau sent the Baghdad representative "a special letter of authorization
in English regarding your appointment and, in a separate envelope, we are
sending you instructions and three circulars on aliya for the immigrants."[28]

Like the aliya bureaus in Europe, the one in Baghdad requested more immigration permits and conducted protracted negotiations with the central aliya
bureau over the number of aliya certificates and the kind of immigrants needed
to build up the country. The answers given to the representative in Baghdad
were identical to those received by his counterparts in Europe. He was asked
to send only the wealthy, because poor immigrants would become a burden
on the settlement institutions. "From this material, you will see that there are
two categories of immigrants: class 1, who lack means, and class 2, who have
means." The representative was instructed to limit class 1 immigrants "in accordance with the country's capacity for absorbing them and the dire financial
situation of the Zionist Organization, which has to support the immigrants in
Palestine so long as they have no work." Class 2 immigrants—that is, those with
means—"have no difficulty at all with immigration. Our representatives in
each location, when contacted with questions by immigrants in this category,
are supposed to assist them as much as possible." Regarding the number of aliya
permits allocated to the office in Baghdad, "we have allocated only twenty-five
certificates . . . despite our tremendous desire to allocate more. The Zionist Organization recently apportioned 1,100 certificates to various centers in eastern
and central Europe, places where hundreds, even thousands, of halutzim are
waiting impatiently for the first opportunity to come to the place of their heart's
desire, after having experienced many trials and tribulations in recent years."[29]

The Zionist representative in Baghdad protested giving preference to halutzim from Europe just because they had undergone "trials and tribulations."
A refugee is a refugee, he said. There was no difference between a Ukrainian
Jew and a Kurdish Jew, whether their homes had been burned and their property looted by the troops of Denikin and Petliura or by the Armenians. The
aliya bureau confirmed that it had received the letter of complaint "regarding
the immigrants and refugees from Persia who are now in Baghdad . . . but

unfortunately the immigration laws have not changed for the better since we last wrote to you."[30] The issue remained on the agenda in Baghdad, with the Zionist representative continuing to pressure the aliya bureau to help bring the refugees to Palestine: "Enclosed is a copy of the telegram that we sent regarding immigrants in several places in Mesopotamia that are unsuitable for settlement. There are about a thousand such persons. One must have mercy on their health. Several children have already died from the heat of the sun."[31]

Additionally, some Iraqi Jews went to Palestine as tourists or immigrants and settled there. In the 1920s, the route from Baghdad to Jerusalem was safer and more accessible than before. "Even when the journey from Baghdad to Palestine was so long—fifty days from Baghdad to Jerusalem and dangerous due to robbers—Easterners would go to prostrate themselves at the tombs of saints, as the Jews of the East do. Now that it has become so short—three days . . . and the cost so low . . . the yearning for the Land of Israel has grown."[32] Middle-class families who had not received immigration certificates bypassed the British immigration policy by entering the country on tourist visas. Obstacles were posed by the Iraqi government, which insisted on a financial bond for each Jewish tourist who set out for Palestine. "Many wealthy families were planning to go to Palestine to celebrate the Sukkot festival. . . . The new decree by the local government blocked their way. Because who would agree to post bond for a tourist. . . . The huge sum that the government is demanding of tourists—more than 70 pounds sterling—denies the middle class the opportunity to go and visit the tombs of the saints."[33]

Middle-class Iraqi Jews had difficulty affording the taxes imposed by the Iraqi government and coping with the hostility of the surrounding society. Other economic factors also spurred them to emigrate:

> Recently extraordinary fervor for emigrating to Palestine has been felt among members of our community, especially the middle class. The dreadful commercial crisis . . . the heavy taxes imposed on merchants and industrialists practically steal the Jews' bread . . . and one after another they are having to close their shops. And woe to the Jew who has a home of his own. He has to pay a municipal tax that is five or even eight times that paid by his Muslim neighbor. . . . The hatred of the Jews being spread among the neighbors by the press, the Jews' bitter enemy, is what has tipped the scales in favor of Zion.[34]

The special correspondent for *Haaretz* in Baghdad noted two additional motivations for emigration: opposition to the Westernization that had altered the traditional character of the Baghdad Jewish community and favorable reports from those who had already gone to Palestine:

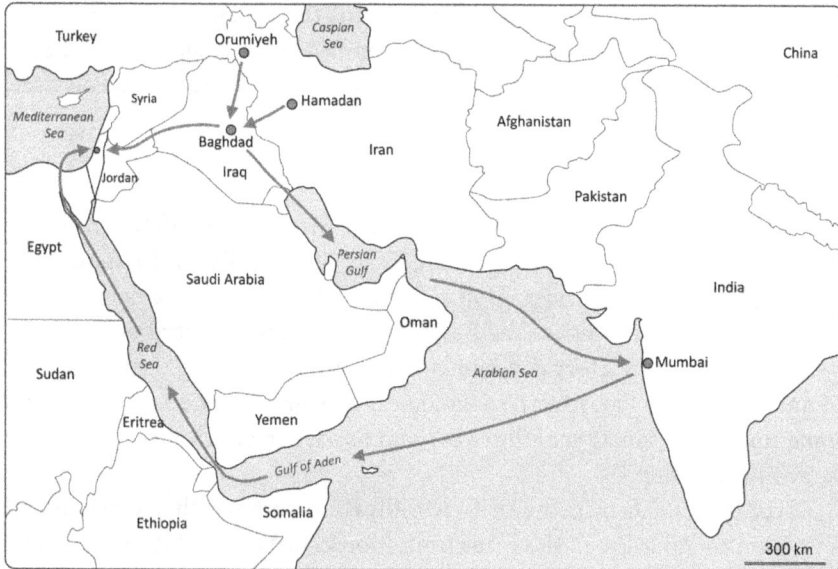

Map 6.1. Routes from Baghdad to Palestine.

A clever Jew who feels things keenly senses his precarious situation in the toxic environment in which he lives. Day after day, he witnesses distressing events inside and outside. The advocates of assimilation, unwilling to give up their status, rule over the community by force. Our community is losing its traditional character and mimicking the "civilization" that is entering via the Alliance. Most of our young people who are educated there learn heretical ways from their teachers, such as smoking on the Sabbath and eating forbidden foods. . . . The encouraging reports from those who have already managed to settle in Palestine have effected a revolution among the masses. More and more tourists, including merchants and industrialists, are going to Palestine to tour the country and investigate economic and commercial conditions there.[35]

If we replace the Iraqi Jew described in this chapter with a Polish Jew, Baghdad with Warsaw, the starving people in Uremiyeh with the starving people from Bolshevik Russia, and the survivors of the pogroms in Iranian Azerbaijan with the survivors of the pogroms in Ukraine, we see that the motivations for migration from Iraq in the 1920s were identical to the motivations for migration from Poland and Ukraine in those same years. More than sixty-seven hundred Jews went to Palestine in the 1920s from Iraq, Iran, and Turkey. The establishment of an aliya bureau in Baghdad and the appointment of an official Zionist movement representative there to handle aliya arrangements made the city a major junction for refugees and immigrants hoping to go on to Palestine.

The Maghreb

The motivations for immigration from North Africa were different from the motivations for immigration from Iraq, Iran, and Kurdistan. In Yemen and the Maghreb there were no pogroms, and Jewish refugees were not a burden on the Jewish communities. The Balfour Declaration and word of the establishment of the Mandatory government in Palestine triggered the resumption of immigration to Palestine for ideological reasons—religious, Zionist, and sometimes a combination of the two—and not due to political persecution or economic hardship.[36]

According to data from the Jerusalem aliya bureau, fewer than two hundred Jews went to Palestine in the 1920s from Morocco, Tunisia, Libya, and Algeria.[37] Despite the small scale of migration, aliya bureaus were established in these countries, usually headed by a community member who was given all the necessary information. For the most part, the aliya bureaus were established in the major cities, and they handled applications from the entire region. The town of Sefrou, about twenty-five kilometers from Fez, was home to a small, affluent Jewish community whose members decided in the early 1920s to go to Palestine. The Zionist association in Fez contacted the Zionist Organization in London and reported that most of the Jews of Sefrou had liquidated their businesses and wanted to migrate. They wished to appoint Yosef Levi—a merchant and Alliance school alumnus who was opposed to the Western reformist ideology of the French education system and who supported Zionism—as the Zionist movement's representative in Fez.[38]

The Zionist Executive agreed to let Levi represent the residents of Fez and outlined what he would have to do as the aliya representative of the Zionist Organization: "This representative must take responsibility for his actions, be decent, have goodwill, and not show favoritism, and he must act strictly in accordance with the immigration instructions." Moreover, they explained, he would be required to send to Palestine only those capable of working: "Strong people, people who have the means to survive for at least one year. Or those who have a trade such as carpenters or blacksmiths. In brief, those who can contribute to the development of the state." Levi was asked not to recommend "people who have only enough for the travel expenses and will have to go begging when they arrive."[39]

From Levi's letter, we see he indeed enforced the Zionist immigration policy and looked for candidates for aliya who had the financial means and occupational skills needed to settle in Palestine:

> For your information, I have long been spreading word that those who lack the necessary means will not be able to obtain a visa for their passport. There are single people who want to serve under the Zionist flag but unfortunately do not have enough money to pay the travel costs. I beg them to be patient. Then there are laborers. I am well aware that before we can send them we have to wait for the country to call for them, which will first require fundraising and a consequent increase in product, the development of big public works companies, and so on. It should be kept in mind that in my work on Zionist campaigns in Fez, Sefrou, Meknes, Rabat, and Jedda in the last three years, I have only recruited comrades associated with the French Zionist Federation.[40]

Similar letters arrived from Marrakesh, from Agudat Zion in Tripoli, and from the Tunisian Zionist Federation.[41] The aliya bureau's responses to the Jews of Sefrou, Marrakesh, Tripoli, and Tunisia resembled those sent to the Zionist representatives in the European aliya bureaus: at that point the economic situation in Palestine precluded the admission of Jews lacking economic means, and they would have to wait until things improved.[42] In a letter to Rabbi Pinhas Halifa Cohen Azour of Marrakesh, the aliya bureau said that immigration to Palestine had been halted "due to the distressing events in Jaffa." After "vigorous [efforts] by the [Zionist] General Council and by the Zionist Commission for Palestine the decree was revoked" and immigration to Palestine resumed, but priority would be given to those already en route, whose entry had been barred due to the riots: "Aliya depends even now, and perhaps even more than before, solely on the financial means that our organization can devote to the employment of the immigrants in Palestine. The Zionist Commission stresses in all its telegrams to us that employing just the laborers who are en route will require tremendous sums of money.... From these details, you will understand on your own that the admission of new halutzim will not be possible until those immigrants who were stopped on the way due to the distressing events have entered the country."[43]

The Zionist Executive's replies were not always received with understanding, and the disappointment was compounded by a sense of discrimination on ethnic grounds. The Tunisian Zionist Federation complained of discrimination in the distribution of aliya permits and about the fact that their request for ten to fifteen aliya permits had been rejected. Y. Beiteli, secretary of the Aliya

Department in Jerusalem, replied that the certificates were distributed fairly based on requests received from the countries of origin and that no orderly request had been received from Tunisia. Furthermore, Beiteli added, the distribution of the semiannual quota had already been completed and only a few aliya certificates remained for skilled construction workers. He explained that due to the great demand for certificates and doubt about whether there were experts in the required trade in Tunisia, the Aliya Department had decided to allocate them only three certificates for qualified candidates.

Sometimes the sense of being unwanted was caused by immigrants telling their relatives about having suffered discrimination. The case of Albert Cohen, who left Tunisia in late 1920, demonstrates the sensitivity of the Maghreb Jewish community in matters affecting their fellows in Palestine. In January 1921, Agudat Zion in Tunisia complained about the antagonistic, unfriendly attitude of the settlement institutions toward a man from Tunis by the name of Albert Cohen. The organization told the Zionist Executive in London that Cohen had complained to his relatives in Tunisia about the problems he was having settling in Palestine and his difficulty finding work. Cohen, they said, had alleged that his difficulties were due to his Tunisian origins. Rather than rejecting the complaint out of hand, the executive asked the Zionist Commission to display sensitivity and see to his needs so that his distress would not appear to stem from ethnic motivations: "It should be noted that the complaints by the Sephardim that they are neglected and even persecuted as Sephardim are general ones. If only to prevent unnecessary grumbling and to ease the minds of our brethren in Tunis regarding the young man in question, it is worth seeing him and getting him a job."[44]

The Zionist Commission absolutely rejected all allegations of discrimination against North African immigrants as well as Albert Cohen's claim. In its reply to the Zionist Executive in London, the commission noted that there was difficulty "regarding our Sephardic brethren. They come as individuals rather than in a group. They do not know Hebrew, they go straight to the cities, especially Jerusalem, and they look for work on their own." The Zionist Commission noted further, "Most of the people coming from these countries are petty merchants and luftmenschen for whom it is hard to find work. We treat all immigrants coming to Palestine with the same attention and goodwill. In fact, because the Sephardim are liable to complain that they are being neglected, we try very hard not to give them any grounds for complaint." As for Cohen, the Zionist Commission reported that in the meantime he had found work to his satisfaction.[45]

The case of Albert Cohen was not singular. Jews from North Africa complained on numerous occasions of ethnic discrimination in medical care, jobs, and even admission into the workers' kitchens. Their letters to their communities triggered grievances and anger vis-à-vis the Zionist establishment's attitude toward Sephardim. These stories and rumors presumably made an impression on people who were considering aliya, deterring them from going ahead with it. The complaints were also sent to the Zionist Executive in London, which passed them on to the Zionist Commission with instructions to review their veracity. The commission conducted an in-depth investigation of every complaint and concluded, "A significant number of Sephardim have entered the country and all of them have received exactly the same treatment and the same assistance in finding work." Spot checks of individual cases found no truth to the complaints: "They complain that they were asked in Rothschild Hospital whether they were Sephardic or Ashkenazi [but] they were told that the questions were solely for statistical purposes. Absolutely no distinction is made between Jews in how they are treated; the same can be said about non-Jewish patients, a small number of whom come to the hospital. As for the food provided to the Hapoel Hatzair house, the kitchen manager, Mrs. Chana Meisel, stated that there is no distinction between Sephardim and Ashkenazim. All immigrants receive exactly the same food."[46]

In a report on Aliya Department activities between March and June 1923, the Zionist Executive addressed the issue of Sephardic immigrants, and the impression given is that there was a condescending attitude toward them. "We want to devote a few words to the type of immigrants coming from Eastern countries (Iran, Yemen, Mesopotamia, Algeria, Morocco, Afghanistan, and so on), who in that period numbered approximately 1,400." On the one hand, such a Jew has "an advantage in aliya because he knows the language of the country (the language of our neighbors), is familiar with their customs and way of life, lives by manual labor, and makes do with little. But on the other hand some of them are having a hard time adjusting psychologically to the conditions of building the country, to life as part of groups based on cooperative foundations."[47] This statement was supposed to be indicative of an egalitarian perspective among the Yishuv leadership based solely on pertinent facts. However, it demonstrates orientalist stereotypes originating in preconceived notions: the immigrants from Islamic countries were perceived as different from the rest of the immigrant population and from the majority society. According to the report, the Jews of Eastern countries made do with little and were familiar with the local customs. This assertion had no basis in fact. Many of the Jews from Islamic countries were unfamiliar with conditions in Palestine, and their encounter with the country was just as complex and difficult as it was for the immigrants from Europe. Some of them had never been accustomed to making do with little; on the contrary, many of them had belonged to the middle class in their countries of origin and had never experienced hardship or lack. The same report also mentioned another category of immigrants:

> Included in this category of immigrant are some who, where they come from, have heard fantastic descriptions of life in Palestine. They have heard the footsteps of the approaching Messiah. They have been told of the Jewish king dwelling on Mt. Zion and bringing about the return to Zion; this Jewish king would meet the immigrants coming to Jerusalem, and so on. These immigrants come to see this with their own eyes, and when they encounter the bitter reality, they sometimes sink into despair and send letters to their countries, spreading untrue reports about the situation and denying every-thing that exists in Palestine. They complain without justification about being treated differently as immigrants from the East, about Western immigrants (Ashkenazim) being given preference, and so on. Unfortunately, some people believe the false rumors and we have had to refute them with facts and figures. We have informed our representatives in those countries; we have demanded that they describe the situation clearly and warn those spreading the pro-paganda not to fire up the people with artificial-fantastic fervor that will be doused an hour after it develops, potentially causing a catastrophe for our work. But our representatives have not always been successful in this task. In some cases the listeners called them spies. They didn't want to hear when the situation was made clear to them. They came anyway. Our aliya bureaus gave them assistance of a different sort, just as they give it to every immigrant who comes to Palestine, in addition to financial support, the cost of transportation to the workplace, and sometimes the disembarkation expenses and the gov-ernment tax. They were given loans to cover rent, work tools, commerce, and so on. It should be noted that the Jerusalem aliya bureau offered assistance this Passover to about one thousand Eastern immigrants.[48]

The report stresses the disparity between the image of Palestine and the reality that immigrants encountered after their arrival. A few of them came to Palestine for Messianic reasons and expected to be welcomed by the Jewish king. According to scholar Yaron Tsur, the Balfour Declaration and word of the establishment of the Jewish home did elicit religious fervor among the Jews of the Maghreb. However, the correspondence between the Zionist representa-tives in the Maghreb and the Zionist Executive in Jerusalem and London shows no evidence of aliya for Messianic reasons but rather attempts to find candi-dates who shared the Zionist worldview.[49] Perhaps some immigrants from the Maghreb were disappointed, but so were the halutzim of the Third Aliya. Many of them, too, left the country or chose to put an end to their lives.[50] In this re-spect, there is an interesting similarity between eastern European immigrants and those from Islamic countries: both were disillusioned with the country they had yearned to reach, and both libeled the country in letters to relatives or slandered it when they returned to their countries of origin.

Despite the feeling of discrimination among Jewish immigrants from North Africa, it seems that the Zionist movement's attitude toward prospective olim in the 1920s was egalitarian. The North African Zionist associations received answers to their questions, and the Zionist Executive tried to explain the objective difficulties in aliya. In its response to a request for information on aliya from Agudat Zion in Tripoli, for instance, the Zionist Commission expressed a positive attitude toward aliya from Libya and satisfaction with the ties formed with the Jews of Tripoli, who were then under Italian rule. "We received your letter of June 9 and are delighted that in your city, too, ties have been established with the Zionist center in London and with us. We will very willingly answer your questions about immigration from time to time. We have delayed our reply to your letter all this time due to the recent events in Palestine, which have brought about fundamental changes in immigration matters."[51]

Further evidence of the Zionist Executive's positive attitude toward aliya from North Africa is its repeated, persistent request that the French authorities stop demanding a financial bond of one thousand francs from every Jew seeking to visit or immigrate to Palestine. Efforts were also made to encourage immigration to Palestine by healthy, productive young people who could participate in building up the country. However, despite the Zionist Executive's favorable attitude toward the awakening of Zionism in the Maghreb, the number of immigrants from there remained low for several reasons: The economic and political situation of the Jews of the Maghreb was relatively good. Unlike the Jews of Iran and Uremiyeh, who arrived in Baghdad as refugees, the Jews of the Maghreb did not suffer from persecution and pogroms. Moreover, Zionist propaganda was banned in North Africa, and the bond demanded of Jews and the limited allocation of aliya permits precluded immigration by more than a few hundred people.

Yemen

About a quarter of the Jewish immigrants from Islamic countries in the first decade of the Mandate arrived from Yemen. Their motivations were similar to those of the immigrants from eastern Europe, Iran, and Kurdistan. In the 1920s, the Jews of Yemen were a persecuted minority among a majority Muslim society. After the riots of 1921 in Jaffa, Imam al-Mutawakkil Yahya banned emigration to Palestine. In 1926, he captured the port city of Hudaydah and blocked the main migration route to Palestine via the Red Sea. In this period, the economic and social position of Yemenite Jewry was undermined, and many sought to leave. Some succeeded in getting out of Yemen and reached Palestine after a long, grueling journey.[52]

In March 1921, the Presidium of the Jewish National Council wrote to the high commissioner asking for his assistance in bringing the Jews of Yemen to Palestine. "If we may be so bold, the Jewish National Council requests that Your Excellency intercede with the British government to ease the living conditions of the Jews in Yemen, as they are in distress . . . there, and also take the necessary steps to ease the restrictions so as to bring them to Palestine." They noted the dire situation of the Jews in Yemen and the decrees imposed by Imam Yahya on the Jews: "This imam's officers have now dredged up from the depths of oblivion an old, foreign, cruel religious edict that even the Turkish government never knew: all Jewish orphans are required to convert. Through force and various acts of violence, they make the Jewish orphans accept the other religion, and if they refrain from doing so and run away from the harassing officers, the heads of the Jewish community are jailed. This occurred in the city of Dhamar, where the community leaders have been held in jail for five months on the charge of helping orphans escape."[53]

From a political standpoint, the situation of the Jews in Yemen was no different from that in Uremiyeh and Ukraine. In all these places, an intolerant regime persecuted the Jews and made their lives unbearable. Because no aliya bureaus were established in Yemen, it is hard to track the motivations and societal composition of the Yemenite migrants or the aliya bureau's attitude toward them. Our limited information comes from the Association of Yemenites, which took care of the immigrants in their first days in the country and helped them settle in. According to this data, 694 Jews came to Palestine from Yemen in 1925 and 1926. Most had families; only twenty-two were single. Eighty-two were farmers, twelve were builders, ten were ritual slaughterers, nine were peddlers, and four were teachers; the rest were laborers with no specific occupation.[54]

In the absence of a Palestine Office in Yemen, the migration of the Yemenite Jews was complicated. They had no one to guide them, make arrangements on their behalf, and, most importantly, see to their welfare during the journey. Yosef Shalom Habara recounts in his memoirs *Bi-Tela'ot Teiman vi-Yerushalayim* (The tribulations of Yemen and Jerusalem) that it took him about five months to reach Palestine after he failed in his first attempt and was forced to return from Aden to Sanaa. "I reached Jerusalem on Rosh Hodesh Elul 5684 [August 30–31, 1924], thereby concluding my journey from Asmara via Massawa, Port Sudan, Khartoum, and Cairo. The journey took about five months. And although I felt great joy over having finally fulfilled my dream, my joy was not complete

Map 6.2. Route from Yemen to Palestine.

because I remembered my wife and three children whom I had left in exile; moreover, my wife was pregnant."[55] Two years after he arrived in Jerusalem, Habara managed to bring his family over via Aden, where they had been waiting for entry visas for Palestine. "My family was delayed in Aden until the end of the month of Kislev for a simple reason: they had no one to accompany them on the ship due to the decree about aliya, and my wife and children could not travel alone. After a long wait in Aden, they were able to resume their journey, and they arrived in Jerusalem—thank God—hale and hearty."[56]

Eliyahu Dobkin, one of the leaders of Hechalutz in Poland, found interesting similarities between the halutzim and the Yemenites, especially with respect to the difficulties they experienced and the obstacles they encountered on their way to Palestine. "There are specific political, legal, and financial barriers to immigration from Russia. We have not fulfilled our obligation with regard to immigration from Russia. The Congress must therefore decide to charge the Zionist Executive with using all means to remove the obstacles from our path and boost immigration from Russia. And the same is true of immigration from

Yemen. There, too, the Jews are being tortured and persecuted unbearably and want to immigrate to Palestine. And Jewish means must be seized with respect to this aliya, too."[57]

The Zionist Executive was aware of the difficulties facing the Yemenite immigrants. In a meeting with Avraham Tabib, Avraham Sarum, and Zecharia Gluska, representatives of the Yemenite Jewish community, the decision was made to try to establish an aliya bureau in Yemen. "About a month ago, at a meeting of the Zionist Executive, Prof. Pick, Mr. Y. Sprinzak, [the British army officer] Kisch, and representatives of the Yemenites discussed enabling the immigration of the orphan refugees in Yemen, who are suffering terribly there economically, spiritually, and politically." Following the meeting, the General Conference of Yemenites in Palestine convened for a serious discussion of immigration from Yemen. It passed several resolutions: "The Conference elected its executive board and charged it with negotiating with the Zionist Executive and the Jewish National Council regarding arrangements for aliya from Yemen."[58]

No aliya bureau was established in Yemen in the 1920s, despite repeated requests from the leadership of the Yemenite Jewish community in Palestine. In 1929, Gluska, chair of the central committee of the Association of Yemenites, accused the Zionist Executive of helplessness with respect to rescuing Yemenite Jewry. He alleged that it was disregarding resolutions of Zionist Congresses and was insensitive to the distress of the Yemenite Jews. "Much has been written and said regarding this question for the past seven years, from the day the dreadful persecutions of our brethren in Yemen resumed." Gluska noted that the 14th Zionist Congress (1925) had already resolved "to open a special aliya office in Aden, but the previous Zionist Executive, loyal to its path, namely, disdain for the Yemenites, ignored this resolution by the Congress, too, and the office in Aden has still not been opened." Meanwhile, conditions in Yemen became worse and "were reported in Palestine and abroad. The decrees of forced apostasy and malicious oppression shocked all of Jewry." Only the Zionist Executive's Aliya Department was not shocked. "[Not] only did it not make any effort to save our tormented, persecuted brethren; it also scorned the resolutions of the Congress: it did not open the aliya office on the Yemeni coast and did not give it the certificates that we had requested to rescue those families that had managed to escape from their tormentors. This disgraceful, inhuman attitude has caused the lives of dozens of families to be cut short on the shores of the Red Sea."[59]

Gluska's accusations regarding the Zionist Executive's attitude toward the persecuted Jews of Yemen are identical to the allegations directed at Zionist policy and the attitude of the Zionist institutions vis-à-vis the refugees of the

Ukrainian civil war. In the 1920s, priority in aliya was given to members of the Zionist youth movements over refugees from Ukraine, Kurdistan, Iran, and Yemen. The Yemenite Jews' criticism of the Zionist Executive was accurate, but that Zionist policy was applied uniformly to all communities. Sometimes the deciding factor was not how much the refugees were suffering—something they all had in common—but how many refugees were thronging the aliya bureaus in Europe and how much pressure was being exerted on Zionist and non-Zionist aid organizations to bring people to Palestine. Like the heads of the European aliya bureaus, Gluska defined the plight of the Jews in Yemen and their motivations for immigration as follows: "We have before us a lot of work and we must be prepared to do it. First and foremost, we must resolve the question of immigration from Yemen, the rescue of our persecuted, tormented brethren who still survive in a remote corner of Yemen."[60] From his perspective they were not olim or even immigrants but survivors seeking to remain alive by escaping from Yemen to Palestine.

Only in 1929, after almost a decade of talk and in full agreement with the leaders of the Yemenite Jewish community in Palestine, did the Zionist Executive dispatch aliya bureau representatives to organize aliya from Yemen.

> With respect to the resumption of aliya, the Zionist Executive expressed its opinion on the appointment of a representative in Aden to organize the immigration of Yemenite Jewry. Based on the investigation of the issue in Aden by R. D. Kesselman, who visited Aden in the winter of 1928, having been given this job by the Zionist Executive, Mr. Ben Zion M. Aharoni, one of the dignitaries of the Jews of Aden, was named the Zionist Executive's official representative on aliya matters vis-à-vis the British commission in Aden. Regarding the certificates given to Mr. Aharoni, it should be noted that the desired order was made in sending the immigrants, the medical inspection, and so on.[61]

Focusing on immigrants from Islamic countries gives us a unique perspective on immigration to Palestine and a context for comparing aliya from various Jewish communities in Palestine and abroad. It is impossible to understand the Third Aliya and Fourth Aliya without addressing the entire range of immigrants who arrived in those years, including those from Islamic countries. Immigration from Asia and North Africa in the 1920s was not uniform. Some of the newcomers were refugees from Iran and Kurdistan who had fled the Armenians and reached Baghdad. In Baghdad, they became a burden on the local Jewish community, which attempted to assist them and send them to Palestine. Others were middle-class Iraqi Jews who went to Palestine to better their financial situation after having fallen on hard times. In North Africa, in contrast, where the Jewish communities had been exposed to Zionism, the immigrants were motivated by Zionist ideology.

From the correspondence between the Palestine Offices in the Maghreb and the Zionist Executive in London and Jerusalem, we see the disparity between the Zionist movement's attitude toward prospective immigrants and the expectations of the applicants themselves. The aliya bureau's replies show that in the first decade of the Mandate, candidates from the Maghreb were being carefully selected and that, as in Europe, the Zionist movement preferred the physically and mentally fit who could adapt to the conditions and needs of the country. However, we can discern a condescending attitude in the Yishuv toward Jews from Islamic countries, which eastern European immigrants did not suffer. Jews from Islamic countries voiced complaints in Palestine, and associations of immigrants from particular towns or regions, like the eastern European landsmanshaften, were formed to contend with the discrimination and condescension.

The causes of migration from North Africa were different from the causes of migration from Yemen and Iran. In the absence of real push factors (political or economic), the Jews of the Maghreb were in no rush to leave for Palestine in the early years of the Mandate. In this sense, the North African Jewish communities were no different from Jewish communities in western and central Europe, who did not migrate to Palestine in large numbers because they were doing well financially, enjoyed equal rights, and had struck roots in the surrounding society. In contrast, we see similarities between the Jewish refugees from Uremiyeh who fled to Baghdad and the Jewish refugees from Ukraine who fled to Odessa and Constantinople. Both refugee populations were products of pogroms and severe manifestations of violence following the breakdown of the old political order during and after World War I.

The Palestine Offices in Iraq and the Maghreb were established at the same time as the ones in Europe, and they assumed responsibility for organizing immigration to Palestine. From the correspondence and requests, we see that the aliya bureaus in London and Jerusalem did not discriminate against Jews from Islamic countries. The answers given to the representatives and applicants were similar; the heads of the Palestine Offices were expected to find young, fit, healthy candidates to build up the country. Certificates were not distributed equally to the various Palestine Offices: eastern European Jews received more than Jews from Asia and Africa. The Palestine Office in Baghdad complained about this because it saw no difference between the refugee populations. The disparity was due to heavier, more extensive pressure exerted on the aliya bureaus by the Ukrainian Jewish refugees.

Conclusion

The book *Land of Refuge* begins with poet Ya'akov Orland, a child survivor of the pogrom in Tetiev. It concludes with poet Isaac Lamdan, who also lived through the bloody pogroms in Ukraine. Lamdan, born in 1899 in the town of Mlynov, in the Volhynia district of Ukraine, spent World War I and the civil war wandering from place to place with his brother, who was later murdered in a pogrom.[1] He arrived in Palestine in 1920, and three years later, he started writing the poem "Masada." This poem, published by Hedim in 1927, was dedicated to his brother Moshe, "him of the pure heart and precious soul, who fell on Ukrainian soil during the slaughter of the Jews" and whose burial place is unknown.

Lamdan's poem, a canonical text for Yishuv society of the 1920s and 1930s, expressed the Yishuv's values and the belief that the Zionist idea would be fulfilled by halutzim joining the growing Zionist revolution in Palestine. They would come en masse, exhausted but determined to save the Jewish people from their suffering and to restore them to their rightful place in history as they rebuilt Palestine from its ruins:

Open thy gates, O Masada, and let me, the fugitive, enter!

At thy feet, I place my disintegrating soul—place it on the anvil of thy rocks and beat it out, shape it and beat it out anew!

For where more can I take this my weary, stumbling body when all the shells of rest have fallen from it?

. . .

Deliver! I shall close my eyes that they be not drawn to this terrible
refuge, and that they be not attracted to its flame.—I pin myself entirely to
the bars of your gates:
   Open them, Masada, and I, the fugitive, shall come![2]

The poem consists of six chapters: "A Fugitive," "To the Wall," "Night Bonfires,"
"Outside the Camp," "When Bonfires Die," and "Not Yet." With tremendous
artistry and linguistic sleight of hand, Lamdan sketched the long history of the
Jewish people from antiquity until the fulfillment of the Zionist idea in Palestine. *Land of Refuge*, from start to finish, is about the first chapter of the poem,
focusing on that Jewish refugee—whether from Europe or from an Islamic
country—in the 1920s. The refugees are the heroes of the epic story of immigration to Palestine in the first decade of the Mandate; it was they who carried on
their backs the Jews' jug of tears, which was unparalleled until the Holocaust.

   Two dramatic events directly and immediately influenced Jewish immigration to Palestine in the 1920s: the civil war in Ukraine, in which about one hundred thousand Jews were murdered or wounded, and the quota laws enacted
by the US Congress in 1921 and 1924. These events impacted eastern European
Jewry and changed the fate of the Jewish people beyond recognition. After the
civil war in Russia ended, the tragedy of Ukrainian Jewry became clear. Scores
of Jewish communities had been looted, destroyed, and put to the torch. Tens
of thousands of Jews had become refugees, seeking asylum in the immigration
countries. Meanwhile, the US administration started limiting the number of
immigrants allowed into the country, especially Jews and Italians. The throngs
of Jews seeking to go to the United States were denied entry visas; they were
rejected even before leaving their countries of origin. Thus, Palestine became
the main destination country for Jewish migrants in the 1920s. In the space
of just two years (1924–1925), some sixty thousand Jews arrived in Palestine,
around the same number as in all thirty years of the First Aliya and Second
Aliya. The US quota laws had more of an impact on immigration to Palestine
than did Zionist ideology, which considered the return of the Jews to their land
to be an essential condition for its success.

   The discussion in this book about immigration to Palestine rather than the
settlement of the newcomers in the country offers several insights that touch
on the Zionist movement in the 1920s:

1. Periodization of immigration to Palestine: Tracking immigration to
   Palestine from the decision-making stage through arrival proves that
   the historiographical periodization of the Third Aliya and Fourth Aliya

is irrelevant. Push factors in the countries of origin, combined with Zionist and British immigration policies, had the greatest impact on immigration to Palestine. Halutzim, immigrants, and refugees arrived in the 1920s in varying proportions. Early in the decade, for instance, large numbers of refugees from Ukraine arrived in Palestine, having fled to Odessa and Constantinople and pressured the Palestine Offices there to let them immigrate. In contrast, in the mid-1920s (the time of the Fourth Aliya), members of Hechalutz and Hashomer Hatzair reached Palestine in growing numbers alongside petty bourgeois Jews.

2. Zionist immigration policy: The pogroms in Ukraine were among the most violent, brutal events in Jewish history until the Holocaust. Jewish communities were destroyed, vanishing without a trace. Tens of thousands of Jews fled their homes, became refugees, and attempted to reach Palestine or anywhere else in the world that would have them. The Zionist movement found itself tested in this tough period, as it had to decide: open the gates of Palestine and assist Jews who had lost everything or close the gates and let in only the wealthy, the fit, and the strong. In other words, it was a choice between the limited absorptive capacity of the developing country and the lives of thousands of Jewish refugees seeking admission. The pogroms took place at a time when immigration to Palestine was almost unrestricted and the Zionist movement had a lot of say in how many immigrants would be allowed in. Weizmann and Sokolow did not take advantage of Commissioner Herbert Samuel's liberal immigration ordinance; instead, at that fateful time for eastern European Jewry, they chose to limit immigration to just one thousand people. For the first time in the history of the Zionist movement, its leaders had the power to influence the scope and human composition of immigration. They chose to restrict it, giving preference to physically and mentally healthy pioneers over the physically and mentally exhausted immigrants and refugees. At the height of the Fourth Aliya, Zionist Organization president Chaim Weizmann said, "Our brothers and sisters from Dzika and Nalewki are flesh of our flesh, but the national home will not be built on the model of these streets in the Jewish Quarter of Warsaw."[3] Itamar Ben-Avi wrote in his newspaper *Doar Hayom*, "At the moment, Palestine is not the answer to the enormous crisis that has struck our nation this year in Russia. We must declare this loudly and openly, paying no attention to outcries against it, no matter who is crying out. The entire fate of our activity here depends on our adherence to this principle without budging

even a hair's breadth. *This national enterprise cannot be established on compassion and mercy.* Where the national revival on the ancestral land is at stake, compassion cannot be put on the scale."

The Zionist leadership's response to the influx of refugees to Palestine was very different from the reaction of American Jewry to the quota law. In the first years of the British Mandate, the Zionist leadership was able to influence immigration policy. It had the power to open up the country and increase the quota of immigrants. Weizmann, as stated, was afraid that masses of exhausted, destitute refugees would become a burden on the Zionist institutions because the country was not ready to absorb so many immigrants. Ironically, the quota instituted by the Zionist movement under Weizmann's leadership was the first of the various laws and regulations restricting immigration after World War I. It limited immigration, reduced its scope, and encouraged only productive, strong, healthy elements to come. In contrast, the American Jewish leadership attempted to amend the quota law so that as many Jews as possible could enter the United States. Weizmann gave precedence to the well-being of Palestine, whereas the leadership of US Jewry focused on the welfare of the Jewish people.

3. Establishment of an immigration system for Palestine: The 1920s were characterized by the organization and administration of immigration to Palestine. The British enacted immigration regulations and orders and made sure the entry procedure was orderly and well documented, as was customary in other immigration countries, especially the United States. At the same time, the Zionist movement established an orderly, organized, hierarchical bureaucracy that handled all immigration arrangements. Palestine Offices were opened in almost all the countries of origin; they were subordinate to the aliya bureau in Jerusalem, which gave them instructions and insisted that they be adhered to. The Zionist immigration apparatus took care of Jewish immigrants and assisted them from the time they decided to migrate until they entered Palestine, and it continued to assist those without means in their first days in the country. The Palestine Offices interviewed prospective immigrants, conducted medical exams, helped obtain entry visas and travel papers, escorted the immigrants on their journey to the port of departure, saw to all their needs while they waited to set sail, handled the shipping of their luggage to Palestine, negotiated with the shipping companies to improve conditions on

the voyage, purchased tickets for the voyage, and essentially handled every problem that arose before and during the journey to Palestine. When the immigrants reached the shores of Palestine, they were welcomed by representatives of the aliya bureaus in Haifa, Jaffa, and Jerusalem, who ensured their entry into the country would be easy and quick. Representatives met them first on board the ship, during British passport control, and accompanied them to the disinfection station and the quarantine camp. Immigrants who had no relatives to help them and who were unfamiliar with the country were housed in immigrant homes, where they were assisted until they acclimatized in their new land.

The Zionist immigration policy created problems for the Palestine Offices. Their staffs were forced to maneuver between pressure from the masses seeking to escape to Palestine and the selective immigration policy that restricted their freedom of action and limited their discretion. The Zionist Executive's instructions were clear, leaving no room for interpretation: undesirable elements (particularly refugees from the pogroms) who were incapable of participating in the building of Palestine and would be burdens were not to be allowed to immigrate. The policy reflected the stance of the Zionist movement, which portrayed itself in the 1920s as the national movement of the Jewish people and not its rescue movement. However, the immigration apparatus had another function as well. Along with providing aid to immigrants and seeing to their welfare, the Zionist movement managed to oversee all stages of immigration to Palestine. The movement restricted and regulated immigration, expedited or delayed it, and most importantly made sure that only "desirable" immigrants came. Hundreds of immigration officials in all the countries of origin of Jewish migration—whether willingly or unwillingly—enforced the selective immigration policy of the Zionist movement, which at the time preferred the welfare of the country over the welfare of the Jewish people. Undesirable immigrants were rejected as early as the interview stage or the medical exams, and their journey to Palestine was delayed or prevented. Immigration officials rejected Bolsheviks, sick people, those with disabilities, the elderly, and people with no occupation and no means, doubting their ability to settle in Palestine and contribute to the country as the Zionist movement demanded. This often sealed immigrants' fate.

4. Immigration from Islamic countries: The Third Aliya and Fourth Aliya
    are identified with migration from eastern Europe, but in those same
    years, Jews also arrived from Islamic countries in Asia and the Maghreb.
    The number of Jews who lived in the Muslim world at the time is esti-
    mated at only 2.5 percent of the total Jewish population, but migrants
    from those countries accounted for 10 percent of total immigration to
    Palestine. Their motivations were similar to those of the eastern Euro-
    pean immigrants: some were refugees from the pogroms in the Uremiyeh
    region of Iran, others were pushed to migrate due to economic hardship,
    some migrated for Zionist or religious reasons, and sometimes there was
    a combination of factors. The Aliya Department's attitude toward migra-
    tion from Islamic countries was ambivalent and tainted by arrogance and
    ignorance; it foreshadowed the State of Israel's attitude toward North
    African immigrants in the 1950s. Aliya certificates were doled out mea-
    gerly to all the Palestine Offices, but a certain preference was given to the
    offices in Europe. When the head of the Baghdad aliya bureau pointed out
    that the Kurdish refugees in his city were suffering terribly and had to be
    sent to Palestine, he was told that the distress of the Jewish refugees from
    Ukraine was greater, so they were being given priority. The motivations
    for the immigration of the Jews of the Maghreb were more ideological
    and thus different from those of the Asian and Yemenite Jews.

Jewish immigration to Palestine is the main topic of this book; its focus is on
the Jewish immigrants, with their hardships, troubles, and vacillations; their
failures and successes; and finally, their grueling journey to Palestine. Whereas
traditional historical scholarship tends to look at migration rather than at the
migrant, this work follows the experiences of the immigrants themselves and
the system that supported them or turned them away. The standard historiographical division into five waves of immigration blurred the heterogeneous
composition of the immigrant population and turned it into a homogeneous,
faceless, nameless mass. The immigrants' stories were jumbled together. The
people lost their individuality and their identity as they were swallowed up in
the hodgepodge of the immigrants over the years, and they faded in the splendor of Zionist ideology. Therefore, to understand the complexity of immigration in general and of immigration to Palestine in particular, we must extricate
the story of the Jewish immigrants from the overarching narrative of Zionism
and the dry data of quantitative statistical research. The individual immigrant
must once again become the protagonist of the drama of immigration—a

drama whose plot is full of ups and downs, great hopes and successes, but also crises and bitter disappointments.

The push factors in eastern Europe and in the Muslim world compelled the Zionist leadership to devise an immigration policy and quickly establish the organizational infrastructure needed to help Jews actualize their decision to migrate. In just a few years, the Zionist leadership managed to instill order in the migration process and regulate it. The infrastructure established in the 1920s and the support for migrants throughout all stages of migration made it possible to turn the Balfour Declaration from words into reality.

The arrival of one hundred thousand immigrants and refugees in the first decade of the Mandate laid the demographic foundations on which the national home in Palestine was built. Sheinkin described the immigrants as "folk pioneers" with a healthy national spirit who went to Palestine; settled there; built buildings and roads; planted; earned a living; and through diligence, determination, and survival instinct created the economic and social foundations for healthy national life.

> Look at the hundreds of skilled tradesmen among the ordinary Jews who are returning. See how energetically they aspire to take any place, how talented they are at adapting to the new conditions, how patiently they and their families quietly overcome all their initial suffering, and how happy they are when they earn a slice of bread. Are these not pioneers? And how many ordinary Jews did the hardest jobs just to stay in the country—pushing wheelbarrows, carrying loads on their shoulders. How many new immigrants with families learned new trades in Palestine, especially construction work, just in order to feed themselves through their own work. Why shouldn't these people be called "pioneers" even if they are already middle-aged and have families? In fact, these people are playing a major part in nation-building. They are the strong stones and the strong material.[4]

Those so-called folk pioneers are the main characters in this book. They include refugees from Ukraine and Uremiyeh, survivors of the pogroms and riots—the homeless, orphans and widows, women who had been raped, the emotionally wounded and fragile. They include immigrants on a grueling journey—those who suffered on the ship and who fell ill on the way, who were detained or sent back, whose suitcases were broken into or stolen. They include ordinary Jews—Polish Jews who had lost their livelihoods, survivors of the famine in Russia under Lenin and Stalin, and survivors of the Bolshevik Yevsektsia. Finally, they include Jews from the fringes of society—the mentally

ill who evaded the doctors' vigilant eyes, people of low morals, thieves, prostitutes, and holders of forged entry visas. Those who didn't make it into the
history books, even as footnotes—this book is about them all.

Standing shoulder to shoulder with the immigrants over the years were
workers in the Zionist migration system: the heads of the aliya bureau, the
staffs of the Palestine Offices, workers in the immigrant homes, port workers,
and so on. Immigration offices were established in the space of a few years in
the Jews' countries of origin, and their employees made the Zionist migration
enterprise a reality. These people's actions, too, have been either forgotten or
else criticized and slandered; they and their stories have been left out of the
chronicles of immigration to Palestine.

The historiography of immigration to Palestine and Israel has probed and
measured immigrants based on their contribution to the Zionist enterprise.
Their task was to settle, build, plow, defend, and sacrifice. So long as they served
the Zionist ideology, their personal stories fit into the overarching narrative of
Palestine, and they found themselves sheltered comfortably within the consen-
sus. But if they exhibited signs of weakness and fatigue, the immigrants became
a historiographical footnote. Weak, disconnected, and skeptical people didn't
serve the Zionist narrative; on the contrary, they were liable to cause cracks
in it and—heaven forbid—even cast doubt on its vitality. When we focus on
refugees and immigrants rather than halutzim and olim, the story of immigration to Palestine becomes more complex and human, centering on the unique
stories of ordinary people.

NOTES

Preface

1. Perec, *Ellis Island*, 23, 53.

Introduction

1. Khodorkov Pogrom, National Library of Israel Photograph Collection, TMA 5490. The album was donated to the National Library in 1936 by Aharon Brzezinsky in the name of Sholem Schwarzbard. In 1927, Schwarzbard had assassinated the Ukrainian nationalist Symon Petliura, one of those responsible for the slaughter of Ukrainian Jewry.

2. Rosenthal, *Megilat ha-Tevah*, vol. 3 (*het–tet*), 15–16. *Megilat ha-Tevah* is arranged alphabetically, and only the first nine letters of the alphabet have been published; the rest of the work is available in the Genazim Archive. On *Megilat ha-Tevah* and its author, see Alroey, "Documenting the Pogroms."

3. Orland, *Kiev*, 31.

4. On Tetiev, see Rosenthal, *Megilat ha-Tevah*, 3:65–90. In a note about the pogrom, Rosenthal wrote, "Of the 124 cities and towns in the Kiev Governorate in which Jews had lived before the war, between 85 and 90 were wiped out. . . . Tetiev suffered more than any other town in the Kiev Governorate. The slaughter there was horrific, both quantitatively and qualitatively. Of the seven thousand people, three-fourths were exterminated. All the victims died in terrible torment: by water and by fire, by the sword and by strangulation, and in all sorts of horrible ways. From Tetiev the affliction spread to the other towns in the area." For more on the pogrom in Tetiev, see Rosenthal, *Tetiever Khurbn*.

5. On the Orlands' journey to Palestine, see Wolf-Monzon, *Bahir ve-Gavoa ke-Zemer*, 1–9.

6. See Orland, "Things Before and After," in *Kiev*, 5.

7. Orland, Ya'akov, *Kiev—Poema; u-Shtei Tiutot-Shir le-Zikhron Tetiev* [Kiev: a poem; and two drafts of a poem in memory of Tetiev] (Jerusalem: Carmel, 1991), 31.

8. Gross, "He'ara."

9. Erez, *Sefer ha-Aliya ha-Shelishit*.

10. See Ben-Avram and Near, *Iyunim ba-Aliya ha-Shelishit*.

11. See Shapira, "Reshitah shel ha-Ha'apala." See also Lissak, "Aliya, Kelita u-Vinyan Hevra."

12. Halamish, *Be-Meruts Kaful*, 15.

13. Halamish, *Mi-Bayit Leumi*, 281.

14. E.g., Halamish, "Yahaso shel Vaitsman." Weizmann's activity in the 1920s is not examined in this article in the context of the violence in eastern Europe. Halamish merely mentions laconically that "in eastern Europe Jews suffered severely due to the war and the pogroms against them in Poland, Ukraine, and elsewhere."

15. Gordon, "Immigration Problems in Palestine."

16. Slutsky, *Mavo*, 15.

17. Halamish, *Be-Meruts Kaful*, 2.

18. Picard, *Olim bi-Mesura*.

19. Yakir, *Toldot ha-Mahlaka la-Aliya*.

1. New Times, New Tunes

1. On the founding of HIAS, see Wischnitzer, *Visas to Freedom*, 27–36. On HIAS on Ellis Island, see Howe, *World of Our Fathers*, 42–46.

2. On HIAS during World War I, see Szajkowski, "American Jewish Overseas Relief," 191–94.

3. See Levitt's letter, September 13, 1915, YIVO, RG 245.3.

4. See letter from Abraham Halevi Lipschitz, November 24, 1914, ibid.

5. Altshuler, "Russia and Her Jews," 14; Frankel, *Jews and the European Crisis*, 8. See also Silber, *Leumiyut Shona*, 7.

6. "Seventh Annual Report of the President of the Hebrew Sheltering and Immigrant Aid Society of America for the Year Ending 31 December 1915," YIVO Archives, 5.

7. On immigration to the United States via Siberia and then China and Japan, see Alroey, "Between the Straits."

8. H. S. Steer, "Report on the Work in the Far East of the Hebrew Sheltering and Immigrant Aid Society of America, 15 October 1920," YIVO Archives, 15.

9. See Wolf Lewkowicz's letter to his nephew: Letter 15, Łódź, February 1, 1924, retrieved from http://web.mit.edu/maz/wolf/. The correspondence spans a period from August 1922 to August 1939, shortly before the outbreak of World War II. The

letters are in the Harvard College Library and the United States Holocaust Memorial Museum in Washington, DC.

10. Bennett, *American Immigration Policies*, 17–18.

11. Ibid., 17.

12. Howe, *World of Our Fathers*, 54.

13. On Louis Marshall's efforts against quota laws, see Silver, *Louis Marshall*, 222–45.

14. On the work of the Dillingham Commission, see Perlmann, *America Classifies the Immigrants*, 104–32.

15. Daniels, *Guarding the Golden Door*, 48–49.

16. Hertzberg, *Jews in America*, 239.

17. Daniels, *Guarding the Golden Door*, 47–48; Perlmann, *America Classifies the Immigrants*, 201–28.

18. Magal Cohen, *Isha Yoshevet ve-Khotevet*, 22.

19. Gorenstein, "Memoir of the Great War," 157–58.

20. Zahra, *Great Departure*, 108.

21. Garland, *After They Closed the Gates*, 87.

22. Jean, "Shayakhut Menuyeret," 122.

23. Ibid., 125.

24. "Mashber ha-Hagira" [The migration crisis], *Ha-Tsefira*, Nov. 14, 1920, p. 3.

25. Ibid.

26. "Khronika Yehudit: Takkanot ha-Kenisa le-Amerika" [Jewish chronicle: regulations for entering America], *Ha-Tsefira*, Dec. 2, 1920, p. 3.

27. On the conference in Prague, see "Jewish Emigration Conference," 1.

28. Wischnitzer, *To Dwell in Safety*, 332.

29. "Ha-Ve'ida le-Inyenei Hagira be-Prag" [The emigration conference in Prague], *Ha-Tsefira*, Sept. 29, 1921, p. 1.

30. Ibid.

31. Emigdirect, *Tsentral-Byuro-Emigdirekt*, 29–30. On the work of the Emigdirect bank, see Szajkowski, "American Jewish Overseas Relief," 214–17.

32. Emigdirect, *Tsentral-Byuro-Emigdirekt*, 31.

33. Linfield, *Jewish Migration*, 20.

34. "Hitahdut ha-Mosdot le-Inyenei Hagira" [The merger of the emigration organizations], *Haaretz*, Apr. 3, 1928, p. 2.

35. "Be-Inyenei Siddur ha-Hagira: Sihat Itona'im im Haver ha-Hanhala ha-Merkazit shel Histadrut ha-Hagira Mar Tscherikower" [Regarding the organizing of emigration: a press conference with a member of the board of the migration association, Mr. Tcherikower," *Doar Hayom*, May 5, 1928, p. 4.

36. Ibid.

37. Wischnitzer, *Visas to Freedom*, 128–29.

38. M. R., "Ha-Trust le-Hagira: Nedida ve-Yashvanut" [The migration trust: migration and settlement]," *Doar Hayom*, Jan. 18, 1927, p. 1.

39. Ibid.

40. Ibid.

41. Ibid.

42. "Ve'ida Itona'it ba-Misrad ha-Artsi Yisraeli be-Varsha" [Press conference in the Palestine Office in Warsaw], *Doar Hayom*, Dec. 1, 1926, p. 2.

43. "3,500 Chalutzim Are Waiting for Permission to Proceed to Palestine," *Jewish Daily Bulletin*, Sept. 23, 1927, pp. 1, 4; "HICEM to Assist in Chaluzim Transportation," ibid., Feb. 6, 1929, p. 2; "HIAS to Seek $500,000 for Emigration to Palestine and South American Countries," ibid., Nov. 9, 1926, p. 5.

44. Palestine Office to Aliya Department of the Zionist Executive, Aug. 9, 1926, CZA, S6, file 474.

45. Memo to HIAS, Sept. 24, 1924, CZA, Z4, file 40664, p. 2.

46. Ibid., p. 3.

2. Town on Fire

1. Letter of protest sent to the Zionist Executive on behalf of thirty-one Ukrainian-Jewish families from the Kiev Governorate, [1923?], CZA, S6, file 443.

2. Ben-Avram and Near, *Iyunim ba-Aliya ha-Shelishit*, 41.

3. Dinur, *Eretz Yisrael bi-Shnat Tarpag*, 158.

4. "Yediot ha-Misrad Eretz Yisrael Merkazi be-Kushta" [News from the central Palestine Office in Constantinople], *Doar Hayom*, February 27, 1922, 4.

5. Zalman Shneor, *Ha'olam*, March 25, 1927.

6. Translation taken from http://soviethistory.msu.edu/1917-2/the-empire-falls/the-empire-falls-texts/first-universal-declaration/, accessed July 4, 2021. See also Abramson, *Prayer for the Government*, 33–66.

7. For a comprehensive study on the Jews in the Ukrainian civil war, see Budnitskii, *Russian Jews*.

8. Gergel, "Di Pogromen in Ukrayne," 112; see also Abramson, *Prayer for the Government*, 109–40.

9. Lucien Wolf archives [1920?], YIVO, RG 348, microfilm 502, 1.

10. Committee of Jewish Delegations, *Pogroms in the Ukraine*, 268.

11. Heifetz, *Slaughter of the Jews*, 179–80.

12. Rosenthal, *Megilat ha-Tevah*, 3:65. A similar number of murder victims is reported in Krimsky, *Barikht*, 6.

13. Gergel, "Di Pogromen in Ukrayne," 106.

14. Gergel, "Pogroms in the Ukraine," 249.

15. Ibid., 251.

16. On the brutality of the pogroms, see Budnitskii, *Russian Jews*, 216–74.

17. Gergel, "Di Pogromen in Ukrayne," 113.

18. Schechtman, "Antishemiut u-Fera'ot," 492.

19. Rosenthal, *Megilat ha-Tevah, mem*, Genazim Archive, file 341, kaf-8074.

20. On the three pogroms in Zhitomir, see *Yizkor (Zhitomir)* (New York, 1921).

21. Rosenthal, *Megilat ha-Tevah, zayin*, Genazim Archive, file 341, kaf-8074.

22. Imri-Fajgenberg, *Megilat Dubova*, 122. The book, originally written in Yiddish in 1921, was translated from the manuscript into French by Leo Motzkin for Shalom Schwarzbard's attorney. Chapters of the book were published in the 1920s in various periodicals.

23. Druyanov, "Shura shel Pega'im," 146.

24. Rosenthal, *Megilat ha-Tevah, peh*, Genazim Archive, file 341, kaf-8074.

25. On the gender aspect of the pogroms, see Alroey, "Sexual Violence"; Astashkevich, *Gendered Violence*.

26. Schechtman, "Antishemiut u-Fera'ot," 493.

27. Litai, "Tseror shel Protokolim," 259.

28. Ibid., 257.

29. Ibid., 256–57.

30. Schechtman, "Antishemiut u-Fera'ot," 494.

31. Koralnik, "Di Iden in Ukrayne," 134–35.

32. Lestschinsky, "Le-Ahar ha-Pera'ot be-Ukraina," 12.

33. Ibid., 13.

34. "Ha-Hagira ha-Yehudit mi-Bessarabia" [Jewish emigration from Bessarabia], *Doar Hayom*, September 29, 1921, 2.

35. "Matzavam ha-Nora shel Sheloshim Elef Pelitim Rusim be-Kushta" [The terrible plight of 30,000 Russian refugees in Constantinople," *Doar Hayom*, November 11, 1921, 2.

36. *Yedies funem Ekzekutiv Komitet fun der Idisher Velt Hilf Konferents* [News from the executive committee of the Jewish World Relief Conference], no. 4, April 3, 1922, YIVO Archives, 1.

37. Ibid., 2.

38. Ibid.

39. Schechtman, "Antishemiut u-Fera'ot," 491.

40. Report of Major Morris, August 18, 1921, National Archives (UK), CO 733, file 6, 12. For more on Morris's trip, see Mossek, *Palestine Immigration Policy*, 45–47.

41. Report of Major Morris, 13.

42. Schapiro, *Communist Party*, 211.

43. Latzky-Bertholdi, "Enut Yehudei Eiropa ha-Mizrahit," 251.

44. Ibid., 254; Lestschinsky, *Ha-Yehudim be-Rusya ha-Sovietit*, 70.

45. Lestschinsky, *Ha-Yehudim be-Rusya ha-Sovietit*, 81.

46. "Ha-Va'ad ha-Poel shel ha-Va'ad ha-Le'umi li-Yehudei Erets Yisrael" [The Executive Committee of the Jewish National Council in Palestine], *Doar Hayom*, June 19, 1922, 3.

47. Zelig Horwitz to Zionist Executive, February 1925, CZA, S6, file 443.

48. On the Jews in Soviet Russia under the NEP, see Galili, "Merhav ha-Pe'ula," esp. 482–84.

49. Lestschinsky, *Ha-Yehudim be-Rusya ha-Sovietit*, 70.

50. Ibid., 71.

51. Ibid.

52. Ibid., 72.

53. On the Yevsektsia, see Altshuler, *Ha-Yevsektsya*. See also Galili, "Merhav ha-Pe'ula," 485–87. Galili maintains that despite the persecution by the Yevsektsia, the Zionist movement was able to function to a significant degree. Though it was not officially allowed by the central government, the authorities tended to turn a blind eye to it. As in the case of the Hebrew teacher described below, such an attitude was able to coexist with persecution and arrests.

54. See Yardeni Bachman and friends to the aliya bureau in Jerusalem, March 2, 1925, CZA, S6, file 443.

55. Pines, "Ha-Matzav ha-Kalkali," 172 (italics mine).

56. Lestschinsky, *Ha-Yehudim be-Rusya ha-Sovietit*, 72–73.

57. Dijour, *Di Moderne Felker-Vanderung*, 67.

58. Mendelsohn, *Zionism in Poland*, 5.

59. Latzky-Bertholdi, "Enut Yehudei Eiropa ha-Mizrahit," 141.

60. Mendelsohn, *Zionism in Poland*, 6.

61. Ibid.

62. Latzky-Bertholdi, "Enut Yehudei Eiropa ha-Mizrahit," 142.

63. Ibid., 143.

64. Ibid., 142.

65. Heller, *Edge of Destruction*.

66. Dijour, *Di Moderne Felker-Vanderung*, 67.

67. Ibid., 69. On Jewish emigration from Poland to Argentina, see Kalczewiak, *Polacos in Argentina*.

68. The exchange of letters was retrieved from http://web.mit.edu/maz/wolf/.

69. See Wolf's letter to his nephew: letter 15, Lodz, February 1, 1924.

70. Ibid.

71. Letter 22, Lodz, July 20, 1924.

72. Letter 29, Lodz, February 21, 1925.

73. Letter 34, Lodz, July 25, 1925.

74. Lestschinsky, *Di Ekonomishe Lage*, 63–64.

75. Ibid., 65.

76. Ibid., 66.

77. Gordon, "Immigration Problems in Palestine," 45.

78. Ibid., 57–59.

79. Ibid., 59–63.

80. Ibid., 48–50.

81. Ibid.

82. See Erez, *Sefer ha-Aliya ha-Shelishit*, 12.

83. Ibid.

84. Ben-Avram and Near, *Iyunim ba-Aliya ha-Shelishit*, 19.

85. Margalit, *Hashomer Hatzair*, 17–21; see also Halamish, *Kibbutz, Utopia and Politics*.

86. Tzahor, *Hazan*, 26.

87. Margalit, *Hashomer Hatzair*, 80.

88. Ben-Avram and Near, *Iyunim ba-Aliya ha-Shelishit*, 19.

89. Gordon, "Immigration Problems in Palestine," 112–13.

90. Ibid., 114.

3. The Gates Open

1. Bartal, "1919: Eretz be-Terem," 26–33.

2. Yogev and Freundlich, *Protokolim*, vol. 1, *Februar 1919–Yanuar 1920* [February 1919–January 1920], 105–6.

3. Yakir, *Toldot ha-Mahlaka la-Aliya*, 6.

4. Moreno, *Encyclopedia of Ellis Island*, xi–xix; Howe, *World of Our Fathers*, 42–50; Anbinder, *City of Dreams*, 329–53.

5. Attias, *Sefer ha-Teudot*, 10.

6. Ibid., 3.

7. Minutes of the Provisional Committee meeting, Nisan 24–26, 5679 (April 24–26, 1919), CZA, L3, file 314.

8. Minutes of the Provisional Committee meeting, Iyar 27, 5679 (May 27, 1919), CZA, L3, file 314.

9. Ibid.

10. Ibid.

11. Immigration council to Zionist Commission, Sivan 13, 5679 (June 11, 1919), CZA, L3, file 314.

12. Minutes of the Provisional Committee meeting, Sivan 19, 5679 (June 17, 1919), CZA, L3, file 314.

13. Shilo, "Tovat ha-Am"; Alroey, *Unpromising Land*.

14. Lilienblum, "Derekh La'avor Golim" [The path of exiles], in *Ketavim Otobiografiyim*, 14.

15. On Sheinkin's information bureau, see Shilo, "Lishkat ha-Modi'in"; Alroey, *Unpromising Land*, 96–102.

16. Sheinkin to Zionist Organization, February 3, 1920, CZA, S4, file 368.

17. Ibid.

18. Sheinkin to Zionist Organization information bureau in Constantinople, April 23, 1920, CZA, S4, file 368.

19. Trifon to Sheinkin, March 30, 1920, CZA, S4, file 368. See also Hayek, *Kefar Giladi*, 21–33. Hayek writes that at a meeting of the Zionist General Council on August 6, 1919, the circular reported the information given at the meeting: "Despite the ban on immigration, people are coming incessantly—now via Beirut" (29).

20. Ibid.

21. Jewish community board in Beirut to Sheinkin, March 30, 1920, CZA, S4, file 368.

22. Trifon to Sheinkin, March 30, 1920, CZA, S4, file 368. On the situation of the immigrants in Beirut, see also Passerby, "Beirut," *Hapoel Hatzair* 8–9 (Nisan 14, 5679 [April 14, 1919]): 24.

23. Zionist Executive in London to Zionist Commission, June 11, 1920, CZA, S6, file 327.

24. Secretary of the Alexandria information bureau to Zionist Commission, June 23, 1921, CZA, S6, file 327.

25. Head office in London to Zionist Commission, November 13, 1919, CZA, L2, file 231, 1–2.

26. Ibid., 2.

27. Ibid.

28. Ibid.

29. Ibid.

30. Shlomo Zacharin, "Derekh Argentina le-Eretz Yisrael" [Via Argentina to Palestine], in Erez, *Sefer ha-Aliya ha-Shelishit*, 201.

31. Ibid.

32. Gurevich, *Statistical Abstract of Palestine*, 54, table 6.

33. Sicron, *Immigration to Israel*, statistical supplement, table A1.

34. Ben-Avram and Near, *Iyunim ba-Aliya ha-Shelishit*, 189. Moshe Mossek states that there are no detailed monthly data on immigration at the beginning of the military regime and therefore data from different sources sometimes has to be compared. According to Mossek, thirteen hundred people immigrated in the ten months from February to December 1919. This number includes returning residents and people who entered the country without a recommendation from the Zionist Organization. See Mossek, "Britania," 10.

35. Gurevich, "15 Shenot Aliya"; Yakir, *Toldot ha-Mahlaka la-Aliya*, 52.

36. *Yediot ha-Mahlaka le-Statistika ule-Informatsia* [News of the Department of Statistics and Information], July 30, 1920, 13.

37. Ibid.

38. Sucker, "Hazon ha-Yamim," 426 (italics mine).

39. On the story of the *Ruslan*, see Rafaeli (Zenzipper), *Ba-Ma'avak li-Geula*, 154–55. See also Erez, *Sefer ha-Aliya ha-Shelishit*, 130–38.

40. Ibid., 134.

41. "Yafo Yom Yom" [Jaffa daily], *Doar Hayom*, Tevet 2, 5680 (December 24, 1919), 3.

42. See Y. Spivak, "Ha-Shayara ha-Rishona" [The first convoy], *Hapoel Hatzair*, Tevet 4, 5680 (December 26, 1919), 7–8.

43. On the *Ruslan* as the *Mayflower*, see Naor, *Mi-Sippurei Eretz Ahavati*, 112.

44. Erez, *Sefer ha-Aliya ha-Shelishit*, 137–38.

45. Due to the storm in Jaffa during disembarkation, not all the passengers on the *Ruslan* managed to disembark. For this reason, there are discrepancies in different sources regarding the number of olim on the ship. Chaim Ridnik stated that 553 olim arrived safely in Jaffa. The passenger log of the *Ruslan*, in contrast, lists 670 passengers: 520 immigrants and 150 returning exiles. See CZA, S6, file 5501.

46. On the ships that arrived in Palestine in 1919, see CZA, L2, file 231.

47. Ibid.

48. "Ha-Pelitim" [The refugees], *Doar Hayom*, January 4, 1920, 2.

49. "Le-Inyenei ha-Sha'a" [On timely matters], *Hapoel Hatzair*, Tevet 4, 5680 (December 26, 1919), 4.

50. Ben-Avi, "Ha-Hat'hala" [The beginning], *Doar Hayom*, Tevet 4, 5680 (December 26, 1919), 1.

51. "Yafo Yom Yom" [Jaffa daily], *Doar Hayom*, January 1, 1920, 2.

52. Ibid.

53. Halamish, "Aliya lefi Yekholet ha-Kelita"; Elam, "Historia Medinit," 194–95.

54. Mossek, *Palestine Immigration Policy*, 8–11; Segev, *Yemei ha-Kalaniyot*, 186–88.

55. Mossek, *Palestine Immigration Policy*, 38.

56. Ibid.

57. Tzippora Weissmann to Aliya Department, Nisan 16, 5685 (April 10, 1925), CZA, S6, file 443.

58. Shifra Wisser to Aliya Deparmtent, February 16, 1925, CZA, S6, file 443.

59. Gurevich, Gertz, and Bachi, *Ha-Aliya*, 25.

60. Ibid.

61. Ben-Avram and Near, *Iyunim ba-Aliya ha-Shelishit*.

62. Metzer, *Jewish Immigration to Palestine*.

63. *Yediot ha-Mahlaka*, July 30, 1920, 13.

64. "Sefinat ha-Nodedim ha-Nitzhiyim" [The ship of the eternal wanderers], *Hapoel Hatzair*, no. 12, January 2, 1920, 15.

65. Ibid.

66. "Hahlatot ha-Ve'ida ha-Shenatit shel Hapoel Hatzair" [Resolutions of the annual conference of Hapoel Hatzair], *Hapoel Hatzair* 12, Tevet 11, 5680 (January 2, 1920), 1.

67. Ibid.

68. Shmuel Yavnieli, "Hovatenu" [Our duty], *Kuntres* 23, Shevat 10, 5680 (January 30, 1920), 3.

69. Lavsky, "Leumiut, Hagira ve-Hityashvut," 157–60.

70. Margalit, "Sugiyat Miyun ha-Olim," 247–48.

71. The disregard of the appeals for rescue aliya and mass immigration is consistent with the claim that many Zionist leaders, including Weizmann, consistently and systematically treated the Yishuv and its leaders with a lack of understanding and sympathy and were dismissive of decisions made in Palestine. On this subject, see Friesel, *Ha-Mediniut ha-Tsiyonit*, 117.

72. Ruppin, "Selection of the Fittest," 67.

73. Yogev and Freundlich, *Protokolim*, 105–6.

74. "Me'et ha-Histadrut ha-Tsiyonit" [From the Zionist Organization], *Hapoel Hatzair*, no. 13, Iyar 23, 5679 (May 23, 1919), 16.

75. Weizmann's fundamental position did not change even in later years. See Meir Chazan's article on Weizmann and the development of the standard impression of the Fourth Aliya. "Hayyim Vaitsman," 454.

76. "Chronika" [Chronicle], *Ha-Olam*, no. 14, January 16, 1920, 14 (italics mine).

77. Ibid.

78. "Asefat ha-Va'ad ha-Poel ha-Gadol" [The meeting of the Large General Council], *Ha-Olam*, no. 21, March 5, 1920, 6.

79. "Me'et ha-Histadrut ha-Tsiyonit." On Weizmann's immigration policy, see Halamish, "Yahaso shel Vaitsman."

80. Ze'ev Tiomkin to Zionist Commission, Tevet 14, 5681 (December 25, 1920), CZA, S6, file 338/1.

81. See, e.g., the report of the aliya committee in Constantinople: "Report on Palestine Emigration Activities in Constantinople during the Period of the 1st June 1920 to the 1st July 1921," CZA, S6, file 338/1.

82. Secretary-general of the Zionist Commission to aliya committee in Constantinople, August 12, 1920, CZA, S6, file 338/1.

83. Katvan and Davidovitch, "Makhshirei ha-Guf veha-Levavot."

84. Katvan, "Mi Ba'al ha-Bayit?" 38–39.

85. Mossek, "Herbert Samuel."

86. Friesel, *Ha-Mediniut ha-Tsiyonit*, 117.

87. Nordau, "Mikhtav li-Yehudei Eretz Yisrael (1919)" [Letter to the Jews of Palestine (1919)], in *Ketavim Nivharim*, 64.

88. Ibid., 64–65.

89. Nordau, "Tseva'a la-Tsiyonut (1920)" [A will for Zionism (1920)], in *Ketavim Nivharim*, 202.

90. "Yafo Yom-Yom [Jaffa daily]," *Doar Hayom*, Tevet 10, 5680 (January 1, 1920), 2 (italics mine).

91. Ben-Avi, "Ha-Hat'hala," 1 (italics mine).

92. See Rosenfeld, *Ha-Kongres ha-Tziyoni ha-Shneim-Asar*, 23–24.

93. Ibid., 21.

94. Ibid., 23.

95. Ibid., 28.

96. Ibid.

97. Shilo, "Tovat ha-Am"; Alroey, *Unpromising Land*, 96–102.

98. Moshe Smilansky, "Li-She'elot ha-Kongres: Ha-Aliya" [On the questions of the Congress: immigration], *Haolam*, 44, August 25, 1921, 1.

99. Menachem Sheinkin, "Hutz me-Halutzim Olim Gam Yehudim Aherim le-Eretz Yisrael" [Jews other than halutzim are also immigrating to Palestine], *Der Tog*, February 12, 1922 (italics mine).

100. Menachem Sheinkin, "Me-Eizeh Sug Mehagrim Netuna Eretz Yisrael," *Der Tog*, June 5, 1922.

101. Ibid.

102. Ibid.

4. Over Troubled Water

1. On information bureaus before World War I, see Alroey, *Ha-Mahpekha ha-Sheketa*, 133–48. On Sheinkin's information bureau, see Shilo, "Lishkat ha-Modi'in."

2. Bylaws of the Palestine Offices, CZA, S81, file 36, 13–14.

3. Ibid., 1. See also Halamish, *Be-Merutz Kaful*, 95.

4. "Palestine Offices and Emigration Representatives," CZA, S81, file 36.

5. "Tazkir Al-Devar ha-Aliya le-Eretz Yisrael, 1927" [Memorandum regarding aliya to Palestine, 1927], CZA, S81, file 37, 19.

6. Ibid.

7. Ibid.

8. Wischnitzer, *To Dwell in Safety*, 160.

9. Palestine Office, *Tätigkeit*, 3.

10. Survey by the Palestine Office in Vienna to the Aliya Department of the Zionist Executive, January 30, 1923, CZA, S6, file 340/1, 1.

11. Ibid., 2.

12. Ibid.

13. Ibid.

14. Ibid., 3.

15. Ibid., 4.

16. Lamdan, *Yoman Yitzhak Lamdan*, 399.

17. World Federation of Hapoel Hatzair and Tze'irei Zion, *Ba-Aliya*, 6.

18. Ibid.

19. "Pe'ulot ha-Misrad ha-Eretzyisre'eli be-Triest bi-Shnat 1924" [Activities of the Palestine Office in Trieste in 1924], CZA, S6, file 443, 2.

20. Ibid., 1.

21. Giuseppe Fano (head of the Trieste office) to Zionist Commission for Palestine, February 2, 1921, CZA, S6, file 339/1.

22. "Pe'ulot ha-Misrad," 1.

23. Ibid.

24. Ibid.

25. "Di Emigratsie keyn Palestine fun Poyln," *Di Idishe Emigratsie* 4 (May 1925): 19; "Din ve-Heshbon: Ha-Misrad ha-Eretzyisre'eli ha-Merkazi le-Polania" [Report: the central Palestine Office for Poland], January 1922, CZA, S6, file 338/2, 1.

26. "Din ve-Heshbon: Ha-Misrad ha-Eretzyisre'eli," 3.

27. Ibid.

28. Ibid.

29. Ussishkin to the central committee of the Zionist Organization in Poland, November 1, 1920, CZA, S6, file 269/1 (emphasis in the original).

30. Shvueli to Aliya Department, August 24, 1923, CZA, S6, file 326/1.

31. Ibid.

32. "Aliyat ha-Tze'irot veha-De'aga Lahen" [Aliya by young women and concern for them], CZA, S81, file 29.

33. Yona Shapiro to the Zionist Executive, January 20, 1925, CZA, S6, file 443.

34. Ibid.

35. "Din ve-Heshbon al Pe'ulot ha-Misrad ha-Eretz-Yisre'eli ha-Merkazi be-Varsha li-Shnat 1922" [Report on the activities of the central Palestine Office in Warsaw, 1922], CZA, S6, file 326/1, 1.

36. Ibid.

37. The Palestine Office and the director of the Labor Department, July 26, 1921, CZA, S6, file 338/2.

38. Ibid.

39. "Du"h ha-Misrad ha-Eretz-Yisre'eli be-Varsha" [Report of the Palestine Office in Warsaw], 1924, CZA, S6, file 4878.

40. Tiomkin to Zionist Commission, Av 10, 5680 (July 25, 1920), CZA, S6, file 338/1.

41. Tiomkin to Ussishkin, eve of Rosh Hashanah 5681 (September 12, 1920), CZA, S6, file 338.

42. "Tazkir" [Memo] (signed by fifteen people), *Hapoel Hatzair*, no. 10–11, December 17, 1920, 19.

43. Ibid.

44. Ibid.

45. Ussishkin to Tiomkin, October 8, 1920, CZA, S6, file 338.

46. Tiomkin to Ussishkin, Marheshvan 10, 5681 (October 22, 1920), CZA, S6, file 338.

47. AJJDC Executive Committee minutes, 1921, American Jewish Archives (hereafter: AJA), MSS COL#3.

48. Memo from the Zionist Organization in Odessa to Dr. J. Kalb in Constantinople, *Hapoel Hatzair*, no. 15–16, Sivan 15, 5679 (June 13, 1919), 1.

49. "Ha-Tena'im veha-Homer shel ha-Aliya ha-Nokhehit" [The conditions and material of the present aliya], March 1925, Pinhas Lavon Institute for Labor Movement Research, IV-211-1-30, 16.

50. Ibid.

51. Yakir, *Toldot ha-Mahlaka la-Aliya*, 130.

52. On Mesila Hadasha, see Yerushalmi, "Mesila Hadasha," 19; Katz, "Mahloket Pnim Tsiyonit."

53. Yerushalmi, "Mesila Hadasha," 19; Katz, "Mahloket Pnim Tsiyonit."

54. "Yediot ha-Misrad Eretz-Yisre'eli Merkazi be-Kushta" [News from the central Palestine Office in Constantinople], *Doar Hayom*, February 27, 1922, 4.

55. "Hahlatot—Ve'idat ha-Misradim ha-Eretzyisre'elim sheba-Gola" [Decisions—the conference of Palestine Offices abroad], CZA, S6, file 398, 1.

56. Ibid.

57. Ibid., 4.

58. Ibid.

59. Minutes of a meeting of the Palestine Office in Warsaw, March 11, 1924, CZA, S6, file 4878, 1.

60. Central Palestine Office, *Moreh-Derekh*, 1.

61. Ibid., 2.

62. Ibid., 2–3.

63. "Yosifon, the Young Pioneer," *Shibolim*, March 30, 1922, 4.

64. Central Palestine Office, *Moreh-Derekh*, 5.

65. "Yosifon," 5.

66. Ibid., 1.

67. "Pe'ulot ha-Misrad," 4.

68. Howe, *World of Our Fathers*, 42–46.

69. Health Council of the Palestine Zionist Executive, *Hora'ot la-Bedika ha-Refu'it*, 1.

70. Ibid., 1–2 (emphasis in the original).

71. Ibid., 3.

72. [1922?], CZA, S6, file 267/1, 4.

73. Ibid.

74. Ibid.

75. Tiomkin to Palestine Office, Jerusalem, August 16, 1921, CZA, S6, file 338/1.

76. Katvan and Davidovitch, "Makhshirei ha-Guf veha-Levavot," 21.

77. Ibid., 21–23.

78. Mordechai Lansky, "Li-She'elat ha-Bikoret ha-Refu'it ba-Misradim ha-Eretzyisre'elim" [On the medical inspections in the Palestine Offices], *Haaretz*, November 18, 1926, 3.

79. Ibid.

80. Katvan and Davidovitch, "Briut, Politika u-Profesionalizm," 59.

81. Ibid., 40–42.

82. "Misrad Eretz-Yisre'eli Merkazi be-Varsha" [The central Palestine Office in Warsaw], November 13, 1929, CZA, S3, file 21.

83. Central Palestine Office, Moreh-Derekh, 9.

84. Menachem Sheinkin to aliya bureaus, September 23, 1920, CZA, S4, file 368.

85. Director of the Haifa aliya bureau to the Aliya Department, August 26, 1926, CZA, S3, file 106.

86. Central Palestine Office for Poland, circular 24, February 1922, CZA, S6, file 3382.

87. Ibid.

88. Ibid. On the cost of the voyage from Poland to Palestine, see also Wrobel Bloom, Social Networks, 150; for the conversion of pounds sterling to present-day values, see http://inflation.iamkate.com/.

89. Central Palestine Office for Poland, circular 24, February 1922, CZA, S6, file 3382.

90. "Ve'idat ha-Misradim ha-Eretzyisre'elim sheba-Gola" [Conference of Palestine Offices abroad], March 25, 1925, CZA, S6, file 398, 6.

91. Central Palestine Office for Poland, circular 24, February 1922, CZA, S6, file 3382.

92. Ya'akov Midrashi, in Erez, Sefer ha-Aliya ha-Shelishit, 178–79.

93. Moshe Smilansky, "Al ha-Saf" [On the threshold], Ben Artzi (weekly for children and teenagers), Tevet 1, 5686 (December 18, 1925), 14.

94. Ibid.

95. Azaryahu, "Formation," 252.

96. Ibid., 256.

97. Ibid.

98. Ibid., 257.

99. Ibid.

100. Schlör, "Tel Aviv," 215–16.

101. Cohen-Hattab, Ha-Mahpekha ha-Yamit.

102. "Pe'ulot ha-Misrad," 3.

103. Central Palestine Office, Moreh-Derekh, 10.

104. Ma'avirim to Louis Marshall, March 30, 1920, American Jewish Archives, Louis Marshall Papers, folder 55/5.

105. Ibid.

106. Mizrachi aliya and labor bureau in Jaffa to Zionist Commission, Elul 6, 5681 (September 9, 1921), CZA, S6, file 341/1.

107. "Pe'ulot ha-Misrad," 7.

108. List of belongings on the Asia, July 19, 1925, CZA, S4, file 340, 20–21.

109. Subbotin, *Bi-Tehum Moshavam*, 51.

110. Ibid., 141.

111. Chaim Lederman to Haifa aliya bureau, August 9, 1925, CZA, S3, file 18.

112. "Ha-Transport" [The transport], CZA, S81, file 30, 4; Luke and Keith-Roach, *Handbook of Palestine*, 110.

113. Central Palestine Office, *Moreh-Derekh*, 8.

114. "Ha-Transport," 2.

115. Ibid. For more on conditions on the voyage, see Segev, *Yemei ha-Kalaniyot*, 190. Segev quotes a British officer who wrote that conditions on these ships were worse than on the slave ships in antiquity.

116. "Ha-Transport," 2.

117. *Shibolim*, Sivan 3, 5682 (May 30, 1922), 20.

118. Zionist Commission to Palestine Office in Trieste, December 22, 1920, CZA, Z4, file 41270.

119. "Ha-Transport," 2.

120. Ibid.

121. Ibid., 10.

122. Alroey, *Ha-Mahpekha ha-Sheketa*, 185.

123. "Ha-Transport," 4.

124. Ibid.

125. Contract between Lloyd Triestino and the Zionist Organization, April 28, 1921, CZA, Z4, file 41270.

126. Zionist Organization, *Din ve-Heshbon ha-Exekutiva shel ha-Histadrut ha-Tsiyonit la-Kongres ha-14*, 259–60.

127. Chaim Katznelson, National Library of Israel (Archives), Schwad file 01 11 100, 2.

128. Ibid., 5.

129. Ibid., 3.

130. Ibid., 5.

131. "Tazkir Va'ad ha-Sefina Trento she-Hifliga be-Hodesh Marheshvan 5682" [Memorandum of the ship's committee on the *Trento*, which sailed in Heshvan 5682 (November 1921)], CZA, S6, file 341/1, 1.

132. Ibid., 2.

133. Ibid., 7.

134. Ibid., 8–9.

135. Ganchovsky, *Ki Tavo'u el ha-Aretz*, 10.

136. Ibid.

137. For the quotations regarding public prayer, Torah study, kosher food, and Sabbath observance, see ibid., 10–11.

138. Mizrachi Federation to Giuseppe Fano, head of the Palestine Office in Trieste, August 1, 1926, CZA, S6, file 498, 2.

139. Ibid.

140. Mizrachi Federation to the Zionist Executive Aliya Department, August 26, 1926, CZA, S6, file 498.

141. Ibid.

142. Circular from the Mizrachi World Center Aliya Department, December 14, 1926, CZA, S6, file 498.

5. Reaching the Shore

1. Smilansky, "Al ha-Saf" [On the threshold], 14.

2. Minutes of the Second Council of the Aliya Department, March 6, 1926, CZA, S81, file 29, 2–3. See also "The Landing of Immigrants," CZA, S81, file 30, 1.

3. "Du"h al Avodat ha-Horada" [Report on the disembarkation work] [1925], CZA, S81, file 30, 1. See also minutes of the Second Council of the Aliya Department, 5–6.

4. Palestine Arab delegation to Winston Churchill, October 24, 1921, National Archives (UK), CO 733, file 16, 509. For more on their opposition to Zionism, see Porath, *Emergence*.

5. "Du"h al Horadat ha-Nos'im bi-Nemal Haifa" [Report on the disembarkation of passengers at Haifa port], July 7, 1921, Lavon Institute, IV-135-5.

6. Ibid.

7. Ibid.

8. Ibid.

9. "Du"h al Horadat ha-Nos'im bi-Nemal Haifa" [Report on the disembarkation of passengers at Haifa port], July 10, 1921, Labor Archives, IV-135-5.

10. Ibid.

11. "Du"h shel Menahel Misrad ha-Hof" [Report by the director of the coastal office] [June 1921?], Labor Archives, IV-135-5.

12. "Ha-Aravim ve-Horadat ha-Olim be-Yafo" [The Arabs and the disembarkation of immigrants in Jaffa], *Ha'aretz*, May 10, 1929, 1.

13. Ibid.

14. Livneh, *Pirkei ha-Aliya ha-Shelishit*, 49–50.

15. Menachem Sheinkin, "Hanhalat Lishkat ha-Aliya be-Eretz Yisrael (Keitsad Kiblu et ha-Olim ve-Kheitzad Tiplu Bahem)" [The management of the aliya bureau in Palestine (how they received the olim and how they handled them)], December 12, 1921, Labor Archives, IV-104-118-13.

16. Director of the Haifa aliya bureau to the Aliya Department, November 10, 1925, CZA, S3, file 42, 2.

17. "Du"h al Avodat ha-Horada," 2.

18. "Hartsa'a al ha-Aliya Derekh Haifa be-Meshekh ha-Shana ha-Aharona (mi-1 be-Mars 1924 ad 26 be-Februar 1925)" [Lecture on aliya via Haifa in the past year (from March 1, 1924, to February 26, 1925), CZA, S6, file 398.

19. "Du"h al ha-Oniyot Trento ve-Konstantsa" [Report on the *Trento* and *Constanţa*], February 26, 1922, CZA, S6, file 318/2, 2.

20. Ibid.

21. "Ha-Garantia Bishvil Olei ha-Oniya Moreno" [The guarantee for the immigrants on the Merano], February 20, 1922, CZA, S6, file 308/3, 1.

22. Ibid., 4.

23. Joshua Gordon to director of the Aliya Department, April 24, 1922, CZA, S6, file 318/1, 1.

24. Menachem Sheinkin to Zionist Commission, Tevet 8, 5681 (December 19, 1920), CZA, S6, file 308/2, 1.

25. Livneh, *Pirkei ha-Aliya ha-Shelishit*, 24–25.

26. Ibid., 48.

27. Ibid.

28. Ibid., 49.

29. Ibid., 50.

30. Ibid.

31. Livneh, *Pirkei ha-Aliya ha-Shelishit*, 54.

32. Ibid., 54–55.

33. Gordon to Pick, April 24, 1922, CZA, S6, file 318/1, 2.

34. Ibid.

35. Minutes of a meeting of the aliya council, December 6, 1921, CZA, S81, file 36.

36. Murray, *Red Scare*; Coben, "Study in Nativism."

37. On Communism and Communists in Palestine in the 1920s, see Dothan, *Adumim*, 37–149. See also Yisraeli, *Mapas*, 15–73.

38. On the bloody riots of May 1921, see Segev, *Yemei ha-Kalaniyot*, 146–66; Giler, "Me'ora'ot Yafo."

39. Giler, *23 be-Nisan*, 63.

40. "Yahaso shel Dr. Kamil Eid el ha-Olim ha-Yehudim" [Dr. Kamil Eid's attitude toward the Jewish immigrants], May 19, 1922, CZA, S6, file 311/3, 1.

41. Report by the Aliya Department, October 1921 to June 1922, CZA, S6, file 275, 4; Levi Shvueli to governor of the Phoenicia-Haifa District, December 21, 1921, CZA, S6, file 308/1, 1.

42. Report by the Aliya Department, October 1921 to June 1922, CZA, S6, file 275, 4.

43. Ibid., 5.

44. Ibid.

45. "Duh meha-Oniya Carnara" [Report from the *Carnaro*], September 24, 1925, CZA, S3, file 42.

46. Director of Haifa aliya bureau to Aliya Department, July 17, 1922, CZA, S4, file 194.

47. Joshua Gordon, "Tazkir be-Inyenei ha-Aliya la-Yeshiva ha-Kelalit" [Memorandum on aliya to the general meeting], December 5, 1921, CZA, S6, file 318/1, 16.

48. On quarantine in Palestine during the Mandate period, see Katvan, "Mi Ba'al ha-Bayit?" 44.

49. Ibid.

50. Beiteli to Pick, October 11, 1925, CZA, S6, file 405, 2.

51. "Hatsa'ot le-Mo'etset Minhal Leshakhot ha-Aliya" [Proposals to the administrative council of aliya bureaus], CZA, S81, file 30, 4.

52. Minutes of the Second Council of the Aliya Department, March 8, 1926, CZA, S81, file 29, 6–7.

53. Ibid., 7.

54. Trei Asar, "Beit ha-Hesger" [The quarantine house], Davar, September 2, 1925, 3.

55. Ibid.

56. Minutes of the Second Council of the Aliya Department, March 8, 1926, CZA, S81, file 29, 7.

57. Shvueli to governor of the Phoenicia-Haifa District, December 21, 1921, CZA, S6, file 308/1, 1.

58. Ibid.

59. Beiteli to Kisch, October 10, 1925, CZA, S6, file 405, 1.

60. Ibid.

61. See Ida Levin's complaint to the aliya bureau, March 18, 1925, CZA, S3, file 48.

62. Ibid.

63. Mottel Y. M. to Tel Aviv aliya bureau, June 30, 1925, CZA, S4, file 340.

64. See Judgment 1172, Av 20, 5685 (August 10, 1925), CZA, S3, file 42.

65. March 3, 1927, National Archives (UK), CO 733, file 133–6, 1.

66. Ibid., 3.

67. "Zikhron Devarim al Devar Bikuri be-Haifa (ba-Oniya Datsia)" [Memorandum on my visit to Haifa (on the Dacia)], May 1, 1926, CZA, S6, file 498, 2.

68. "Mahane ha-Karantina" [The quarantine camp], September 13, 1923, CZA, S6, file 311/2, 1.

69. "Hesderim ba-Karantina" [Arrangements in quarantine], October 11, 1923, CZA, S6, file 311/2, 2.

70. March 3, 1927, National Archives (UK), CO 733, file 133–6, 4.

71. Ibid., 2.

72. Protest by passengers from the Barga, March 17, 1925, CZA, S3, file 3.

73. See letter from the board of the Society of Polish Jews, March 29, 1925, CZA, S3, file 3.

74. Ze'ev Leibowitz, director of the Jerusalem aliya bureau, to the Aliya Department, Kislev 19, 5682 (December 20, 1921), CZA, S6, file 315/1, 1.

75. Government health department to Joshua Gordon, January 20, 1922, CZA, S6, file 315/1.

76. Joshua Gordon to director of the Aliya Department, January 3, 1922, CZA, S6, file 315/1.

77. General secretariat of the Zionist Executive to the administration of the home for the mentally ill, November 24, 1921, CZA, S6, file 315/1.

78. Joshua Gordon to director of the Aliya Department, December 5, 1921, CZA, S6, file 315/1.

79. "Hartsa'a al ha-Aliya Derekh Haifa be-Meshekh ha-Shana ha-Aharona (mi-1 Mars 1924 ad 28 be-Februar 1925)" [Lecture on aliya via Haifa in the past year (from March 1, 1924, to February 28, 1925)], CZA, S6, file 398.

80. Feigenbaum to director of the aliya bureau, January 25, 1922, CZA, S3, file 85.

81. Ibid.

82. Levi Shvueli to Aliya Department, January 1, 1924, CZA, S3, file 85.

83. Gordon to director of the Aliya Department, January 9, 1922, CZA, S6, file 315/1, 2.

84. Gordon to directors of the aliya bureaus, July 30, 1926, CZA, S3, file 106.

85. Gordon to director of the Aliya Department, May 5, 1922, CZA, S6, file 316/1.

86. Gordon to director of the Aliya Department, December 20, 1921, CZA, S6, file 316/1, 2.

87. Gordon to director of the Aliya Department, February 15, 1922, CZA, S6, file 316/1.

88. Ibid.

89. Seinfeld to Gordon, CZA, S6, file 315/1.

90. Gordon to director of the Aliya Department, December 20, 1921, CZA, S6, file 316/1, 2.

91. "Zikhron Devarim al Devar Bikuri be-Haifa," 2.

92. "Tazkir al Devar ha-Aliya le-Eretz Yisrael" [Memorandum on immigration to Palestine], CZA, S81, file 37, 2.

93. Yakir, *Toldot ha-Mahlaka la-Aliya*, 68.

94. Report by the director of the Jaffa aliya station, January 15, 1922, CZA, S6, file 308/2.

95. See Sheinkin, "Hanhalat Lishkat ha-Aliya."

96. Efter to Ruppin, August 9, 1920, CZA, S6, file 308/1.

97. On the violence in May 1921, see Segev, *Yemei ha-Kalaniyot*, 146–66.

98. See testimony of Rachel Kaufman, May 18, 1921, CZA, L4, file 831-het, 14–15. On the riots at the immigrant home, see Giler, "Me'ora'ot Yafo," 1–9.

99. Giler, "Me'ora'ot Yafo," 15.

100. On Rubinow, see Shehory-Rubin and Shvarts, *Hadasa*, 21–23.

101. Ibid., 21.

102. Letter to Rubinow, July 10, 1921, CZA, S6, file 308/2, 1.

103. Ibid., 2.
104. Gordon to Zionist Commission, November 17, 1921, CZA, S6, file 308/2.
105. Gordon to Eder, January 15, 1922, ibid.
106. Tel Aviv municipality to aliya bureau, January 31, 1922, ibid.
107. Dizengoff to Gordon, October 14, 1923, CZA, S4, file 212.
108. Erez, *Sefer ha-Aliya ha-Shelishit*, 2:639.
109. Memorandum regarding a new camp for immigrants in Haifa, CZA, S6, file 308/1.
110. Jewish National Fund to Zionist Executive, May 18, 1922, CZA, S6, file 311/3.
111. Bat Galim neighborhood committee to aliya bureau, May 31, 1922, ibid.
112. "Hagigat Beit ha-Olim be-Haifa" [Celebration for the immigrant home in Haifa], *Doar Hayom*, November 30, 1923, 6.
113. Dr. Bershizen to immigrant home in Haifa, October 13, 1925, CZA, S3, file 48.
114. "Ha'ataka—Beit ha-Aliya" [Relocation—immigrant home] [1925], ibid.
115. [Joshua Gordon], "Kabbalat ha-Olim (Tazkir le-Va'adat ha-Malaria be-Yafo)" [Greeting the immigrants (memo to the malaria committee in Jaffa)], March 15, 1923, CZA, S6, file 275, 4.
116. Battalion for the Defence of the Language to Aliya Department, Tammuz 29, 5683 (July 13, 1923), CZA, S4, file 212.
117. Director of the Netzah Yisrael educational institution to Levi Shvueli, Adar 1, 5685 (February 25, 1925), CZA, S3, file 13.
118. Director of the Haifa aliya bureau to the Aliya Department in Jerusalem, December 31, 1925, CZA, S3, file 42.
119. Ibid.
120. Director of Haifa aliya bureau to Aliya Department, December 21, 1925, ibid.
121. Ibid.
122. See Joshua Gordon to Aliya Department, September 19, 1926, CZA, S3, file 106.
123. Yosef Aharonovich, "Lishkat ha-Aliya be-Yafo" [The aliya bureau in Jaffa], *Hapoel Hatzair*, no. 4, November 25, 1921, 1.
124. Zvi Livneh, "Beit Olim u-Veit Okhel la-Halutzim" [An immigrant home and dining house for halutzim], in Erez, *Sefer ha-Aliya ha-Shelishit*, 2:554; Livneh, *Pirkei ha-Aliya ha-Shelishit*, 29–34.
125. Observer, "Liskhat ha-Aliya be-Haifa" [The aliya bureau in Haifa], *Doar Hayom*, April 30, 1925, 4.
126. [Gordon], "Kabbalat ha-Olim," 2.
127. Ibid., 1.
128. Ibid. (emphasis mine).

6. Invisible Immigration

1. Livneh, *Pirkei ha-Aliya ha-Shelishit*, 186.
2. Erez, *Sefer ha-Aliya ha-Shelishit*, 4.

3. Shoham, "Meha-Aliya ha-Shelishit."

4. Ben-Avram and Near, *Iyunim ba-Aliya ha-Shelishit*, 170.

5. Chaim Arlosoroff, "Le-Ha'arakhat ha-Aliya ha-Revi'it (1925)" [Estimation of the Fourth Aliya (1925)], in Arlosoroff, *Kitvei Chaim Arlosoroff*, 107. See also Chazan, "Hayyim Vaitsman"; Shoham, "Meha-Aliya ha-Shelishit."

6. Ruppin, *Ha-Sotsiologya shel ha-Yehudim*, 60; Segall, *Die beruflichen und sozialen Verhaltnisse*.

7. Shvueli to Aliya Department in Jerusalem, December 27, 1925, CZA, S3, file 42.

8. Ibid.

9. Ibid.

10. Zionist Organization, *Din ve-Heshbon ha-Exekutiva shel ha-Histadrut ha-Tsiyonit la-Kongres ha-15*, 231.

11. Ibid., 232; "Ha-Aliya mi-Teiman" [Immigration from Yemen], *Davar*, March 17, 1929, 1.

12. Amir, *Na'ar ha-Ofanayim*, 122.

13. Ya'akobi and Hakhami, *Nash Didan*, 43.

14. Yedidya and Cohen, "Aliyat Yehudim," 87.

15. Ibid., 88–89.

16. Ya'akobi and Hakhami, *Nash Didan*, 45.

17. Testimony of Ovadia Yedidya, in Yedidya and Cohen, "Aliyat Yehudim," 92.

18. Ya'akobi and Hakhami, *Nash Didan*, 67.

19. Ibid., 119–20.

20. Benzion, *Me-Iran umi-Makedonia*, 9–13.

21. Zalman Rubashov, "Uremiyeh," *Davar*, September 6, 1960.

22. Mesopotamian Zionist Association to Zionist Commission, Av 29, 5681 (September 2, 1921), CZA, S6, file 327/1.

23. Mesopotamian Zionist Association to Zionist Commission, Marheshvan 12, 5682 (November 13, 1921), CZA, S6, file 327/1.

24. Mesopotamian Zionist Association to Zionist Commission, Tevet 22, 5682 (January 22, 1922), CZA, S6, file 327/1.

25. "Reshimat Mehagrei u-Felitei Yehudei Paras be-Baghdad" [List of Persian Jewish immigrants and refugees in Baghdad], Tevet 15, 5682 (January 15, 1922), CZA, S6, file 327/1.

26. Reply of the aliya bureau to the Mesopotamian Zionist Association, Adar 2, 5682 (March 2, 1922), CZA, S6, file 327/1.

27. Aliya bureau to April 8, 1921, CZA, Z4, file 41747, 1.

28. Ibid.

29. Ibid., 2.

30. Jerusalem aliya bureau to president of the Zionist Organization in Iran (Baghdad), March 17, 1922, CZA, Z4, file 41747.

31. Zionist representative in Baghdad to Jerusalem aliya bureau, August 9, 1922, CZA, Z4, file 41747.

32. Zionist representative in Baghdad to Jerusalem aliya bureau, September 17, 1924, CZA, Z4, file 41747.

33. Ibid.

34. Nesher, "Yedi'ot me-Aram Naharayim" [News from Mesopotamia], *Haaretz*, September 2, 1924, 2.

35. Ibid.

36. On immigration from Fez to Palestine (the "Exodus from Fez"), see Tsur, *Kehila Keru'a*, 58–61; Cohen, "Lyautey." On Zionism in Morocco shortly before World War I, see Yehuda, "Ha-Pe'ilut ha-Tsiyonit be-Maroko."

37. Gil, *Dappei Aliya*, 28.

38. On Yosef Levi, see Tsur, *Kehila Keru'a*, 58.

39. Jews of Serfou to London aliya bureau, November 9, 1920, CZA, Z4, file 41501, 2.

40. Ibid., 4.

41. See, e.g., letter from Rabbi Pinhas Halifa Cohen Azour of Marrakesh requesting information about immigration to Palestine, July 28, 1921, CZA, Z4, file 41501; extensive correspondence between the Tunis Jewish community and the aliya bureau, CZA, Z4, file 41621; correspondence between the Jews of Tripoli and the London aliya bureau, CZA, Z4, file 41625.

42. London aliya bureau to the Jews of Sefrou, December 14, 1920, CZA, Z4, file 41501.

43. Secretary for aliya to Azour, July 28, 1921, CZA, Z4, file 41501.

44. On Albert Cohen, see Yakir, *Toldot ha-Mahlaka la-Aliya*, 136.

45. Ibid.

46. Zionist Commission to Dr. Kalb, June 21, 1921, CZA, S6, file 338/1.

47. "Duh al Devar Pe'ulot Mahleket ha-Aliya be-Meshekh Asara Hodashim— Yuni–Mars 1923" [Report on the Aliya Department's activities over ten months, June–March {March–June?} 1923], CZA, S81, file 35, 9–10.

48. Ibid.

49. Tsur, *Kehila Keru'a*, 58.

50. On the dream and the awakening to harsh reality among halutzim of the Second Aliya and Third Aliya, see Alroey, "Halutsim Ovdei Derekh?"

51. Zionist Commission to Agudat Zion in Tripoli, July 6, 1921, CZA, S6, file 338/1, 1.

52. Eraqi Klorman, *Traditional Society in Transition*, 87–116; Eraqi Klorman, *Yehudei Teiman*, 233–39.

53. Presidium of the Jewish National Council to High Commissioner, February 23, 1921, in *Sefer ha-Te'udot*, 44–45.

54. Zionist Organization, *Din ve-Heshbon ha-Exekutiva shel ha-Histadrut ha-Tsiyonit la-Kongres ha-15*, 240.

55. Habara, *Bi-Tela'ot Teiman vi-Yerushalayim*, 141.

56. Ibid., 154.

57. Eliyahu Dobkin, "Din ve-Heshbon shel Va'adat ha-Aliya" [Report of the aliya committee], *Ha'aretz*, August 19, 1929, 3.

58. "Le-Siddur ha-Aliya mi-Teiman le-Eretz Yisrael (me-Hoda'ot ha-Hanhala ha-Tsiyonit)" [On the organization of aliya from Yemen to Palestine (taken from announcements by the Zionist Executive)], *Doar Hayom*, March 21, 1923, 4.

59. "Aharei Arba Shanim (Likrat ha-Ve'ida shel Hitahdut ha-Teimanim)" [After four years (in advance of the conference of the Association of Yemenites)], *Doar Hayom*, March 17, 1929, 3.

60. Ibid.

61. Zionist Organization, *Din ve-Heshbon ha-Exekutiva shel ha-Histadrut ha-Tsiyonit la-Kongres ha-16*, 193.

Conclusion

1. On Yitzhak Lamdan, see Avidov Lipsker, "Mavo: . . . ad Masada" [Introduction: . . . up to Masada] in Lamdan, *Yoman Yitzhak Lamdan*, 11–73.

2. Isaac Lamdan, *Masada*, in Yudkin, *Isaac Lamdan*, 207.

3. Chazan, "Hayyim Vaitsman," 454.

4. Menachem Sheinkin, "Be-Eizeh Sug Mehagrim Netuna Tikvat Eretz Yisrael" [On what kind of immigrants does Palestine's hope depend], June 1, 1922, Labor Archives, IV-104-118-13.

BIBLIOGRAPHY

Collections and Archives

National Library of Israel Photograph Collection

Khodorkov Pogrom   TMA 5490

National Library of Israel (Archives)   Schwad file 01 11 100

Genazim Archive

Megilat ha-Tevah   341

National Archives (UK)

Colonial Office: Palestine Original Correspondence   CO 733

Pinhas Lavon Institute for Labor Movement Research

Jewish Labor Movement in Palestine   IV-135-5
IV-104-118-13
General Federation of Jewish Labour   IV-211-1-30

Central Zionist Archives (CZA)

Palestine Office, Jaffa, Tel Aviv, Jerusalem   L2
Zionist Commission for Palestine, Jerusalem   L3
Zionist Commission for Palestine, Jaffa   L4
Aliya Bureau, Haifa   S3
Aliya Bureau, Tel Aviv   S4
Aliya Department   S6
Office of Hermann Pick (director of the Aliya Department, 1922–1927)   S81
Zionist Organization and Jewish Agency headquarters, London   Z4

YIVO

Foreign Relations Department, HIAS   RG 245.3
Lucien Wolf   RG 348

American Jewish Archives (AJA)

Louis Marshall Papers

Press Sources

Daily Newspapers

Doar Hayom; Davar; Der Tog; Haaretz; Ha-Tsefira; Jewish Daily Bulletin

Periodicals

Di Idishe Emigratsie; Ben Artzi; Ha-Olam; Hapoel Hatzair; Yediot ha-Mahlaka le-Statistika ule-Informatsia [News of the Department of Statistics and Information]; *Ma'abarot; Kuntres; Shibolim; Statistical Abstract of the United States*

Documents, Reports, and Official Publications

Attias, Moshe, ed. *Sefer ha-Teudot shel ha-Va'ad ha-Leumi le-Knesset Yisrael be-Eretz Yisrael, 5678–5708* [Documents of the Jewish National Council]. Jerusalem: Jewish National Council, 1963.

Central Palestine Office. *Moreh-Derekh Bishvil ha-Olim le-Eretz-Yisrael* [Guide for immigrants to Palestine]. Warsaw: Central Palestine Office, 1924/25.

Committee of Jewish Delegations. *The Pogroms in the Ukraine under the Ukrainian Governments (1917–1920)*. London: Bale, 1927.

Emigdirect. *Tsentral-Byuro-Emigdirekt, Faraynigter Idisher Emigratsie-Komitet (Emigdirekt)—Di Arbet far di Yorn 1921–1925* [The Emigdirect central office: United Jewish emigration committee (Emigdirect)—the work in the years 1921–1925]. Berlin: Emigdirect, 1925.

Ganchovsky, E. M., ed. *Ki Tavo'u el ha-Aretz: La-Oleh le-Tsiyon vala-Metzapeh Lir'otah* [When you enter the Land: to immigrants to Zion and to those who look forward to seeing it]. Jerusalem: Mizrachi Palestine Fund, 1935/36.

Gurevich, David. *Statistical Abstract of Palestine, 1929*. Jerusalem: Keren Hayesod, 1930.

Health Council of the Palestine Zionist Executive. *Hora'ot la-Bedika ha-Refu'it shel ha-Olim be-Hutz la-Aretz* [Instructions for the medical examination of immigrants]. Jerusalem: Immigration Department of the Palestine Zionist Executive, Hamadpis, 1926.

Jewish World Relief Conference. "The Jewish Emigration Conference in Prague." In *Bulletin of the Executive Committee of the Jewish World Relief Conference*. Paris: n.p., 1921.

Krimsky, Yosef. *Barikht iber der Lage fun di Ukrayner Flikhtlinge un Yesomim* [Report on the situation of the Ukrainian refugees and orphans]. New York, 1920.

Luke, Harry Charles, and Edward Keith-Roach. *The Handbook of Palestine.* London: MacMillan, 1922.

Palestine Office. *Die Tätigkeit des Wiener Palästina-Amtes.* Vienna: Palestine Office, 1922.

Rosenfeld, S., ed. *Ha-Kongres ha-Tziyoni ha-Shneim-Asar* [The 12th Zionist Congress]. Warsaw: Achiasaf, 1921.

Sefer ha-Te'udot shel ha-Va'ad ha-Leumi li-Khneset Yisrael be-Eretz Yisrael 5678–5708, 1918–1948 [Book of documents of the Jewish National Council in Palestine, 1918–1948]. Jerusalem: R. C. Hacohen, 1963.

Segall, Jakob. *Die beruflichen und sozialen Verhaltnisse der Juden in Deutschland.* Berlin: M. Schildberger, 1912.

World Federation of Hapoel Hatzair and Tze'irei Zion. *Ba-Aliya: Sekira Kelalit* [Aliya: an overview]. Vienna: Union, 1920/21.

Yogev, Gedalya, and Yehoshua Freundlich, eds. *Ha-Protokolim shel ha-Va'ad-ha-Poel ha-Tsiyoni 1919–1929* [Minutes of the Zionist General Council, 1919–1929]. Tel Aviv: Tel Aviv University and Hakibbutz Hameuchad, 1975.

Zionist Organization. *Din ve-Heshbon ha-Exekutiva shel ha-Histadrut ha-Tsiyonit la-Kongres ha-14 (Helki)* [Report of the Zionist Organization Executive to the 14th Congress (partial)]. London: Zionist Organization, 1925.

Zionist Organization. *Din ve-Heshbon ha-Exekutiva shel ha-Histadrut ha-Tsiyonit la-Kongres ha-15* [Report of the Executive of the Zionist Organization to the 15th Congress]. London: Zionist Organization, 1927.

Zionist Organization. *Din ve-Heshbon ha-Exekutiva shel ha-Histadrut ha-Tsiyonit la-Kongres ha-16* [Report of the Executive of the Zionist Organization to the 16th Congress]. London: Zionist Organization, 1929.

Memoirs, Testimonies, and Works of Fiction

Amir, Eli. *Na'ar ha-Ofanayim* [Bicycle boy]. Tel Aviv: Am Oved, 2018.

Arlosoroff, Chaim. *Kitvei Chaim Arlosoroff* [Writings of Chaim Arlosoroff]. Tel Aviv: A. Y. Shtiebl, with the participation of the Mapai central committee, 1933/34–1934/35.

Benzion, Yehoshua. *Me-Iran umi-Makedonia li-Yerushalayim: Sipureihen shel Mishpehot Ben-Eliahu u-Menahem* [From Iran and Macedonia to Jerusalem: the stories of the Ben-Eliahu and Menahem families]. Jerusalem: published by the family, 2002.

Dijour, Ilja. *Di Moderne Felker-Vanderung* [The modern migration of peoples]. Berlin: HIAS-Emigdirect, 1929.

Dinur, Ben-Zion. *Eretz Yisrael bi-Shnat Tarpag* [Palestine in 1922/23]. Jerusalem: Mishana Leshana, 1923/24.

Druyanov, Alter. "Shura shel Pega'im" [A series of attacks]. *Reshumot* 3 (1922/23): 132–236.

Erez, Yehuda, ed. *Sefer ha-Aliya ha-Shelishit* [The book of the Third Aliyah]. Tel Aviv: Am Oved, 1964.

Habara, Yosef Shalom. *Bi-Tela'ot Teiman vi-Yerushalayim* [The tribulations of Yemen and Jerusalem]. Jerusalem: self-published, 1969/70.

Heifetz, Elias. *The Slaughter of the Jews in the Ukraine in 1919*. New York: Seltzer, 1921.

Howe, Irving. *World of Our Fathers*. New York: Harcourt Brace Jovanovich, 1976.

Imri-Fajgenberg, Rachel. *Megilat Dubova: Toldot Ir she-Avra u-Vatla min ha-Olam* [The scroll of Dubova: the history of a city that is no more]. Tel Aviv: La'am, 1940.

Lamdan, Yitzhak. *Yoman Yitzhak Lamdan* [Yizhak Lamdan's diary]. Ramat Gan: Bar-Ilan University, 2015.

Lilienblum, Moshe Leib. *Ketavim Otobiografiyim* [An autobiography]. Jerusalem: Mossad Bialik, 1970.

Litai, A. "Tseror shel Protokolim" [A bunch of minutes]. *Reshumot* 3 (1922/23): 237–63.

Livneh, Zvi. *Pirkei ha-Aliya ha-Shelishit: Mi-Kenisat ha-Britim la-Arets ad Ve'idat ha-Histadrut (5679–5681)* [The Third Aliya: from the entry of the British to Palestine until the General Federation of Jewish Labour conference (1918/19–1920/21)]. Tel Aviv: Gadish, 1957/58.

Magal Cohen, Adva. *Isha Yoshevet ve-Khotevet: Rachel Tauber* [A woman sitting and writing: Rachel Tauber]. Jerusalem: privately printed, 2011.

Naor, Mordechay. *Mi-Sippurei Eretz Ahavati: Eretz Yisrael ba-Shanim 1850–1950* [Tales from my beloved country]. Tel Aviv: Ministry of Defense, 1985.

Orland, Ya'akov. *Kiev—Poema; u-Shtei Tiutot-Shir le-Zikhron Tetiev* [Kiev: a poem; and two drafts of a memorial poem to Tetiev]. Jerusalem: Carmel, 1991.

Rafaeli (Zenzipper), Aryeh. *Ba-Ma'avak li-Geula: Sefer ha-Tsiyonut ha-Rusit mi-Mahpekhat 1917 ad Yamenu* [The struggle for redemption: Russian Zionism from the 1917 revolution until today]. Tel Aviv: Davar, 1956.

Rosenthal, Eliezer David. *Megilat ha-Tevah: Homer le-Divrei Yemei ha-Pera'ot veha-Tevah ba-Yehudim be-Ukraina, be-Rusya ha-Gedola uve-Rusya ha-Levana* [Scroll of slaughter: historical material on the pogroms and the slaughter of the Jews in Ukraine, Russia, and White Russia]. Vol. 3 (*het–tet*). Jerusalem: Havura, 1930/31.

Rosenthal, Eliezer David. *Tetiever Khurbn*. New York: American Representatives of the All Russian Jewish Public Committee, 1922.

Ruppin, Arthur. "The Selection of the Fittest." In *Building Israel: Selected Essays, 1907–1935*. New York: Schocken, 1949.

Schechtman, Joseph. "Antishemiut u-Fera'ot" [Antisemitism and pogroms]. *Reshumot* 3 (1922/23): 470–502.

Sucker, Y. [Yitzhak Laufbahn]. "Hazon ha-Yamim" [Vision of the days]. *Ma'abarot* 10–11 (1919/20).

Ya'akobi, Ora, and Avraham Hakhami. *Nash Didan: Toldot Yahadut Urmia (Azerbaijan ha-Iranit)* [Nash Didan: the history of the Jews of Orumiyeh (Iranian Azerbaijan)]. N.p.: n.p., 2007.

Yudkin, Leon I. *Isaac Lamdan: A Study in Twentieth-Century Hebrew Poetry.* London: Horovitz, 1971.

Scholarly Books and Articles

Abramson, Henry. *A Prayer for the Government: Ukrainians and Jews in Revolutionary Times, 1917–1920.* Cambridge, MA: Harvard University Press, Ukrainian Research Institute and Center for Jewish Studies, 1999.

Alroey, Gur. "Between the Straits: Jewish Immigration to the United States and Palestine, 1915–1925." *East European Jewish Affairs* 47 (2017): 150–68.

Alroey, Gur. "Documenting the Pogroms in Ukraine, 1918–1920: Eliezer David Rozenthal's Megilat Hatevah." *Galed* 24 (2014): 63–102.

Alroey, Gur. "Halutsim Ovdei Derekh? Sugiyat ha-Hitabdut al Seder Yomah shel ha-Aliya ha-Shniya veha-Shelishit." *Yahadut Zemanenu* 13 (1998/99): 209–41.

Alroey, Gur. *Ha-Mahpekha ha-Sheketa: Ha-Hagira ha-Yehudit meha-Imperia ha-Rusit, 1875–1924* [The quiet revolution: Jewish emigration from the Russian Empire, 1875–1924]. Jerusalem: Zalman Shazar Center, 2008.

Alroey, Gur. "Sexual Violence, Rape, and Pogroms, 1903–1920." *Jewish Culture and History* 18, no. 3 (2017): 313–30.

Alroey, Gur. *An Unpromising Land: Jewish Migration to Palestine in the Early Twentieth Century.* Stanford, CA: Stanford University Press, 2014.

Altshuler, Mordechai. "Russia and Her Jews: The Impact of the 1914 War." *Wiener Library Bulletin* 27 (1973–1974): 12–16.

Altshuler, Mordechai. *Ha-Yevsektsya bi-Vrit ha-Mo'atsot 1918–1930: Bein Le'umiyut le-Komunizm* [Between nationalism and communism: the Evsektsiia in the Soviet Union, 1918–1930]. Tel Aviv and Jerusalem: Sifriyat Poalim and the Hebrew University of Jerusalem, 1980.

Anbinder, Tyler. *City of Dreams: The 400-Year Epic History of Immigrant New York.* Boston: Houghton Mifflin Harcourt, 2016.

Astashkevich, Irina. *Gendered Violence: Jewish Women in the Pogroms of 1917 to 1921.* Boston: Academic Studies, 2018.

Azaryahu, Maoz. "The Formation of the 'Hebrew Sea' in Pre-State Israel." *Journal of Modern Jewish Studies* 7, no. 3 (2008): 251–67.

Bareli, Avi, and Nahum Karlinsky, eds. *Kalkala ve-Hevra bi-Yemei ha-Mandat: 1918–1948* [Economy and society in Mandatory Palestine, 1918–1948]. Sede Boker: Ben-Gurion University Press, 2003.

Bartal, Israel. "1919: Eretz be-Terem." In *Between Collection and Museum: From the Peremen Collection through the Tel Aviv Museum*, by Batia Donner, 26–33. Tel Aviv: Tel Aviv Museum of Art, 2002.

Ben-Avram, Baruch, and Henry Near. *Iyunim ba-Aliya ha-Shelishit: Dimui u-Metsiut* [Studies in the Third Aliyah (1919–1924)]. Jerusalem: Yad Izhak Ben-Zvi, 1995.

Bennett, Marion T. *American Immigration Policies.* Washington, DC: Public Affairs, 1963.

Budnitskii, Oleg. *Russian Jews between the Reds and the Whites, 1917–1920.* Philadelphia: University of Pennsylvania Press, 2012.

Chazan, Meir. "Hayyim Vaitsman ve-Hivatsrut Dimuyah shel ha-Aliya ha-Revi'it be-Reshit Yameha" [Chaim Weizmann and the creation of the Fourth Aliya image and character]. *Zion* 76, no. 4 (2011): 453–80.

Coben, Stanley. "A Study in Nativism: The American Red Scare of 1919–20." *Political Science Quarterly* 79, no. 1 (1964): 52–75.

Cohen, David. "Lyautey veha-Tsiyonut be-Maroko (1912–1925)" [Lyautey and Zionism in Morocco]. *Kivunim* 18 (1982/83): 105–53.

Cohen-Hattab, Kobi. *Ha-Mahpekha ha-Yamit: Ahizat ha-Yishuv ha-Yehudi ba-Yam uve-Hofei Eretz Yisrael, 1917–1948* [Maritime revolution: the Yishuv's hold on the sea and shores of the Land of Israel, 1917–1948]. Jerusalem: Yad Izhak Ben-Zvi, 2019.

Daniels, Roger. *Guarding the Golden Door: American Immigration Policy and Immigration since 1882.* New York: Hill and Wang, 2004.

Dothan, Shmuel. *Adumim: Ha-Miflaga ha-Komunistit be-Eretz Yisrael* [Reds: the Communist Party in Palestine]. Kefar Sava: Shevna ha-Sofer, 1991.

Elam, Yigal. "Historia Medinit, 1918–1922" [Political history, 1918–1922]. In *Toldot ha-Yishuv ha-Yehudi be-Eretz Yisrael me-az ha-Aliya ha-Rishona: Tekufat ha-Mandat ha-Briti* [History of the Jewish Community in Eretz-Israel since 1882: the period of the British Mandate], edited by Moshe Lissak, Gabriel Cohen, and Israel Kolatt, 2:139–222. Jerusalem: Israel Academy of Sciences and Humanities and Mossad Bialik, 1994.

Eraqi Klorman, Bat-Zion. *Traditional Society in Transition: The Yemeni Jewish Experience.* Leiden: Brill, 2014.

Eraqi Klorman, Bat-Zion. *Yehudei Teiman: Historya, Hevra, Tarbut* [The Jews of Yemen: history, society, culture]. Ra'anana: Open University, 2004–2008.

Frankel, Jonathan, ed. *The Jews and the European Crisis, 1914–1921.* New York: Oxford University Press, 1988.

Friesel, Evyatar. *Ha-Mediniut ha-Tsiyonit le-Ahar Hatsharat Balfur, 1917–1922* [Zionist policy after the Balfour Declaration, 1917–1922]. Tel Aviv: Hakibbutz Hameuchad, 1977.

Galili, Ziva. "Merhav ha-Pe'ula shel ha-Tsiyonim be-Rusya ha-Sovietit bi-Shnot ha-Esrim" [Openings for Zionist activity in Soviet Russia in the 1920s]. *Iyunim Bitkumat Israel* 14 (2004): 479–508.

Garland, Libby. *After They Closed the Gates: Jewish Illegal Immigration to the United States, 1921–1965.* Chicago: University of Chicago Press, 2014.

Gergel, N[ahum]. "Di Pogromen in Ukrayne in di Yarn 1918–1921" [The pogroms in Ukraine in the years 1918–1921]. In *Shriftn far Ekonomik un Statistik* [Papers on economics and statistics], edited by Jacob Lestschinsky, vol. 1. Berlin: YIVO, 1928.

Gergel, Nahum. "The Pogroms in the Ukraine in 1918–1921." *YIVO Annual of Jewish Social Science* 6 (1951): 237–52.

Gil, Benjamin. *Dappei Aliya: Sheloshim Shenot Aliya le-Eretz Yisrael, 1919–1949* [Aliya pages: thirty years of Aliya to the Land of Israel, 1919–1949]. Jerusalem: Jewish Agency for Israel, Aliya Department, 1949/50.

Giler, Samuel. "Me'ora'ot Yafo, May 1921 (5681): Erua Mifne be-Sikhsukh ha-Yehudi Aravi" [The 1921 riots in Jaffa: a turning point in the Jewish-Arab conflict]. Master's thesis, University of Haifa, 2019.

Giler, Samuel. *23 be-Nisan 5681, ha-Yom Bo Atsru Pa'amei Mashiah* [Nisan 23, 5681, the day the footsteps of the Messiah stopped]. N.p.: self-published, n.d.

Gordon, Joshua. "Immigration Problems in Palestine," 1923. Available in the National Library of Israel.

Gorenstein, Lillian. "A Memoir of the Great War." *YIVO Annual of Jewish Social Science* 20 (1991): 125–83.

Gross, Nachum. "He'ara le-Inyan Halukatan li-Tekufot shel Toldot ha-Yishuv bi-Tekufat ha-Mandat" [A note on the periodization to the history of the Yishuv during the Mandatory Period]. *Cathedra* 18 (1981): 174–77.

Gurevich, David. "15 Shenot Aliya" [15 years of immigration]. *Aliya: Kovets le-Inyenei Aliya*, Nisan 2, 5695 (April 5, 1935): 44.

Gurevich, David, Aaron Gertz, and Roberto Bachi. *Ha-Aliya, ha-Yishuv yeha-Tenua ha-Tiv'it shel ha-Ukhlusiya be-Eretz Yisrael* [The Jewish population of Palestine]. Jerusalem: Jewish Agency Statistics Department, 1944/45.

Halamish, Aviva. "Aliya lefi Yekholet ha-Kelita ha-Kalkalit: Ha-Ekronot ha-Manhim, Darkei ha-Bitsua veha-Hashlakhot ha-Demografiot shel Mediniut ha-Aliya bein Milhemot ha-Olam" [Immigration according to the economic absorptive capacity: the guiding principles, the implementation, and the demographic ramifications of the British and the Zionist immigration policy in Palestine between the world wars]. In Bareli and Karlinsky, *Kalkala ve-Hevra,* 179–216.

Halamish, Aviva. *Be-Meruts Kaful Neged ha-Zeman: Mediniyut ha-Aliya ha-Tsiyonit bi-Shnot ha-Sheloshim* [Dual race against time: Zionist immigration policy in the 1930s]. Jerusalem: Yad Izhak Ben-Zvi, 2006.

Halamish, Aviva. *Kibbutz, Utopia and Politics: The Life and Times of Meir Yaari, 1897–1987.* Translated by Lenn Schramm. Brighton, MA: Academic Studies, 2017.

Halamish, Aviva. *Mi-Bayit Leumi li-Medina ba-Derekh: Ha-Yishuv ha-Yehudi be-Eretz-Yisrael bein Milhemot ha-Olam* [From national home to a state in the making: the Jewish community in Palestine between the world wars], vol. 1. Ra'anana: Open University, 2004.

Halamish, Aviva. "Yahaso shel Vaitsman la-Aliya bein Milhemot ha-Olam" [Weizmann and Jewish immigration between the world wars]. In *Vaitsman: Manhig ha-Tsiyonut* [Weizmann: the leader of Zionism], edited by Uri Cohen and Meir Chazan, 261–98. Jerusalem: Zalman Shazar Center for Jewish History, 2016.

Hayek, Drora. *Kefar Giladi—Sha'ar ha-Aliya: Ha-Ha'apala ha-Yabashtit mi-Gevul ha-Tsafon 1919–1946* [Kfar Giladi—an unknown gate to the illegal immigration: the illegal immigration from the northern border to the Land of Israel in 1919–1946]. Reut: Efi Meltzer, 2015.

Heller, Celia. *On the Edge of Destruction: Jews of Poland between the Two World Wars.* New York: Columbia University Press, 1977.

Hersch, Liebmann. "International Migration of the Jews." In *International Migrations,* edited by Imre Ferenczi and Walter F. Willcox, 471–520. New York: National Bureau of Economic Research, 1929–1931.

Hersch, Liebmann. "Jewish Migrations during the Last Hundred Years." In *The Jewish People: Past and Present,* produced by Central Yiddish Culture Organization, 1:407–30. New York: Jewish Encyclopedic Handbooks, 1946.

Hertzberg, Arthur. *The Jews in America: Four Centuries of an Uneasy Encounter: A History.* New York: Simon & Schuster, 1989.

Jean, Yaron. "Shayakhut Menuyeret" [Belonging on paper: Jews and travel papers in Europe between the two world wars]. *Zmanim: A Historical Quarterly* 133–34 (2016): 122–31.

Kalczewiak, Mariusz. *Polacos in Argentina: Polish Jews, Interwar Migration, and the Emergence of Transatlantic Jewish Culture.* Tuscaloosa: University of Alabama Press, 2020.

Katvan, Eyal. "'Mi Ba'al ha-Bayit?' Ha-Karantina u-Vedikat ha-Olim be-Sha'arei Eretz-Yisrael 1918–1929" [Who is the landlord? Quarantine and medical examinations for immigrants at the gates of Eretz-Israel (1918–1929)]. *Korot* 20 (2010): 37–71.

Katvan, Eyal, and Nadav Davidovitch. "Briut, Politika u-Profesionalizm: Ha-Bedika ha-Refu'it le-Mu'amadim la-Aliya le-Eretz Yisrael, 1925–1928" [Health, politics, and professionalism: medical examination of Jewish immigrants to Palestine, 1925–1928]. *Israel* 11 (2007): 31–60.

Katvan, Eyal, and Nadav Davidovitch. "Makhshirei ha-Guf veha-Levavot: Ha-Rof'im Bodkei ha-Olim le-Eretz Yisrael bein Shtei Milhemot ha-Olam" [Medical inspection of immigrants to Eretz-Israel during the interwar period]. *Korot: The Israeli Journal of the History of Medicine and Science* 20 (2010): 19–36.

Katz, Yossi. "Mahloket Pnim Tsiyonit al Hityashvut Yehudit mi-Huts le-Eretz Yisrael: 'Parshat Turkiya' 1911–1912" [Internal Zionist discord over Jewish settlement outside Palestine: the Turkey affair, 1911–1912]. *Zion* 49, no. 3 (1983/84): 265–88.

Kaznelson, Reuben. *L'Immigrazione degli ebrei in Palestina nei tempi moderni*. Bari and Rome: F. Casini, 1931–1939.

Koralnik, I. "Di Iden in Ukrayne" [The Jews in Ukraine]. *Bleter far Idishe Demografie, Statistik un Ekonomik* 3 (1923).

Latzky-Bertholdi, Ze'ev. "Enut Yehudei Eiropa ha-Mizrahit veha-Aliya la-Aretz" [The suffering of eastern European Jewry and immigration to Palestine]. *Ahdut ha-Avoda* 8, no. 2 (1930).

Lavsky, Hagit. *The Creation of the German-Jewish Diaspora: Interwar German-Jewish Immigration to Palestine, the USA, and England*. Berlin: Walter de Gruyter, 2017.

Lavsky, Hagit. "Leumiut, Hagira ve-Hityashvut: Ha-Im Hayta Mediniut Klita Tsiyonit?" [Nationalism, immigration, and settlement: was there a Zionist absorption policy?]. In Bareli and Karlinsky, *Kalkala ve-Hevra*, 153–77.

Lestschinsky, Jacob. *Di Ekonomishe Lage fun Yidn in Poyln* [The economic situation of Polish Jewry]. Berlin: Victoria, 1931.

Lestschinsky, Jacob. *Ha-Yehudim be-Rusya ha-Sovietit: Mi-Mahpekhat Oktober ad Milhemet ha-Olam ha-Sheniya* [The Jews in Soviet Russia: from the October Revolution to World War II]. Tel Aviv: Am Oved, 1942/43.

Lestschinsky, Jacob. "Le-Ahar ha-Pera'ot be-Ukraina" [After the pogroms in Ukraine]. *Kuntres* 96 (Tishre 1921): 12–16.

Linfield, H. S. *Jewish Migration: Jewish Migration as a Part of World Migration Movements, 1920–1930*. New York: Jewish Statistical Bureau, 1933.

Lissak, Moshe. "Aliya, Kelita u-Vinyan Hevra Yehudit be-Eretz Yisrael bi-Shnot ha-Esrim (1918–1930)" [Aliya, absorption, and building a Jewish society in Palestine in the 1920s (1918–1930)]. In *Toldot ha-Yishuv ha-Yehudi be-Eretz Yisrael me-Az ha-Aliya ha-Rishona: Tekufat ha-Mandat ha-Beriti* [The history of the Jewish community in Eretz-Israel since 1882: the period of the British Mandate]. Edited by Moshe Lissak, Gabriel Cohen, and Israel Kolatt, 2:41–125. Jerusalem: Israel Academy of Sciences and Humanities, Mossad Bialik, 1989/90–2008/09.

Margalit, Elkana. *Hashomer Hatzair: Me-Adat Ne'urim le-Marxism Mahapkhani (1913–1936)* [Hashomer Hatzair: from youth community to revolutionary Marxism (1913–1936)]. Tel Aviv: Hakibbutz Hameuchad, 1985.

Margalit, Meir. *Ha-Shavim be-Dim'a: Ha-Yerida bi-Tekufat ha-Mandat ha-Beriti* [Tearful return: immigration from Palestine under the British Mandate]. Jerusalem: Carmel, 2018.

Margalit, Meir. "Sugiyat Miyun ha-Olim be-Reshit Tekufat ha-Mandat: Ideologia, Mediniut u-Vitsua" [Selective immigration at the start of the Mandate period: ideology, policy, and implementation]. *Yahadut Zemanenu: Shenaton le-Iyun ule-Mehkar* 13 (1998/99): 243–80.

Mendelsohn, Ezra. *Zionism in Poland: The Formative Years, 1915–1926*. New Haven, CT: Yale University Press, 1981.

Metzer, Jacob. *Jewish Immigration to Palestine in the Long 1920s: An Exploratory Examination*. Jerusalem: Maurice Falk Institute for Economic Research in Israel, 2007.

Moreno, Barry. *Encyclopedia of Ellis Island*. Westport, CT: Greenwood, 2004.

Mossek, Moshe. "Britania u-Mediniut ha-Aliya le-Eretz Yisrael, 1918–1928" [Britain and immigration policy in Palestine, 1918–1928]. Master's thesis, Hebrew University of Jerusalem, 1971.

Mossek, Moshe. "Herbert Samuel ve-Itsuv ha-Defusim shel Mediniut ha-Aliya." In *Pirkei Mehkar be-Toldot ha-Tsiyonut* [Studies in the history of Zionism], edited by Yehuda Bauer, Moshe Davis, and Israel Kolatt, 286–310. Jerusalem: Zionist Library of the Zionist Executive and Institute of Contemporary Jewry, Hebrew University of Jerusalem, 1976.

Mossek, M[oshe]. *Palestine Immigration Policy under Sir Herbert Samuel: British, Zionist, and Arab Attitudes*. London: F. Cass, 1978.

Murray, Robert K. *Red Scare: A Study in National Hysteria, 1919–1920*. New York: McGraw-Hill, 1964.

Nordau, Max. *Ketavim Nivharim* [Selected writings], vol. 4. Jerusalem and Tel Aviv: Mitzpeh, 1961/62.

Perec, Georges. *Ellis Island*. With Robert Bober. New York: New Press, 1995.

Perlmann, Joel. *America Classifies the Immigrants: From Ellis Island to the 2020 Census*. Cambridge, MA: Harvard University Press, 2018.

Picard, Avi. *Olim bi-Mesura: Mediniut Yisrael Klapei Aliyatam shel Yehudei Tsefon Afrika, 1951–1956* [Cut to measure: Israel's policies regarding the aliyah of North African Jews, 1951–1956]. Sede Boker: Ben-Gurion Research Institute for the Study of Israel and Zionism, Ben-Gurion University of the Negev, 2013.

Pines, Dan. "Ha-Matzav ha-Kalkali shel ha-Yehudim bi-Vrit ha-Mo'atsot" [The economic situation of the Jews in the USSR]. *Ahdut ha-Avoda* 2 (June 1930).

Porath, Yehoshua. *The Emergence of the Palestinian-Arab National Movement, 1918–1929*. London: Cass, 1974.

Ruppin, Arthur. *Ha-Sotsiologya shel ha-Yehudim* [The sociology of the Jews]. Tel Aviv: A. Y. Shtiebl, 1930/31.

Schapiro, Leonard. *The Communist Party of the Soviet Union*. New York: Random House, 1960.

Schlör, Joachim. "Tel Aviv: (With Its) Back to the Sea: An Excursion into Jewish Maritime Studies." *Journal of Modern Jewish Studies* 8, no. 2 (2009): 215–35.

Segev, Tom. *Yemei ha-Kalaniyot: Erets Yisrael bi-Tekufat ha-Mandat* [Palestine under the British]. Jerusalem: Keter, 1999.

Shapira, David. "Reshitah shel ha-Ha'apala: Shenot ha-Mimshal ha-Tseva'i 1918–1920" [The beginning of illegal immigration: the years of military government, 1918–1920]. In *Ha'apala: Me'asef le-Toldot ha-Hatsala, ha-Beriha, ha-Ha'apala u-She'erit ha-Peleta* [Illegal immigration: a collection on the history of rescue, escape, illegal immigration, and the survivors], edited by Anita Shapira, 15–43. Tel Aviv: Shaul Avigur Inter-University Project for the Study of Illegal Immigration, Tel Aviv University, 1990.

Shehory-Rubin, Zipora, and Shifra Shvarts. *"Hadasa" li-Veri'ut ha-'Am: Pe'ilutah ha-Beriutit-ha-Hinukhit shel "Hadasa" be-Eretz Yisrael bi-Tekufat ha-Mandat ha-Beriti* [Hadassah: for the health of the people]. Jerusalem: Zionist Library, 2003.

Shilo, Margalit. "Lishkat ha-Modi'in shel Sheinkin be-Yafo bi-Tekufat ha-Aliya ha-Sheniya" [The information bureau of Menahem Sheinkin in Jaffa during the Second Aliya period]. *Zionism* 17 (1993): 39–69.

Shilo, Margalit. "Tovat ha-Am o Tovat ha-Aretz: Yahasah shel ha-Tenua ha-Tsiyonit la-Aliya bi-Tekufat ha-Aliya ha-Sheniya" [Changing attitudes in the Zionist movement toward immigration to Eretz-Israel (1904–1914)]. *Cathedra* 46 (1987): 109–22.

Shoham, Hizky. "Meha-Aliya ha-Shelishit la-Aliya ha-Sheniya uva-Hazara: Hivatsrut ha-Haluka li-Tekufot lefi ha-Aliyot ha-Memusparot" [From the Third Aliya to the Second, and back: on the creation of the periodization of the numbered immigrations (aliyot)]. *Zion* 77, no. 2 (2012): 189–222.

Sicron, Moshe. *Immigration to Israel, 1948–1953*. Jerusalem: Falk Project for Economic Research in Israel and Central Bureau of Statistics, 1957.

Silber, Marcos. *Leumiyut Shona, Ezrahut Shava: Ha-Ma'amats Lehasagat Otonomia li-Yehudei Polin be-Milhemet ha-Olam ha-Rishona* [Different nationality, equal citizenship! The efforts to achieve autonomy for Polish Jewry during the First World War]. Tel Aviv: Tel Aviv University, 2014.

Silver, Matthew M. *Louis Marshall and the Rise of Jewish Ethnicity in America: A Biography*. Syracuse, NY: Syracuse University Press, 2013.

Slutsky, Yehuda. *Mavo le-Toldot Tenu'at ha-'Avoda ha-Yisre'elit* [Introduction to the history of the labor movement in Israel]. Tel Aviv: Am Oved, 1973.

Subbotin, Andrei Pavlovich. *Bi-Tehum Moshavam shel ha-Yehudim: Kit'ei Mehkar Kalkaliyim be-Ma'arav Rusya uvi-Drom Ma'aravah, Kayitz 1887* [In the Jewish Pale of Settlement: economic research in southern and southwestern Russia, summer 1887]. Tel Aviv: Kadima, 2020. Originally published as *V cherte evreiskoi osedlosti*. St. Petersburg: Ekonomicheskii Zhurnal, 1888–1890.

Szajkowski, Zosa. "Private and Organized American Jewish Overseas Relief and Immigration (1914–1938)." *American Jewish Historical Quarterly* 57, no. 2 (December 1967): 191–253.

Tsur, Yaron. *Kehila Keru'a: Yehudei Maroko veha-Leumiyut 1943–1954* [Torn community: Jews of Morocco and nationalism, 1943–1954]. Tel Aviv: Am Oved, 2001.

Tzahor, Ze'ev. *Hazan—Tenu'at Hayyim: Hashomer Hatzair, ha-Kibbutz ha-Artzi, Mapam* [Ya'akov Hazan—biography]. Jerusalem: Yad Izhak Ben-Zvi, 1997.

Wischnitzer, Mark. *To Dwell in Safety: The Story of Jewish Migration since 1800.* Philadelphia: Jewish Publication Society of America, 1948–1949.

Wischnitzer, Mark. *Visas to Freedom: The History of HIAS.* Cleveland, OH: World, 1956.

Wolf-Monzon, Tamar. *Bahir ve-Gavoa ke-Zemer: Ya'akov Orland: Poetika, Historia, Tarbut* [Ya'acov Orland: poetics, history, culture]. Sede Boker: Ben-Gurion University of the Negev, 2016.

Wrobel Bloom, Magdalena M. *Social Networks and the Jewish Migration between Poland and Palestine, 1924–1928.* Frankfurt: PL Academic Research, 2016.

Yakir, Moshe. *Toldot ha-Mahlaka la-Aliya shel ha-Histadrut ha-Tsiyonit: Ha-Shanim ha-Rishonot 1919–1927* [The history of the Zionist Organization Aliya Department: the early years, 1919–1927]. Jerusalem: Jewish Agency for Israel, Aliya Department, 2006.

Yedidya, Ovadia, and Amnon Cohen. "Aliyat Yehudim le-Eretz Yisrael mi-Kurdistan ha-Parsit umi-Turkiya ha-Mizrahit le-Ahar Milhemet ha-Olam ha-Rishona" [Jewish immigration to Palestine from Persian Kurdistan and eastern Turkey after World War I]. *Pe'amim* 5 (1980): 87–93.

Yehuda, Zvi. "Ha-Pe'ilut ha-Tsiyonit be-Maroko Erev ha-Protektorat." In *Yahadut Tsefon Afrika ba-Me'ot 19, 20: Iyunim be-Toldoteha, be-Tarbutah, uve-Hevratah* [North African Jewry in the nineteenth and twentieth centuries], edited by Michel Abitbol, 96–108. Jerusalem: Ben-Zvi Institute for the Study of Jewish Communities in the East, 1980.

Yerushalmi, Eliezer. "Mesila Hadasha: Tahanat Ma'avar le-Eretz Yisrael" [Mesila Hadasha: a way station en route to Palestine]. *Et-mol* 8, 1, 45 (1982): 18–19.

Yisraeli, G. Z. [Walter Laqueur]. *Mapas: P.K.P.-Maki: Korot ha-Miflaga ha-Komunistit be-Yisrael* [The SWP: PCP-Maki: The history of the Communist Party in Israel]. Tel Aviv: Am Oved, 1952/53.

Zahra, Tara. *The Great Departure: Mass Migration from Eastern Europe and the Making of the Free World.* New York: W. W. Norton, 2016.

INDEX

Page number in italics refer to illustrations.

GUR ALROEY is a historian of Jewish history in modern times. Since 2021 he has been Provost of the University of Haifa. His main fields of research are Jewish migration in the late nineteenth century and early twentieth century, early Zionism, and the territorial ideology. Professor Alroey is author of three books in English: *Bread to Eat and Clothes to Wear: Letters from Jewish Migrants in the Early Twentieth Century*; *An Unpromising Land: Jewish Migration to Palestine in the Early Twentieth Century*; and *Zionism without Zion: The Jewish Territorial Organization and Its Conflict with the Zionist Organization*.

FOR INDIANA UNIVERSITY PRESS

Tony Brewer *Artist and Book Designer*

Gary Dunham *Acquisitions Editor and Director*

Anna Francis *Assistant Acquisitions Editor*

Brenna Hosman *Production Coordinator*

Katie Huggins *Production Manager*

Nancy Lightfoot *Project Manager/Editor*

Dan Pyle *Online Publishing Manager*

Pamela Rude *Senior Artist and Book Designer*

Stephen Williams *Marketing and Publicity Manager*

www.ingramcontent.com/pod-product-compliance
Lightning Source LLC
Chambersburg PA
CBHW020337270326
41926CB00007B/215